D0712914

JOSEPH CONRAD
IN CONTEXT

Joseph Conrad's Polish background, his extensive travels and his detached view of his adopted country, Britain, gave him a perspective unique among English writers of the twentieth century. Combining Continental and British influences, and Victorian and modernist styles, he was an artist acutely responsive to his age, and his works reflect and chronicle its shaping forces. This volume examines the biographical, historical, cultural and political contexts that fashioned his works. Written by a specialist, each short chapter covers a specific theme in relation to Conrad's life and work: letters, Modernism, the sea, the Polish and French languages, the First World War and many other topics. This book will appeal to scholars as well as to those beginning their study of this extraordinary writer. It shows how this combination of different contexts allowed Conrad to become a key transitional figure in the early emergence of British literary Modernism.

ALLAN H. SIMMONS is Reader in English Literature at St Mary's University College, Twickenham, London. He has published many books and articles on Conrad over twenty years. He is one of the General Editors of The Cambridge Edition of the Works of Joseph Conrad, General Editor of *The Conradian* and co-General Editor of *Conrad Studies*.

JOSEPH CONRAD
IN CONTEXT

EDITED BY
ALLAN H. SIMMONS

CAMBRIDGE
UNIVERSITY PRESS

CAMBRIDGE UNIVERSITY PRESS

Cambridge, New York, Melbourne, Madrid, Cape Town, Singapore,
São Paulo, Delhi, Dubai, Tokyo

Cambridge University Press
The Edinburgh Building, Cambridge CB2 8RU, UK

Published in the United States of America by Cambridge University Press, New York

www.cambridge.org
Information on this title: www.cambridge.org/9780521887922

© Cambridge University Press 2009

First published 2009

Printed in the United Kingdom at the University Press, Cambridge

A catalogue record for this publication is available from the British Library

ISBN 978-0-521-88792-2 Hardback

Contents

Illustrations

Notes on contributors

AMAR ACHERAÏOU has published extensively on modernist, postmodernist and postcolonial literatures. The author of *Rethinking Postcolonialism: Colonialist Discourse in Modern Literatures and the Legacy of Classical Writers* (2008), his *Conrad and the Reader: Questioning Modern Theories of Narrative and Readership* is forthcoming from Palgrave (2009) and he is currently editing a volume on *Joseph Conrad and the Orient*.

KATHERINE ISOBEL BAXTER is Research Assistant Professor in Cross-Cultural Studies in English at the University of Hong Kong. In 2004, she won The Joseph Conrad Society of America's Bruce Harkness Young Conrad Scholar Award. Her publications include *Conrad and the Performing Arts*, edited with Richard J. Hand (2009), and *Conrad: The Contemporary Reviews* (forthcoming), for which she is a co-editor.

MARTIN BOCK is Professor of English at the University of Minnesota Duluth and a trustee of The Joseph Conrad Society of America. He is author of *Crossing the Shadow-Line: The Literature of Estrangement* (1985) and *Joseph Conrad and Psychological Medicine* (2002).

ADDISON BROSS is Professor of English at Lehigh University, Bethlehem, Pennsylvania. He has published articles on Conrad in *Nineteenth-Century Fiction, Conradiana, The Conradian: The Journal of the Joseph Conrad Society (UK)* and several volumes of the Conrad: Eastern and Western Perspectives series. His translation of selections from the memoirs of Tadeusz Bobrowski was published in 2009.

MARIO CURRELI is Professor of English at the Università di Pisa. He is the author, editor or translator of more than thirty volumes by or about Conrad, the Romantics and the Scriblerians. A founding member of The Joseph Conrad Society (UK) and of its Italian counterpart, he has taught at Exeter University and in Florence.

LAURENCE DAVIES is Honorary Senior Research Fellow in English at Glasgow University and President of The Joseph Conrad Society (UK). He serves on the Board of The Cambridge Edition of Joseph Conrad and is General Editor of *The Collected Letters of Joseph Conrad* (9 vols.; 1983–2007). His other work includes *Cunninghame Graham: A Critical Biography*, with Cedric Watts (1979).

STEPHEN DONOVAN is a senior lecturer in English at Uppsala University, Sweden. His publications include *Joseph Conrad and Popular Culture* (2005), an edition of *Under Western Eyes* (2007) and *Conrad First: The Joseph Conrad Periodical Archive*, an open-access digital archive of Conrad's serial publications (www.conradfirst.net). He is currently a visiting lecturer at the University of Indonesia, Jakarta, and working on a book on Conrad and the sea.

LINDA DRYDEN is Reader in Literature at Napier University, Edinburgh. The co-editor of the *Journal of Stevenson Studies* and of *Stevenson and Conrad: Writers of Land and Sea* (forthcoming 2009; with Stephen Arata and Eric Massie), she has published numerous articles on Conrad and is the author of two monographs, *Joseph Conrad and the Imperial Romance* (2000) and *The Modern Gothic and Literary Doubles: Stevenson, Wilde and Wells* (2003).

ROBERT FOULKE is Professor Emeritus and former Chair of the English Department at Skidmore College, Saratoga Springs, New York. In addition to many articles on Conrad's voyage fiction, he has published *The Sea Voyage Narrative* (2002) and he served as Literary Editor of *The Oxford Encyclopaedia of Maritime History* (4 vols., 2007), which includes his articles on sea literature and Conrad.

ROBERT HAMPSON is Professor of Modern Literature in the Department of English of Royal Holloway College, University of London. A former editor of *The Conradian*, his publications include *Joseph Conrad: Betrayal and Identity* (1992) and *Cross-Cultural Encounters in Conrad's Malay Fiction* (2000). The author of numerous articles, he has also edited 'Heart of Darkness', *Lord Jim* (with Cedric Watts), *Victory* and *Nostromo*.

RICHARD J. HAND is Professor of Theatre and Media Drama at the University of Glamorgan, Wales. He is the author of *The Theatre of Joseph Conrad: Reconstructed Fictions* (2005) and other publications on Conrad with a special interest in adaptation and the performance media. In 2000 he directed the world première of Conrad's play *Laughing Anne*.

Aside from works on Conrad, he has published studies of Grand Guignol theatre, of radio drama and on specific figures ranging from Ambrose Bierce to Frank Zappa.

OWEN KNOWLES is Senior Research Fellow at the University of Hull. He is editing *Youth, Heart of Darkness and The End of the Tether* for The Cambridge Edition of the Works of Joseph Conrad. Co-editor of *Heart of Darkness and The Congo Diary* with Robert Hampson (2007), he has also co-edited Volumes VI and IX of *The Collected Letters of Joseph Conrad* (2002 and 2007).

JOHN LESTER schooled in England but attended the University of Canterbury in New Zealand for both undergraduate and post-graduate studies. His doctoral dissertation concerned the purposes of Joseph Conrad's religious terminology and was published in 1988 as *Conrad and Religion*. He has contributed several essays to Conradian journals. He was Head of English at Havering College of Further and Higher Education for some years and, now semi-retired, still teaches there on a part-time basis.

MICHAEL LEVENSON is William B. Christian Professor of English at the University of Virginia and author of *A Genealogy of Modernism* (1984), *Modernism and the Fate of Individuality* (1991), *The Spectacle of Intimacy* (2000; co-author Karen Chase) and the forthcoming *Modernism*. He is also the editor of *The Cambridge Companion to Modernism* (1999).

DAVID MILLER was born in Edinburgh, and educated in Canterbury and at the University of Cambridge, where he read Theology and Religious Studies. He is a director of the literary agency Rogers, Coleridge & White, Ltd. He has contributed to *The Conradian, English Literature in Transition*, the *Times Literary Supplement*, the *Daily Telegraph* and *La Vanguardia*.

GENE M. MOORE teaches at the Universiteit van Amsterdam. His major publications include *Conrad's Cities* (1992), *Conrad on Film* (1997), *The Oxford Reader's Companion to Conrad* (with Owen Knowles, 2000) and a casebook on 'Heart of Darkness' (2004). He was co-editor of the last two volumes of *The Collected Letters of Joseph Conrad* (2007), and is currently at work on a critical edition of Conrad's *Suspense*.

MARY MORZINSKI has published and presented papers extensively on the language of Joseph Conrad. From 2001 to 2006 she was Executive Editor of *Joseph Conrad Today*, the semi-annual publication of The Joseph

Conrad Society of America. A former Professor of English at the University of Wisconsin-La Crosse, she now resides in Montana, teaching and editing online.

M. S. NEWTON has taught for University College London and Princeton, and currently teaches for Universiteit Leiden. He is the author of *Savage Girls and Wild Boys: A History of Feral Children* (2002) and a book in the British Film Institute's Film Classics series on *Kind Hearts and Coronets* (2003). He has edited Edmund Gosse's *Father and Son* (2004) and Conrad's *The Secret Agent* (2007).

RICHARD NILAND completed his doctorate at Oxford University and is the author of *Conrad and History* (forthcoming). He has published on Conrad in *The Conradian* and *The Polish Review*, and is a co-editor of *Conrad: The Contemporary Reviews* (forthcoming).

VÉRONIQUE PAULY lives in Paris and teaches British literature at the Université de Versailles – Saint-Quentin and the École Polytechnique. She wrote her doctoral thesis on the aesthetics of perception in Conrad's fiction, and has published articles on Conrad as well as on eighteenth- and twentieth-century British fiction. In 2007, she edited *Nostromo* for the Penguin Black Classics series.

ANDREW PURSSELL, a research student at Royal Holloway College in the University of London, is working on a thesis about space and empire in the fiction of Joseph Conrad and Graham Greene. He has published on both writers, and is a committee member of The Joseph Conrad Society (UK).

MATTHEW RUBERY is Lecturer in Victorian Literature at the University of Leeds. The author of *The Novelty of Newspapers: Victorian Fiction after the Invention of the News* (forthcoming), he has contributed to *The Cambridge Companion to Victorian Literature and Culture* (forthcoming).

ALLAN H. SIMMONS, Reader in English Literature at St Mary's University College, Twickenham, London, is General Editor of *The Conradian*, and has recently published *Joseph Conrad* (2006) and *Conrad's 'Heart of Darkness': A Reader's Guide* (2007). He has co-edited *Lord Jim* with J. H. Stape, and *The Nigger of the 'Narcissus' and Other Stories* with Gail Fraser and J. H. Stape (both 2007).

J. H. STAPE, Research Fellow at St Mary's University College, Twickenham, London, is the author of *The Several Lives of Joseph*

Conrad (2007) and General Editor of the seven Conrad volumes in Penguin Classics (2007). Editor of *The Cambridge Companion to Joseph Conrad* (1996) and co-editor of Volumes VII and IX of *The Collected Letters of Joseph Conrad* (2004 and 2007), he has also edited *Note on Life and Letters* (2004) and *A Personal Record* (2008) in The Cambridge Edition of Joseph Conrad.

AARON ZACKS, a doctoral candidate in English at the University of Texas at Austin and an intern in the Technology and Digital Services section at that university's Harry Ransom Center, is at work on a dissertation entitled 'Publishing Short Stories: Magazines, Short Story Collections, and British Literary Modernism in Conrad, Joyce and Woolf'.

Preface

This volume locates Conrad within the contexts that contribute to a better understanding of his life, work and growing reputation. As its title, *Conrad in Context*, suggests, its focus is both the artist and the circumstances from which he emerges and to which he responds. With his insider/outsider status in England and English literature, Conrad's writings have long needed the comprehensive historical, social, political and intellectual placement afforded here. Addressing subjects germane to Conrad's times and writing, the individual chapters provide a comprehensive study of the context for his writings. It is hoped that they will foster and help to fashion future scholarship on this remarkable author.

Joseph Conrad acknowledged the multifaceted nature of his life, writing in a letter that 'Homo duplex has in my case more than one meaning' (*CL* 3:89). Born Józef Teodor Konrad Korzeniowski in Berdyczów in Podolia, part of the Polish Commonwealth that had been annexed to the Russian Ukraine in 1793, he would travel the world as a merchant seaman, rising to the rank of master in the British Merchant Service, before making his reputation as an English novelist, writing in his third language. By 1894, when his literary career began, Conrad had acquired a wide experience of other European cultures and of European colonialist expansion, particularly in the Far East and in Africa. Little wonder that Henry James would write to him admiring 'the prodigy of your past experiences': 'No one has *known* – for intellectual use – the things that you know, and you have, as the artist of the whole matter, an authority that no one has approached.'[1]

Biographers have responded to this multiplicity: Frederick R. Karl entitled his biography *Joseph Conrad: The Three Lives* (1979); more recently, J. H. Stape improved upon this with *The Several Lives of Joseph Conrad* (2007). In addition, there have been psychological and economic biographies, and still the subject – partly a matter of surviving records but partly because of his fundamental reticence – remains elusive, and no doubt will continue to do so.

Ever wary of categorization – whether as a 'sea writer' or a 'national' English novelist – the trans-national Conrad is also a transitional figure in the development of the novel: a late-Victorian who helped usher in the flowering of literary Modernism, he brought a distinctly Continental inflection to bear upon the tradition of English letters, making it less insular and more self-aware than it had been in the past. Recognized by his literary peers as a leading writer of the generation, he nevertheless struggled to make headway with the book-buying public until 1914, when, ironically, most of his best work was behind him. Coincidentally, he perhaps typifies the 'duplex' role of the major artist: of and yet always ahead of his time.

The historical, political and artistic parameters of Conrad's life (1857–1924) invite contextual consideration of the work. He shares his birth year with Elgar, with the Indian Mutiny, and with the publication of Dickens's *Little Dorrit*; his death year with Lenin, the formation of the first Labour government in Britain, and the publication of E. M. Forster's *A Passage to India*. Put another way, the writings that have ensured Conrad's enduring fame were not produced in a vacuum. His timeless contribution to letters had a time-bound dimension that, when exposed, reveals him to be intricately involved in his age's changing habits and rules, while making of these enabling contexts for his art.

I should like to express my thanks to the contributors to this volume. A watchword in Conrad studies is 'solidarity', and their fellowship, co-operation and patience has provided a living example of this. I would also like to take this opportunity to remember Michael Lucas, friend and Conradian, who died before completing his contribution to this book. I owe special thanks to Mary Burgoyne, who kindly shared with me her discovery of the Waterman pen advertisement in the *Scotsman*. I am also indebted to the curators and librarians who have helped me secure the illustrations in this volume. In particular, I should like to express my gratitude to Adrienne Leigh Sharpe, Public Services Assistant, The Beinecke Rare Book and Manuscript Library, Yale University; Helen Fisher, Archivist, Special Collections, University of Birmingham; Thomas Lisanti, Manager, Photographic Services and Permissions, The New York Public Library, Astor, Lenox and Tilden Foundations; Melissa Atkinson, Picture Library, National Portrait Gallery, London; Professor Jolanta Dudek, Director of the Jagiellonian University Joseph Conrad Research Centre, Cracow; and Mariko Finch, Copyright Licensing Administrator, Design and Artist Copyright Society. I would also like to thank Christine Jarvis at St Mary's University College, Twickenham, for her patient professionalism.

Finally, it is my privilege to acknowledge the Cambridge University Press production team: thanks to Linda Bree, Maartje Scheltens, Rosina di Marzo and Leigh Mueller, preparing this volume for print has been a pleasure.

ALLAN H. SIMMONS

St Mary's University College, Twickenham, London

NOTE

1. Leon Edel, ed., *Henry James Letters*. Vol. IV: *1895–1916* (Cambridge, MA: Belknap Press, 1984), p. 419.

Abbreviations

Unless otherwise indicated, all references to Conrad's works are to Dent's
Collected Edition (1946–55), and use the following abbreviations:

AF	*Almayer's Folly*
AG	*The Arrow of Gold*
C	*Chance*
I	*The Inheritors*
LE	*Last Essays*
LJ	*Lord Jim*
MS	*The Mirror of the Sea*
N	*Nostromo*
NLL	*Notes on Life and Letters*
NN	*The Nigger of the 'Narcissus'*
OI	*An Outcast of the Islands*
PR	*A Personal Record*
Re	*The Rescue*
Ro	*The Rover*
Rom	*Romance*
S	*Suspense*
SA	*The Secret Agent*
SL	*The Shadow-Line*
SS	*A Set of Six*
T	*Typhoon and Other Stories*
TH	*Tales of Hearsay*
TLS	*'Twixt Land and Sea Tales*
TU	*Tales of Unrest*
UWE	*Under Western Eyes*
V	*Victory*
WT	*Within the Tides*
Y	*Youth: A Narrative and Two Other Stories*

References to Conrad's letters are to *The Collected Letters of Joseph Conrad* (9 vols., Cambridge University Press: 1983–2007), General Editors Frederick R. Karl and Laurence Davies with Owen Knowles, Gene M. Moore and J. H. Stape. This edition is abbreviated as *CL*.

Chronology

Allan H. Simmons

1857

3 December — Józef Teodor Konrad Korzeniowski (Nałęcz coat-of-arms) born in Berdyczów (officially, Berdychiv) in the Ukraine to Apollo Korzeniowski and Ewelina (or Ewa), née Bobrowska, Korzeniowska.

1859

— The Korzeniowski family moves to Żytomierz following Apollo's financial failure as an estate manager.

1861

May — By this time JC's father has moved to Warsaw, ostensibly to establish a literary journal, but more likely to involve himself in clandestine political activities.

October — Ewa Korzeniowska and her son join Apollo in Warsaw.

20 October — Apollo Korzeniowski arrested for anti-Russian conspiracy and imprisoned in Warsaw's Citadel. Ewa is subsequently arrested too.

1862

9 May — Apollo and Ewa Korzeniowski are sentenced to exile in Russia and, with JC, escorted to Vologda, 300 miles north-east of Moscow.

1863

January — The Korzeniowskis are allowed to move south, to Chernikhov, near Kiev.

Summer — Ewa and her son are permitted a three-month leave for medical treatment.

1865	
18 April	Ewa Korzeniowska dies of tuberculosis.
1866	
Summer	JC stays with his maternal grandmother, Teofila Bobrowska, at Nowochwastów, during which visit he is frequently unwell.
Autumn	Accompanied by Teofila Bobrowska, JC returns to Chernikhov; nervous fits and epileptic symptoms necessitate visits to Kiev for treatment.
1867	
Spring	Suffering from German measles, JC travels to Żytomierz for treatment.
1868	
February	Seriously ill, Apollo Korzeniowski is permitted to leave Russia; he and his son settle in Lemberg in Austrian Poland.
1869	
February	Korzeniowski and son move to Cracow.
23 May	Apollo Korzeniowski dies. JC is looked after by a friend of his father's, Stefan Buszczyński, and his grandmother.
1870	
2 August	Teofila Bobrowska appointed JC's official guardian.
1871	
	Tadeusz Bobrowski, JC's maternal uncle, becomes increasingly important in overseeing his upbringing. JC studies with a tutor, Adam Pulman, a medical student.
1873	
May	JC visits Switzerland and northern Italy with Pulman.
1874	
October	JC takes position with Delestang et Fils, a shipping firm in Marseilles.
15 December	Sails as a passenger on the *Mont-Blanc* to Martinique.

1875

23 May	Arrives back in France.
25 June – 23 December	Sails again to Martinique, this time as apprentice in the *Mont-Blanc*.

1876

10 July – 15 February	Sails as steward in the *Saint-Antoine*, again to the Caribbean.

1877

According to JC's own and dubious account, this period includes an ill-fated gun-running expedition in the Carlist cause. According to Tadeusz Bobrowski, JC's difficulties during this period include gambling losses in Monte Carlo.

1878

Late February	Whether in a duel (his own version) or, more likely, a self-inflicted cry for help, JC is shot in the chest.
Early March	Learning that JC is wounded, Bobrowski travels to Marseilles, where he settles his nephew's debts. It is decided that JC will join the British Merchant Service.
24 April	JC sails in an unknown capacity in the *Mavis*, a British steamer bound for the Sea of Azov via Constantinople. He touches English soil for the first time when the *Mavis* arrives back at Lowestoft on 10 June.
11 July – 23 September	Makes three voyages as ordinary seaman in the *Skimmer of the Sea* between Lowestoft and Newcastle.
15 October	Departs from London as an ordinary seaman in the *Duke of Sutherland*, bound for Australia on a voyage that will take just over a year, including a five-month stay in Sydney.

1879

19 October	JC arrives back in London.
12 December	Sails as ordinary seaman in the *Europa* to various Mediterranean ports.

1880

30 January   JC returns to London, lodging near Finsbury
                    Park. He meets G. F. W. Hope, his first
                    English friend.

May   Moves to 6 Dynevor Road, Stoke Newington,
                    London.

28 May   Passes his second-mate's examination.

22 August   Sails as third mate in the *Loch Etive*, bound for
                    Australia.

1881

25 April   Returns to London.

19 September   Signs on as second mate in the *Palestine*,
                    whose frustrated attempts to leave England
                    and eventful voyage to Bangkok form the
                    basis of 'Youth'.

1883

March   The *Palestine*'s cargo of coal spontaneously
                    combusts off Sumatra, forcing the crew to row
                    to Bangka Island.

2 April   A court of inquiry in Singapore exonerates the
                    captain and crew of the *Palestine*. JC stays in
                    Singapore before returning to England via the
                    Suez Canal.

Late July   Travels to Marienbad to visit Tadeusz
                    Bobrowski.

13 September   Sails as second mate in the *Riversdale* for
                    Madras; en route she stops at Port Elizabeth,
                    in South Africa, from 7 December to 9
                    February.

1884

6 April   The *Riversdale* arrives in Madras. Following a
                    dispute with her captain, JC is discharged and
                    travels by train to Bombay.

28 April   Signs on as second mate in the *Narcissus*,
                    returning to Europe, at Dunkirk, on 16
                    October.

3 December   Passes first-mate's examination at the second
                    attempt.

1885

27 April   Sails as second mate in the *Tilkhurst* from
                            Hull to Singapore and Calcutta, stopping for a
                            month (13 May to 10 June) at Penarth, where
                            he meets Joseph Spiridion and his family.
22 September   Arrives in Singapore.
19 October   The *Tilkhurst* begins her return voyage.
19 November   Stops in Calcutta for seven weeks.

1886

12 January   The *Tilkhurst* leaves Calcutta.
16 June   JC signs off in Dundee, and immediately
                            travels to London.
19 August   Becomes a naturalized British subject.
10 November   Passes his master's examination at the second
                            attempt.
28 December   Sails as second mate in the *Falconhurst* for
                            Penarth.

1887

2 January   Signs off *Falconhurst* in Penarth.
18 February   Sails from Amsterdam as first mate in the
                            Highland Forest, bound for Java. He signs off
                            for medical treatment in Singapore, on 1 July,
                            having sustained an injury during the voyage.
August   Signs on as first mate in the *Vidar* in which he
                            makes four trading trips between Singapore
                            and Dutch East Indies ports on Borneo and
                            Celebes. During these trips he meets Willem
                            Karel Olmeijer, prototype for Kaspar
                            Almayer.

1888

4 January   Signs off the *Vidar* in Singapore.
9 February   Sails from Bangkok in the *Otago* as master: his
                            only command.
7 May   Arrives in Sydney.
May–July   Makes round trip to Melbourne.
7 August   Takes the *Otago* via the Torres Strait to Port-
                            Louis, Mauritius, where he stays for seven
                            weeks, departing on 21 November.

1889

4 January	Arrives back in Melbourne.
13 February	Sails to Minlacowie, South Australia, where he remains for about a month.
26 March	The *Otago* arrives in Port Adelaide, where JC resigns his command.
3 April	JC departs for Europe via the Suez Canal, a passenger on the SS *Nürnberg*.
14 May	Arrives in Southampton. Back in London, JC takes rooms at 6 Bessborough Gardens, Pimlico.
2 July	JC's release from the status of a Russian subject is officially gazetted.
Autumn	Begins writing *Almayer's Folly*.
November	Travels to Brussels to be interviewed by Albert Thys of the Société Anonyme Belge pour le Commerce du Haut-Congo.

1890

February–April	Returns to the Ukraine to visit Tadeusz Bobrowski, stopping in Brussels on the way to visit his distant cousin, Aleksander Poradowski, who is terminally ill, and his wife Marguerite.
May–December	Travels to Africa, serving as second-in-command, and temporarily as captain, of the steamship *Roi des Belges* on the Congo River. Apart from meeting Roger Casement, JC finds the whole ordeal 'repellent'. Falling seriously ill, he returns to Europe.

1891

January	Arrives back in London.
March	Suffering from malaria, rheumatism and neuralgia, JC is a patient in the German Hospital, Dalston.
21 May – 14 June	Spends three weeks in Champel-les-Bains, near Geneva, for medical treatment.
Summer	Manages warehouse of Barr, Moering & Co., London. Moves to new lodgings at 17 Gillingham Street, near Victoria Station.

21 November	Sails as first mate in the *Torrens* for Australia.
1892	
2 September	Arrives back in London.
25 October	Again sails as first mate in the *Torrens* to Australia. A passenger, W. H. Jacques, becomes the first reader of *Almayer's Folly* in manuscript.
1893	
24 March	The *Torrens* leaves Adelaide for the return voyage to London, during which JC meets John Galsworthy and Edward Lancelot ('Ted') Sanderson.
26 July	Arrives back in London.
August–September	Visits Tadeusz Bobowski in the Ukraine.
November–December	JC joins the *Adowa* as second mate. The steamer, chartered by the Franco-Canadian Transport Company to carry emigrants from France to Canada, sails from London to Rouen, but remains idle when these plans do not materialize as the company fails.
1894	
17 January	JC signs off the *Adowa*. Unknown to him, this marks the end of his sea career.
10 February	Tadeusz Bobrowski dies.
24 April	Completes first draft of *Almayer's Folly*.
August–September	Revisits Champel-les-Bains for hydrotherapy and begins writing *An Outcast of the Islands*.
October	JC learns that *Almayer's Folly* has been accepted by Unwin. He meets the publisher on 8 October and then, or soon afterwards, also meets Edward Garnett, who will become his friend and mentor.
November	JC meets his future wife, Jessie George.
1895	
8 March	Visits Marguerite Poradowska in Brussels.
29 April	*Almayer's Folly* published by T. Fisher Unwin (3 May by Macmillan in America).

May	Back in Champel-les-Bains for medical treatment, JC forms a romantic attachment with young Frenchwoman Émilie Briquel.
18 September	*An Outcast of the Islands* delivered to Unwin. Begins work on *The Sisters* (never finished).

1896

February	JC proposes marriage to Jessie George.
March	JC abandons work on *The Sisters* in favour of 'The Rescuer' (later *The Rescue*). This ill-fated novel will occasion a major creative crisis for JC, and he will return to it intermittently across his career, not finishing it until 1919.
4 March	*An Outcast of the Islands* published by Unwin (15 August by Appleton in America).
24 March	Marries Jessie George in a registry office in Hanover Square. The couple leave the following day for a five-month honeymoon in Brittany, taking a house on Île-Grande.
May–August	JC writes 'The Idiots' (*Savoy*, October (*TU*)), 'An Outpost of Progress' (*Cosmopolis*, June–July 1897 (*TU*)) and 'The Lagoon' (*Cornhill*, January 1897 (*TU*)), and begins work on *The Nigger of the 'Narcissus'*. The German publisher Tauchnitz takes up *An Outcast of the Islands* for inclusion in its *Collection of British Authors* (1896).
2 September	The Conrads return to England, where they set up their first home in Victoria Road, Stanford-le-Hope, Essex.
27 October	JC sends an inscribed copy of *An Outcast of the Islands* to Henry James, initiating their friendship.
22 December	The Conrads leave to spend Christmas with Joseph Spiridion and his family in Cardiff.

1897

17 January	Completes *The Nigger of the 'Narcissus'* (*New Review*, August–December).
February–April	Writes 'Karain: A Memory' (*Blackwood's*, November (*TU*)).

13 March	The Conrads move to a new home, Ivy Walls, just outside Stanford-le-Hope.
Summer	Writes 'The Return' (unserialized (*TU*)).
26 November	JC first meets R. B. Cunninghame Graham.
30 November	*The Nigger of the 'Narcissus'* published by Dodd Mead in America, under the title *The Children of the Sea* (2 December by Heinemann in Britain).
1898	
15 January	JC's first son, Alfred Borys Leo Conrad, born.
26 March	*Tales of Unrest* published by Scribner's in America (4 April by T. Fisher Unwin in Britain).
May–June	Writes 'Youth' (*Blackwood's*, September (*Y*)) and 'Jim: A Sketch', precursor to *Lord Jim*.
26 October	The Conrads move to a new home at Pent Farm, in Postling, near Hythe, Kent, sublet to them by Ford Madox Ford.
1899	
14 January	*The Academy* awards *Tales of Unrest* a 50-guinea prize.
6 February	Completes 'The Heart of Darkness' (*Blackwood's*, February–April (*Y*)). JC spends much of the year writing *Lord Jim*.
October	Serialization of *Lord Jim* begins in *Blackwood's* (October 1899 to November 1900). Begins collaborating with Ford on *The Inheritors*.
1900	
14 July	Completes a draft of *Lord Jim*.
Late September	Begins 'Typhoon'.
3 October	JC's association with the literary agent, J(ames) B(rand) Pinker, begins. It will last twenty years.
9 October	*Lord Jim* published by Blackwood (in America by Doubleday, McClure, 31 October).
1901	
11 January	Completes 'Typhoon' (*Pall Mall*, January–March 1902 (*T*)).
10 May	Completes 'Falk' (unserialized (*T*)).

1 June	*The Inheritors* published by McClure, Phillips (by Heinemann in Britain, 26 June).
1902	
16 January	Finishes 'To-morrow' (*Pall Mall*, August (*T*)).
13 July	Awarded £300 by the Royal Literary Fund.
4 September	*Typhoon* published as a separate volume by Putnam in America.
October	Completes 'The End of the Tether' (*Blackwood's*, July–December (*Y*))
13 November	*Youth: A Narrative and Two Other Stories* published by Blackwood (by McClure, Phillips in America on 8 February 1903).
1903	
January	JC begins work on *Nostromo*, which will occupy the coming year.
22 April	*Typhoon and Other Stories* published by Heinemann (in America, McClure, Phillips publish *Falk, Amy Foster, To-morrow – Three Stories* in October).
16 October	*Romance*, JC's second collaboration with Ford, published by Smith, Elder (2 May 1904 by McClure, Phillips in America).
1904	
January	Jessie Conrad falls and injures both her legs, leading to a permanent disability. JC begins work on the semi-autobiographical essays that will comprise *The Mirror of the Sea*, and *One Day More*, a one-act adaptation of 'To-morrow'.
6 February	JC's bank, Watson and Co., collapses.
Early April	By this date Conrad has secured the services of Lilian M. Hallowes who will remain with him as his secretary, on and off, for the rest of his career.
June	Receives a Royal Literary Fund award of £200.
14 October	*Nostromo* published by Harper (by the same publisher in America on 23 November).

November–December	The Conrads in London where Jessie undergoes a leg operation.
1905	
13 January	The Conrads travel to Capri for a four-month visit.
March	Awarded £500 from the Royal Bounty Fund.
25–27 June	*One Day More* performed by the Stage Society at the Royalty Theatre, London.
Mid-October	Finishes 'Gaspar Ruiz' (*Pall Mall*, July–October 1906 (*SS*)).
Mid-November	The Conrads spend the rest of the year in London, where Borys is hospitalized with scarlet fever.
End December	'An Anarchist' completed (*Harper's Magazine*, August 1906 (*SS*)).
1906	
January	'The Informer' completed (*Harper's*, December (*SS*)).
11 February	The Conrads depart for a two-month stay in Montpellier, where JC begins 'Verloc', which will develop over the year into *The Secret Agent*.
21 February	'The Brute' completed (*Daily Chronicle*, 5 December (*SS*)).
May	Collaborates with Ford on *The Nature of a Crime* (*English Review*, April–May 1909).
2 August	JC's second son, John Alexander Conrad, born.
4 October	*The Mirror of the Sea* published by Methuen (by Harper in America on the same day).
4 December	Completes 'Il Conde' (*Cassell's Magazine*, August 1908 (*SS*)).
16 December	The Conrads leave to winter in Montpellier.
1907	
11 April	Completes 'The Duel' (*Pall Mall*, January–May 1908 (*SS*)).
15 May	With both sons ill, the Conrads leave Montpellier for Champel-les-Bains.

10 August	The Conrads arrive home to confront their financial crisis.
12 September	*The Secret Agent* published by Methuen (and by Harper a couple of days later). During this month, the JCs move to their new home in Someries, Luton, Bedfordshire.
29 October	JC adds his name to a letter in *The Times* attacking theatrical censorship.
December	Begins 'Razumov' (later *Under Western Eyes*).

1908

January 1908–10	*Under Western Eyes* expands over the next two years, occasioning a rift between JC and Pinker, to whom he is already deeply in debt.
Late January	'The Black Mate' completed (*London Magazine*, April (*TH*)).
April	Receives a grant of £200 from the Royal Literary Fund.
6 August	*A Set of Six* published by Methuen (15 January 1915 by Doubleday, Page in America).

1909

14 February	The Conrads move into rented rooms, above a butcher's shop, in Aldington, near Hythe, Kent.
Mid-July	JC's debt to Pinker now stands at £2,250.
December	JC breaks off from *Under Western Eyes* to write 'The Secret Sharer' (*Harper's*, August–September 1910 (*TLS*)). Crisis with Pinker over the novel deepens, with the agent demanding more regular copy and JC threatening to destroy the manuscript.

1910

26 January	Completes *Under Western Eyes*. A row with Pinker the following day, when JC delivers the MS, leads to a two-year estrangement. At the end of the month, JC suffers a physical and mental breakdown that renders him invalid for the next three months.
24 June	The Conrads move to Capel House, Orlestone, Kent.

July	Writes book reviews for the *Daily Mail*.
9 August	JC is granted an annual Civil List pension of £100.
September	Completes 'A Smile of Fortune' (*London Magazine*, February 1911 (*TLS*)) and 'Prince Roman' (*Oxford and Cambridge Review*, October 1911 (*TH*)).
December	Completes 'The Partner' (*Harper's*, November 1911 (*WT*)).

1911

February	Completes 'Freya of the Seven Isles' (*Metropolitan*, New York, April 1912 (*TLS*)).
22 September	Borys joins HMS *Worcester*, a nautical training ship.
5 October	*Under Western Eyes* published by Methuen (19 October by Harper in America).

1912

19 January	*A Personal Record* published by Harper (in Britain by Eveleigh Nash at the end of the month, as *Some Reminiscences*).
15 April	The manuscript of 'Karain', bound for the American collector John Quinn, goes down with the *Titanic*.
13 August	JC purchases his first car, 'the puffer', a second-hand Cadillac.
14 October	*'Twixt Land and Sea* published by J. M. Dent (3 December by Hodder and Stoughton, Doran in America).
December	Completes 'The Inn of the Two Witches' (*Pall Mall*, March 1913 (*WT*)).

1913

	Revisions of *Chance* and composition of *Victory* occupy much of the year.
September	Publication of *Chance* delayed by bookbinders' strike.
14 December	Completes 'The Planter of Malata' (*Metropolitan*, New York, June–July 1914 (*WT*)).

1914

January — Completes 'Because of the Dollars' (*Metropolitan*, New York, September (*WT*)).

15 January — Publication of *Chance* by Methuen (26 March by Doubleday, Page in America).

25 July — The Conrads travel to Poland, where the general mobilization of Austria soon forces them to move to unmilitarized territory. They stay for nine weeks with JC's distant cousin, Aniela Zagórska, in Zakopane in the Tatra Mountains.

2 November — The Conrads arrive back in England, via Austria and Italy, travelling from Genoa to London on the SS *Vondel*.

1915

24 February — *Within the Tides* published by J. M. Dent (15 January by Doubleday, Page in America).

27 March — *Victory* published by Doubleday, Page (24 September by Methuen in Britain).

20 September — Borys reports for basic training in the Army Service Corps.

1916

March — Completes 'The Warrior's Soul' (*Land and Water*, 29 March 1917 (*TH*)).

April — Begins preparing 'Author's Notes' for Doubleday's Collected Edition of his works.

11 September — Travels to Ramsgate on naval inspection for the Admiralty, initiating a series of tours of naval bases this year.

30 October — Completes 'The Tale' (*Strand Magazine*, October 1917 (*TH*)).

November — A ten-day mission in the North Sea in the 'Q' ship, *Ready*.

1917

19 March — *The Shadow-Line* published by J. M. Dent (27 April by Doubleday, Page in America).

July — Begins *The Arrow of Gold*, the first of the novels to be largely dictated.

25 November	The Conrads leave for a three-month stay in London where Jessie has major surgery on her leg.
1918	
May	Meets 'G. Jean-Aubry', who will become JC's first biographer.
24 June	The Conrads return to London for a seven-week stay during which Jessie's leg is operated on.
Autumn	Returns to *The Rescue*.
10 October	Borys is hospitalized in Rouen suffering from shell-shock.
1919	
26 March	B. Macdonald Hastings's stage version of *Victory* opens at the Globe Theatre, London, running until 14 June.
12 April	*The Arrow of Gold* published by Doubleday, Page (6 August by T. Fisher Unwin in Britain).
23 May	Sells film rights to four novels for $20,000.
25 May	Finishes a draft of *The Rescue*.
2 October	The Conrads move to Oswalds, in Bishopsbourne, near Canterbury.
December	The Conrads spend the month in Liverpool where Sir Robert Jones operates on Jessie.
1920	
21 May	*The Rescue* published by Doubleday, Page (24 June by J. M. Dent).
September–October	Collaborates with J. B. Pinker on *Gaspar the Strong Man*, a film script of 'Gaspar Ruiz' (*SS*).
10 December	Completes a draft of *Laughing Anne*, a two-act dramatization of 'Because of the Dollars' (*WT*). Collected editions begin publication in England (Heinemann) and in America (Doubleday).
1921	
23 January	The Conrads leave for a nine-week visit to Corsica, where they are joined by the Pinkers and Miss Hallowes.

25 February	*Notes on Life and Letters* published by J. M. Dent (22 April by Doubleday, Page in America).
Summer	Translates Bruno Winawer's Polish play *Księga Hioba* into English (as *The Book of Job*).

1922

8 February	J. B. Pinker dies of pneumonia in New York.
2 September	Borys marries, but the news is kept from JC for nine months.
2 November	Stage version of *The Secret Agent* opens at the Ambassadors Theatre, London, running for only ten performances.

1923

21 April	JC leaves Glasgow on the *Tuscania* for a promotional visit to America, arriving in New York on 1 May and departing on the *Majestic* on 2 June. Based at the home of F. N. Doubleday, on Oyster Bay, Long Island, JC also enjoys a motor-tour of New England with his hosts. Generally fêted, he is interviewed by American journalists and gives a reading from *Victory* to an invited audience.
9 June	Arrives back in England at Southampton.
1 December	*The Rover* published by Doubleday, Page (3 December by T. Fisher Unwin in Britain).

1924

11 January	JC's grandson, Philip James, son of Borys, is born.
March	Sits for bust by Jacob Epstein.
27 May	Declines offer of a knighthood from Sir Ramsay MacDonald.
3 August	Dies of a heart attack at 8.30 a.m., aged sixty-six.
7 August	Buried in Canterbury Cemetery.
26 September	*The Nature of a Crime* published by Duckworth (on the same day by Doubleday, Page in America).
21 October	*Laughing Anne & One Day More: Plays by Joseph Conrad* published by Castle (8 May 1925 by Doubleday, Page).

17 November	*The Times* reports the gross value of Conrad's estate as £20,045.
1925	
23 January	*Tales of Hearsay* published by T. Fisher Unwin (on the same day by Doubleday, Page in America).
15 September	*Suspense*, unfinished, published by Doubleday, Page (16 September by J. M. Dent).
1926	
3 March	*Last Essays* published by J. M. Dent (26 March by Doubleday, Page).
1928	
June	*The Sisters* fragment published in the *Bookman* (New York).

PART I

Life and Works

CHAPTER I

Life

J. H. Stape

The story of Conrad's life has been the subject of intense scholarly research since Jocelyn Baines' *Joseph Conrad: A Critical Biography* (1959).[1] Prior to that, a mainly hagiographical approach dominated, with biographies by Conrad's wife and his friends Richard Curle and Jean-Aubry benefiting from first-hand observation of their subject and usefully preserving materials that might otherwise have been lost, but, for all their intimacy, falling short on accuracy and completeness.[2] Several myths of Conrad's own creation have needed demolition, and during the past half-century biographers have constructed a more nuanced picture of a man whose life has long been a focus of interest and speculation on the part of those who read his fiction.

Born in Berdyczów in 1857 (3 December) in the central Ukraine, formerly Polish but then under Russian rule, to Polish parents of the gentry class, Józef Teodor Konrad Korzeniowski, the only child of a writer and ardent nationalist, died in the village of Bishopsbourne near Canterbury in 1924 (3 August), a British subject and a widely renowned author. He had turned to writing in his third language after a career in the French and English Merchant Navies that took him to the Caribbean, the Far East, Australia and Africa, providing him with a stock of impressions and experiences that he drew upon for his writings.

Conrad, who spoke of his own duality – 'Homo duplex in my case has more than one meaning' (*CL* 3:89) – saw himself as having led three lives: as Pole, seaman and writer. However useful at first sight, these categories fall short of delineating his complexities of temperament and experience, nor are they water-tight: Conrad had begun writing even while at sea, and although aspects of a Polish identity – language and Roman Catholicism – were abandoned in the transition to England, the values and attitudes of his native culture, as well as memories of a difficult childhood and youth in Russian and Austrian Poland, not only remained with him throughout adulthood but also influenced his outlook and work. In his impressionist autobiography *A Personal Record* (serialized 1908–9; 1912), he declares his intention to present 'a coherent justifiable personality both in its origins and its action' (xxi); the work itself depicts a chameleon, multiplex self confronting vicissitude, the coherence imposed by artistic design.

A sickly child and an orphan at the age of eleven, Conrad had already experienced radical displacement in his native environment, and attachment to a geographic locale was not an option open to him. Condemned to exile for their political activities, his parents took him to Vologda, in northern Russia, and, after his mother's premature death of tuberculosis in 1865, his father, Apollo Korzeniowski (1820–69), wandered in several Galician towns with his son before ending up in Cracow where he died a broken man.

Thereafter the ward of his maternal grandmother and maternal uncle, Tadeusz Bobrowski (1829–94), a landowner in the Ukraine, Conrad lived in Lemberg (now L'viv) and Cracow before leaving for Marseilles and a career at sea in 1874, at sixteen. His education was mainly through private schooling and tutoring, and his childhood and adolescence, periods of rapidly shifting ties, severe emotional upheaval and traumatic loss, were punctuated by physical and nervous illnesses. Political tensions provided the backdrop for his youth: the Polish nation-state had ceased to exist with the Third Partition of 1795, and her peoples, fragmented, lived under Prussian, Austrian and Russian domination. To be Polish, then, was a cultural, not a national, identity, and until he took up British nationality in August 1886 Conrad was the Tsar's subject.

The son of political criminals, Conrad's prospects in Austrian Poland were limited, and his choice of a career at sea, pursued from 1874 to 1894, not only fulfilled a youthful ambition but also, and much more importantly, provided him with the exotic locales that he would draw on for his writing. In the event, the choice proved troubled. In France, his nationality barred him from long-term employment after he made a few voyages to the French Antilles; in England, his decision to climb the ranks from ordinary seaman to a captaincy went mainly unrewarded as employment opportunities shrank. The so-called 'Long Depression' of the 1890s, an abundant labour supply and technological change that saw an increase of tonnage but a contraction in the number of ships reduced the number of berths. These difficult labour conditions, exacerbated by the Great Dock Strike of 1889, forced Conrad to seek employment with a Belgian company in Africa, an experience that shattered his health, while the moral degradation he witnessed in the Congo's economic exploitation disgusted him. By way of compensation, the ordeal provided him with material for 'An Outpost of

Progress' and 'Heart of Darkness'; it also profoundly altered his world-view, allowing him to speak powerfully to contemporary and later audiences.

Having obtained his professional credentials, Conrad rarely found a berth commensurate with his qualifications, and he generally did not get along well with the captains over him, perhaps his happiest years at sea being those in the crack clipper, the *Torrens* (1891–3), taking passengers to Australia. During Conrad's time at sea, he put down deep roots in England, despite being necessarily absent for long periods, particularly on voyages to Australia. His closest friendships, with Fountaine Hope (G. F. W. Hope, 1854–1930) and Phil Krieger (Adolph Philip Krieger, *c.* 1850–1918), were with men engaged in business, although Hope had also been at sea. One suspects that emotional solitude characterizes Conrad's early life in England and in English ships, where his intellectual interests and manner set him apart, and his habit of reading, taken up in childhood, stood him in good stead. He read deeply and widely in contemporary French literature, a profound influence on his work and outlook.

In the event, authorship proved a wiser choice than the sea. Although no less precarious than seamanship, at least before achievement and recognition, Conrad's writing career opened as literacy rates climbed, new audiences were created and both the high- and low-brow ends of the market expanded. The happy few could enjoy large incomes (Kipling and Arnold Bennett are cases in point) in an increasingly professionalized market in which the new institution of the literary agent, legal contracts, better copyright conditions and literary associations secured a writer's interests, and, if not wholly effacing the past's unstable conditions, at least mitigated them.

A self-proclaimed 'artist' contemptuous of 'the Democracy of the bookstalls' (*CL* 5:173), Conrad's aesthetic posture ensured that financial security eluded him from the outset of his career, in 1895, until 1914. During the long wait for a popular audience, he none the less managed to place himself at the forefront of the day's writers, particularly with early works like *The Nigger of the 'Narcissus'* (1897) and *Lord Jim* (1900). He created for himself a profile as a sea-writer at a time when England's emotional attachments to and financial interests in the sea were still strong. This label increasingly became a sore point, with advantages as regards audience recognition but proving much too confining and narrow as a definition of his work.

Despite gratifying recognition from the literary elite and intelligentsia, Conrad was not spared the hard necessity of providing for himself and his family, and had to supplement his income with loans from friends with deep pockets (particularly John Galsworthy) and grants: a Royal Bounty Grant in 1905, a Royal Literary Fund award in 1908 and a Civil List pension of £100, held from 1910 to 1917 when circumstances permitted him to resign it. In 1900, Conrad placed his literary affairs under professional management, becoming a client of the highly successful J. B. Pinker (1863–1922), who also acted for Henry James, Arnold Bennett, John Galsworthy and, briefly and unhappily, D. H. Lawrence. Allowing Pinker to place his work on the open market and arrange contracts worked well up to a point, but it also led to increased stresses and strains. Never accurately predicting his output or able to keep to deadlines, Conrad almost always fell behind as projects grew and expanded beyond his original estimates. In time this *modus operandi* collapsed altogether, the writer so deeply in debt to his agent as to place into question Pinker's business acumen. Conrad was, however, fortunate in his choice of agent, who, over the years, played many parts – generous banker, father-figure, general factotum and, ultimately, friend.

Marrying in 1896 (24 March), Conrad's choice lit upon a lower-middle-class woman (her father was warehouseman to a book-dealer in Lambeth), Jessie Emmeline George (1873–1936), twelve years his junior and, when he met her, working for a typewriter manufacturing company.[3] His previous romantic attachments, also to younger women – in Mauritius to Eugénie Renouf, and to Émilie Briquel, a Frenchwoman he met in Geneva – were apparently serious, but scant available evidence discreetly conceals their emotional depth. Some biographers also argue for an attachment to Marguerite Poradowska (née Marguerite-Blanche-Marie Gachet de la Fournière, 1848–1937), a distant marriage relation (in letters, 'Tante Marguerite'), widowed shortly after they first met, a bluestocking and established novelist resident in Brussels and Paris.

Jessie Conrad, the second child in a family of nine children, proved a largely maternal figure to her husband, to whom in due course she bore two sons (Alfred Borys Leo) (1898–1978) and John Alexander (1906–82). Not perhaps temperamentally, or by his childhood experience, particularly prepared for paternity or domestic life, Conrad none the less seems to have enjoyed aspects of bourgeois family life, proving a dutiful and affectionate husband and father.[4]

Living in the countryside after their marriage – the Conrads rented homes in Essex, Bedfordshire and, mainly, Kent – was cheaper than life in the metropolis, and even periods on the Continent – Capri in 1905, Montpellier in the winters of 1906 and 1907 – were partly motivated by economics, daily life then being cheaper abroad. Conrad was, however, never provident; a history of overspending and even economic recklessness dates back to his period in Marseilles. In time, his makeshift solutions brought him to breaking-point. Plagued by ill-health in his early childhood, by nervous complaints in adolescence and depression of varying severity in adulthood, for which he resorted to hydropathic cures in Switzerland, in early 1910 he suffered a complete breakdown and took several months to recover fully. Given the patterns he had established by mid-life, it seems almost predictable.[5] One factor in this as well is the collapse of his friendship with his sometime collaborator, Ford Madox Hueffer (later Ford).

Following his recovery, Conrad's work became generically and stylistically more conventional, one eye cannily fixed upon a wider audience that would include women: then, as now, the majority of readers. With *Chance* (1913), he abandoned the philosophical and political interests that so dominate *Nostromo* (1904) – perhaps the novel he most agonized over – *The Secret Agent* (1907) and *Under Western Eyes* (1911) to take up domestic issues in an English setting, including the topic of women's suffrage, then being fought out in the streets as well as in Parliament.

In late July 1914, after a seven-year absence from the Continent, the Conrads made an ill-advised trip to Austrian Poland that nearly ended in disaster. Caught up by the outbreak of the First World War, they took refuge in the mountain resort of Zakopane, making their way back to England via Vienna and Genoa, with the help of influential friends. Conrad, an enemy alien of reputation, had narrowly missed being interned for the war's duration. Wholeheartedly supportive of Britain, he was deeply moved by the conflict. His son Borys, who received a commission, was shell-shocked and gassed in France.

Conrad complained that the war drained his fitness for work, although he managed to revise *Victory* (1915) and to write *The Shadow-Line* (1917), fictions that return to the Far East settings of his distant past, as *The Arrow of Gold* (1919) does to the South of France of his youth. A writer mainly of retrospective impulse, Conrad also returned to the Far East in *The Rescue* (1920), finally finishing a work abandoned on his honeymoon in 1896. Now successful and established, he enjoyed a large audience, his work selling particularly well in America as the result of skilful, even muscular, marketing by his publisher F. N. Doubleday. He could also count on American interest in European culture, then still vibrant and engaged.

There is ample evidence of artistic enervation as Conrad's career entered its final years, both in the loosening of the prose and in the clumsy plotting. Ill-health accounts for some of this failing grasp: as gout afflicted his hands, he employed a secretary, Lilian M. Hallowes. He also saddled himself with *Suspense*, a novel set in Genoa with the exiled Napoleon on Elba poised to return to France. The novel grew fitfully as he picked at other projects – a dramatization of *The Secret Agent* (1922) that was quickly withdrawn and

The Rover (1923), originally a short story set in the South of France that grew into a novel – and remained unfinished on his death.

Conrad's final years saw both him and his wife in chronic ill-health, and, rather than enjoying his achievement, Conrad was incapable of rest, ceaselessly worrying over his finances and preoccupied about his family's welfare after his death. Still, he enjoyed a comfortable later life, renting a large house with extensive grounds maintained by a staff of domestics and gardeners and riding in a chauffeured motor-car. John was sent to Tonbridge School and enjoyed private tutoring in mathematics and a stint in France to acquire the language.

An effort to ensure his posthumous fame was the collected editions of his work published in England (Heinemann) and America (Doubleday) in 1920–1, for which he wrote a series of short prefaces. In 1921, he and his wife sojourned in Corsica, a trip made to soak up atmosphere for *Suspense*, and in the spring of 1923 Conrad made a long-delayed trip to the United States, a publicity campaign orchestrated by Doubleday. New York's social and cultural elite lionized him, and he visited Boston and Yale University. In what his hostess described as 'a very delicate state of health',[6] he was simultaneously exhausted and stimulated by the round of new impressions and by American vigour and generosity.

Returning home (June) to news that Borys had secretly married in the previous autumn, Conrad bravely faced this turn of affairs, but his son, never quite recovered from the war, also proved to be in the hands of money-lenders. Tensions were papered over, aided by the birth of a grandson in January 1924, although Jessie Conrad, wounded by her son's increasingly erratic behaviour, never reconciled herself to her daughter-in-law, Joan King.[7] Even as Conrad's family life took an unhappy turn, he was offered – but graciously declined – a knighthood (1924) by the new Labour government of Ramsay MacDonald, following a line taken by Galsworthy and Kipling, and consistent with his refusal of honorary degrees from Oxford, Cambridge, Durham, Liverpool, Edinburgh and Yale.

Conrad's family life was difficult in his last years. Hugh Walpole described the atmosphere of a disastrous weekend at Oswalds, the Conrads' last home, in 1922: 'State of things really awfully bad. J. C. much worse – shrivelling up, looks like an old monkey and does nothing all day. The house divided absolutely into two camps and who is speaking the truth I really don't know.'[8] By way of compensation there were a number of friendships, especially with younger men, including Richard Curle, a Scot long settled in England, who nursed literary ambitions but worked in journalism. Conrad was also especially close to Jean-Aubry, a Norman of literary and musical tastes resident in London and widely connected on the Paris cultural scene. Conrad's friendship with Edward Garnett, his early literary mentor, intensified again as the two men aged, as did his friendship with Pinker.

A deeply private man, Conrad's choice of country life allowed him to mix in literary circles when it suited him, even though he was fully at ease in the great world and courtly, even punctilious, in manner and dress. (T. S. Eliot remarked to Stravinsky that Conrad was 'a Grand Seigneur, the grandest I have ever met'.)[9] Oswalds, the former dower house of Bourne Park set in the rolling Kentish countryside, none the less opened its doors wide to a select circle of friends, with Curle and Aubry frequent visitors. Conrad's wife made friends in the neighbourhood, but aside from Sir John Millais, the painter's grandson and Conrad's chess partner, Conrad took slight interest in local affairs.

On his death, Conrad was recognized as one of the most important writers of his day. The broad outlines of his life have now been securely established, but tracts of it remain fundamentally unknowable. Frustratingly little evidence survives from the earlier periods, and when Conrad turned to writing, his life-story inevitably became the story of the conception and writing of his books. In rehearsing the surviving facts, which, *contra* Marlow in *Lord Jim*, do reveal important things, there are intractable interpretive problems. The gap yawns wide between the inner and outer man, for Conrad was particularly adept at adopting the carapace that late-Victorian and Edwardian protocols and his gentry background urged on him. His life-story is sometimes more truly grasped in the sideways glance or in the fissures of a larger, seemingly coherent picture.

NOTES

1. For a survey of biographies, see J. H. Stape, 'Conrad Biography as a Fine Art', *The Conradian*, 32.2 (2007), 57–75.
2. See the chapter by David Miller in the present volume, and Owen Knowles and Gene M. Moore, *Oxford Reader's Companion to Conrad* (Oxford: Oxford University Press, 2000), pp. 35–7. See both for bibliographical details of the writings by Jessie Conrad, Curle and Jean-Aubry mentioned here.
3. She was not, as all biographical accounts assume, a typist. Conrad mentions her working for the American Caligraph Company, in fact a manufacturer, not a typing agency.
4. For a full discussion, see David Miller, 'The Unenchanted Garden: Children, Childhood, and Conrad', *The Conradian*, 31.2 (2006), 28–47.
5. In *Joseph Conrad and Psychological Medicine* (Lubbock: Texas Tech University Press, 2002), Martin Bock discusses in detail the nature of Conrad's illnesses and the therapies upon which he relied.

6. Florence Doubleday, *Episodes in the Life of a Publisher's Wife* (New York: privately printed, 1937), p. 67.

7. Quickly troubled, the marriage had collapsed by 1932, and ended in an official separation in 1935; see Jessie Conrad to Walter and Helen Tittle, 31 December 1935, The Harry Ransom Humanities Research Center, The University of Texas at Austin.

8. The Diaries of Hugh Walpole, The Harry Ransom Humanities Research Center, diary entry: 5 February 1922.

9. Igor Stravinsky, *Themes and Conclusions* (London: Faber & Faber, 1972), p. 71.

CHAPTER 2

Chronology of composition and publication

Katherine Isobel Baxter

Accounting for Conrad's writing and publishing, we come up against a variety of problems, not least of which are his own reports of his compositional practice, at times forgetful, at others inventive.[1] This is particularly so when examining Conrad's first steps as a writer: whilst the basic facts of *Almayer's Folly*'s composition given in *A Personal Record* may be roughly accurate, if unverifiable, Conrad's account of the manuscript's precarious journey through Europe and the Belgian Congo is sketched symbolically, drawing together disparate geographies and experiences, creating a sense of inevitability to his emergence as a writer.

What *is* clear is that Conrad had little trouble placing his first novel, and his choice of publishers was, we may presume, hardly haphazard. In 1894, when Conrad submitted the manuscript, Unwin's titles were decidedly global in their subject matter, including Rodway's *In the Guiana Forest* (1895), Mackie's *The Devil's Playground: A Story of the Wild North West* (1894) and Baron Conway's *Climbing and Exploration in the Karakoram-Himalayas* (1894), amongst many others. Moreover, Unwin's list did not shy away from books showing the shabbier side of colonialism, particularly in the East, notably Louis Becke's *By Reef and Palm* (1894). Thus Conrad's novel, of European colonialism in Malaya, fitted easily into Unwin's broader publishing strategy.

Conrad may well have done his research beforehand, but he could not have anticipated that his submission would lead to a lifelong friendship with Edward Garnett, a senior reader for Unwin. Garnett's enthusiasm for *Almayer's Folly* (published in April 1895, and in May with Macmillan in the USA) encouraged Conrad to continue with a second story, 'Two Vagabonds', which, developing into *An Outcast of the Islands*, was published by Unwin the following year. *An Outcast of the Islands* makes use of protagonists from *Almayer's Folly* to narrate a prior story, creating the second volume of what was to become, with *The Rescue*, a trilogy-in-reverse. All three drew on Conrad's own experience in the Far East. In response to Hugh Clifford's criticism of their accuracy, Conrad claimed that these tales were not intended as ethnographic and topographical studies.[2] Conrad's interest lies instead with the psychology of his European and Malayan protagonists. This interest sets these novels apart from much colonial fiction of the time, which tended either towards the ethnographic style that Clifford expected or towards heroic romps through generically 'savage' environments.

His intention to complicate the romance genre with psychological explorations proved almost impossible to master in his next novel.[3] In *The Rescue* Conrad set out to write a novel where the 'psychological phenomena are the foundation of the structure – and being the foundation must remain out of sight. Only action shall be visible.' Yet this was also to be a 'romance' in which 'nothing fantastic will happen'.[4] Such paradoxical aims made work on *The Rescue* painfully slow, despite Garnett's initial enthusiasm for early sections of the manuscript.[5]

Struggling to develop the novel, Conrad broke off from it several times, initially to write short stories.[6] Escaping from one writing project to another became a familiar pattern in Conrad's writing career and is one reason why, despite an output that averaged almost one volume a year, he constantly felt that he was working slowly. 'The Idiots', written in May 1896, was followed two months later by 'An Outpost of Progress', and in August by 'The Lagoon'. The first two reveal something of Conrad's early experimentalism in subject matter and treatment. The ironic detachment that colours his narration was not typical in mainstream fiction of the time, however, and the more conventional tone of 'The Lagoon' may well have been a conscious response to rejections of 'The Idiots' by *Cornhill* and *Cosmopolis* that summer.[7]

During the summer of 1896 another story, *The Nigger of the 'Narcissus'*, occupied Conrad, and that autumn he laid aside *The Rescue* to work on it further. By January 1897 he completed a draft, and whilst revising it composed 'Karain'. These two pieces brought significant changes. With the help of Sydney S. Pawling he switched publishers for *The Nigger of the 'Narcissus'*, negotiating not only better terms with Heinemann (Pawling's employer) but also serialization in the artistically prestigious *New Review*. Serialization prior to book issue became a standard practice, enabling Conrad to earn greater revenues from his work. Meanwhile 'Karain' was placed with *Blackwood's Magazine*, initiating a publishing relationship that dominated the next five years of his career. A thoroughly established and establishment magazine, *Blackwood's* provided Conrad with a financially and artistically secure forum for his work. Here he serialized all three stories from the *Youth* volume (which itself appeared under the Blackwood imprint in due course), as well as *Lord Jim*.

This period of association with *Blackwood's* saw Conrad developing increasingly complex narrative techniques. Already in *The Nigger of the 'Narcissus'* he had experimented with an unstable narrative voice. In 'Youth', 'Heart of Darkness' and *Lord Jim* this voice bifurcated to create the audible and active narrator, Marlow, and a predominantly tacit and inactive frame narrator. As *Lord Jim* expanded, from the initial short story (serialized in *Blackwood's* as he wrote) to a full-blown novel, so Conrad expanded the range of voices contributing to the narration of Jim's life.[8]

Alongside his *Blackwood's* fiction he also produced the stories collected in the 1903 *Typhoon* volume, all but 'Falk' appearing separately in magazines prior to the collection's publication: 'Amy Foster' appeared in the *Illustrated London News*, 'To-morrow' appeared in *Pall Mall* as did 'Typhoon', which was also serialized in the *Critic* in the USA. These stories, simpler in their narrative structure than the *Blackwood's* fiction, nevertheless encompass with disarming dispassion problematic topics such as ethnicity and cannibalism.

The placement of these stories was largely as a result of another crucial encounter, this time with the literary agent J. B. Pinker. Like most authors of the period, Conrad had negotiated his own terms with publishers, relying on advice from friends in the business such as Garnett. At the turn of the century, however, as international syndication became regulated, and as a result more favourable for authors, literary agents appeared on the scene able to negotiate on their clients' behalf with multiple publishing houses across the globe. Pinker already represented several of Conrad's friends and acquaintances when their association began in 1900. Until his death in 1922 when he was succeeded by his son, Eric, Pinker came to act as agent, mentor, banker and friend for Conrad.

Meanwhile, Conrad continued to experiment, most notably through collaboration with Ford Madox Ford (then Hueffer). One result was *The Inheritors*, Conrad's only published attempt at science fiction. Heavily influenced by H. G. Wells, the novel's satire of London's publishing scene hardly made it available to a broad audience. In contrast, *Romance* (1903), based upon a true incident, made full use of adventure-fiction tropes – pirates, a beautiful girl, tropical islands. Ironically the volume to which Ford contributed least during this period has also stirred most discussion about his involvement. For whilst there is little doubt that *Nostromo* (1904) is almost entirely Conrad's own work, Ford's later claims, as well as manuscript evidence, indicate an element of contribution, even if only as an amanuensis.[9]

During the first decade of the twentieth century Conrad supported a
wife, and eventually two children, through writing, supplemented at times
by literary grants.[10] His work of this period divides roughly into two
categories: that written for fast cash, and that written with an eye to critical
reception. Thus, whilst working on *Nostromo* he also churned out, often by
dictation to Ford, many of the articles later collected in *A Mirror of the Sea*.
Conrad also made his first foray into drama in this period, adapting 'To-
morrow' as *One Day More* in 1904.[11] Following *Nostromo* he began work on
Chance, reviving his narrator Marlow, only to set the novel aside repeatedly
in favour of various short stories, which could be sold for immediate
magazine publication. One of these, 'Verloc', started in 1906, eventually
displaced work on *Chance* and, whilst continuing other short stories and
collaboration with Ford on *The Nature of a Crime*, Conrad developed it into
The Secret Agent.[12]

Towards the end of the decade he became embroiled in another lengthy
story, initially entitled 'Razumov'. To Pinker's annoyance work progressed
slowly, interrupted both by financial needs, which caused Conrad to rustle
up material for quick publication (as with 'The Black Mate' published in
London Magazine in April 1908), and by the need to escape the novel's
claustrophobic plot (as when he paused to write 'The Secret Sharer' in
December 1909, a story which evidently gave him much pleasure[13]). Further
interruptions, and tensions with Pinker, were caused by his contributions to
Ford's new journal, *English Review*. Conrad wrote a series of autobiographical sketches, 'Some Reminiscences', for the first seven issues, before falling
out with Ford over further contributions. While the arrangement lasted, the
money from these sketches was useful, and there was literary kudos to be
gained from publication in a journal that wore its aesthetic credentials on its
sleeve.

To aid the progress of 'Razumov' Conrad hired a typist, Lilian
M. Hallowes, so that he could continue when stricken with gout, which
made writing painfully difficult. He had hired her previously in similar
circumstances when he was working on *Nostromo*. His reengagement of her
marked a slow but steady move towards dictation as the gout increasingly
impinged on his writing capacity. A further benefit was that, since Miss
Hallowes could type from dictation, his manuscripts no longer needed to be
typed-up for submission.

At the beginning of 1910 he finally finished 'Razumov', now *Under
Western Eyes*. The novel had taken two years to write and, whilst in 1908
A Set of Six appeared in Britain and the United States, 1909 had only seen
the *English Review* contributions. Moreover, since Conrad circumvented his

agent in his payment for these 'Reminiscences', Pinker had essentially earned nothing from him in a year. When he submitted *Under Western Eyes* to Pinker in person, a row ensued that soured their relationship for two years, during which Robert Garnett (Edward's brother) and John Galsworthy acted as go-betweens and to some extent agents for Conrad until his full rapprochement with Pinker in 1912.

As he revised *Under Western Eyes*, Conrad attempted to revive both *The Rescue* and *Chance*, whilst producing various short stories and book reviews for the *Daily Mail*. In October 1911 *Under Western Eyes* was published, swiftly followed in January 1912 by *Some Reminiscences* (published in the United States under its more familiar title, *A Personal Record*). At the same time *Chance* took off and by the end of March he had a complete draft. *Chance* was serialized in the *New York Herald* between January and June 1912, and he immediately began work on his next novel, *Victory*, initially called 'Dollars'. In the meantime Conrad found a new way to supplement his income through the sale of manuscripts to a wealthy American lawyer, John Quinn. Quinn's initial purchases were the relatively old manuscript of *An Outcast of the Islands* and, by contrast, 'Freya of the Seven Isles', a story completed only a few months prior to the sale of its manuscript. In the second half of the year *'Twixt Land and Sea* appeared, collecting together short stories written during and after the composition of *Under Western Eyes*. This increased productivity allowed Conrad to clear the air and some of his debts with Pinker, although the following year saw less come out in print, *Chance*'s appearance in book form being delayed until 1914 due to a British bookbinders' strike.

Conrad's productivity continued over the next two years. Completing a draft of *Victory* in the summer of 1914, he also continued to turn out short stories, which could be published immediately in magazines, sold in manuscript form to Quinn and later collected in volume form. Thus, by the end of February 1915, *Within the Tides* appeared, followed a month later by *Victory*, with Conrad already at work on *The Shadow-Line*. During 1916 he worked mainly on smaller pieces of journalism and fiction, and began to prepare 'Author's Notes' for a collected edition of his works, under discussion with Doubleday since 1913. In the summer André Gide discussed translating Conrad into French, and Basil Macdonald Hastings approached him about adapting *Victory* for the stage. The market success of *Chance* and *Victory* allowed Conrad to trade on his name and, through his agent, he became financially adept at making the most from any work he did. Already in 1915 he had sold film options on *Romance*, and when they ran out without a production he was able to resell options on the same book to Lasky-Players, in 1919.[14] In March 1917, *The Shadow-Line* appeared and he began work on *The Arrow of Gold*, relying heavily by this time on dictation. The novel, revisiting material set aside long before in 'The Sisters', took a year to complete. Unusually for Conrad, and doubtless testament to his new-found financial security, he worked on little else at the same time. Thereafter, with *The Arrow of Gold* completed, he returned finally to that other long-ignored manuscript, *The Rescue*, picking up the story where he had left off twenty years previously.

Attempts to stage Hastings' adaptation of *Victory* finally came off, with a successful three-month run at London's Globe Theatre in 1919. No doubt inspired by the play's success, that autumn Conrad turned his attention to adapting *The Secret Agent*, having completed a full draft of *The Rescue* earlier in the year. Publication of *The Arrow of Gold* and the sale of film options on four novels ensured a profitable year. In the summer of 1920, *The Rescue* finally appeared in book form.

The 1920s saw Conrad repeat his publishing pattern of the early 1910s. Alongside *Suspense*, which remained unfinished at his death, he worked on a wide range of projects, including a collection of his occasional essays, *Notes on Life and Letters*; a stage adaptation of 'Because of the Dollars'; a collaboration with Pinker to adapt 'Gaspar Ruiz' for the cinema;[15] and a translation from Polish of Bruno Winawer's play, *Księga Hioba*. Thus Conrad remained productive during the last years of his life, and, although he struggled to make headway with *Suspense*, he did complete one final novel, *The Rover*, which appeared in 1923. In this relatively short novel he mastered Mediterranean material of the sort which continued to elude his control in *Suspense*.

Conrad died in the summer of 1924. That autumn his earlier collaboration with Ford, *The Nature of a Crime*, finally appeared in book form, as did his two plays, *Laughing Anne* and *One Day More*. In 1925 his last short stories (of which *The Rover* was initially intended to be one) were collected as *Tales of Hearsay*, and *Suspense* was published with an introduction by Richard Curle, Conrad's friend and executor. Eventually, in 1926, *Last Essays* appeared, edited and introduced once again by Curle, collecting together Conrad's journalism since the publication of *Notes on Life and Letters*, alongside scraps of previously unpublished material, such as his 'Congo Diaries'. The work of Conrad's last years is frequently dismissed by critics as lacking the original flair which marks the first part of his career. Yet, whilst the aesthetic value of this later work is perhaps less obvious, his continued productivity and his forays into film and theatre indicate that he remained eager to experiment with emerging and avant-garde forms and genres.

NOTES

1. The major problem, of course, is lack of material evidence: although a great number of Conrad's manuscripts, typescripts, proofs, galleys, etc., survive, much is also lost, particularly evidence of tentative early drafts, and stories toyed with but which remained unwritten.
2. See Hugh Clifford, 'Mr. Conrad at Home and Abroad', *Singapore Free Press*, 1 September 1898, p. 142. For Conrad's response, see Conrad to William Blackwood, 13 December 1898, *CL* 2:130.
3. As *An Outcast of the Islands* was in press Conrad did briefly pursue another story. Provisionally entitled *The Sisters*, it did not take off but provided ideas that were recycled in *Nostromo* and later *The Arrow of Gold*.
4. See Katherine Isobel Baxter, '*The Rescuer* Synopsis: A Transcription and Commentary', *The Conradian*, 31.1 (2006), 117–27, p. 127.
5. See Garnett to Conrad, 17 June 1896, in *A Portrait in Letters: Correspondence to and about Conrad*, ed. J. H. Stape and Owen Knowles (Amsterdam and Atlanta, GA: Rodopi, 1995), pp. 24–5.
6. There is no evidence that Conrad took similar breaks from writing *Almayer's Folly* and *An Outcast of the Islands*, but this does not mean he didn't.
7. 'The Idiots' finally appeared in *Savoy*, 6 October 1896.
8. This technique reached its apogee in *Nostromo*.
9. A portion of Part II, Chapter 5 is in Ford's hand in the manuscript.
10. Conrad received £300 from the Royal Literary Fund in 1902, £500 from the Royal Bounty Fund in 1905, and an annual Civil List pension of £100 from 1910 to 1917.
11. The Stage Society, a company known for tackling 'difficult' plays, gave *One Day More* a five-performance run at London's Royalty Theatre in June 1905. For a full discussion of Conrad's drama, see Richard J. Hand, *The Theatre of Joseph Conrad: Reconstructed Fictions* (London: Palgrave, 2005).
12. Composed in 1906 and serialized in 1909, *The Nature of a Crime* did not appear in book form until the end of 1924, following Conrad's death.
13. For his opinion of the story, see Conrad to Edward Garnett, 5 November 1912, *CL* 5:128.
14. Paramount's production, *The Road to Romance*, eventually appeared in 1927.
15. As far as we know Conrad was the first major British author to write a film adaptation.

CHAPTER 3

Language

Mary Morzinski and Véronique Pauly

That Joseph Conrad achieved his literary success in a language that was not his first or even second (but quite probably his fourth, following Polish, French and most likely Russian) is a truly impressive feat. Vestiges of his languages emerge in various forms throughout his writing. Below, Mary Morzinski explains how the sounds of Polish transferred to his English pronunciation, how differences between the English and Polish verbal systems surface in his writing and how circumventing the lack of inflections in English creates what many readers recognize as 'foreign flavour' in his style. Véronique Pauly discusses his Gallicisms, common French phrases directly translated into English, in Conrad's stories.

CONRAD'S POLISH AND ENGLISH

One consequence of the mutability of Poland's geographical and political boundaries is that it intensifies the importance of language as a characteristic of national and cultural identity. Ukrainian, Belorussian, Lithuanian, Latvian, Yiddish, Prussian, Russian, German, Austrian German and Polish were all languages or dialects that could be heard during the country's factious history, and, growing up with parents who were ethnic Poles in a territory once Polish, Conrad would most likely have been aware at a young age of multiple linguistic, to say nothing of cultural, differences.

Polish remained the language of the *szlachta*, the gentry class to which Conrad's father and mother belonged, and was the language of his home. The Slavic languages belong to a single family and include not only Polish but also Czech, Slovak and Sorbian (Western Slavic); Russian, Belorussian and Ukrainian (Central Slavonic); and Serbian, Croatian, Slovenian, Bulgarian and Macedonian (Southern Slavonic). They are related in sound, grammar and vocabulary but for the most part are mutually unintelligible.

Common features of Slavic languages include phonemic palatalization, complex consonant clusters, inflections and perfective and imperfective verbal aspect. Although we have only a few reports of Conrad's speech, there is evidence that features of Polish phonology transferred to his spoken English.[1] Ford Madox Ford claimed that Conrad's pronunciation was so faulty at times that he was difficult to understand, while Edward Garnett attributes Conrad's frequent mispronunciation of words to the fact that he had only read them in books rather than heard them.[2]

Whereas the grammatical structure of a target language can be learned at any age, the sounds of a language are best learned in childhood. Conrad heard and spoke French at an early age, but English came to him later, probably not in its spoken form until he was nineteen. Consequently, his spoken English revealed the 'negative transfer' noted by those who found him difficult to understand. In Polish, voiced consonants in word final position are devoiced ([b] becomes [p], [d] becomes [t], [v] becomes [f], [z] becomes [s], and so on).

This feature was evident in Conrad's speech when he reportedly pronounced 'have' as 'half', for example. The Polish vowel system is much simpler than that of English, with only one sound per letter. This contrasts with English vowels, which may have several sounds per letter. For example, *u* has different renderings in 'sun', 'sugar', 'unique' and 'tune', while, in addition, the [u] sound is spelled at times with *oo*, as in 'moon', or *ou*, as in 'soup'. In Polish, on the other hand, *u* is always pronounced with the sound in 'tune'. Therefore, Conrad used that sound to rhyme 'good' [gut] and 'blood' [blut].

Another example of negative transfer, or interference, evident in Conrad's speech is shared by many non-native speakers learning English. The sound made by the spelling *th* in English exists in few other languages and is therefore difficult for learners to make. Native speakers of Germanic languages typically substitute either [t]/[d] or [f]/[v], while native speakers of the Romance and Slavic languages typically substitute [s]/[z], as did Conrad.[3]

In Conrad's writings, we see numerous examples of transfer, particularly from verbal aspect and Polish syntax.[4] In the ancestral development of languages from Proto-European, aspect was a major distinguishing characteristic. It became important in the Slavic languages, whereas tense is emphasized in the Germanic ones. English can express actions or states taking place in the previous past, the recent past, the immediate past, the past including or excluding the present moment, the present or the future, whereas, in contrast, Polish tense only designates now, before now and after now.

Aspectually, however, Polish has a much greater spectrum of semantic distinctions. The perfective/imperfective opposition can indicate whether an action has been completed or is ongoing; whether it is habitual, frequentative or durative; and whether it is deliberate or unintended. One consequence of this difference between the two verbal systems is that a single expression in Polish may have up to seven renderings in English. For example, 'I was taking', 'I (often) took', 'I have been taking', 'I have (often) taken', 'I have (at some time or other) taken', 'I had (often) taken' and 'I had been taking' are all translated by one Polish word: *brałam*.

Although Conrad's grasp of English temporal distinctions notably improved during his writing career and with his longer residence in England, certain forms continued to be problematic throughout his life. For example, while the differences between 'I wrote', 'I have written' and 'I had written' are significant in English, Polish native speakers would have no means of making such a distinction. The following examples demonstrate Conrad's mismanagement of the English forms of 'have':

He has been dead once before, and came to life to die again now. (*AF*, 109)

… and I dragged him by the feet; in through the mud I have dragged him … (*AF*, 96)

The last shriek died out under him in a faint gurgle, and he had secured the relief of absolute silence. (*AF*, 160)

I wanted nothing more. I've had a prize for swimming my second year in the *Conway*. (*TLS*, 258)

Such examples are more frequently found in *Almayer's Folly* than in Conrad's later writings, although they even appear in his last works.

In addition to verbal aspect, another major area of transfer in Conrad's writing is in syntax. Polish is an inflected language, meaning that the grammatical identification of a word (person, number, case, tense) is built into the form, or morphology. English, on the other hand, has lost its inflections and relies upon word order to determine who did what to whom. The flexibility of Polish word order transferred to Conrad's writing as awkwardly worded sentences, not necessarily ungrammatical, but definitely lending a 'foreign flavour'. In the following examples, subject and object have been inverted from normal English word order: 'Hermann, I would find in his shirt-sleeves' (*T*, 113), 'The young man Leonard he had met in town' (*OI*, 34) or 'But the resources of sagacity I did not review' (*C*, 136).

When the verb precedes the subject, adjectival and adverbial complements often seem out of place as well:

Over the white rims of berths stuck out heads with blinking eyes. (*NN*, 8)

… neither ran he much risk of being suddenly lassoed on the road … (*N*, 97)

And yet upon them will depend, more than once, the very life of the ship. (*MS*, 13)

These two features of Conrad's language – verbal aspect and word order – demonstrate the most prevalent evidence of the influence of Polish on his written English. They are an important reason for his enigmatic style, the result of an inter-language expressed through an expert command of English with underpinnings of Polish syntax. The knowledge of these two languages along with French blended into a linguistic mastery that only a writer with Conrad's genius could claim.

A variety of reasons have been projected to explain why Conrad wrote in English rather than French or Polish, many having political and psycho-logical significance. His own words in *A Personal Record* are frequently quoted to answer these claims:

The truth of the matter is that my faculty to write in English is as natural as any other aptitude with which I might have been born … English was for me neither a matter of choice nor adoption. The merest idea of choice had never entered my head. And as to adoption – well, yes, there was adoption; but it was I who was adopted by the genius of the language. (vii)

Regardless of his reasons for choosing English as his literary language, the fact is that he was fluent in English, French and Polish. French seems to have been his preference for discussing philosophical topics, and he used Polish in personal correspondence with Polish relatives and acquaintances. It was in English, however, that his characters came to life and struggled with their moral dilemmas, and it was in that language, his third, that Conrad revealed his world-view and expressed his art.

CONRAD'S FRENCH

'*N'oublie pas ton français, mon chéri*' (Don't forget your French, my darling). Such was the affectionate advice given to the six-year-old Józef Korzeniowski by 'good, ugly Mlle. Durand', his governess at Nowochwastów, the estate of his Uncle Tadeusz' parents-in-law when, in November 1863, after a three-month 'leave' granted to his mother, whose health was declining, mother and son were sent 'back to exile' (*PR*, 65). In this exile, Conrad acquired, thanks to his poet-and-translator father, a bookish knowledge of French and French literature; in particular, as he relates in *A Personal Record*, it was by reading aloud the proofs of his father's translation of Victor Hugo's

Les Travailleurs de la mer that he got his 'first introduction to the sea in literature' (72).

Years later, when his desire to go to sea could no longer be opposed, Marseilles offered a sensible destination. Apart from his having distant connections there, Conrad's command of the language would no doubt have proved decisive. In that port, Conrad acquired the Provençal twang noted by Paul Valéry and G. Jean-Aubry in their tributes to the writer published in the *Nouvelle Revue Française* to mark his death.[5] Both also praised his faultless grammar (not, in fact, true), his rich vocabulary and, in particular, his knowledge of French nautical terms, as well as the sheer pleasure and natural ease with which he conversed in his second language.

Later testimonies qualify and even contradict this glowing report. St-John Perse described Conrad's French as 'dreadful', and René Rapin, in his introduction to his edition of Conrad's letters to Marguerite Poradowska, noted that Conrad made 'frequent and at times serious mistakes' and concluded that, for all its general naturalness, 'as he himself bemoaned, Conrad's French was that of a foreigner'.[6] J. H. Stape makes a similar point, arguing that Conrad's decision not to write in French was, after all, the only pragmatic move he could make since he was already no longer in France when he launched his literary career, and 'that language, with which he had had little daily contact for years, was growing remote to him'.[7] For all its general fluency, Conrad's French was not flawless. Apart from spelling mistakes and omitted accents, it suffers mainly from a certain stiffness, enhanced in his letters by a habit of mistakenly capitalizing the second-person form of address, '*Vous*', as a typographical mark of respect.[8]

The most striking use Conrad made of his knowledge of French arguably occurs in *Lord Jim* in which Marlow's encounter with the French Lieutenant is rendered in highly Gallic English. Marlow's translation of the French Lieutenant's words is peppered with untranslated French words – *merci, voilà, cassis à l'eau* – and also incorporates Gallicisms. The text sometimes supplies the original French in brackets: 'one does what one can (*on fait ce qu'on peut*)' (108), or the delightful, if overly literal, 'I have rolled my hump (*roulé ma bosse*)' (112). But while the former is easily understood, the latter may remain obscure for the reader unfamiliar with French: the only explanation Marlow provides is that this is a 'slang expression' (meaning that one has 'knocked about the world').

The same applies to other Gallicisms not referred back to the original, such as 'one does one's possible' (109) – easily understood, to be sure – or 'make good countenance' (113), the meaning of which may not be immediately clear to all. Marlow's incorporation of Gallicisms is even more puzzling when it is associated with a Gallicism that occurs in a narrative break in Marlow's rendering of this conversation: 'he submitted himself passively to a state of silence' (110). Is this Marlow's or Conrad's? Later in the novel, Conrad takes this hybridization of language a step further with the 'half caste' master of the brigantine whose 'flowing English seemed to be derived from a dictionary compiled by a lunatic' (183). His hilarious 'weapons of crocodile' (183) – a cross-breeding between the French phrase '*larmes de crocodile*' (crocodile tears) and '*armes de crocodile*', meaningless in French – is an instance of language gone quite mad.

Conrad's rendering of Franco-English encounters repeatedly leads to these forms of contamination. In *The Rover*, for instance, Peyrol's conversation with Symons is, quite logically, peppered with French words, for, as Conrad tells us, 'it was ages since he had uttered a sentence in English' (128). Less logical, however, are the Gallicisms in Peyrol's conversations with Lieutenant Réal – when, for instance, Peyrol asks Réal whether he has 'a little friend of any sort' (205) (derived from *une petite amie*, meaning a 'girlfriend', whereas 'kind' would arguably be more idiomatic English than 'sort', possibly derived from *sorte*). Whether these are to be viewed as part of a stylistic strategy aimed at giving local colour to a story staged in Southern France is unclear.

Conrad's French was at times very much an Englishman's. His use of the phrase '*à propos des bottes*' ('to no apparent purpose') in *Under Western Eyes* (42), *Chance* (142) and *Victory* (8) is a vivid case in point. The expression circulated in English in this incorrect form – '*à propos des*' instead of '*à propos de*' – and there is 'strong evidence that Conrad knew the idiom in the form in which it circulated in English rather than (for the most part) in French'.[9] The grammatical mistake that Anglicized this French expression was indeed Conrad's as well, as is evidenced in a letter to Jean-Aubry in which he expresses his indignation at Gide's suggestion that *The Arrow of Gold* be translated by a woman: '*Il me jette en pature a un tas des femmes qui lui font des histoires*' (He's throwing me to a lot of women who become fussy with him (*CL* 6:502–3)).[10] Conrad's use of '*à propos des bottes*' thus illustrates the apparent paradox that he was most English when outwardly very French.

Conrad professed a lofty idea of the French language, possibly on the grounds that 'of all the countries in Europe it is with France that Poland had the most connection' (*PR*, 121). In 1906, he called French '*la pierre de touché* [*sic*] *de l'expression – sinon de la pensée elle-même*' (the cornerstone of expression – if not of thought itself (*CL* 3:383)), and in 1918, refuting 'the absurd legend set afloat by Hugh Clifford' that he 'had hesitated between

English and French as a writing language', he stated that 'If I had been offered the alternative I would have been afraid to grapple with French which is crystallized in the form of its sentences and therefore more exacting and less appealing ... But there was never any alternative offered and even dreamed of' (*CL* 6:227–8).

Conrad's silence about the other obvious choice available to him – writing in Polish – is telling. But beyond this, whether there actually was something in the nature of the French language that daunted him, or whether these statements constitute a rationalization of what was, after all, the only correct decision given his circumstances, is debatable. French, therefore, was to remain, as Zdzisław Najder has stated it, 'the language of social immediacy and also a language of theoretical discourse'.[11] But Conrad's propensity to lapse into French in conversation, along with his admiration for French writers – Flaubert, Maupassant, Anatole France and Mérimée, among others[12] – did not help to counteract the misconception about his origins that made critics and journalists view him as a 'Slavic' writer with 'Gallic manners'.[13]

NOTES

1. 'Transfer' is the linguistic term referring to the influence of a native language on a target language (second or tertiary language being learned). Many languages share certain features, such as sounds, grammatical patterns and cognates, with other languages. The extent to which two languages share the same features determines positive transfer while the extent to which the features of two languages differ determines negative transfer, or 'interference'. Languages belonging to the same family share more features than languages belonging to different families.

2. Ford Madox Ford, *Joseph Conrad: A Personal Remembrance* (London: Duckworth, 1924), p. 34; Edward Garnett, *Letters from Joseph Conrad 1895–1924* (London: Nonesuch, 1928), p. xix.

3. E. Pugh, 'Joseph Conrad as I Knew Him', *T. P.'s and Cassell's Weekly*, 23 August 1924, p. 575.

4. For a detailed discussion of this topic, see Mary Morzinski, *Linguistic Influence of Polish on Joseph Conrad's English*, ed. Wieslaw Krajka. Conrad: Eastern and Western Perspectives 3 (Lublin: Maria Curie-Skłodowska University; New York: Columbia University Press, 1994).

5. Georges Jean-Aubry, 'Souvenirs (fragments)', and Paul Valéry, 'Sujet d'une conversation avec Conrad', in *Hommage à Joseph Conrad, La Nouvelle Revue Française*, 135 (1 December 1924), 21–3, 30–8.

6. St-John Perse cited in Zdzisław Najder, *Joseph Conrad: A Chronicle*, trans. Halina Carroll-Najder (Cambridge: Cambridge University Press, 1983), p. 560; René Rapin, 'Le français de Joseph Conrad', in *Lettres de Joseph Conrad à Marguerite Poradowska* (Geneva: Droz, 1966), p. 53 (my translation).

7. J. H. Stape, *The Several Lives of Joseph Conrad* (London: Heinemann, 2007), p. 57.

8. Conrad's admiration for Henry James, as well as his fear of making mistakes in English, led him to converse with the great master and to write to him in French, invariably addressing him as '*cher maître*'.

9. Jeremy Hawthorn, 'À Propos "À propos de(s) bottes"', *L'Époque Conradienne*, 32 (2006), 41–8, p. 43.

10. The omitted accents are Conrad's. In correct French, the phrase should read: '*il me jette en pâture à un tas de femmes qui lui font des histoires.*'

11. Najder, *Joseph Conrad: A Chronicle*, p. 223.

12. On French influences, see Yves Hervouet, *The French Face of Joseph Conrad* (Cambridge: Cambridge University Press, 1990), and Owen Knowles, 'Conrad, Anatole France, and the Early French Romantic Tradition: Some Influences', *Conradiana*, 11.1 (1979), 41–61.

13. See, for instance, James Huneker, 'A Visit to Joseph Conrad, the Mirror of the Sea', *New York Times* (Magazine), 17 November 1912, p. 4.

CHAPTER 4

Letters

Gene M. Moore

Joseph Conrad wrote some 5,000 letters in three different languages, nearly all of them now available in the nine volumes of *The Collected Letters*.[1] They constitute a kind of diary in epistolary form, providing countless contexts for tracing the development of Conrad's works and the preoccupations of his daily life. His reclusive habits and the need to make a living effectively chained him to his writing-desk, so that the letters were not only a relief from the agony of composition but a primary mode of communication with the world beyond (or even with the world close at hand: there is one in-house letter from Conrad, bedridden with gout upstairs at Capel House, to his wife Jessie, who lay recovering from knee surgery in her bedroom downstairs; *CL* 6:346). As Zdzisław Najder has observed, 'Conrad's social contacts consisted mainly of an exchange of letters.'[2]

Like his literary career, Conrad's epistolary career began late, and he began writing letters in English later still. All the letters from the first forty years of his life fit into the first volume of *The Collected Letters*. Before the publication of his first novel in 1895, Conrad had only two regular correspondents. He wrote in Polish to his guardian Tadeusz Bobrowski, his mother's brother, an earnest, ironic uncle who administered an estate south-west of Kiev called Kazimierówka and loved his adventurous nephew like a wayward son, not only sending him a regular allowance and sound (but often unheeded) advice, but speeding to Marseilles at news of his attempted suicide. Conrad's letters to his uncle were lost when Kazimierówka was 'burned down by rabble' in 1917,[3] although some of Bobrowski's replies survive. There are many important years for which no letters by Conrad exist, among them 1887 and 1888, when he reached the farthest point of his Malay navigation and first took command of a ship. In 1890, shortly before he went to the Congo, he met a distant cousin, a newly widowed novelist named Marguerite Poradowska – the 'Aunt' of 'Heart of Darkness' – and sent her letters in French from various ports of call, such as Kazimierówka and Kinshasa and Adelaide. Together with Bobrowski's letters, the 109 surviving letters to Poradowska offer the most detailed first-hand account of Conrad's years of literary apprenticeship.

Conrad became a writer of English letters only shortly before he became an author of English tales. From Calcutta he wrote to a friend in Lowestoft in a cool and cynical mode: 'I look with the serenity of despair and the indifference of contempt upon the passing events' (*CL* 1:17). This was written before he had been to Borneo and the Congo. Seven years later, he began a much warmer and more confident discourse with former passengers who had spent three months in his company on the *Torrens*: with a cotton merchant named Redmayne and his daughter, who played the piano, or with a restless young barrister named Galsworthy. Once he settled in England, married and became a published author, the pace and range of his correspondence increased accordingly. From 1890, the year of his Congo journey, only 19 letters survive; by 1900, the year of *Lord Jim*, there are 95, a nearly five-fold increase. In 1910 he suffered a nervous breakdown, yet he still managed to send 89 letters, all but a few written by hand. As Conrad's reputation expanded, so too did his correspondence, so that in 1920 the acclaimed author sent some 285 letters, most of them typed from dictation.

Many of his correspondents were his literary *confrères*, like Hugh Clifford, Stephen Crane, Ford Madox Ford, Cunninghame Graham, W. H. Hudson, Henry James, H. G. Wells or Edith Wharton, men and women who knew about writing and shared with Conrad an impressive range of cultural references, not to mention French. His literary correspondence reveals Conrad as a versatile performer, not only expressing ideas or conveying information but playing with idiom and register and ironic self-mockery, taking liberties with his non-native tongue even as he uses it to complain or to express annoyance. It has been said that Conrad felt in Polish, thought in French, and wrote in English, but the letters belie such a neat division: Conrad often used French (or Italian, or Latin) expressions in his letters to Polish or English correspondents. He mixed not only languages but also epistolary conventions. For example, in Polish (as in German), it is customary and respectful to capitalize the pronouns used for one's addressee. Conrad extended this courtesy by addressing his correspondents as 'You' or 'Vous' in capitals of widely varying sizes, both relative and absolute.[4]

Writing letters also liberated Conrad from the perpetual embarrassment of his erratically accentuated English, which left him shy of formal public occasions where he was at risk of being misunderstood.[5] As he told one of his French translators in 1911, 'My pronunciation is rather defective to this day. Having unluckily no ear, my accentuation is uncertain, especially when in the course of a conversation I become self-conscious' (*CL* 4:409). But if his spoken accent was uncertain, he claimed, not without reason, that 'Idiomatically I am never at fault' (*CL* 8:38); and in his letters he could give free rein to his command of the language, playing with various accents and multi-cultural and multi-linguistic references, dipping into slang or citing not only Shakespeare and the Bible but also tags from characters by Dickens or Turgenev. And, along with literary matters, Conrad's letters also contain evidence of his sympathies and antipathies in politics, his opinions about the Boer War or the Russian Revolution or the cause of Polish independence, or his feelings about the real Kurtzes and Holroyds and Vladimirs of this world.

They display a wide range of emotion, at times so wide as to suggest that his cries of agony or despair are in large measure rhetorical performances to be understood not literally but almost therapeutically. The letters also reveal Conrad's likes and dislikes in a range of more casual modes, especially his dislikes: 'I hate machinery' (*CL* 2:4); 'I hate babies' (*CL* 2:33); 'I hate photographs anyhow!' (*CL* 2:140); 'I hate restraint' (*CL* 2:373); 'I hate T. F. U[nwin] more than ever' (*CL* 3:39); 'I don't eat strawberries because by a merciful dispensation of Providence I detest the things' (*CL* 3:340); 'I hate to have my portraits published' (*CL* 3:496); 'I hate parading in the capital in a gout-boot' (*CL* 4:170); 'I hate the autumn season' (*CL* 5:129); 'I hate paperasses [paper scraps] of all kinds' (*CL* 5:303). They also record his shifting relations with his correspondents: the cooling of his relations with Ford, or his cautious warming to the Doubledays. In 1910, when Conrad's agent – 'Dear Pinker' – let slip an ill-considered reference to Conrad's accent, the tone of Conrad's letters instantly froze, thawing only gradually after two years had passed from 'Sir' to 'Dear Sir' or 'Dear Mr. Pinker' to 'My dear Sir' and finally to 'My dear Pinker' (*CL* 5:24–40).

The largest number of Conrad's letters, more than one-fifth of the total, are those to Pinker, and have chiefly to do with the business of authorship. At the beginning of his career, Conrad was obliged to negotiate directly with his publishers or their agents, with T. Fisher Unwin, Sydney S. Pawling of Heinemann or William Blackwood's London editor David S. Meldrum, while his wife helped to prepare typed copies of his work for submission. These early letters represent Conrad as a natural aristocrat who depends upon others for the management of his mundane affairs, and as an author congenitally unable to plan ahead, to foretell how much more time and effort a given text would require. His inability to meet deadlines, or to live within his means, obliged him to adopt a posture of apology and self-justification that became habitual over time, and, as his gout grew worse with age, he complained increasingly about his health. At times Conrad seems himself to wonder why he cannot manage things better, as when in 1908 he told Pinker 'Nobody can say I have a vice – gambling or drink to lead me astray. It may be that I don't *count* my money very well' (*CL* 4:24).

In the new century Conrad began to receive typed letters from his publishers, but it was considered rude to type a personal letter even though his increasing correspondence made writing by hand ever more burdensome. He eventually found help in the form of an agent, and his first typed letter dates from 1903, announcing to his three publishers that henceforth Mr. James Brand Pinker of Effingham House, Arundel Street, would represent him in all business matters relating to his literary work and collect all revenues on his behalf (*CL* 3:19). Pinker modernized Conrad's business practices, finding him a typist and having other typists prepare multiple copies of Conrad's texts for submission to magazines or publishers. Soon Pinker also had a telephone (*CL* 3:177).

Conrad's letters bear first-hand testimony to the processes and conventions of the literary market-place, and chronicle the elaboration of a system designed to maximize the number of times a given work could be brought to the market for profit. His later works appeared first in serial publications separately in England and the United States, then as books published and reprinted in various British and American editions. With recognition came plans for collected editions in England and America; and a collector's market developed for essays privately reprinted as pamphlets, or for de luxe editions of his stage adaptations. Conrad found that he could also make money by selling the film rights to his works, and he was surprised to discover that collectors would pay cash for the drafts and scraps from his writing-desk, sometimes even in advance of work actually done. This expanding process necessarily took up a great deal of time and epistolary attention.

Fame came late to Conrad, and never ceased to puzzle him. His health was never robust, and the increasing demands of the management of his literary estate, even with the help of Pinker and then of Pinker's son Eric, took a heavy toll. Conrad always wrote slowly, and was handicapped by increasingly frequent episodes of gout, sometimes so severe that he could not hold a pen at all. After 1917 the letters are usually the products of dictation to Conrad's secretary, Miss Lilian M. Hallowes, with Conrad inscribing the opening and closing salutations along with his signature, and sometimes adding a handwritten postscript or appended paragraphs. The letters in French and Polish were necessarily handwritten. Conrad's habit of correcting typescripts also extended to the letters, which he would amend by hand, so that the recipient can usually see his first thought as well as his second. The demands of Conrad's growing reputation eventually meant that to the agony of composition was added the sheer physical pain of marketing the personal touch: he agreed to sign each of the 1,000 copies of T. Werner Laurie's limited edition of the stage adaptation of *The Secret Agent* (*CL* 8:24, 28), and the collector George T. Keating offered him $1,000 to add personal inscriptions to his copies of Conrad's American first editions (*CL* 8:284).

Conrad was seriously in debt throughout most of his writing career. He broke even only with the success of *Chance* in 1914 and its confirmation with *Victory* a year later, a success which attracted film-makers and stage adaptors to his works and tempted him also to recycle his works in more lucrative forms. By the age of sixty he achieved solvency, but his financial worries were by then too deeply ingrained to be assuaged, and he could never quite learn to live within his means, or to convince himself that his income would be adequate to cover the needs of his sons or his wife's medical expenses. These worries about health and money also find copious expression in the letters, to such an extent that Ford Madox Ford, upon reading the letters published by Jean-Aubry in 1927, was moved to ask:

Which was Conrad? The bothered, battered person who wrote innumerable, woeful, tactful, timid letters ... or the amazing being that I remember? With a spoken word or two he could create a whole world and give to himself the aspect of a returned Sir Francis Drake emerging from the territory of the Anthropophagi and the darkness of the Land of Fire.[6]

What indeed is the connection between the 'bothered, battered' writer of letters and the dazzling teller of tales? The simple answer is that Conrad was both, but that the practical conventions of letter-writing obliged him to limit his epistolary yarn-spinning to brief anecdotes or sketches from memory, as when he mentioned to Hugh Clifford an encounter with a Sulu slave-trader who 'endeavoured to split my skull with a horrid wood-chopper' (*CL* 2:226).

A relatively small part of the correspondence is devoted to the art of writing, and only rarely does Conrad provide a glimpse behind the scenes into the secrets of his craft, either responding to queries about his own works or giving advice to others. He deferred to Clifford's more extensive knowledge of the Malay world, for example, yet felt that Clifford's overly explicit phrasing in his Malay stories left too little to the reader's imagination:

words, groups of words, words standing alone, are symbols of life, have the power in their sound or their aspect to present the very thing you wish to hold up before the mental vision of your readers. The things 'as they are' exist in words; therefore words should be handled with care lest the picture, the image of truth abiding in facts should become distorted – or blurred. (*CL* 2:200)

Conrad sometimes wrote to translators or reviewers to correct what he saw as errors in their interpretations. He chided Edward Garnett for making far too much of the 'Slavic' element in his works, and Richard Curle for drawing specific links between ships and stories that left too little to the reader's imagination. Yet he was not above seeking advice from those whose opinions he respected, valuing Garnett's criticism of *The Rover* and his comments on dialogue in the first draft chapters of *Suspense*, which Garnett found artificial and anachronistic.

Conrad was surprised to discover that collectors were willing to pay for his manuscripts and for inscribed copies of his works, but he would surely have been even more surprised to discover that his personal letters – including those marked 'Private and Confidential' – would someday be brought to the market and find their way into published volumes for all the world to read. Ethically and legally, letters were considered private unless their author authorized their publication, and after the writer's death correspondents were expected to observe a decent interval before selling letters or making their contents public. A large number of Conrad's manuscripts and typescripts were auctioned in New York in November 1923 when John Quinn sold his Conrad collection, but none of Conrad's letters to Quinn were included in the sale. Nor were letters included in the sale of J. B. Pinker's effects in December 1924, nor in the Hodgson sale the following March, when Conrad's widow and his executors brought his literary remains to the auction block. The line between letters and inscriptions in books can be difficult to draw, but it seems that the first sale of Conrad's letters took place in June 1925, nearly a year after his death, when four letters to the impresario Joseph Benrimo appeared in a catalogue of London bookseller Frank Hollings.

In 1927, the first scholarly edition of Conrad's letters in English appeared in the form of G. Jean-Aubry's two-volume biography, *Joseph Conrad: Life & Letters*, complete with footnotes and indexes, but silently omitting trivial or personal remarks. The following year, Conrad's many letters to Sir Sidney and Lady Colvin were auctioned in 103 lots, and both Edward Garnett and Richard Curle published volumes containing their own correspondence with Conrad, also sanitized (but not completely: the publication of Conrad's wry remarks about Ford (*CL* 2:257) prompted Ford to send Garnett a long letter of reproach). Since that time, Conrad's letters have been sold and published with regularity, although they have been slow to figure largely in scholarly argument. Edward W. Said's dissertation, published in 1966, was among the first scholarly books to make extensive use of the available correspondence.

Now that virtually all the letters are in print, there remains the question of their relevance to the meaning of Conrad's works. As against the *mots justes* of Conrad's fictions, the letters contain a good many *mots injustes*, spontaneous expressions of shifting moods, and a good many assertions that Conrad might well have lived to regret, but to his credit they contain nothing truly dishonourable and remain a delight to read. They help us to understand many things about the tone of his times, the conception and production of his fictions and about his immense difficulties in making a living as an author, but whether the contexts they provide can reveal the figure in Conrad's carpet remains to be seen.

NOTES

1. For comparison, there exist some 10,423 letters by Henry James and nearly 12,000 by Charles Dickens. Some Conrad letters were auctioned decades ago and remain unlocated, while others survive only in transcription or translations. The Beinecke Rare Book and Manuscript Library at Yale holds half a letter to Edward Garnett torn vertically down the middle (*CL* 1:304).

2. Najder, *Joseph Conrad: A Life*, trans. Halina Carroll-Najder (Rochester: Camden House, 2007), p. 247.

3. Najder, *A Life*, p. 494n. Who were these 'rabble', one wonders, and how much did they have in common with the peasants who had ransacked the estate of Conrad's great-uncle Nicholas in 1863 (*PR*, 58–63)?

4. *The Collected Letters* attempt to reproduce Conrad's inconsistent capitals in both English and French, while letters in Polish are given only in English translation with lower-case pronouns. Capitalization may be a visible expression of respect in some of Conrad's manuscripts, as in *An Outcast of the Islands*, where the initial letter of 'Captain' seems to vary in size according to the speaker.

5. In their autobiographies, both F. N. Doubleday and William Lyon Phelps expressed amazement that a man who spoke English so badly could manage to write it so well. No recordings of Conrad's voice are known to exist, but an echo of his accent is recorded in the mistakes Miss Hallowes would sometimes make while taking dictation, for example typing 'lover's fears' for Conrad's 'lower spheres'.

6. Ford Madox Ford, 'The Other House', in *Critical Essays*, ed. Max Saunders and Richard Stang (New York: New York University Press, 2004), p. 272.

CHAPTER 5

Literary influences

Owen Knowles

'Books are an integral part of one's life', wrote Conrad in *A Personal Record* (73), an autobiographical reminiscence that, among other things, evokes the symbolism of books and writers in marking the key formative stages of his life. To the Polish-born creative writer who began a literary career in England in 1895, 'books' carried an especially resonant symbolic force: they provided him with entry to a new vocation, to a community of fellow writers and to supporting traditions that would take the place of those he had moved away from.

The range and quality of the literary influences that consequently come to shape his novels require some prefatory general remarks. In the first place, his richly allusive works point to a range of reading so wide and various that all of his influences cannot be included here. To mention only one area, his astonishingly omnivorous reading of the works and authors central to the evolution of Western mythology – classical writers, the Bible, Shakespeare, Cervantes, Goethe and so on – has a formidable impact upon all of his work: so, for example, 'Heart of Darkness' is a *bricolage* making creative use of numerous shards or traces from historical literatures; in *Lord Jim* echoes from both Shakespeare's *Hamlet* (1601) and Goethe's play *Torquato Tasso* (1790) suggest their wider influence in the novel; *Victory* owes a primary debt to Shakespeare's *The Tempest* (1611) and a subsidiary one to John Milton's *Comus* (1634). Second, some of his formative influences were of a long-standing kind, dating back to his childhood reading in Poland and including not only Polish writers,[1] but also the tempting worlds of escape available through such authors as Frederick Marryat, Charles Dickens, Fenimore Cooper and Louis Garneray. Finally, the formative influences upon Conrad's fiction tend to enforce the image of a writer richly poised on the borderline between varying national literary traditions – a writer described by one of his friends as having the 'resources of a mind steeped in the modern literature of Europe, especially in that of France'.[2] As this description indicates, French writing and writers form a major part of his literary inheritance. Generally his reading in nineteenth-century French literature exposed him to an exciting generic range of writing – for example, the exotic novel, French symbolist writings and the more experimental Naturalism being developed in the 1890s; and it embraced most of the major nineteenth-century French novelists, including Stendhal, Prosper Mérimée, Victor Hugo, Honoré de Balzac, Alphonse Daudet, Pierre Loti and Émile Zola.[3]

Two French writers, Gustave Flaubert (1821–80) and Guy de Maupassant (1850–93), are of particular importance as the presiding guardians overseeing Conrad's birth as a writer. In *A Personal Record*, he describes his final year as a seaman in Rouen, on the eve of his transformation into a full-time writer, secretly 'scribbling' at his first novel, *Almayer's Folly*. That Rouen should also have been Flaubert's birthplace and the setting for many scenes in *Madame Bovary* (1857) is for Conrad a talismanic fact: he goes on to imagine himself, a humble believer, watched over by 'the shade of old Flaubert', and concludes, 'Was he not, in his unworldly, almost ascetic, devotion to his art a sort of literary, saint-like hermit?' (2). The semi-religious character of the description is especially telling in suggesting both the high altar at which Conrad worshipped and the shaping influence upon him of Flaubert's elevated notion of the 'artist' as a semi-reclusive and single-minded anchorite. A similar sense of the artistic pursuit as a high mission was to shape every detail in Conrad's first manifesto, the 'Preface' to *The Nigger of the 'Narcissus'*: here, the 'strenuously aspiring' artist is pictured as occupying a 'lonely region of stress and strife', responding with 'unswerving devotion' to the demands of his art and abandoning the known 'gods' in pursuit of the truth within 'the core of each convincing moment' (x–xi).

The combined evidence from all of Conrad's writings – letters, essays and novels – also suggests that here was a writer fully alert to the new poetics that Flaubert had established for the novel – including a narrative authority founded on impersonality and authorial self-abnegation, ideals of heightened visuality, the pursuit of *le mot juste* and the quest for refined principles of structure. The issue of Flaubert's influence upon Conrad the practitioner is more problematic, not least because, as Conrad himself pointed out, no sensible writer would ever have the temerity to think of 'imitating', or even closely emulating, a figure as great as Flaubert. Nevertheless, Conrad, particularly in his early phase, can be felt to make an important general compact with the tradition established by the 'master', whose influence in his work is everywhere sensed, but not often directly seen. *Lord Jim* is perhaps the novel where the influence of *Madame Bovary* reaches full fruition, notably felt in Conrad's refined techniques (of, for example, montage and visual evocation). Additionally, Jim, like his predecessor Almayer, can fruitfully be regarded as a study in *Bovaryisme*, a condition named by later commentators after Emma Bovary and associated with a personality type driven by the habit of romantic fantasy and sublimating wish-fulfilment. Conrad's portrait of the chivalric Jim may occasionally echo Cervantes' *Don Quixote* (1605–15), but his chief debt is to Flaubert's more analytic presentation of a kind of quixoticism that develops into something perilously akin to a personality disorder or retrogressive obsession, which ultimately leads the dreamer into a painful collision with, and final defeat by, the constraints of commonplace reality.

Conrad had first read Flaubert during his sea career, commenting after his 're-reading' of *Madame Bovary* in 1892 that the French master had 'enough imagination for two realists' (*CL* 1:111); in 1894, he was to begin his engagement with the works of Flaubert's chief disciple. Where Flaubert had compelled awed admiration, Maupassant prompted the excited Conrad into more immediate practical emulation. During the early part of his career, from 1897 to 1904, he was deeply immersed in Maupassant's works. In 1894, his close study of the latter's *Pierre et Jean* (1888) left him in 'profoundest despair': 'It seems nothing, but it has a technical complexity which makes me tear my hair. One feels like weeping with rage while reading it' (*CL* 1:185). Again, Maupassant and Flaubert appear to have provided a keystone in his early collaboration with Ford Madox Ford, as the latter records: 'But that which really brought us together was a devotion to Flaubert and Maupassant. We discovered that we both had *Félicité*, *St.-Julien l'Hospitalier*, immense passages of *Madame Bovary*, *La Nuit*, *Ce Cochin de Morin*, and immense passages of *Une Vie* by heart.'[4] In 1903, Conrad was even further immersed in Maupassant's works as he helped Ford's wife, Elsie Martindale, to translate the French writer's stories, a task that left him 'astonished at the Maupassantesque style one can give to English prose' (*CL* 3:54).

This 'saturation' left Conrad with an ineradicable admiration for the French writer's grown-up integrity of vision, which he described in terms that echo his own ideals: 'He is merciless and yet gentle with his mankind … he looks with an eye of profound pity upon their troubles, deceptions and misery. But he looks at them all. He sees – and does not turn away his head. As a matter of fact he is courageous. Courage and justice are not popular virtues' (*NLL*, 29). The width, depth and subtlety of Maupassant's 'seeing' were, in Conrad's assessment, always linked with the French writer's technical refinement, economy of means and what he termed 'the picture-producing power of arranged words' (*CL* 2:435). His stated ideal in the

'Preface' to *The Nigger of the 'Narcissus'*, of making the reader '*see*' (x), may thus be read as testifying to his own sense of having inherited Maupassant's exacting legacy, that of employing acts of visual seeing which, through the agency of *le mot juste* and stringent selection, become the very condition for sharply penetrating *in*sight. Like Conrad in his 'Preface', Maupassant also emphasizes acts of significant perception as a form of rescue-work:

> The skill of his plan will not therefore consist in emotion or charm, in a beguiling opening or a thrilling catastrophe, but in the ingenious grouping of changeless little facts from which the real meaning of the work will emerge … and throw into relief in a special way all those that might have remained unnoticed by the unobservant onlookers, and which give the book its meaning and value as a whole.[5]

The description here offers striking anticipation of effects developed in some of Conrad's more 'poetic' stories from the pre-1900 phase of his career, such as *The Nigger* and 'Heart of Darkness'. Excluding the convention of 'thrills', 'charm' and obvious 'catastrophe', these works develop an alternative method that he and Ford termed '*progression d'effet*'.[6] The phrase is full of implication: it suggests a scrupulous attention to the 'small', whether it be a fleeting glimpse, an image or an observed detail, but it also embraces the wider effects that arrive through their careful selection and plastic grouping – effects of narrative tempo, singleness of impression and coherence of effect. Conrad's relish in extending the possibilities of the 'Maupassantesque' into the language and form of his fiction, particularly during the period 1896–1906, makes the French writer the most important single influence upon his practice.

Unlike the impact of Flaubert and Maupassant, which occurred at the beginning of Conrad's literary career and constituted a form of discipleship, the influence of a third French writer, Conrad's celebrated contemporary Anatole France (1844–1924), essayist, novelist and a Nobel Prize laureate in 1921, was of a later date, slower in effect, and more diffuse. It is not for that reason less important, but simply different, and its patterns more difficult to anatomize. Although Conrad valued France as an artist, the chief source of his admiration lay elsewhere. It was predominantly the *intellectual* quality and sceptical probity of France's work that attracted him when, in his essay of 1904 on the writer, he stressed that the 'proceedings of France's thought compel our intellectual admiration' and went on to admire the quality of a mind combining 'Pyrrhonic philosophy … Benedictine erudition … and most humane irony' (*NLL*, 40, 42).

France's *La Vie littéraire* (1888–92), a four-volume series of essays sensitively attuned to contemporary European artistic and intellectual movements, stands out as a major formative influence. Among the spoils he gathered from France's essays were scores of aphorisms, generalizations and *obiter dicta* on life and art that often appear in his work as more or less directly translated borrowings. Some of these debts suggest that France was at times a *maître à penser*, a decisive influence upon Conrad's way of regarding the world; elsewhere it seems truer to say that what Conrad takes over from France's essays are not attitudes and beliefs, but a body of reflective wisdoms that supplement his own deeply held convictions or are transplanted into new dramatic contexts. Another pattern of influence is evident in Conrad's habit of garnering from France's biographical sketches in *La Vie littéraire* germinating ideas for characters and states of mind in his fiction: in particular, France's essays on the French writers Prosper Mérimée and Benjamin Constant as flawed individuals whose multiple potential selves are destructively at odds with each other provided suggestive blueprints for the characters of Decoud (in *Nostromo*) and Heyst (in *Victory*), as well as for the maladies of life-denying scepticism that blight their lives. In both novels, these influences are supplemented by yet more from France's other works, notably *Le Lys rouge* (1894), whose heroine Thérèse is a major shaping force in the presentation of Lena in *Victory*.

Conrad's French inheritance partly helps to explain why, in his essay of 1904, 'A Glance at Two Books' (*LE*, 132–7), he should choose to dissociate himself from the 'national' English novelist in order implicitly to align himself with a line of conscious 'artist'-craftsmen. Yet two English writers had held a long-standing appeal dating back to his youth in Poland. Frederick Marryat (1792–1848), the widely popular seaman-turned-writer, is perhaps an unexpected name to find among Conrad's later literary influences, as he himself tacitly acknowledges when, in his essay 'Tales of the Sea', he describes an affiliation based upon the attraction of opposites: 'To the artist his work is interesting as a completely successful expression of an unartistic nature' (*NLL*, 53). If, in part, Conrad's later devotion to the creator of *Peter Simple* (1834) and *Mr Midshipman Easy* (1836) had a sentimental basis, it also rested upon his recognition of Marryat's position as the progenitor of the English sea story, *the* 'writer of the Service' (54) and the creator of a national mythology. 'Youth' owes a not inconsiderable debt to Marryat, and when the youthful Marlow describes events on board the *Judea* as 'the deuce of an adventure – something you read about' (*Y*, 12), he might well have in mind the early-nineteenth-century 'enslaver of youth' (*NLL*, 53). If in part the older and more sceptical Conrad was to revalue the appeal of Marryat, he would never lose respect for – or deny his debt to – the latter's portrayal of the 'honourable but conventional' code that underpins the life of the nameless collective crew, 'the spirit animating the crowd of obscure men who knew how to build for their country such a shining monument of memories' (*NLL*, 54).

The other English writer to evoke his warmest affection was Charles Dickens, whose *Nicholas Nickleby* (1839) had the special significance for Conrad of a work that first introduced him to English imaginative literature, albeit in Polish translation. Chief among his early favourites, however, was *Bleak House* (1853), 'a work of the master for which I have such an admiration, or rather such an intense and unreasoning admiration, dating from the days of my childhood, that its very weaknesses are more precious to me than the strengths of other men's work' (*PR*, 124). Dickens is recalled here as less of an influence in the conventional sense than a long-standing English friend, who had not only charmed the young Conrad, but presumably also spoken intimately – as a writer whose works often dealt with the spectacle of abandoned or psychologically orphaned children – to an isolated orphan in Poland.

Conrad's later fictional debt to Dickens has been described as a legacy 'too extensive and too profound ever to be more than adequately charted'.[7] An appropriate starting-point would be with *The Secret Agent* and *Chance*. Significantly, both have London settings and incorporate, even while they modify, the rich urban mythologies associated with *Bleak House*. *The Secret Agent*, in particular, evokes a cityscape as part-jungle and part-subaqueous world remarkably similar to the one Conrad associated with Dickens: 'that wonder city, the growth of which bears no sign of intelligent design, but many traces of freakishly sombre fantasy the great Master [Dickens] knew so well how to bring out' (*NLL*, 152). Along with this, the novel displays a marked Dickensian relish for comic-grotesque visualization in the portrayal of the anarchists and bureaucratic functionaries, who are often treated with a frosty sarcasm reminiscent of the opening chapters of *Our Mutual Friend* (1864). Another Dickens novel, *Little Dorrit* (1857), seems to preside over *Chance*, where the relationship between Flora and her father, described at one point as 'Figures from Dickens – pregnant with pathos' (162), recalls the relationship between Amy Dorrit and her incarcerated father. In all of these cases, the recognizable Dickensian effects in Conrad's work – thumbnail caricature, grotesque effects and moments of pathos – are invariably boldly announced and savoured by the adept *pasticheur* as a form of respectful homage. Elsewhere, there may even be an element of the affectionate joke in Conrad's play with Dickens, as when he shows MacWhirr in 'Typhoon' with his Dickensian 'gamp' or assigns the name 'Toodles' to one of the characters in *The Secret Agent*. In these cases, playfulness and pastiche also signify the measure of Conrad's detachment from Dickens, one allowing him to keep his cherished predecessor at arm's length in order to develop more stringently impersonal forms and styles.

Given Conrad's inherited antipathy to all things Russian, it might be expected that he would be largely immune to influences from its writers. The works of Ivan Turgenev (1818–83) prove to be an exception. Having first read some of Turgenev's novels as a youth in Poland, Conrad re-immersed himself in the writer's works during the early part of his literary career (1895–1900), when he regularly received Constance Garnett's pioneer translations. When, in 1917, Edward Garnett collected his prefaces to his wife's translations in a single volume, Conrad readily agreed to write a foreword and there described the Russian 'artist' in terms comparable to those he reserved for his revered favourites, Flaubert and Maupassant. In this essay (*NLL*, 45–8), Conrad seeks to underplay Turgenev's Russianness by placing him within a wider 'Western' context congenial to the English reader and emphasizing his cosmopolitanism, humanism and political liberalism. Several specific links between the writings of the two authors have been discussed by Paul Kirschner,[8] including Conrad's planning of a series of sea sketches (later *The Mirror of the Sea*) as a work 'in the spirit of Turgenev's Sportsman's Sketches' (*CL* 3:132) with the possible title of *A Seaman's Sketches*. As several other critics have pointed out, Turgenev's basic division of mankind into two fundamental types – as signalled in his 1860 lecture 'Hamlet and Don Quixote: The Two Eternal Human Types' – as well as his conception of the 'superfluous man' – as embodied in Lermontov's Chulkaturin in 'The Diary of a Superfluous Man' (1850) – are likely to have had a pivotal significance for the creator of Martin Decoud, Razumov and Axel Heyst.

Conrad's essay on Turgenev also shows this Russian novelist figuring as an antitype to his contemporary, Fyodor Dostoevsky (1821–81). The stress upon Turgenev as a 'Western' artist is influenced – and indeed partly shaped – by Conrad's recurrent need to use him as a bulwark against, and a stick to beat, the 'convulsed terror haunted' and Slavonic Dostoevsky: 'All his [Turgenev's] creations, fortunate and unfortunate, oppressed and oppressors are human beings, not strange beasts in a menagerie or damned souls knocking themselves to pieces in the stuffy darkness of mystical contradictions' (*NLL*, 48, 47). Thus heatedly demonized and apparently exorcized, the Dostoevsky constructed by the essay nevertheless tends to emerge with the charismatic force of a dangerous, but tempting, Mephistopheles.

The part played by Dostoevsky in *Under Western Eyes* forms an intri-guingly elusive chapter in the history of Conrad's literary influences. His turn

towards 'things Russian' in this novel of 1911 was destined to engage the
deepest sensitivities of a writer of Polish origin, as well as to involve unresolved
tensions in his Polish inheritance. As the novel's preface also implies, the
decision to deal with Russian life entailed a further challenge to his inherited
convictions in demanding a greater detachment than he had ever before been
called upon to make. Yet the claim to detachment would always be tested by
another powerful 'haunting' felt in the novel's agitated dialogue with
Dostoevsky and the world of his *Crime and Punishment* (1866). Too complex
to examine within a brief essay, this dialogue would seem to speak of an
unusually intense 'anxiety of influence', deriving from what one critic
describes as 'Conrad's intense unconscious identification with the hated
Russian novelist'.[9] Dostoevsky's magnetic influence in the novel creates a
shiftingly tense field of positive and negative attraction: the author of *Crime
and Punishment* is so powerful a determinant of the novel's created world as to
be virtually its co-creator; paradoxically, however, *Under Western Eyes* also
testifies to Dostoevsky's power in the very complexity of the anxious precautions taken (through its Western narrator and other distancing devices) to
disavow his influence and, thereby, attempt to repudiate, exorcize or re-direct
the power of a 'haunting' precursor.

The history of Conrad's own wide and varied influences is complemented by his powerful generative influence upon later twentieth-century
writers. T. S. Eliot's use of a fragment from 'Heart of Darkness' as an
epigraph to his poem 'The Hollow Men' (1925) foreshadows the way in
which that work alone has become a seminal force in modern literature,
inspiring numerous emulations, adaptations and counter-novels. The later
'rediscovery' of his psychological and political insights in other of his works
has also ensured that his 'line' in the twentieth century – from André Gide
and F. Scott Fitzgerald through Graham Greene and William Golding to
V. S. Naipaul – is a remarkably powerful one: to re-contextualize Conrad's
own words, his 'books are an integral part of life' in the present.

NOTES

1. For the influence of Polish literature upon Conrad's work, see Andrzej Busza,
   'Conrad's Polish Literary Background and Some Illustrations of the Influence of
   Polish Literature on his Work', *Antemurale*, 10 (1966), 109–255.
2. R. B. Cunninghame Graham, 'Preface', *Tales of Hearsay*, p. ix.
3. A full survey of Conrad's French legacy can be found in Yves Hervouet's *The
   French Face of Joseph Conrad* (Cambridge: Cambridge University Press, 1990).
4. Ford Madox Ford, *Joseph Conrad: A Personal Remembrance* (London:
   Duckworth, 1924), p. 36.

5. Guy de Maupassant, 'The Novel', in *Pierre and Jean*, trans. Leonard Tancock (Harmondsworth: Penguin, 1987), p. 25.
6. The term is given fuller description in Ford, *Conrad*, p. 210.
7. Jeremy Hawthorn, *Joseph Conrad: Narrative Technique and Ideological Commitment* (London: Arnold, 1990), p. 136.
8. Paul Kirschner, *Conrad: The Psychologist as Artist* (Edinburgh: Oliver & Boyd, 1968), pp. 240–52.
9. Jeffrey Berman, 'Introduction to Conrad and the Russians', *Conradiana*, 12.1 (1980), 6; see also Keith Carabine, *The Life and the Art: A Study of Conrad's 'Under Western Eyes'* (Amsterdam and Atlanta, GA: Rodopi, 1996), pp. 64–96.

CHAPTER 6

Biographies and memoirs

David Miller

In her portrait of Sonia Brownell (1918–80), the widow of George Orwell
(Eric Blair), Hilary Spurling recounts the instant when 'George had been so
infuriated by a life of Joseph Conrad written by his widow that he hurled it
across the room, saying to Sonia (who was mystified): *"Never do that to me".*'[1]

Conrad laid no similar strictures upon posterity, although it seems
unlikely that he would have been comfortable with others unearthing the
private facts behind his public life. Within two months of his funeral in
August 1924, others had become opportunistically intrusive. Ford Madox
Ford rushed into print *Joseph Conrad: A Personal Remembrance* (1924), while
one of Conrad's literary executors, Richard Curle, privately published *Joseph
Conrad's Last Day* (later incorporated as the final chapter of *The Last Twelve
Years of Joseph Conrad* (1928)). Galsworthy wrote a portrait for a French
audience, later collected in *Castles in Spain & Other Screeds* (1927).

Two years later, Conrad's widow, Jessie, published the first of her books
about her husband. These memoirs were undoubtedly written to take
advantage of the high interest in her late husband, whilst also feeding her
(still undocumented) financial extravagances and the debts undoubtedly
incurred by her eldest son. *My Father: Joseph Conrad* by Borys Conrad
(1970) had the same genesis differently expressed: ready cash. John Conrad's
book, *Joseph Conrad: Times Remembered* (1981), gently enticed from him by
Richard Curle, its dedicatee, was published some time after Curle's death in
1968, but, perhaps more tellingly, three years after that of Borys, when John
presumably felt free to set the family record straight.

None of these intimate memoirs are especially revealing of their ostensible subject, 'Joseph Conrad'. There is scant mention of his nervous
collapse during the writing of *Under Western Eyes* in any, and no mention
of his acute financial anxieties, nor the family ructions over Borys' secret
marriage, massive debts or imprisonment for fraud in 1927. Given the
time in which they were written, one should perhaps not expect breaches
of an Edwardian family's confidences. Seen with today's eyes – and as a

whole – these books are fascinating for their range of inconsistencies, differing emphases and, above all, their silences.

Jessie Conrad's books, *Joseph Conrad as I Knew Him* (1926) and *Joseph Conrad and his Circle* (1935), are consistently odd. To take but two examples: there is much mention of her revulsion for Ford, while her feelings for Conrad's secretary are constrained through teeth-clenched flattery – writing that Miss Lilian M. Hallowes 'used to declare that the proofs [of Conrad's works] would be found imprinted on her heart when she died. It may be so, she was a very efficient proof-reader, I believe.'[2] This catty remark colours something Hugh Walpole hinted at in a diary entry of early October 1921: 'Too many women in this house and too many secret feelings'.[3] Jessie's penchant for name-dropping, factual inaccuracy and a whiff of emotional concealment pervade both books.

While we should not doubt Conrad's widow's desire to add to or aid her husband's reputation, and we can understand her necessity to make money, a different course to attain both may have been advisable. Her second book was perhaps snobbishly and misogynistically dismissed. Edward Garnett wrote to her in July 1935 calling it 'the most detestable book ever written by a wife about her husband ... your *tone* is common ... that of a landlady or manageress of an hotel who kept house for him for years'. Jessie Conrad defended herself, declaring: 'I made life for Conrad more possible ... I can claim to have been a success as *his* wife ... He has made his mark, and made it my dear Edward with no *inconsiderable* help from me',[4] a reality to which Conrad attested in the letters he wrote to his wife from New York and during the last full summer of their lives.

The Conrads' first son rarely rises to emotion in his lacklustre, self-serving and wilfully elusive memoir. At one point Borys recalls leaving his father alone, when his mother was away having an operation on her knee in 1917: 'J. C. embraced me with emotion instead of giving me the usual slap on the shoulder and firm handclasp. I think this one of the unhappiest moments of my life.' Borys veiled not only the 1927 case against him and his debts but also his relationship with Joan King. He later wrote that he had intended to tell his parents about his marriage but 'that I shrank from doing so may have been partly due to the realization of J. C.'s deep concern for my future welfare'.[5]

John Conrad's memoir has been unduly neglected as it is both beautifully written and well observed: his is the most sincere book by a member of Conrad's direct family. The sub-title to *Joseph Conrad: Times Remembered* should give a clue: '*Ojciec jest tutaj*' (Polish for 'Father is here'), a declaration only made true once his mother and brother had gone.

In a revealing anecdote about things left unsaid, John recalls:

The Rescue was the first book written by my father that I read and when I had
finished it I asked him to sign it for me which he did 'To John with his father's love,
1920.' He handed it back to me. 'Now get out.' I left the room closing the door
quietly and as I walked away heard him blow his nose with terrific violence. At no
time did he like to show emotion but on this occasion I believe he came very close
to it.

John's memory of the day continues with his being summoned into his
father's study after lunch to be told by his father that the signed copies of
first editions given to Jessie would one day pass to him: 'A few years after his
death I learnt that the books had been acquired by an American book
collector and so I have only one book of my father's stories inscribed to me
personally.' John pondered that 'it never occurred to me that my father's
wishes would be ignored and so few of the personal things of JC's should
be retained'.[6]

Whilst John alone depicts their father's diverse love for his sons, *Joseph
Conrad: Times Remembered* more movingly reveals a son's love for his father
whilst best fleshing out the Conrads' real family life: Conrad flicking bread-
pellets when bored at the dinner table, making paper-boats, playing chess or
building with Meccano, taking his 'kids' to the theatre ('JC never rode a
bicycle though he thoroughly enjoyed the "trick" cyclists at circuses' (110)),
and the reason for the Cigarette Jug – John recalled that 'before we got a
willow-patterned jug for cigarette ends and a plain cream-coloured jug with
a lid for the tea several mix-ups occurred … Luckily no harm was done'
(161).

The introduction to Edward Garnett's volume *Letters from Conrad: 1895–
1924* is similarly and refreshingly intimate.[7] Other Conrad memoirs perhaps
not as well known as they should be were collected by Martin Ray in *Joseph
Conrad: Interviews and Recollections* (1990), an inestimably valuable book
that sets out to give us the author in sixty or so fragments of recollections,
replicating Conrad's fractured identity. Ray collected such gems as the
moment when Edward Garnett commented on Conrad's 'snug bachelor
quarters' in Gillingham Street: 'As soon as he had placed me in an easy-chair
Conrad retired behind some mysterious screen and left me to study the
cosiness of the small firelit room, a row of French novels, the framed
photograph of an aristocratic lady and an engraving of a benevolent impos-
ing man on the mantelshelf. On a little table by the screen lay a pile of neat
manuscript sheets.'[8] As revealing is Garnett's comment on Conrad's 'great
quickness of eye'. Dining at the Café Royal one night, Garnett 'asked him,

after a painted lady had brushed haughtily past our table, what [Conrad] had specially noticed about her. "The dirt in her nostril", he replied instantly.' E. V. Lucas is quoted not quoting Conrad: 'Efforts to get him to express his real opinions of other writers were usually fruitless, although you could tell by his silences how the land lay.' And Fred Arnold, in a letter of 8 June 1958 to the *Daily Telegraph,* recalled that the Fleur-de-Lys was 'Joseph Conrad's "favourite" local pub' in Canterbury, where 'he would take up the seat tacitly reserved for him to the right of the window' and 'chat for an hour or so in his forceful and staccato fashion' over 'a healthy master mariner's ration of his favourite gin'.[9]

Read in one sitting, Ray's anthology presents Conrad in a mosaic of flickering puzzles and enigmas, questions and anxieties that are, somehow, as reflective of its subject as any biography yet published. The volume was recently supplemented with Ray's posthumous *Joseph Conrad: Memories and Impressions – An Annotated Bibliography* (2007), which provides glimpses from others of the author in his last years, particularly during his 1923 visit to the United States. One observation comes from Conrad's American champion, F. N. Doubleday, who wrote to John Quinn: 'how he ever had the nerve to leave England in his condition beats me' (38).[10]

As Conrad's wife and some of his close friends hurried – perhaps with indecent haste – into print, his executors encouraged Gérard Jean-Aubry (1882–1950) in compiling the two-volume *Joseph Conrad: Life and Letters* (1927), a work that proffers intimacy through letters but in its commentary (translated by Desmond MacCarthy) meanders into hagiography with no real biographical focus, as did the same writer's later *The Sea Dreamer: A Definitive Biography of Joseph Conrad* (tr. 1957).

No real biographical study appeared after John Dozier Gordan's *Joseph Conrad: The Making of a Novelist* (1940) until Jocelyn Baines, an editor working in a London publishing house, published his *Joseph Conrad: A Critical Biography* (1960), an account – critical and biographical – that remains exemplary, although it too often, and too unquestioningly, uses the fiction to illuminate Conrad's life. The publication of Jerry Allen's *The Sea Years of Joseph Conrad* (1965) coincided with Norman Sherry's *Conrad's Eastern World* and *Conrad's Western World* (1966 and 1971, respectively), works that delve into particular corners of Conrad's experience. These volumes were followed by Frederick R. Karl's gargantuan *Joseph Conrad: The Three Lives* (1979) and by Zdzisław Najder's *Joseph Conrad: A Chronicle* (1983, updated 2007).

What do these studies tell us? As with memoir, biography can reveal more about the author than the subject. The most recent English-language biographer, J. H. Stape, in *The Several Lives of Joseph Conrad* (2007), and the first, Baines, are reassuringly absent from the pages of their books, both of which are centred on telling 'a' or 'the' story of a life: Baines offering relatively uninspired critical appreciations of the work, and Stape concentrating on the life. Norman Sherry was splendidly described by one Conradian as 'flat-footed' in his quest to locate a biographical gem 'under every frangi-pangi tree in the Malay Archipelago'.

Karl's and Najder's respective approaches are exhaustive and, for some readers, exhausting in their respective emphases: Conrad's decline and Conrad's Polishness. Both are painstakingly scrupulous biographers, 'who start with the ancestors, aim for the gravestone, and chew methodically and in chronological order through every available fact in the manner of a tortoise going through a particularly tough piece of lettuce' (Sam Leith, *The Spectator*, 18 April 2007). Yet other biographers get bogged down by theory, detail or fantasy. Most notably, Jeffrey Meyers' scissors-and-paste job retains its notoriety due to his fantasy of Conrad philandering with the 'yum-yum' Jane Anderson – an 'affair' with no basis in fact. Refreshingly, Owen Knowles' *A Conrad Chronology* (1989) provides simply that: a month-by-month account of the facts – personal, financial, medical and professional.

Despite this – and notwithstanding the completion of *The Collected Letters of Joseph Conrad* (9 vols., 1983–2007) – it is hard not to think that Conrad biography remains what it has always been: a self-limiting genre, constrained by the opaque nature of its subject who can, as Knowles states, 'disappear from view for long periods'.[11] Karl bizarrely suggested, two years before his own 1,000-page *Three Lives* was published, that no more need to be said about Conrad as 'very little remains to be said'.[12] Much remained to be said, obviously. Reviewing Stape's portrait, Philip Hensher wrote perceptively: 'despite the fascination of his work and the dramatic stuff of his life, Conrad has yet to inspire a dazzling biography' (*Daily Telegraph*, 23 August 2007); and jointly reviewing Najder's revised account and Stape's volume, Michael Gorra bluntly questioned 'the possibility of anyone writing a genuinely great biography of Conrad' (*Times Literary Supplement*, 29 February 2008, p. 4).

Primary sources tell the reader and scholar more than anything else written long after the events and assist in 'getting to know' Conrad. His own memoirs are biographically and artistically evasive: whilst neither *The Mirror of the Sea* (1906) nor *A Personal Record* (1912) are soul-shattering in their 'revelations' – little about a childhood in the Ukraine and Poland, less about the time spent in France, nothing about marriage – and both have moments of personal mythologizing, these misty recollections and his immediate family's own unreliable memoirs will always be more illuminating, as they give us shards from a mirror, not a definitive constructed portrait of the artist as a young, or even an old, man. The facts of Conrad's life will always remain an unsolvable puzzle, especially given its cultural, linguistic, geographical, financial and, last but by no means least, psychological components.

In *Things Fall Apart* (1958) one of Conrad's more critical readers, Chinua Achebe, wrote: 'There is no story that is not true.'[13] What studies of Conrad's life – or, as Stape usefully has it, 'several' lives – reveal is that there is no story without its truths. Stape subsequently suggested Conrad biography now needed 'more than assiduous archival research' and may need to 'call upon the methods and insights of art'.[14] Man cannot live by criticism alone, prone as it is to reel out of control: too much has been read into and much written about 'Heart of Darkness' since Achebe's notable 1974 lecture at the University of Massachusetts. Conrad biography needs to guard against similar over-production, especially as it seems we know enough now about the facts of the life of 'Joseph Conrad'.

In the months after his death in August 1924, things seemed different, but since then nearly twenty biographical studies of the man have been published, half during the last decade, with three volumes – the revised Najder, Stape and Schenkel – appearing in 2007 alone. The necessity for *another* biography – of this Ukrainian-born ethnic Pole who spoke French as his second language and died a British 'gentleman' having been lionized for his English prose internationally – has, for the next generation at least, been rendered redundant.

Conrad the novelist who captured humanity somehow still, superbly, evades us as a man. The more obsessive reader and some scholars will always fret about who taught Conrad how to spell, which woman he first loved, the details of his suicide attempt, how he mended John's bicycle, how he dined at the Mont Blanc Restaurant, why he married Jessie George, what brand of cigarettes he smoked and what he ate in Oswald's the night before he died – when it rained and rained, and a week later, when the sun blazed on his funeral cortège driving through the streets of Canterbury busily bedecked with fluttering flags for its Annual Cricket Week (not, like Chekhov's did, in a van marked 'OYSTERS', twenty years earlier in a different place, telling us the same intangible things about a different genius), when real folk noticed the passing of a man who wrote and lived amongst them: a chap who shopped, drank whisky or gin in pubs and died tired, adrift from both his children and no longer capable of writing at his best.

One can only *imagine* his sons at that funeral, only dream up the sight of his wheel-chaired widow watching as the hearse crunched over the gravel at Oswald's, watching it drive away with their children in the car behind, or wonder how much and for how long Miss Hallowes sobbed. We are left with the empty husk of a man, traces of an accidental author who wrote words which, he once stated, 'are the great foes of reality'. Conrad wrote of his art in 1901 that it 'demands from the writer a spirit of scrupulous abnegation. The only legitimate basis of creative work lies in the courageous recognition of all the irreconcilable antagonisms that make our life so enigmatic, so burdensome, so fascinating, so dangerous – so full of hope' (*CL* 2:348–9). Biography and memoir are full of abnegation, enigma, danger, burden, hope, hate – but sometimes they betoken love.

NOTES

1. Cited in Hilary Spurling, *The Girl from the Fiction Department: A Portrait of Sonia Orwell* (London: Hamish Hamilton, 2002), pp. 149–50.
2. Jessie Conrad, *Joseph Conrad as I Knew Him* (London: Heinemann, 1926), pp. 227–8.
3. In Martin Ray, ed., *Joseph Conrad: Interviews and Recollections* (London: Macmillan, 1990), p. 137.
4. In J. H. Stape and Owen Knowles, eds., *A Portrait in Letters: Correspondence to and about Conrad* (Amsterdam and Atlanta, GA: Rodopi, 1996), pp. 256, 257.
5. Borys Conrad, *My Father: Joseph Conrad* (London: Calder & Boyars, 1970), pp. 127, 57.
6. John Conrad, *Joseph Conrad: Times Remembered* (Cambridge: Cambridge University Press, 1981), pp. 167–8.
7. Edward Garnett, ed., *Letters from Conrad: 1895–1924* (London: Nonesuch, 1928), pp. v–xxxiii.
8. Garnett, *Letters from Conrad*, p. 76.
9. Garnett, *Letters from Conrad*, pp. 81, 85, 220.
10. Martin Ray, ed., *Joseph Conrad: Memories and Impressions – An Annotated Bibliography*, Conrad Studies 7 (Amsterdam and New York: Rodopi, 2007), p. 38.
11. In J. H. Stape, ed., *The Cambridge Companion to Joseph Conrad* (Cambridge: Cambridge University Press, 1996), p. 1.
12. Frederick R. Karl, 'Conrad Studies', *Studies in the Novel*, 9.3 (1977), 326–32, pp. 326–7.
13. Chinua Achebe, *Things Fall Apart* (London: Heinemann, 1958), p. 99.
14. J. H. Stape, 'On Conrad Biography as a Fine Art', *The Conradian*, 32.2 (Autumn 2007), 57–75, p. 73.

CHAPTER 7

Portraits and illustrations

J. H. Stape

The iconographic record for Joseph Conrad, despite lacunae during his sea career, is remarkably complete, extending from his early childhood to very shortly before his death. This oeuvre embraces several major media – the oil portrait, the pastel, the pen-and-ink sketch, the portrait bust and portrait medallion, as well as formal and informal photographs and caricatures.

The sheer number of surviving artefacts suggests that, at the least, Conrad was not averse to having his image preserved and circulated. Whilst this was occasionally a matter of bowing to marketing pressures, it is of a piece with Conrad's sense of his Modernism; not insignificantly, when asserting that of his own work, he called to witness two painters, Rodin and Whistler (*CL* 2:418).

The work of several of the period's significant artists is represented, including the caricaturist Max Beerbohm (1872–1956), the portraitist William Rothenstein (1872–1945) – a personal friend of the writer – the American sculptor Jacob Epstein (1880–1959) and the American artist Walter Tittle (1883–1966). Among important photographers who aimed their cameras at Conrad were the pioneering Polish photographer Walery Rzewuski (1837–88), the American Alvin Langdon Coburn (1882–1966), George Charles Beresford (1864–1938) and the society photographer Malcolm Arbuthnot (1874–1967).

Drawings by personal friends form another category. Ellen ('Nellie') Heath (1873–1962), the companion of Conrad's friend Edward Garnett, produced an accomplished portrait of Conrad in 1898 at the outset of his career (Leeds Art Gallery). The Scottish artist Muirhead Bone (1876–1953) produced several pen-and-ink sketches of the writer; and the Irish landscape and portrait artist Alice S. Kinkead (1871–1926), with whom the Conrads became acquainted on Corsica, painted portraits of both Conrad and his wife, Jessie.

On the whole, the iconographic record displays Conrad in formal mode, and at times literally in formal dress. The more domestic and personal side of his personality is revealed almost exclusively in photographs taken by amateurs. Most of the professional portraits were commissioned, but the formal temper of the age, one in which the boundaries of public and private life were distinct, suited Conrad's own. His refusal to appear before his public 'en pantoufles' [in slippers] ('Author's Note', *NLL*, vi) also frequently governs most of the images taken or made of him for public distribution. These show him personally composed and, socially, as conventionally middle-class.

CHILDHOOD AND YOUTH

The earliest known image of Conrad, a somewhat idealized one, survives only in a photographic reproduction by Maryan Dederko of Warsaw (Yale). Dressed in a smock, the subject, seated, holds a whip. A somewhat older child appears in an 1862 studio photograph. Dressed in a belted and decorated smock and wearing three-quarter length trousers, Conrad stands with a whip in his left hand (*CL* 1:Plate 1). This was taken during the same session as photographs of his father and mother (Yale): the identical high-backed chair, capped by an eagle, figuring in all three photographs. The surviving example is apparently a reproduction made by a Warsaw photographic studio (Yale).

A photograph of Conrad at age six, by Stanisław Krakow, a Polish photographer in Vologda (Yale), survives with the first known composition in the future writer's hand, a note to his maternal grandmother. A photograph of Conrad at seven or eight seated on a horse was taken in Chernikhov by F. Schlegel (Yale). Whilst there are individual photographs of Conrad, his father and mother, no pictures of the family group are known.

Perhaps the most evocative photograph of the younger Conrad was that taken by Walery Rzewuski in his Podwale Street *atelier* in Cracow shortly before Conrad left for Marseilles in 1874 (Yale). The portrait shows the young man dressed in a suit and wearing a bow-tie, his sensitive eyes and wide forehead prominent. Particularly noted for his portraits, Rzewuski (also a city councillor) managed to elicit from his youthful sitter a look of seriousness and determination while avoiding stiffness and self-consciousness.

Only one image is known of Conrad from the period 1878 to 1891, the exception being a studio portrait taken at Le Havre by Charles Potier in 1882 (Yale). Remembered for his documentary photographs of the city's shipping and port, Potier failed to engage his sitter, and the portrait has a slightly awkward quality.

EARLY CAREER

With the exception of Potier's photograph, the only known picture of Conrad during his career at sea sees him posing with five apprentices aboard the *Torrens* (1891–3) in the Port of London (Yale). Taken by Donald Madrid of Artists Illustrators, Ltd, of 17 Fleet Street, the photograph features a heavily bearded Conrad, in uniform, standing in the group's centre. Formal portraits of Conrad and of his then-fiancée, Jessie George, were, according to Jessie Conrad's note on the photographs, taken 'on the eve' of their wedding on 24 March 1896 (Yale). An informal photograph of Conrad with Stephen and Cora Crane commemorates a visit to the Cranes at Ravensbrook in 1898 (Texas). Another informal snapshot of the time shows Conrad getting into his motor-car (Texas).

On Conrad's turn to writing the number of portraits of him prolifer-ates, his career coincident with the rise of the professionalization of authorship, involving the more aggressive advertising of literary works, as well as the creation of public interest in writers' private lives. The oil portrait by 'Nellie' Heath testifies to Conrad's self-awareness of his pro-fessional and class status (such portraits generally being reserved for the solidly middle class and those above). Two other portraits were likewise the work of acquaintances. Conrad sat for Georg Sauter (1866–1937), John Galsworthy's brother-in-law and then an artist of some reputation, in December 1902 (location unknown); and in August 1903, he acceded to Will Rothenstein's request to include a portrait of him in a series of notable figures, with the artist producing a pastel (National Portrait Gallery; bequest of Edmund Gosse).

The most important photographic session of Conrad's early career was that with Beresford in 1904 at the photographer's Knightsbridge studio. The session yielded at least five appealing portraits of the mature Conrad by a photographer who notably portrayed Virginia Stephen (later Woolf) and J. M. Barrie. A photograph of Conrad in profile, unsigned but obviously by Beresford, served as the frontispiece to Thomas Nelson & Sons' edition of *A Personal Record* (1916) and highlighted the work's autobiographical character.

MID-CAREER

As Conrad's fame grew, the need for images of him to accompany advertise-ments of his work expanded; however, many that his agent supplied to publicists dated to earlier in his career.

An undated photograph by Frank Wells, of Conrad and H. G. Wells seated across from one another, must have been taken prior to 1910 and the collapse of the friendship. The well-known American painter John Singer Sargent (1856–1925) produced a charcoal drawing in 1911, showing Conrad uncharacteristically heavy in the face and tight of lip (photograph: Texas). The writer and illustrator Henry Major Tomlinson (1873–1958) made four informal pencil sketches of Conrad (undated but possibly summer 1912; Private collection).

Will Cadby produced no less than eighteen shots of Conrad in September 1913, at the request of Alfred A. Knopf. Two known products of this session depict Conrad seated, dressed in a suit and jauntily sporting a checked waistcoat.[1] Around this time a number of stagey informal photographs that might best be called 'Conrad at home' were also produced (photographer unknown). These show Conrad seated at his desk in Capel House; sitting in the checked suit and boots of a country squire; being served tea by his wife in their sitting-room; and even playing cards with John and Jessie.

A few amateur photographs of the period round out the iconographic record of Conrad in mid-career. One of Conrad and his son Borys as a cadet, with Captain Edmund Oliver, testifies to his fatherly role (Texas). The arrival of callers occasioned informal photographs: the July 1911 call by André Gide and Valery Larbaud, the June 1914 call by the American writer Ellen Glasgow and the visit by the American journalist Jane Anderson (in 1916 or 1917) are among the occasions commemorated. The Conrads' sojourn in Poland during July–October 1914 resulted in a touching photograph of Conrad and his eight-year-old-son John (Reading University), a snapshot of Conrad with his cousin Aniela Zagórska and an appealing and dramatic sketch by Dr Kazimierz Górski, made on 23 August at Zakopane.

The American sculptor Jo Davidson (1883–1952) sculpted the first bust of Conrad in March 1916 (National Portrait Gallery; bequest of Edmund Gosse). A friend of Conrad reputedly found it 'a *tour de force* of searching modeling, instinct with life and splendidly characteristic'.[2] Alexander Coburn, who attended one of the sittings, took 'about a dozen shots' (*CL* 5:566).

LATER PORTRAITS

Conrad's meeting with the novelist Hugh Walpole in January 1918 led to a chalk-and-wash portrait being done soon after by Walpole's partner, the American-born stage designer and artist Percy Anderson (1851?–1928) (National Portrait Gallery; gift of Sidney Colvin). A more significant encounter was with Walter Tittle, who did two lithograph portraits of Conrad.[3] A dry-point etching (1922), half-length and signed in the plate, is at the San Francisco Art Museum. Tittle did another dry-point etching in 1924 (National Portrait Gallery).

Conrad's peregrinations are variously recorded. There are photographs of him alone as well as with crew members in the Q-ship HMS *Ready* (November 1916, Yale). Photographs of him in Corsica in early 1921, including one with his agent, J. B. Pinker (Yale), record the holiday. His tour of New York and New England led to the creation of several images by Muirhead Bone, who made dry-point etchings, while press photographers greeted Conrad on his arrival (Library of Congress). Their endeavours include a photograph for the *Daily Mail* of Bone, Conrad and the *Tuscania*'s captain, David Bone (British Library; Texas).

What is on record of the mature man is a carefully controlled and meticulously managed public image that fails to capture the tense, excitable side of Conrad's character, testified to by several of his contemporaries and close friends. The keynote of these formal efforts stresses, with rare exception – notably the bust by Jacob Epstein – tranquillity, dignity and worldly success. This formality is marked in the photographs taken during a session with Malcolm Arbuthnot in July 1919, of whose fourteen shots (*CL* 6:449) only a handful are known.

The American medallist Theodore Spicer-Simpson (1871–1959) included Conrad in his series *Men of Letters of the British Isles: Medallions from the Life* (1924), the writer sitting for him in July 1921 for photographs for a portrait medallion (castings: University of Miami; British Library; Yale; photograph: Berg Collection). Initially hesitant about this project, Conrad, in the event, found both the artist and his work congenial. The drawing by 'Quiz' (Powys Evans, 1899–1981) for the *London Mercury* (1922) displeased its subject, with Conrad objecting to the 'thick nose' and 'disagreeable expression' (*CL* 7: Plate 1). A photograph of Conrad on the set of *The Secret Agent* was published in *The Times* to promote the play (27 October 1922).

Epstein's bust, made from sittings in March 1924, is by common consent the most artistically significant portrait of Conrad.[4] The sittings at Oswalds were tense, with Conrad ill and nervous. Although the sitter was pleased with the result, which he found 'marvellously effective', he seems to have found Epstein himself uncongenial, a feeling returned by the sculptor, with Epstein describing Conrad as hysterical and histrionic.[5] Alice S. Kinkead's portrait (Private collection; sold Sotheby's, December 2006), painted in April 1924, is the work of a journeyman artist, displaying no marked degree of originality or artistic flair. The aged Conrad is presented in a flattering light, but the formal pose has an effect of lifelessness. (She also painted a portrait of Jessie Conrad during May–June 1921.)[6] Another late portrait (undated), by Bruce Cameron,[7] was possibly done not from the life but from the best-known and most iconic formal photographic portrait of Conrad in his late years, that by James Craig Annan (1864–1946) of T. R. Annan & Sons of Glasgow. The portrait shows Conrad as austere and withdrawn, capturing the essential loneliness and solemn melancholy evident in his writing.

Amateur snapshots taken at Oswalds offer an antidote to this formality, Conrad appearing with friends and relatives and in a relaxed, even genial, mood. These include photographs with Karola Zagórska (National Library of Poland), Conrad with distant cousins and Conrad with J. B. Pinker at his agent's home in Reigate, Surrey. A photograph with Jean-Aubry in Oswalds' gardens (Yale) shows the two friends in conversational mood. This, as well as other informal portraits, featured on postcards made by the Conrads.

The very last images of Conrad contrast sharply. One with his wife shows a worn, extremely ill man who unmistakably bears the marks of physical suffering (Collection Mario Curreli; gift of Borys Conrad). Another shows Conrad seated in his garden, the writer leaning back, holding a cigarette in a gout-bandaged hand, and displaying a man in supremely serene mood about to quit the world.

CARICATURES

Conrad the artist *par excellence* was the subject of several genial caricatures. Most notable among these are the no less than five by Max Beerbohm: a pencil sketch of Conrad as puppet in the hands of Henry James (Joseph Conrad Society (UK) Collection); a drawing published in the *Bookman* in 1911 (13 August, p. 208); Conrad's inclusion among the worthies at Edmund Gosse's seventieth-birthday celebrations ('The Birthday Surprise', 1919); Conrad's inclusion in the series 'The Young Self and the Old Self' (Private collection); and 'Somewhere in the South Pacific', featuring Conrad in dress clothes on a beach contemplating a snake crawling through a skull (late 1920).[8] A caricature by David Low (1891–1963) of September 1923 playfully suggests a small Conrad fronting the vast universe (Lilly Library). The American caricaturist Ralph Barton (1891–1931), famous for his New York celebrity and high-society work, produced perhaps the most daring send-up of Conrad. Entitled merely 'Sea Captain Smoking

Cigarette on Deck', the drawing presents as an almost bloated and grumpy-looking gent in relaxed repose aboard ship (Private collection; date unknown).

Originals and copies of Conrad's portraits and photographs are widely scattered in museums, libraries and private hands. Major iconographic holdings are at the National Portrait Gallery, London, and the Beinecke Rare Book and Manuscript Library, Yale University. Libraries with major Conrad collections (for example the Berg Collection at the New York Public Library, the Lilly Library at Indiana University, the University of Texas at Austin) hold visual materials.

The Coburn Collection is at George Eastman House, Rochester, New York, and photographs of Conrad on his arrival in America (1923) are in the Library of Congress. Stephen Conrad inherited photograph albums from his father, Philip (Borys Conrad's only child). The Joseph Conrad Society (UK) holds a few original photographs. The University of California, Los Angeles, and the University of Arizona also have Conrad items, the latter related to Tittle.

No systematic descriptive census of Conrad photographs and portraits has been undertaken, and only a handful of professional descriptions of the iconic record (medium, measurements, etc.) exists. The richly illustrated short biographies by Norman Sherry and Chris Fletcher give a photographic record of Conrad's life and locations; photographs from diverse sources provide illustrative material for the standard biographies and scholarly resources, including, importantly, *The Collected Letters of Joseph Conrad*.[9] Martin Ray's *Joseph Conrad: Interviews and Recollections* brings together memoirs of several artists (Rothenstein, Cadby, Davidson, Tittle, Bone, Epstein) for whom Conrad sat. A brief survey of the ground covered is offered by Knowles and Moore.[10]

The hunt for unknown images of the writer has led to individual 'finds' being announced to the scholarly community. John S. Lewis located two informal snapshots.[11] Jeremy Hawthorn, believing Conrad had greeted the *Titanic*'s seamen on their arrival in England, merely set off a hare, as did Claudine Lesage, who claims that Conrad appears in a photograph with Edith Wharton at Toulon in 1921.[12] Allan H. Simmons has established the provenance of a photograph of Conrad on his arrival in New York in the collection of The Joseph Conrad Society (UK).[13]

NOTES

1. The frontispiece to Ford Madox Ford's *Joseph Conrad: A Personal Remembrance* (London: Duckworth, 1924) gives the photographer as Cadby. *CL* 5:Plate 1 wrongly attributes it to Warrington Dawson (to whom Conrad inscribed it). In another from the same session, Conrad is standing (Jessie Conrad's *Joseph Conrad and his Circle* (London: Jarnolds, 1935), facing p. 161).

2. 'New Portrait Busts by Jo Davidson', *Vanity Fair*, June 1916, p. 56.

3. See Richard P. Veler, 'Walter Tittle and Joseph Conrad', *Conradiana*, 12 (1980), 93–104; Jessie Conrad to Walter Tittle, Letters 1922–35 (University of Texas at Austin).

4. Apparently six castings were planned: see Muirhead Bone to Hugh Walpole, 7 February 1924 (University of Texas at Austin). Two busts are on public display (National Portrait Gallery and Museum of Canterbury); Sotheby's sold another in December 2006.

5. Conrad to Curle, 25 March 1924 (*CL* 8:33), and Jacob Epstein, *Let There be Sculpture: An Autobiography* (London: Michael Joseph, 1940), pp. 91ff.

6. Stephen Conrad Collection; for dating, see letters dated 7 May (*CL* 9:237) and 30 June 1921 (*CL* 7:306).

7. The drawing, in the Museum of Canterbury, graces the dust-jacket of John Conrad's *Joseph Conrad: Times Remembered* (Cambridge: Cambridge University Press, 1981).

8. Reproduced as follows: Owen Knowles and Gene M. Moore, *Oxford Reader's Companion to Conrad* (Oxford: Oxford University Press, 2000), p. 33; Ann Thwaite, *Edmund Gosse: A Literary Landscape* (London: Secker & Warburg, 1984), between pp. 440 and 441 (two sketches); *Conradiana*, 4.1 (1972), 62; Max Beerbohm, *A Survey* (London: Heinemann, 1921).

9. Norman Sherry, *Conrad* (London: Thames and Hudson, 1972; rpt 1988), and Chris Fletcher, *Joseph Conrad* (London: The British Library, 1999).

10. 'Portraits and Other Images', in Knowles and Moore, *Oxford Reader's Companion to Conrad*, pp. 288–90.

11. John S. Lewis, '"Artless Photos": Two Previously Unknown Photographs of Joseph Conrad', *Conradiana*, 8 (1976), 203–8.

12. Jeremy Hawthorn, 'Joseph Conrad and the Surviving *Titanic* Seamen and Firemen: A New Photograph', *The Conradian*, 16.2 (1999), 38–45; Claudine Lesage, *Magazine Littéraire* (March 1992), 27.

13. Allan H. Simmons: '"Something that hasn't been knocking about": A New Conrad Photograph', *The Conradian*, 27.2 (2000), 88–90. This photograph has appeared on the cover of *The Conradian* since 2003.

PART II
Critical Fortunes

CHAPTER 8

Critical responses: contemporary
Allan H. Simmons

Conrad's critical and economic fortunes stand in inverse, even ironic, relation to each other. Showing Edward Garnett the manuscript of *An Outcast of the Islands* (1896), his second novel, Conrad declared: '*I won't live in an attic!*'[1] None the less, the first half of his career was spent supplementing the income from his work with loans from friends; outright gifts from John Galsworthy; subsidies from his patient agent, James Brand Pinker, to whom Conrad's debt eventually totalled some £2,700; awards from various bodies, including the Royal Literary Fund in 1902 and the Royal Bounty Fund in 1905; and, from 1910, an annual pension. Hardly surprisingly, H. G. Wells quipped that Conrad 'ought to be administered by trustees'.[2]

At the same time, Conrad was composing the works, from *The Nigger of the 'Narcissus'* (1897) to *Under Western Eyes* (1911), upon which, critics generally agree, his critical reputation now rests. But also generally agreed is that the transformation of his economic fortunes, with the publication of *Chance* in 1914, coincided with some deterioration in the quality of the work across his final creative decade. Thomas C. Moser's claim, in 1957, that the trajectory of Conrad's writing-life is best understood in terms of achievement-and-decline had already been voiced by such contemporaries of the author as Henry James and Virginia Woolf. And while reaping the rewards of the knock-on effect of *Chance*, Conrad could note the irony, commenting to Galsworthy of *Within the Tides* (1915): 'this vol is not so much art as financial operation. You have no idea how much these second rate efforts have brought in ... The Planter alone earned eight times as much as Youth, six times as much as Heart of Darkness' (*CL* 5:455). At the beginning of his career, Conrad had been paid £20 for the copyright of *Almayer's Folly* (1895). In 1923, a year before the author's death, John Quinn, who had begun buying Conrad's papers in 1911, auctioned his collection. The sale realized over $100,000.

I

The earliest reviews of *Almayer's Folly* and *An Outcast of the Islands* proclaimed the arrival of a powerful new talent. The politician and newspaper owner T. P. O'Connor declared Conrad to be 'a writer of genius' in the *Weekly Sun* of 9 June 1895, in a review that occupied a page and a half, spread over nearly eight broad-sheet columns, and in which Conrad confessed himself 'buried … under an avalanche of compliments' (*CL* 1:229). A year later, in an unsigned review in the *Saturday Review* of 16 May 1896, H. G. Wells wrote: '*An Outcast of the Islands* is, perhaps, the finest piece of fiction that has been published this year, as *Almayer's Folly* was the finest that was published in 1895.' Alongside such plaudits, many reviewers reacted to Conrad's use of the Malay archipelago as his locale by trying to identify him with contemporaries, like Robert Louis Stevenson and the Australian Louis Becke, noted for their 'exotic' fictions. The *Daily News* review of *Almayer's Folly* declared that Conrad had 'annexed the island of Borneo' while the *Spectator* review predicted that he 'might become the Kipling of the Malay Archipelago'.[3]

Presciently, the reaction to Conrad's first few volumes already delineated areas of interest and contention that would continue to shape response to his work. Foremost among these is the question of Conrad's style, found to be both a virtue and a vice. Reminding one that critical reception itself was in transition, with belletristic general comments about fine writing giving way to more robust and trenchant criticism, there is widespread praise for Conrad's descriptive powers, while his prolixity is censured.

To the *Daily Record*, Conrad's style in *An Outcast of the Islands* 'seems to be permeated with the languor of a sultry clime'; while the *Bookman* links the pace of *Almayer's Folly* to its setting: 'The slow, vague mysterious East has cast its spell over Mr Conrad, with results not conducive to the interests of the volatile European reader.'[4] Style is thus a function of subject and setting, with the *Newcastle Daily Chronicle* describing Conrad's technique as 'psychological impressionism' (10 April 1896). At times, style *is* content, at others in opposition to it. To the *Bradford Observer*, 'Even Michel Angelo would not have worked to much purpose with sandstone for material' (22 May 1896). And Wells, too, saw the novel as 'not so much told as seen intermittently through a haze of sentences'. His comparison of Conrad's style to 'river-mist' anticipates E. M. Forster's review of *Notes on Life and Letters* (1921), in which he claimed that 'the secret casket of his genius contains a vapour rather than a jewel'.[5]

The number of notices and reviews Conrad's works attracted from the outset was impressive: between them, *Almayer's Folly* and *An Outcast of the Islands* received over seventy; *The Nigger of the 'Narcissus'*, published in America as *The Children of the Sea*, garnered that many on its own. Responsible for providing Conrad with a sizeable proportion of his income, the American market is crucial to any sense of his early reception. The following periodicals (a by no means exhaustive list) carried reviews of *The Nigger of the 'Narcissus'*: *Boston Evening Transcript, Brooklyn Eagle, Chicago Daily Inter Ocean, Chicago Tribune, Cleveland Leader, Detroit Free Press, Indianapolis News, New York Times* and *New York Tribune, St Paul Pioneer Press* and the *Toledo Blade*.

Conrad's belief that *The Nigger of the 'Narcissus'* had 'certain qualities of art that make it a thing apart' (*CL* 1:334) was endorsed by the critics, who he found to be 'unexpectedly appreciative', while Garnett recalled 'a general blast of eulogy'.[6] The novelist Israel Zangwill in the *Academy* voiced the reservations of many: 'The tale has no plot and no petticoats' (1 January 1898), but, at a moment when the sea was a national obsession on both sides of the Atlantic, these were outweighed by its strengths. American novelist and journalist Harold Frederic summed up the feeling when he claimed that Conrad 'gives us the sea as no other story-teller of our generation has been able to render it', while, to the *Daily Chronicle* reviewer, 'There may be better tales of the sea, but we have never read anything in the least like it.'[7]

As ever, Conrad's style drew attention – and divided opinion: 'it is doubtful if a sentence in his book could be bettered' according to Boston's *Saturday Evening Gazette*; Chicago's *Daily Inter Ocean*, however, found the style 'unpolished to a painful degree'. But what was never in doubt was the sheer power of the writing: 'the school of fiction-brutality', according to the *Illustrated London News*. And while critics finally discovered Conrad's humour – 'hitherto unsuspected' according to James Payne (in the *Illustrated London News*) – his capacity to bring high art to bear on low subject matter led the *Court Journal* to suggest that the 'audacious uncompromising naturalism' would induce '"mental dyspepsy" in those whose literary appetites are at all inclined to be delicate'.[8] The novella drew repeated comparison with Stephen Crane's *The Red Badge of Courage* and Stevenson's 'The Ebb Tide'. As proof of how far and how quickly Conrad had come already, Arnold Bennett could speak of 'the Conrad Manner'[9] at home while, abroad, the *Daily Pioneer Press* (St Paul) of 14 August 1898 wrote: '*The Children of the Sea* being from the pen of Joseph Conrad is a powerful study of its subject … In Mr. Conrad's hands, it is needless to say, all the possibilities of the situation are fully developed' (p. 17). The idea that

his third novel could arouse such expectations is indicative of his international reception. This sense of a recognizable style – 'Conradese' as the
author himself put it – reached its apogee in 1912 when Conrad found
himself 'agreeably guyed' in Max Beerbohm's parody, itself a token of
recognition, of his early style in *A Christmas Garland.*

II

Conrad's attitude to criticism could be censorious, as in his well-known
antipathy to the Irish critic Robert Lynd.[10] Early in his career, he wrote to
Blackwood that 'the blind distribution of praise or blame ... which is the
very essence of "periodical" criticism seems to me to be a work less useful
than skirt-dancing and not quite as honourable as pocket-picking' (*CL*
2:215–16). Yet he knew the importance of good notices, pronouncing
himself 'the spoiled child of the critics' (*CL* 2:313) in the wake of *Lord
Jim*'s favourable reception. Placing Conrad 'into the front rank of living
novelists' (*Speaker*, 24 November 1900), *Lord Jim* earned comparisons with
Henry James, as critics differed over the success of its narrative method. It is
safe to say that, with *Lord Jim*, Conrad had 'arrived'. The *Speaker*
announced that it 'more than fulfilled' the 'extravagant' prophecies made
about the author of *The Nigger of the 'Narcissus'*; the *Manchester Guardian*
declared it 'a book to make the world wider and deeper'; while the *Spectator*
despaired of conveying an adequate sense of the style, portraiture and 'the
subtlety of psychological analysis ... in Mr Conrad's latest and greatest
work'.[11] *Lord Jim* would set the critical standard for novels to follow.

Edward Garnett proved indispensable in steering Conrad's reception
among the critics. For instance, when the *Youth* volume was published in
1902, it was the title story that reaped most of the plaudits until Garnett
identified 'Heart of Darkness' as 'the high-water mark of the author's
talent'.[12] As Conrad noted, 'The ruck takes its tone from you' (*CL* 2:468).
If Garnett's opinion guided critical response at home, Conrad also had his
champions abroad. Among these was William L. Alden, whose 'London
Letter' in the *New York Times Saturday Review of Books and Art* reads at
times like a campaign to sell Conrad to an American readership.[13] In 1898,
for instance, Alden's column returned to *The Nigger of the 'Narcissus'* on at
least four occasions.

The publication of *Typhoon* in 1903 consolidated Conrad's place with the
critics. The titular story's representation of the storm scene was acknowledged to be unsurpassed and to show Conrad 'writing in the fullness of his
power', by the *Manchester Guardian*. Indeed, the reviewers seemed to have

run out of superlatives, with the *Academy* suggesting that 'before such distinct achievement criticism may well lay down its arms'.[14] These would be taken up again over the next decade, however, which saw the publication of Conrad's great trilogy of political novels.

Even where critics respond positively to these works, which stand at the heart of Conrad's achievement, he is repeatedly cast as a 'difficult' author, one who eschews the conventions of plot construction, chronology and narration – 'a law unto himself' as the *Athenaeum* had pronounced in its review of *Lord Jim*. The *Times Literary Supplement* declared *Nostromo* (1904) a 'critical mistake'; the *Morning Post* found *The Secret Agent* (1907) 'too sordid to be tragic and too repulsive to be pathetic'.[15] Still achieving distinctly ordinary sales, Conrad complained to Galsworthy: 'there is something in me that is unsympathetic to the general public ... Foreignness, I suppose' (*CL* 4:9). This speculation concealed no little ire, for criticism had begun to cite Conrad's background as a means of accounting for the difficulty of his works. Even Garnett referred to him as 'an alien of genius' and his 'Slav thought and feeling'. Again, 'the ruck' followed, with the *Glasgow News*, for instance, now finding in Conrad's prose something 'Slavonic'.[16] Conrad fulminated at having 'been so cried up of late as a sort of freak, an amazing bloody foreigner writing in English' (*CL* 3:488).

Conrad remained a 'difficult' writer, whose style and subject matter – male preserves of seafaring, Empire and politics – led to Wells chiding him as early as May 1896 for not making 'the slightest concessions to the reading young woman who makes or mars the fortunes of authors'.[17] The publication of *Chance*, with its central character a heroine, Flora de Barral, would answer this criticism. By the time that Conrad commented to Doubleday upon its 'remarkable reception' on 29 January 1914, a fortnight after publication, the novel was already in its fifth printing. Unsurprisingly, Conrad's publishers cashed in, and American reprints of *Almayer's Folly* and *The Nigger of the 'Narcissus'* were quickly planned. With no little irony, the inverse balance between literary fame and fortune persisted, only reversed this time: as the public bought Conrad's books at last, so the cognoscenti found them lacking. In particular, Henry James's public criticism of *Chance* stung, while Garnett suggested that the figure of the lady on the dust-jacket did much to sell the novel.

III

In his 'Author's Note' to *Chance* (1920), Conrad declared his aversion to writing 'for a limited coterie' as inconsistent with his belief 'in the solidarity of all mankind in simple ideas and in sincere emotions'. But on first publication Conrad privately admitted to misgivings about the chorus of praise, telling Galsworthy: 'I can't even pretend I am elated. If I had Nostromo, The Nigger or Lord Jim, in my desk or only in my head I would feel differently no doubt' (CL 5:365).

The return of Marlow in Chance, together with the return to the exotic locales in subsequent work, pleased the critics. In its review of 'Twixt Land and Sea (1912), the Spectator applauded Conrad for returning 'with fresh vigour to his earlier course'.[18] As Conrad assumed the position of Grand Old Man of English Letters, each new literary venture – allegory in Victory (1915), the supernatural in The Shadow-Line (1917) – drew further praise. It had become unfashionable to criticize Conrad. As Norman Sherry put it, critics of the later Conrad 'seem incapable of finding anything wrong with the work. Evaluation is being replaced by adoration.'[19] That said, while Victory and The Shadow-Line were fêted, there was an increasing sense among critics that Conrad had written himself out. In the New Statesman, for instance, Gerald Gould spoke of the 'fatigued air of delicacy' in Victory (2 October 1915).

The work produced in the post-war years attracted a curious mixture of flattery and over-praise, on the one hand, and, on the other, much criticism that would be reformulated in terms of the achievement-and-decline theory decades later. In his review of The Arrow of Gold (1919), novelist J. D. Beresford found 'a just perceptible falling away from the abilities of the artist, who gave us, say, Lord Jim'.[20] The Glasgow Evening News pronounced Conrad's next work, The Rescue (1920), 'Mr Conrad's masterpiece'. But, while concurring – 'his finest work' – the London Mercury yet posed the question of 'whether the wider reputation had not come … to a writer whose best work was already done'. Summarizing the views of many, Rose Macaulay claimed that 'Mr Conrad's sure touch with men always a little fails him with women'.[21] Perversely, reviewers now also criticized Conrad's novels for brevity and being straightforward. The Times predicted for the reader of Conrad's last completed novel, The Rover (1923), 'enjoyment unmitigated by any necessity for intellectual strivings', while, in the New Statesman, Raymond Mortimer described it as 'downright bad'.[22] The posthumously published Suspense (1925) fared even worse, as P. C. Kennedy, also in the New Statesman, claimed that, were it not known to be written by Conrad, no one would attribute it to an author of 'genius', thus removing the attribute bestowed at the beginning of Conrad's career.

Alongside the contemporary reviews that attended the publication of his novels, articles and books written during Conrad's lifetime had already begun to fashion an early critical response to his work. Following in the footsteps of Garnett, other friends, such as Hugh Clifford and Arthur Symons, while promoting Conrad to the book-buying public, were engaged in testamentary acts, helping to fashion his critical reputation.[23] Reprints of Conrad's works also afforded the opportunity to rethink their worth. Thus, in her *Times Literary Supplement* review on the reissue of *Lord Jim*, Virginia Woolf could argue, 'It is not a question of luxury, but of necessity: we have to buy Mr Conrad; all our friends have to buy Mr Conrad' (26 July 1917).

The first full-length study, Richard Curle's *Joseph Conrad: A Study* (1914), was authorized and read by Conrad himself. While attempting to make the 'unEnglish' Conrad accessible to English readers, Curle makes the claim for *Nostromo* as the author's highest achievement and argues that this 'romantic realist' belongs to a European tradition. A year later, in the United States, Wilson Follett's *Joseph Conrad: A Short study of his intellectual and emotional attitude toward his work and of the chief characteristics of his novels* (1915) appeared. In a letter to Pinker, Conrad described it as 'the first intelligent attempt to understand the fundamental ideas of my work' (*CL* 5:576). Hugh Walpole's *Joseph Conrad* followed in 1916 and, in the same year, chapters on Conrad appeared in two critical works: John Freeman's *The Moderns: Essays in Literary Criticism* and William Lyon Phelps's *Advance of the English Novel*.

By the time of his death eight years later, critical analysis of Conrad's work had begun. Ruth M. Stauffer's *Joseph Conrad: His Romantic-Realism* (1922) attempts to locate Conrad in twin traditions – Stevenson's, on the one hand, and that of Maupassant and Zola, on the other – and to demonstrate how their fusion influenced his fundamental approach to plot, character and setting. A critical fascination till the last, in a letter to Ernst P. Bendz, with whose *Joseph Conrad: An Appreciation* (1923) he was taking issue, Conrad wrote wryly: 'Some of my critics have perceived my intention; the last of them being Miss Ruth Stauffer' (*CL* 8:37). The reverberations of that 'Some' echoed through his writing career, and beyond.

NOTES

1. Edward Garnett, ed., *Letters from Conrad: 1895 to 1924* (London: Nonesuch Press, 1928), p. xiii.
2. Owen Knowles and Gene M. Moore, *Oxford Reader's Companion to Conrad* (Oxford: Oxford University Press, 2000), p. 143.
3. *Daily News*, 25 April 1895, p. 6; *Spectator*, 19 October 1895, p. 530.
4. *Daily Record*, 2 May 1896, p. 2; *Bookman*, September 1895, p. 176.
5. H. G. Wells, unsigned review, *Saturday Review*, 16 May 1896, pp. 509–10; E. M. Forster, *Abinger Harvest* (Harmondsworth: Penguin, 1967), p. 152.

6. Letter to Edward Garnett, 7 January 1898 (*CL* 2:9); Garnett, ed., *Letters from Conrad: 1895 to 1924*, p. xx.

7. *Saturday Review*, 12 February 1898, p. 211; *Daily Chronicle*, 22 December 1897, p. 3.

8. *Saturday Evening Gazette*, 16 April 1898, p. 6; *Daily Inter Ocean*, 2 April 1898, p. 10; *Illustrated London News*, 8 January 1898, p. 50; *Court Journal*, 11 December 1897, p. 2086.

9. Arnold Bennett, *Journals of Arnold Bennett, 1896–1928*, ed. Newman Flower, 3 vols. (London: Cassell, 1932), vol. 1, p. 64.

10. See Richard Niland, '"Who's that fellow Lynn?"; Conrad and Robert Lynd', *The Conradian*, 33.1 (Spring 2008), 130–44.

11. *Speaker*, 24 November 1900, p. 215; *Manchester Guardian*, 29 October 1900, p. 6; *Spectator*, 24 November 1900, p. 753.

12. *Academy and Literature*, 6 December 1902, p. 606.

13. See Owen Knowles and J. H. Stape, 'Conrad's Early Reception in America: The Case of W. L. Alden', *The Conradian*, 33.1 (Spring 2008), 145–57.

14. *Manchester Guardian*, 23 April 1903, p. 10; *Academy*, 9 May 1903, p. 464.

15. *Times Literary Supplement*, 21 October 1904, p. 320; *Morning Post*, 19 September 1907, p. 2.

16. Edward Garnett, unsigned review, *Nation*, 28 September 1907, p. 1096; *Glasgow News*, 3 October 1907, p. 5.

17. J. H. Stape and Owen Knowles, eds., *A Portrait in Letters: Correspondence to and about Conrad* (Amsterdam: Rodopi, 1996), p. 21.

18. *Spectator*, 16 November 1912, p. 815.

19. Norman Sherry, ed., *Conrad: The Critical Heritage* (London: Routledge & Kegan Paul, 1973), p. 30.

20. *Everyman*, 9 August 1919, pp. 425–6.

21. *Glasgow Evening News*, 5 August 1920, p. 2; *London Mercury*, August 1920, pp. 497–8; Rose Macaulay, *Time and Tide*, 9 July 1920, p. 188.

22. *The Times*, 3 December 1923, p. 15; *New Statesman*, 15 December 1923, p. 306.

23. Hugh Clifford, 'The Genius of Mr Conrad; *North American Review* (June 1904), 842–52; Arthur Symons, 'Conrad', *Forum* (April 1915), 579–92.

CHAPTER 9

Critical responses: 1925–1950

Owen Knowles

The scores of obituaries marking the occasion of Conrad's death in 1924 represent a collective and consensual memorial to the great writer, many of them wishfully envisioning a reputation so powerful as to be immune from the vagaries of passing time. But from a point of hindsight, such laudation seems to underestimate both the speed of changing literary tastes and the natural tendency of a younger post-First World War generation, in both Britain and America, to turn away from the example of its elders. In fact, Conrad's reputation during the entire period 1925–50 was subject to marked fluctuations, and its changing history divides into three more or less distinct phases: one of posthumous public acclaim (1925–9); a second of neglect and uncertain stocktaking (1930–9); and a third involving a dramatic rediscovery of his works during the Second World War and its aftermath (1940–50).

Writings during the five years after Conrad's death were largely dominated by his close friends and admirers who, highly conscious of their role as guardians of his reputation, made concerted efforts to fashion his posthumous legacy. Many of the labours of G. Jean-Aubry, Edward Garnett, Richard Curle and R. B. Cunninghame Graham involved valuable and necessary rescue-work: the publication of his letters, the collecting of his scattered shorter works and essays, and the preservation of essential biographical materials. Deaths of the famous also, of course, occasion memorial reminiscences, and Conrad's attracted scores of them – by his wife, close friends, distant admirers, artists, old seamen colleagues and fleeting acquaintances.[1] Understandable though such homage was, its overpowering hagiography threatened to be counter-productive in creating the false impression that Conrad's reputation needed to be artificially boosted by over-zealous admirers. The period 1928–9 alone saw the publication of two volumes of letters; an intimate reminiscence by Richard Curle of the writer's later career, celebrating his 'picturesque', many-sided personality and recording in awed tones the events of the final day of his life; and a handsome effort in fine book-making, George T. Keating's *A Conrad*

Memorial Library (1929), a volume combining bibliography and numerous essays by the entire community of Conrad's friends and admirers, and designed to stand as a grand memorial monument to the 'master'.[2]

As early as 1924, John Galsworthy had sounded a warning note: 'It does disservice to Conrad's memory to be indiscriminate in praise of his work. Already, in reaction from this wholesale laudation, one notices a tendency in the younger generation to tilt the nose skyward and talk of his "parade".'[3] Galsworthy here seems more alert than others to the possible neglect or necessary stocktaking that inevitably follows upon a writer's death. But he was clearly also attuned to the swiftly changing tastes of a younger generation of readers who, formed by experiences and memories of the First World War and now exposed to a second wave of Modernist writers (among them T. S. Eliot, Ezra Pound, James Joyce and Virginia Woolf), increasingly tended to regard Conrad as an exotic romancer, sturdy philosopher of the sea or patricianly late-Victorian. During the lean inter-war years of Conrad's faltering popularity (1930–9), the prevailing imagery was of a reputation 'waning', 'contracting' and in some danger of 'eclipse'. In his 1934 overview of the period's fiction, Hugh Walpole noted this sharp break with the pre-war generation of writers: his judgement that 'there has been no Conradian influence – no, simply none at all', sounded out like a lament and possible epitaph.[4]

A fuller sense of why Conrad was thought to be 'unfashionable' by a younger generation emerges in the period's scattered attempts at stocktaking. In 'Conrad After Five Years' (1930), the American Marxist critic Granville Hicks began by arguing that Conrad was ill-advised to turn away from sea fiction, where problems of the sea and seafaring men were perfectly adapted to the world-view of a primarily 'philosophic' writer. Having inexplicably set aside *Nostromo*, *The Secret Agent* and *Under Western Eyes* as extraneous to Conrad's 'real' achievement, Hicks moved effortlessly to the view that, while Conrad's sea stories allowed him access to 'what is central in our civilization', his range of subjects seemed peripheral to present tastes – 'too simple for sophisticates, too barbaric for humanists, not barbaric enough for new primitivists'. He was, Hicks concluded, now largely regarded as being out of touch: he excluded modern women (and women readers); he depreciated intellect in a scientific age; and he ignored complicated sexual involvements and social reform.[5]

While the novelist Elizabeth Bowen proved to be more open to the possibility of a Conrad revival, she nevertheless felt compelled in a review of 1936 to echo the current state of disaffection: 'Conrad is in abeyance. We are not yet clear how to rank him; there is an uncertain pause.' She continued:

Conrad is suspect for the very magnificence that had us under its spell. We resist verbal magic now. His novels are, in the grand sense, heroic: now we like our heroics better muffled – the terse tough heroics of the Hemingway school. His dramatic, ironic sense of fate is out of accord with our fatalism. Most vital of all, perhaps, he seems to be over-concerned with the individual: with conscience, with inner drama, with isolated endeavour. Romantic individualism is at a discount now.[6]

To this list, George Orwell added one further possibility: that while Conrad's unfashionability was ostensibly based upon objections to his 'florid style and redundant adjectives', it was in reality a matter of his being regarded as a gentleman, 'a type hated by the modern intelligentsia'.[7] Even the stalwart Richard Curle in reviewing the problem of 'Conrad and the Younger Generation' (1930) was forced to admit that the writer, now widely seen as 'too involved in his approach, too sumptuous in his language ... too conventional in his attitude', was invariably held up by younger readers as appealing to 'some false need of the [present] age' for the exotic and picturesque.[8]

If the picture was not totally bleak – Gustav Morf's psychoanalytic study of Conrad's Anglo-Polish dualism (1930) and Thomas Mann's essay on *The Secret Agent* (1926), first translated into English in 1933,[9] offered fresh and independent approaches – it generally remains true that during this period Conrad was also not particularly fortunate in his defenders, whose well-meaning intentions did not translate into significant revaluation. In part, the problem lay in the fact that defences of Conrad in Britain were too much the exclusive property of the writer's two friends and acolytes, Richard Curle and G. Jean-Aubry. But another aspect of the problem lay in the persistence of a belletristic tradition of criticism that rarely allowed for the more rigorous assessment that the debate required. For example, Edward Crankshaw's *Joseph Conrad: Some Aspects of the Art of the Novel* (1936), opened with the bracing recognition that the dozen years since Conrad's death had been 'the empty period ... between adulation and settled regard' and promised a study 'starting from scratch and made in a spirit as free from prejudice and preconception as maybe'.[10] Yet the study is always hampered by its form as a freely wandering, extended essay that, in eschewing any close analysis or steady focus, is finally notable as one of the last examples of the belletristic tradition of Conrad criticism. Valuable though parts of it remain, it was always unlikely to succeed in persuading the unconverted or in attracting new readers.

The period 1940–50 proved to be a crucial watershed in the early formation of Conrad's 'modern' reputation. That such a revaluation should coincide with the Second World War and its aftermath is certainly no accident. An increasing number of critics and readers seem to have felt subliminally that many of Conrad's darkly pessimistic intuitions of apocalypse and of the destructive effects of *Weltpolitik* were more in accord with a later period of history than with earlier decades. He was, in short, discovered to be a 'modern' and 'prophetic' writer in ways that, it was felt, spoke intimately to the collective consciousness of a generation who were living through the Second World War or coming to terms with its legacy. Bringing with it a new sense of critical urgency and mission in reclaiming Conrad's works for changed audiences, this rediscovery marks a significant moment in the history of the writer's reception, the effects of which were first felt among British critics of the early 1940s and then quickly developed by their American counterparts. Another significant development was also under way: the belletristic tradition was in rapid and terminal decline, and academic criticism emergent, in both Britain and America (along with associated calls for Conrad to be taught in school and college classrooms[11]). Indeed, evidence of this increasing professionalization was clear as early as 1940, with John Dozier Gordan's landmark study, *Joseph Conrad: The Making of a Novelist*, which broke new ground in the kind and depth of scholarly interest brought to Conrad's manuscripts and other unpublished materials, in this case in order to follow his emergence from amateur to professional writer, culminating in *Lord Jim*. Still an indispensable source-book, Gordan's pioneer work marked the beginning of serious scholarly study of Conrad's works and anticipated their passage into academe.

The bare outlines of a more 'modern' revaluation were first evident in M. C. Bradbrook's *Joseph Conrad: Poland's English Genius*, an eighty-page 'ordinance map' surveying the phases of Conrad's career.[12] Too brief to be especially revealing, this study remains interesting on two grounds. First, the account of Conrad's strengths as one of the greatest writers of his time (including the judgement that 'Heart of Darkness' was the 'masterpiece' of his early period (27)) combined with the call for a more rigorous revaluation of the decline that appears to overtake his work after *Victory*: 'Conrad's later novels are for the most part sound, careful, but incurably listless works. They are exercises in the manner of Conrad' (68). Second, along with this call, its wartime sense of the relevance and aptness of the writer's political wisdom struck a new note: 'Whatever else in Conrad has dated, his politics are contemporary' (8). Of the power of *Under Western Eyes*, Bradbrook wrote: 'No wonder the book was unpopular in 1911. It might have been equally unpopular in 1931, but at the moment its premises are familiar.

Conrad's political writings are few, but almost without exception they are apt to the present time' (9). This excited discovery culminated in the ambitious claim that Conrad was a type of writer belonging 'not to the past but the future' (77).

By far the most decisive interventions of the period belong to two critics, F. R. Leavis in Britain and Morton D. Zabel in America. Leavis's 'Revaluations: Joseph Conrad' first appeared in *Scrutiny* in 1941 and was later collected in *The Great Tradition* (1948), a dominant, widely influential and – until the mid-1970s – inescapable work in Conrad criticism. Leavis's exciting recovery of Conrad identified him as 'among the very greatest novelists in the language – or any language' (226) and the natural inheritor of the tradition of the English novel that includes Jane Austen, George Eliot and Henry James. The placement of Conrad in such a line led Leavis to emphasize the moral and social richness of Conrad's sea fiction as testimony to his commitment to British national traditions ('his genius was a unique and happy union of seaman and writer' (189)). This account was complicated (in ways that do not always seem to square happily with Leavis's underlying thesis) by his recognition that, with the appearance of *Nostromo*, the writer seemed to take his place in an altogether different tradition: in the latter novel, he claimed, 'Conrad is openly and triumphantly the artist by *métier*, con-scious of French initiation and of fellowship in craft with Flaubert' (190).

To this critic also belonged the first memorably argued construction of a Conrad canon and the case for a major period extending from 'Typhoon' (1902) to *The Shadow-Line* (1917) (with *Nostromo* and *The Secret Agent* identified as the writer's two indisputable classics). Just as tenaciously argued, Leavis's negative verdicts were also to reverberate widely in later criticism. His downgrading of the early Marlow narratives from Conrad's *Blackwood's Magazine* period – 'Youth', 'Heart of Darkness' and *Lord Jim* – was both challenging and combative. Most famously, the encounter with 'Heart of Darkness' yielded a very mixed report, in which admiration for some of the story's local descriptive effects was outweighed by the severest of judgements on the 'cheapening' effect of popular magazine styles – particularly, the 'adjectival and worse than supererogatory insist-ence' upon inexpressible mystery that suggests a writer at times 'intent on making a virtue out of not knowing what he means' (180). As such pungent judgements indicate, Leavis's critical method was also essential to the urgency of the case being made: his approach was teacherly in its use of demonstration-by-quotation, more stringently focused upon the texts themselves, and espoused varieties of practical criticism in the search for clear discrimination and evaluation.[13]

Almost simultaneously, the American critic Morton D. Zabel was engaging with Conrad's fiction in a number of pioneering articles and prefaces, later collected in *Craft and Character: Text, Method and Vocation in Modern Literature*.[14] Between Leavis and Zabel there were many underlying similarities: both were impatient with the moribund state of Conrad criticism, urged on by the need to establish a secure basis for his reputation, and intent upon highlighting a canon of his best work, including, in Zabel's case, the writer's shorter stories in his anthology *The Portable Conrad*.[15] But, that said, their critical emphases proved to be markedly different. Where Leavis had looked back to Conrad's British antecedents and forebears as a way of establishing his classic status, part of Zabel's case rested upon his linking of Conrad with more recent European writers. Seen as part-originator of a more dangerously radical modern tradition, Conrad thus forcefully emerged as 'our' contemporary, his preoccupation with extreme moral isolation, the 'trapped sensibility' and lonely recognition making him akin to Franz Kafka, Thomas Mann, André Gide and the French existentialists: 'The ambiguity of truth, the conflict of appearance and reality, the rival claims of the secret and the social self – these are now integral to modern fiction in its major manifestations' (17). Where Leavis had stressed a pattern of moral significances and controlled intelligence in Conrad's best work, Zabel was strikingly open to the possibility of his fiction being 'always more than the sum of his conscious motives and critical intelligence' (12) and of his development as an artist as reproducing 'the ordeal of self-mastery and spiritual exoneration which he dramatized repeatedly in the lives of his heroes' (22). And, it should be added, Zabel differed from Leavis in regarding 'Heart of Darkness' and *Lord Jim* as central to Conrad's contribution to modern fictional method, 'his imposition of the processes and structures of psychological experience (particularly the experience of recognition) on the form of the plot' (14).[16]

It is difficult to over-estimate the galvanizing effect of these two major figures, who, quickly attracting younger admirers, largely helped to shape the contrasting character of future British and American criticism during the following decades.[17] By the late 1940s, a number of articles by younger critics, such as Douglas Hewitt, Albert J. Guerard and R. W. Stallman, proved to be trial-runs for highly influential studies that were to appear in the 1950s. Along with this reviving critical interest, Conrad's works were now also being made available and freshly introduced in new portable anthologies and large-scale popular editions, notably Dent's Collected Edition that began appearing from 1947. Conrad's 'rediscovery' was clearly gathering powerful momentum.

As a final coda, two writers in particular – E. K. Brown in 1945 and George Orwell in 1949 – stand out as representative spokesmen for this decade: combining a backward look at a recent history of neglect with confident prophecy for the future, they testify to a strikingly re-invigorated view of Conrad's place and rank in twentieth-century literature:

Of Conrad little is heard. I believe that before thirty years have passed, the world of his imagination will fascinate the general reader as surely as it did twenty years ago; and that the close critical analysis of his work, which has barely begun, will take a large place in the interpretation of fiction.[18]

I regard Conrad as one of the best writers of this century, and – supposing that one can count him as an English writer – one of the very few true novelists that England possesses. His reputation, which was somewhat eclipsed after his death, has risen again during the past ten years, and I have no doubt that the bulk of his work will survive … [He had] a sort of grown-upness and political understanding which would have been almost impossible to a native English writer at that time.[19]

NOTES

1. For a comprehensive listing of reminiscences, see Martin Ray, ed., *Joseph Conrad: Memories and Impressions – An Annotated Bibliography*, Conrad Studies 1 (Amsterdam and New York: Rodopi, 2007); extracts from some are reprinted in *Joseph Conrad: Interviews and Recollections*, ed. Martin Ray (Basingstoke: Macmillan, 1990).
2. Works mentioned in this paragraph are as follows: *Letters from Conrad: 1895 to 1924*, ed. Edward Garnett (London: Nonesuch Press, 1928); *Joseph Conrad: Lettres françaises*, ed. G. Jean-Aubry (Paris: Gallimard, 1929); Richard Curle, *The Last Twelve Years of Joseph Conrad* (London: Sampson Low, Marston, 1928); George T. Keating, ed., *A Conrad Memorial Library: The Collection of George T. Keating* (Garden City, NY: Doubleday Page, Doran, 1929).
3. John Galsworthy, 'Reminiscences of Conrad' (1924), rpt in Galsworthy's *Castles in Spain & Other Screeds* (London: Heinemann, 1928), p. 81.
4. Hugh Walpole, 'England', in *Tendencies of the Modern Novel* (London: Allen & Unwin, 1934), p. 15.
5. *New Republic*, 61 (8 January 1930), 192–4.
6. 'Conrad', *Spectator*, 156 (24 April 1936), 758, rpt in Bowen's *Collected Impressions* (London: Longmans Green, 1950), pp. 151–3.
7. George Orwell, 'Recent Novels', *New English Weekly*, 9 (23 July 1936), 294–5, rpt in *The Collected Works of George Orwell*. Vol. x: *A Kind of Compulsion 1903–1936*, ed. Peter Davison (London: Secker & Warburg, 1998), pp. 490–3.
8. *Nineteenth Century*, 107 (1930), 104.
9. Gustav Morf, *The Polish Heritage of Joseph Conrad* (London: Sampson Low, Marston, 1930); Mann's essay was translated in *Past Masters and Other Papers*, trans. H. T. Lowe-Porter (London: Secker & Warburg, 1933), pp. 234–47.

10. Edward Crankshaw, *Joseph Conrad: Some Aspects of the Art of the Novel* (London: John Lane, 1936), pp. 1, 2.

11. In 1947, R. C. Churchill called for Conrad's works to be included in the English school curriculum immediately after Shakespeare and Dickens: see his 'Conrad in School', *Journal of Education*, 79 (May 1947), 130.

12. Bradbrook, *Joseph Conrad: Poland's English Genius* (Cambridge: Cambridge University Press, 1941).

13. All page references in these two paragraphs are from Leavis's *The Great Tradition, George Eliot, Henry James, Joseph Conrad* (London: Chatto & Windus, 1948).

14. *Craft and Character: Text, Method and Vocation in Modern Literature* (New York: Viking Press, 1958).

15. Morton D. Zabel, ed., *The Portable Conrad* (New York: Viking Press, 1947).

16. All page references in this paragraph are from Zabel's 'Joseph Conrad: Chance and Recognition', *Sewanee Review*, 53 (1945), 1–22.

17. The present survey has restricted itself to British and American criticism. For a corresponding view of Conrad's reputation in Poland – particularly during his 'lean years' of neglect (1945–55) and later renaissance – see Adam Gillon, *Conrad and Shakespeare and Other Essays* (New York: Astra Books, 1976), pp. 211–38.

18. E. K. Brown, 'James and Conrad', *Yale Review*, 35 (1945), 285.

19. George Orwell, 'Conrad's Place and Rank in English Letters', *Wiadomości*, 10 April 1949, rpt in *The Collected Essays, Journalism and Letters of George Orwell*, ed. Sonia Orwell and Ian Angus (London: Secker & Warburg, 1968), p. 489.

CHAPTER 10

Critical responses: 1950–1975

Richard Niland

Following his positioning as a major English novelist by F. R. Leavis in *The Great Tradition* (1948), Conrad became a central figure in academic literary criticism in the 1950s and 1960s with the publication of a series of seminal works on the writer. With studies by Thomas C. Moser, Albert J. Guerard and Edward Said, the period saw the beginning of the Conrad industry in international academe, with several biographies undertaken or written and the hunt for every possible scrap of extant Conradiana under way. This resulted in societies and journals dedicated to Conrad's life and works in Britain, France, Poland and the United States; the first steps in the daunting but now completed collected letters of Conrad; and a stubbornly unassailable interpretation of Conrad's literary career, captured in the title of Moser's influential *Joseph Conrad: Achievement and Decline* (1957). The period between 1950 and 1975 also saw groundbreaking work on Conrad's life by Zdzisław Najder, Norman Sherry and Hans van Marle and, with the unprecedented attention given to his life and works by gifted international scholars, these years constitute a true golden age of Conrad criticism.

In the aftermath of the Second World War, philosophical and political criticism, conscious of the catastrophic results of nationalist and supremacist ideologies throughout the world, adopted Conrad as a writer transcending national boundaries, one representative of a sceptical voice on international politics. Hannah Arendt's *The Origins of Totalitarianism* (1951), 'written against a background of both reckless optimism and reckless despair', isolated 'Heart of Darkness' as 'the most illuminating work on actual race experience in Africa',[1] with Arendt frequently citing Conrad's vision of imperialism as 'the merry dance of death and trade' in her overview of repressive political power. Written before the widespread growth of post-war prosperity in the Western world, Arendt foreshadowed the emergence of later criticism acknowledging Conrad as a prophetic voice on the disasters of the first half of the twentieth century.

The same year saw Robert Penn Warren deem *Nostromo* Conrad's 'supreme effort', and the American poet/critic argued that Conrad should,

against the view of F. R. Leavis and E. M. Forster, be considered a 'philosophical novelist', whose masterpiece was 'one of the few mastering visions
of our historical moment and our human lot'.[2] Albert J. Guerard's *Conrad
the Novelist* (1958) also registered the importance of contemporary history in
evaluating Conrad's psychological and political immediacy: 'It has taken the
full aftermath of the Second World War to make me recognize the political
insights of *Nostromo, The Secret Agent,* and *Under Western Eyes,* and their
pertinence for our own time.'[3]

Thomas C. Moser's *Joseph Conrad: Achievement and Decline* emerged
from the writer's research at Harvard University alongside Guerard, and it
represents a pivotal moment in Conrad studies, pointing forward to later
academic/departmental studies of Conrad, while sharing aspects of an earlier tradition of *belles-lettres* criticism. Unburdened by the extensive cross-
referencing of subsequent monographs, Moser engaged with the relatively
small contemporary field of Leavis, Guerard, Douglas Hewitt, Edward
Crankshaw and Morton D. Zabel, promoting archetypal interpretations
of the intricate psychology of Conrad's stories. Conrad was 'England's most
complex novelist', and Moser aimed to 'give insight into a great writer's
creative strengths and weaknesses'. In an influential but hardly novel
interpretation (Moser noted Guerard's 'account of Conrad's "anti-climax"'
and John Galsworthy's selective praise of Conrad), 'Love's Tangled Garden'
emerged as Conrad's 'Uncongenial Subject'. The writer's career journeyed
from early achievement to 'The Exhaustion of Creative Energy', and Moser
sought to explain 'the degeneration of Conrad's prose style', believing
Chance to be 'the first clearly second-rate work that pretended to be of
major importance'.[4] Contrary to later critical perspectives, after theoretical
schools reliant on contemporary European philosophy emerged in
Anglophone universities, Moser eschewed exhaustive, overly ingenious
analysis in favour of an opinionated evaluation, a critical style that would
gradually disappear during coming years. For example, *The Secret Agent* and
Under Western Eyes were 'clearly serious, respectable novels, but they
seemed to lack that particular magic one thinks of as "Conradian"'.[5]

In *Conrad the Novelist,* Albert J. Guerard sought 'to express and define
my response to a writer I have long liked and admired'.[6] Following Moser's
trajectory, Guerard adopted a psychoanalytic reading, with Conrad's characters becoming manifestations of the writer's psyche. However, influen-
tially, and contrary to Moser, Guerard believed *The Shadow-Line* stood as
'Conrad's last important work of fiction'. Guerard commented on Conrad's
recent adoption as a student-friendly author, his short fiction now the
subsistence diet of undergraduates. Exploring 'spiritual and moral isolation'

in 'The Secret Sharer', he noted that 'These matters (the preoccupation of so many college freshmen today) were then unfamiliar enough, and it is safe to say that in 1947 the large majority of critics in America did not read Conrad at all ... The ten years have brought a more substantial rediscovery than I dared hoped for.'[7] Praising recent critics such as Morton D. Zabel, Penn Warren, Moser, Dorothy Van Ghent, Douglas Hewitt and M. C. Bradbrook, Guerard also signalled the departure of the first generation of Conradians. Guerard highlighted the unreliability of G. Jean-Aubry's *The Sea Dreamer* (1957; a translation of his earlier *Vie de Conrad*), 'because it takes almost no notice of work done in the last twenty-five years',[8] and lamented the textual irregularities of *Joseph Conrad: Life and Letters* (1927), thereby challenging prospective biographers.

A more scrupulous approach to documenting Conrad and his works led to the first modern life, Jocelyn Baines' *Joseph Conrad: A Critical Biography* (1960). Indebted in part to the pioneering research of Zdzisław Najder, Baines brought Conradian biography to an authoritative and objective level, writing with the required temporal and emotional distance from his subject. As J. H. Stape notes, Baines was 'self-consciously writing the life of a man whose work was attaining "classic" status'.[9] Baines marked the beginning of a decade that produced an outpouring of research and detailed documentary evidence contradicting Conrad's maxim to Richard Curle that explicitness is fatal to all glamour. Norman Sherry, in *Conrad's Eastern World* (1966), and later *Conrad's Western World* (1970), along with Jerry Allen's *The Sea Years of Joseph Conrad* (1967), launched a trend for following in the biographical footsteps of the writer, tracking real-life sources for characters esoterically mythologized in contemporary/post-modern academic criticism, and later in popular film, notably Francis Ford Coppola's *Apocalypse Now* (1979). Sherry also presented a selective grouping of contemporary critical responses to Conrad in *Conrad: The Critical Heritage* (1973), while bibliographical works on writings about Conrad materialized in the shape of Theodore G. Ehrsam's *A Bibliography of Joseph Conrad* (1969) and Bruce E. Teets and Helmut E. Gerber's *Joseph Conrad: An Annotated Bibliography of Writings About Him* (1971). Significant critics of the history of English literature also turned their attention to Conrad. Ian Watt, author of the seminal *Rise of the Novel* (1957), wrote extensively on Conrad's intellectual background throughout the period, culminating in his important study *Conrad in the Nineteenth Century* (1979).

As Tony Judt notes, the 1960s were 'the great age of Theory', and in an 'age of vastly expanded universities, with periodicals, journals and lecturers urgently seeking "copy", there emerged a market for "theories" of every kind – fuelled not by improved intellectual supply but rather by insatiable consumer demand'.[10] Between 1950 and 1975, close to 3,000 books, essays or articles were published on Conrad. Conrad's work, with its striking engagement with colonial and postcolonial political contexts, and its Flaubertian concern with the *mot juste*, invited and challenged new critical schools. In 1968, Bernard C. Meyer unveiled his *Joseph Conrad: A Psychoanalytic Biography*, which, as Chinua Achebe later noted, followed 'every conceivable lead (and sometimes inconceivable ones) to explain Conrad',[11] while Paul Kirschner's *The Psychologist as Artist* (1968) conversely sought to systematize Conrad's psychological reflections. Conrad's writings seemed adapted for theoretical readings, with the author's tri-lingual, tri-cultural heritage an open field for critics eager to perform semantic acrobatics.

Previously condemned features of Conrad's literary and philosophical style, captured in E. M. Forster's critique that Conrad made a virtue out of incoherence, acquired a new value, as English literary and cultural criticism of the 1960s and 1970s believed 'Difficulty became the measure of intellectual seriousness.'[12] Conrad's experimental use of narrative proved a convenient resource for critics exploring the emerging discipline of narratology, given a working vocabulary by the publication of Gérard Genette's study of Proust, *Figures III*, in 1972. Increasingly, Conrad was removed altogether from studies of his texts. The period, which had opened with Jean-Paul Sartre's *What is Literature?* (1948), and now influenced by the structuralist perspectives of Claude Lévi-Strauss and Michel Foucault, questioned 'What is an Author?', looking with supercilious scepticism on 'man-and-his-work criticism',[13] ultimately leading to a post-structuralist insistence on the subjectivity and socially/politically constructed nature of all perspectives. However, major studies of Conrad's politics by Avrom Fleishman and Eloise Knapp Hay remained traditional in their political focus, and later conspicuous in their lack of engagement with contemporary theory, locating Conrad's politics in a tradition of European thought indebted to Burke and Rousseau.

A generation of critics who would become important voices in Derrida-influenced deconstructionist theory also began to investigate Conrad's work. J. Hillis Miller's *Poets of Reality: Six Twentieth-Century Writers* (1966) devoted considerable attention to Conrad as a writer who pointed 'the way toward the transcendence of nihilism by the poets of the twentieth century'.[14] Conrad was a novelist 'of imperialism', one connected by Miller to a nihilistic tradition of European literature including Dostoevsky, Mann, Gide, Proust and Camus, but also grounded in 'the narrower limits of the

English novel' to a 'native tradition' following Dickens, George Eliot, Trollope, Meredith and Hardy in his representation of reality (6). One of the most influential literary and cultural voices of the twentieth century, Edward Said, published his doctoral work as *Joseph Conrad and the Fiction of Autobiography* (1966), and Said continually refined his interpretations of Conrad, using *Nostromo* as a central text in his reflections on writing and textuality in *Beginnings: Intention and Method* (1975). Said captured the evolving approach to literature of the period and its pertinence to Conrad's multi-layered narratives: 'A text, then, seems more essentially just itself – a text, with its own highly specialized problematics – than a representation of anything else.'[15]

Alongside a flowering of theoretical criticism on Conrad appeared a concerted drive by Polish literary scholars to reposition the importance of Conrad's Polish heritage. While Conrad had been given increased attention in Polish literary journals since his death, and not forgetting that he remained a cult writer in Poland during the Second World War, the process of bringing the full complexity and extensive documentary evidence of Conrad's Polish background to an international readership began in the 1950s. In November 1957, the international face of Polish literature and opposition to Communism, Czesław Miłosz, wrote on 'Joseph Conrad in Polish Eyes' in the *Atlantic Monthly*. The issue also featured an essay by Conrad critic Edward Crankshaw on 'Russia's Imperial Design', arguing that Russian foreign policy was exhausted. Miłosz focused on Conrad's anti-Russian credentials, noting intellectual and political continuity between Apollo Korzeniowski and his son. While Miłosz asserted that 'Conrad is an English writer and the Poles have never tried to assimilate him into their literature',[16] Conrad nevertheless emerged as an international reminder of cultures behind the Iron Curtain. For Miłosz, the

Polish reader, then, has a strange feeling as he trips constantly over things that have a familiar ring. Certain themes, and even the rhythms of certain passages in his novels, are reminiscent of verse lines very close to him, whose sources, upon reflection, can be named. What happened in Conrad was the perfect fusing of two literatures and two civilizations.[17]

Conrad undoubtedly proved a magnetic figure for the political dissident Zdzisław Najder. The scope of the material he presented to English-language readers and the authority with which he assessed Conrad's relationship to the culture of nineteenth-century Eastern Europe was of monumental importance for understanding Conrad's early life, and Najder's contribution to this field is unlikely to be superseded. *Conrad's Polish*

Background (1964), in its magisterial unveiling of primary documents, signalled that Conrad now belonged to a second generation of critics and thinkers; further removed in time, yet his complexities somehow better known. The reluctance of Conrad's own remaining contemporaries to release their guarded proximity to the writer was revealed in Richard Curle's review of Najder for the *Contemporary Review*. Noting the increasing 'outflow of books' on Conrad, Curle praised Najder's 'masterly' introduction to this seminal volume, but appeared to downplay its importance. Condemning the prolixity of Tadeusz Bobrowski's 'decidedly tedious' letters,[18] Curle appeared dismissive of one of the emerging stars of Conradian biography and scholarship, namely Bobrowski himself, who would feature largely in Najder's later *Joseph Conrad: A Chronicle* (1983), and whose translated voice illuminated aspects of Conrad's Polish past previously beyond the reach of the Anglophone critic. As Bobrowski and his cultural milieu assumed centre-stage in Conrad studies, the field saw an increase in work devoted to the political, cultural and literary arena of Conrad's Polish youth. Important voices in this respect were Andrzej Busza, in his 'Conrad's Polish Literary Background' (1966), and Adam Gillon, who refined the earlier work of Gustav Morf (who would re-enter the fray in 1970), and challenged the overwhelming Anglicization of Conrad's achievement.

While detailed feminist readings and Fredric Jameson's major Marxist interpretation, *The Political Unconscious: Narrative as Socially Symbolic Act* (1981), would come later, the period closed with the rise of postcolonial perspectives on Conrad. These years witnessed the dismantling of the British Empire, highlighting the difficulties of bringing civil and political order to the real-world settings of Conrad's fiction, most of which gained political autonomy between 1960 and 1975. Nigerian novelist Chinua Achebe's Chancellor's Lecture at the University of Massachusetts in February 1975, later published in the *Massachusetts Review* (1977), embodies, alongside Edward Said's *Orientalism* (1978), the academic postcolonial explosion, a reordering of centuries of control by the imperialist voice over stunted indigenous vernaculars. Achebe outlined the tendency in 'Western psychology to set up Africa as a foil to Europe, as a place of negations at once remote and vaguely familiar'. 'Heart of Darkness' was 'constantly evaluated by serious academics', but Achebe accused Conrad of 'inducing hypnotic stupor in his readers through a bombardment of emotive words and other forms of trickery', ultimately 'playing the role of purveyor of comforting myths'.[19] Keen to unveil supremacist views on Conrad's part, Achebe rather coyly avoided treating the larger implications of Conrad's tale. Achebe's reading of the dispossession of language from Africans, Marlow's perception of grunts and noises, has become increasingly misguided; social developments in a monolingual British establishment culture a hundred years after Conrad's time mean that the average Englishman (if such is what Marlow represents) would have the same perceptions today, not just in 'darkest Africa' but in Paris or Rome. Achebe discounted Conradian irony, believing 'Joseph Conrad was a thoroughgoing racist', and English departments in American universities were attacked for prescribing a work 'in which the very humanity of black people is called in question'. Achebe's polemical assessment of 'Heart of Darkness' was perhaps credible: 'Conrad saw and condemned the evil of imperial exploitation but was strangely unaware of the racism on which it sharpened its iron tooth.'[20]

However, it is important to attribute to Achebe a strong degree of post-colonial *ressentiment* towards the departed colonial Other, as states such as his native Nigeria – which experienced civil war between 1967 and 1970, a series of military dictatorships and a scramble for newly discovered oil wealth – disintegrated and suffered ethnic and civil strife sometimes beyond the brutal excesses of the colonizer. Falling prey to corrupt governmental practices and an inability to adopt the alien European tradition of the nation-state, indigenous abuse easily matched the inhumane control of former Empires. Conrad's work, an obvious critique of imperialism and inhumanity in its original context, was dragged into the postcolonial era as an example of the pervasive and irredeemable malignity of the colonial enterprise. Nevertheless, Achebe brought some controversial attention to a writer whose biography refused to throw up any salaciously marketable revelations, and Conrad's racial and political views proved a cornerstone of literary debate during the next quarter-century.

The International Conrad Conference in Kent in 1974, the papers of which were edited by Norman Sherry, captured the breadth of critics working between 1950 and 1975.[21] Conrad now represented a stable sub-industry within international academe, evidenced by the foundation of the Joseph Conrad Society UK (1973), the Joseph Conrad Society of America (1974) and the Société Conradienne Française (1975), with their respective journals, *The Conradian*, *Conradiana* and *L'Époque Conradienne*. Present at the 1974 international gathering were Guerard, Tony Tanner, Ian Watt, Eloise Knapp Hay, Edward Said, Zdzisław Najder, Edward Crankshaw, Andrzej Busza, Avrom Flieshman, Frederick R. Karl, Thomas C. Moser, Ugo Mursia and Adam Gillon. Following diverse methodologies and inter-pretative strategies, the conference embodied a quarter-century's achieve-ment in recognizing Conrad's position as a major European writer.

NOTES

1. Hannah Arendt, *The Origins of Totalitarianism* (1951; London: Allen & Unwin, 1958), pp. vii, 185.
2. Robert Penn Warren, *Selected Essays by Robert Penn Warren* (London: Eyre & Spottiswoode, 1951), pp. 32, 58.
3. Albert J. Guerard, *Conrad the Novelist* (Cambridge, MA: Harvard University Press, 1958), p. xi.
4. Thomas C. Moser, *Joseph Conrad: Achievement and Decline* (Cambridge, MA: Harvard University Press, 1957), pp. 1, 2, 8.
5. Moser, *Joseph Conrad: Achievement and Decline*, p. 2.
6. Guerard, *Conrad the Novelist*, p. ix.
7. Guerard, *Conrad the Novelist*, pp. xiii, xi.
8. Guerard, *Conrad the Novelist*, p. xii.
9. J. H. Stape, 'On Conradian Biography as a Fine Art', *The Conradian*, 32.2 (2007), 57–75, p. 59.
10. Tony Judt, *Postwar: A History of Europe since 1945* (London: Pimlico, 2005), pp. 398–9.
11. Chinua Achebe, *Hopes and Impediments: Selected Essays* (London: Heinemann, 1988), p. 10.
12. Judt, *Postwar*, p. 480.
13. Michel Foucault, *The Foucault Reader* (London: Penguin, 1981), p. 101.
14. J. Hillis Miller, *Poets of Reality: Six Twentieth-Century Writers* (London: Oxford University Press, 1966), p. 6.
15. Edward W. Said, *Beginnings: Intention and Method* (New York: Basic Books, 1975), p. 11.
16. Czesław Miłosz, 'Joseph Conrad in Polish Eyes', *Atlantic Monthly*, 200.5 (November 1957), 219–28, p. 224.
17. Miłosz, 'Polish Eyes', p. 226.
18. Richard Curle, 'Son of Poland', *Contemporary Review* (October 1964), 552.
19. Achebe, *Hopes and Impediments: Selected Essays*, pp. 2, 3.
20. Achebe, *Hopes and Impediments: Selected Essays*, pp. 8, 10, 13.
21. Norman Sherry, ed., *Joseph Conrad: A Commemoration: Papers from the 1974 International Conference on Conrad* (London: Macmillan, 1976).

CHAPTER 11

Critical responses: 1975–2000

Andrew Purssell

In 1977, Frederick R. Karl proclaimed Conrad a writer 'about whom very little remains to be said'. In reaction, William Bonney contended that to 'scrutinize Conrad's fiction any further' remained anything but 'futile'. The sheer weight of Conrad criticism amassed since suggests plenty were in agreement – so much so, indeed, that Cedric Watts surmised that 'the customary formula' for critical books on Conrad was to 'defend the need for yet another book'.[1] What the attitude typified by Karl's pronouncement foreclosed itself to, furthermore, were those developments in critical and literary theory which, in the 1980s and 1990s, had as profound an impact on Conrad studies as on the broader study of literature.

Appearing just after Karl, *Joseph Conrad: The Major Phase* (1978) by Jacques Berthoud redresses critical opinion of Conrad – from E. M. Forster's 'notorious verdict that Conrad is misty in the middle as well as at the edges', to C. B. Cox's that '"there is no clear development of ideas" throughout his work'. Conrad, Berthoud concludes, 'is a much more intellectually coherent figure than the one criticism has accustomed us to'. Key to demonstrating this intellectual coherence, as the title suggests, is the consolidation of the idea of a 'major phase': Berthoud hereby draws upon one critical commonplace – the familiar narrative of 'achievement and decline' – to challenge another. Conrad's 'major theme', posited here as 'the problem of individual identity' ('the question of what the "real" self is – where it is located, and how it is to be understood'), is contextualized in the shift from a Romantic 'concern with individual experience' to a 'behaviourist, structuralist, Marxist emphasis on its determinants'. In this 'move from private intentions to public systems', it is not 'individual consciousness' that matters but the 'idea of a social role'.[2]

In scope and influence, Ian Watt's *Conrad in the Nineteenth Century* (1979) is a landmark study. Concentrating almost exhaustively on Conrad's career up to 1900 and the early fiction up to *Lord Jim*, Watt takes up 'such matters as Conrad's relationship to his Polish past, to the Romantic movement, to the popular and highbrow traditions and to the treatment of time in narrative' – historical considerations that help determine 'the nature and the originality of Conrad's narrative methods more clearly', and how these methods reflect 'Conrad's sensitiveness to the fundamental social and intellectual conflicts of this period'.[3] Out of this comes the coinage 'delayed decoding', which, deriving from a perceived overlap between Conrad and Impressionism, describes the represented gap in Conrad's fiction between sensory experience and cognitive understanding.

Fredric Jameson's analysis of the function of romance in *Lord Jim* and *Nostromo* in *The Political Unconscious* (1981), a work as knotty as it was fêted, marked another important and influential intervention, not least as it sustained within its Marxist, materialist frame a complex engagement with post-structuralism, then beginning to take hold. Proposing that, 'as with few other modern writers', Conrad's narratives project 'a bewildering variety of competing and incommensurable interpretive options', Jameson provocatively regards Conrad as not 'an early modernist', but rather 'an anticipation of that quite different thing we have come to call … post-modernism'.[4]

Frederick R. Karl's *Joseph Conrad: The Three Lives* (1979) is perhaps the most ambitious of the critical biographies to appear in the late 1970s and 1980s, interleaving Conrad's life and works, and drawing on unpublished correspondence to create an in-depth – albeit at times highly speculative – psychological portrait. Zdzisław Najder's *Joseph Conrad: A Chronicle* (1983) conversely disfavours viewing Conrad through his works, emphasizing a more 'concrete' brand of scholarly biography. Published the same year, his *Conrad Under Familial Eyes* translates for an English-speaking audience hitherto inaccessible Polish biographical materials, enlarging the picture of Conrad's cultural heritage. Complementarily, Yves Hervouet's *The French Face of Joseph Conrad* (1990) details the influence on Conrad of writers in French, his second language (including Flaubert, Maupassant and Anatole France). *Joseph Conrad: A Literary Life* (1989) by Cedric Watts, though grounded in little documentary research, examines Conrad's life from a professional perspective. Like his earlier *A Preface to Conrad* (1982),[5] it blends biographical with contemporary cultural contexts, focusing on Conrad's often fraught relationship with an expanding Edwardian publishing industry, the importance of its serial markets and the role and rise of the literary agent.

Alongside such examinations of Conrad's relation to writing as a profession are several devoted to technical aspects of Conrad's writing itself. Evoking Forster's classic complaint that the 'secret casket of Conrad's genius contained a vapour rather than a jewel', Allon White suggests in *The Uses of Obscurity* (1981) that Conradian 'narrative is only a hint or a clue to some immense secret enclosed within it'. Whereas Forster bemoaned, White sets out to explain ambiguity in Conrad, finding the looping, recalcitrant nature of Conrad's storytelling to be characteristic of the fictions of early Modernism – part of 'the new, fiercely difficult kind of writing' that heralded 'the collapse of realism'.[6]

Appearing just after Edward Said's chapter on Conrad in *The World, the Text, and the Critic* (1983), and approaching narrative from a Freudian perspective, Peter Brooks' influential study *Reading for the Plot* (1984) contextualizes Conradian issues 'concerning endings, authority, repetition and the transaction of narratives' in a '"crisis" in the understanding of plots and plotting' brought about by Modernism. Thus 'Heart of Darkness' 'displays an acute self-consciousness about the organizing features of traditional narrative, working with them still, but suspiciously, with constant reference to the inadequacy of inherited orders of meaning'.[7] Put simply, Conrad's narrative approach tessellates with some of the wider concerns of, and crises in, contemporary Western thought. In this regard, Brooks' volume recalls the argument made by White: that the true 'meaning' of Conradian narrative lies in an un-locatable 'elsewhere', forever just beyond knowledge.

Drawing upon the linguistic theory of Mikhail Bakhtin, Aaron Fogel's *Coercion to Speak: Conrad's Poetics of Dialogue* (1985), after beginning with Conrad's often overlooked short fiction 'The End of the Tether', proceeds to give detailed analysis of three of the 'major' fictions: *Nostromo, The Secret Agent* and *Under Western Eyes*. Pointing up the socio-political elements of language production, coercive or 'forced' dialogue, it emerges, is instrumental to the act of storytelling itself – the task of which for Conrad is 'to *make you see*' (*NN*, x; emphasis added).[8]

Heavily influenced by Gérard Genette, Jakob Lothe's *Conrad's Narrative Method* (1989) is less concerned with situating Conrad narratologically in his ideological context than considering narrative hermetically, on its own terms. Citing Edward Said (a recurrent figure in late Conrad criticism), Lothe argues that the 'greatness' of Conrad's fiction is in 'its presentation', not just 'what it was representing'. Developing the argument of his earlier *Joseph Conrad: Language and Fictional Self-Consciousness* (1979), Jeremy Hawthorn's *Joseph Conrad: Narrative Technique and Ideological Commitment* (1990) explores the tension between the 'extreme flexibility' of Conrad's narrative discourse, and the 'rootedness' of his characters' 'moral and human commitment', finding in it an expression of the paradox that 'although recognizably modernist in many ways' Conrad was 'both more contemporary and more old-fashioned than his modern peers'.[9]

Rather than take Conrad's famous claim 'I am *modern*' (31 May 1902; *CL* 2:418) at face value, then, much energy has been spent trying to plot his ambivalent relation to late-Victorian and early-modernist culture. While many studies claim Conrad for Modernism, others, such as Daphna Erdinast-Vulcan's *Joseph Conrad and the Modern Temper* (1990), cautiously reiterate that ambivalence. Building on the distinction drawn by Conrad in his 'The Ascending Effort' (1910) 'between pre-modernity and modernity – between a cosmos made to man's measure and a universe which is alien, meaningless and indifferent' – she extracts from his famous description of himself as Homo duplex another sense, of 'a modernist at war with modernity'.[10] Hence Conrad's fascination with remote, exotic settings, where Western forms of 'modernity' had yet to intrude.

Conrad's complex engagement with race and Empire has similarly been the source of much – occasionally heated – discussion. In a well-known 1975 lecture, Chinua Achebe dismissed 'Heart of Darkness', arguing that it reduces Africa 'to the role of props for the break-up of one petty European mind'. Insisting 'Conrad was a thoroughgoing racist', Achebe's dismissal significantly altered the landscape of Conrad scholarship. Indeed, it is through Achebe that Conrad lives up to, half a century after penning, his own playful epithet: 'Conrad controversial' ('Author's Note', *NLL*, vi). Achebe implicitly questioned Conrad's canonical place, sealed by F. R. Leavis' *The Great Tradition* (1948), by questioning that of 'Heart of Darkness', 'perhaps the most commonly prescribed novel [*sic*] in twentieth-century literature courses in … American universities'. In fact, because it approached the text from a singularly psychoanalytical perspective – and thus *made it about* 'the break-up of one petty European mind' – it is to this North American context and a received interpretation of 'Heart of Darkness', as much as the text itself, that Achebe responds.[11] Nonetheless, Achebe's remains a key intervention for its anticipation of a shift in Western literary theory in the 1980s and 1990s towards issues of culture, race and colonialism, following the publication in 1978 of Edward Said's path-breaking *Orientalism*. From just such a postcolonial perspective, Conrad's 'Africa' presents less a personal than a prevailing, contemporary European view of the continent, as some have pointed out. Having tackled Conrad's interrogation of colonialist discourse in *Conrad and Imperialism* (1983), Benita Parry went on to suggest that 'Heart of Darkness', on a deeper level, is a representation of the *failure of representation*. As such, Marlow's self-conscious narrative struggle posits Africa as a space that cannot 'be fixed, named and possessed in the language available to imperialism's explanatory system'.[12]

Coming between Andrea White's *Joseph Conrad and the Adventure Tradition* (1993) and Linda Dryden's *Joseph Conrad and the Imperial Romance* (2000) – two studies at either end of the 1990s to connect genre and imperial discourse – Imperialism also provides a key point of reference for Christopher GoGwilt's *The Invention of the West: Joseph Conrad and the Double-Mapping of Europe and Empire* (1995). Its crux is that Conrad's fiction registers a contemporary crossing of imperialist and political discourse, by which the traditional 'ground' of debate about political and historical development shifted 'from Europe to an idea of "the West"'. Sensitized – like Robert Hampson's *Cross-Cultural Encounters in Joseph Conrad's Malay Fiction* (2000) – both to Conrad's own writings on geography and to the role of space in cultural experience, GoGwilt's reconstruction of how the West produced itself in Conrad's contemporary moment likewise tessellated with a critical debate then taking shape in the 1990s, centring on the deconstruction 'of the concept, the authority, and assumed primacy of the category of "the West"'. Thus Conrad has a claim to be a writer as much of *post*colonial as of colonial literature (recalling Jameson's claiming of Conrad for *post*modernism over modernism) in so far as the former, as Elleke Boehmer puts it, is 'that which critically scrutinizes' rather than merely 'coming after' Empire.[13]

Concerned with psychological and political identity in Conrad, Robert Hampson's *Joseph Conrad: Betrayal and Identity* (1992) follows up earlier studies by Paul Kirschner, Eloise Knapp Hay and Avrom Fleishman. While tracing how Conrad's ideas of political and social identity were shaped by contemporary debates in psychology, Hampson rejects a Freudian interpretive frame on methodological grounds (as 'limited to the recognition of "signs" and the decoding of those signs according to an *a priori* system'), finding the existential psychology pioneered by R. D. Laing better suited to literary analysis.[14] Like other recent studies, *Betrayal and Identity* challenges the influential achievement-and-decline model by concentrating on Conrad's early and late fiction – whose valences, Hampson argues, Thomas C. Moser's achievement-and-decline model is methodologically ill-equipped to unpack.

Susan Jones' *Conrad and Women* (1999) similarly suggests that the very idea of a 'major phase', privileging 'a narrow band of texts … focused on male experience', has nourished a view of Conrad as someone who wrote solely from and about masculine experience. Instead, Jones emphasizes Conrad's later experimentation with popular forms such as the romance

(*Chance*), historical novel (*The Rover*, *The Arrow of Gold*) and sensation fiction (*Suspense*), which, as well as addressing female experience and subjectivity, are moreover keyed to women as readers. In addition to these previously overlooked audience and publication contexts, Jones offers new perspectives on Conrad biography, including the creative influence of his distant cousin by marriage, Marguerite Poradowska, redressing the conventional view of Conrad as one 'who looked to women only for domestic and moral support'.

Another gender-inflected study, Andrew Michael Roberts' *Conrad and Masculinity* (2000), meanwhile builds on pioneering, feminist critiques of gender in Conrad during the 1980s by Karen Klein and Nina Pelikan Straus, and the coalescence during the 1990s of debates around Conradian masculinity. Roberts draws on recent theoretical elaborations of gender as culturally produced rather than biologically determined (by Eve Sedgwick, Gayle Rubin and Luce Irigaray). He also takes a biographical tack, arguing that Conrad's representations of masculinity are informed by a scepticism of identity born of his experience of cultural displacement and marginality. This creates an overarching and 'highly problematic sense of masculinity as fractured, insecure and repeatedly failing in its attempts to master the world'.[15]

Another project begun in this period was ongoing at its close. The year 1983 saw the publication of the first volume of *The Collected Letters of Joseph Conrad* (covering 1861–97), the first fruits of a massive endeavour involving a number of leading Conradians that would last a quarter of a century, and range over some 5,000 letters – many previously unpublished and accessible only in archival and private collections – across nine volumes (the last two appearing in 2007). Representing the definitive edition of Conrad's correspondence, *The Collected Letters* is also perhaps *the* crucial piece of Conrad scholarship of the last twenty-five years. Together with The Cambridge Edition of the Works of Joseph Conrad (begun in 1990) – which on completion will provide a critical edition of Conrad's entire corpus, including the non-fiction – it demonstrates the consistence of academic investment in, and thus the continued importance of, Conrad studies.

NOTES

1. Frederick R. Karl, 'Conrad Studies', *Studies in the Novel*, 9.3 (Fall 1977), 326; William W. Bonney, *Thorns and Arabesques: Contexts for Conrad's Fiction* (Baltimore, MD: Johns Hopkins University Press, 1980), p. ix; Cedric Watts, Review of R. A. Gekoski, *Conrad: The Moral World of the Novelist*, in *The Yearbook of English Studies*, 11 (1981), 341.

2. Jacques Berthoud, *Joseph Conrad: The Major Phase* (Cambridge: Cambridge University Press, 1978), pp. 187–96.
3. Ian Watt, *Conrad in the Nineteenth Century* (London: Chatto & Windus, 1980), pp. ix–x.
4. Fredric Jameson, *The Political Unconscious: Narrative as Socially Symbolic Act* (London: Methuen, 1981), p. 219. For a counter-response, see Jacques Berthoud, 'Narrative and Ideology: A Critique of Fredric Jameson's *The Political Unconscious*', in *Narrative: From Malory to Motion Pictures*, ed. Jeremy Hawthorn (London: Edward Arnold, 1985), pp. 101–15.
5. Frederick R. Karl, *Joseph Conrad: The Three Lives – A Biography* (London: Faber & Faber, 1979); Zdzisław Najder, *Joseph Conrad: A Chronicle* (Cambridge: Cambridge University Press, 1983); Zdzisław Najder, *Conrad Under Familial Eyes* (Cambridge: Cambridge University Press, 1983); Yves Hervouet, *The French Face of Joseph Conrad* (Cambridge: Cambridge University Press, 1990); Cedric Watts, *Joseph Conrad: A Literary Life* (Basingstoke: Macmillan, 1989); Cedric Watts, *A Preface to Conrad* (London: Longman, 1982).
6. Allon White, 'Conrad and the Rhetoric of Enigma', in *The Uses of Obscurity: The Fictions of Early Modernism* (London: Routledge and Kegan Paul, 1981), pp. 108–29, 2–9.
7. Edward Said, 'Conrad: The Presentation of Narrative', in *The World, the Text, and the Critic* (Cambridge, MA: Harvard University Press, 1983), pp. 90–110; Peter Brooks, 'An Unreadable Report: Conrad's "Heart of Darkness"', in *Reading for the Plot: Design and Intention in Narrative* (Oxford: Clarendon Press, 1984), p. 238.
8. Aaron Fogel, *Coercion to Speak: Conrad's Poetics of Dialogue* (Cambridge, MA: Harvard University Press, 1985).
9. Jakob Lothe, *Conrad's Narrative Method* (Oxford: Clarendon Press, 1989), p. 3; Jeremy Hawthorn, *Joseph Conrad: Narrative Technique and Ideological Commitment* (London: Edward Arnold, 1990), pp. ix–xii.
10. Daphna Erdinast-Vulcan, *Joseph Conrad and the Modern Temper* (Oxford: Oxford University Press, 1990), pp. 1–6.
11. Chinua Achebe, 'An Image of Africa: Racism in Conrad's "Heart of Darkness"', *Massachusetts Review*, 18.4 (1977), 782–94; rpt in Joseph Conrad, *Heart of Darkness*, ed. Robert Kimbrough (New York: W. W. Norton and Company, 1988), pp. 257–9. Achebe originally used the words 'bloody racist'; see *Research in African Literatures*, 9.1 (1978), 1–15. For a response, see Cedric Watts, '"A Bloody Racist": About Achebe's View of Conrad', *Yearbook of English Studies*, 13 (1983), 196–209.
12. Edward Said, *Orientalism* (New York: Pantheon Books, 1978); Benita Parry, *Conrad and Imperialism: Ideological Boundaries and Visionary Frontiers* (London: Macmillan, 1983); Benita Parry, 'Narrating Imperialism: *Nostromo*'s Dystopia', in *Cultural Readings of Imperialism: Edward Said and the Gravity of History*, ed. Keith Ansell Pearson, Benita Parry and Judith Squires (London: Lawrence and Wishart, 1997), p. 231.

13. Andrea White, *Joseph Conrad and the Adventure Tradition: Constructing and Deconstructing the Imperial Subject* (Cambridge: Cambridge University Press, 1993); Linda Dryden, *Joseph Conrad and the Imperial Romance* (Basingstoke: Macmillan, 2000); Christopher GoGwilt, *The Invention of the West: Joseph Conrad and the Double-Mapping of Europe and Empire* (Stanford: Stanford University Press, 1995), p. 33; Robert Hampson, *Cross-Cultural Encounters in Joseph Conrad's Malay Fiction* (London: Palgrave, 2000); Elleke Boehmer, *Colonial and Postcolonial Literature* (Oxford: Oxford University Press, 1995), p. 3.
14. Robert Hampson, *Joseph Conrad: Betrayal and Identity* (Basingstoke: St Martin's Press, 1992), p. 9.
15. Susan Jones, *Conrad and Women* (Oxford: Clarendon Press, 1999), pp. 2–4; Karen Klein, 'The Feminist Predicament in Conrad's *Nostromo*', in *Brandeis Essays in Literature*, ed. John Hazel Smith (Waltham, MA: Brandeis University, 1983), pp. 101–16; Nina Pelikan Straus, 'The Exclusion of the Intended from Secret Sharing in Conrad's "Heart of Darkness"', *Novel*, 20 (1987), 123–37; Andrew Michael Roberts, *Conrad and Masculinity* (Basingstoke: Macmillan, 2000), p. 3.

CHAPTER 12

Dramatic and other adaptations

Richard J. Hand

Usually perceived as a creator of literary fictions that are complex in style, ambitious in theme and groundbreaking in narrative strategy, Conrad is also the creator of original and highly engaging *stories*. This aspect of his writing explains his perennial appeal to adapters across a range of performance media including theatre, film, television, radio and music. Conrad himself recognized the dramatic essence of his fiction. Despite his denunciations of the theatre – for example describing actors as '*wrongheaded lunatics pretending to be sane*' (*CL* 1:419) and his dismissal of theatre's 'inferior poetics' as 'capable of falsifying the very soul of one's work both on the imaginative and on the intellectual side'[1] – the dramatic arts are not as distant from his oeuvre as such comments seem to imply.

Shakespeare's plays were central to Conrad's artistic identity. As a child his first encounter with literature included England's national playwright – his father, Apollo Korzeniowski, having translated *A Comedy of Errors* and *The Two Gentlemen of Verona* into Polish. It comes as no surprise then that Shakespeare occupies an important place in the intertextual framework of Conrad's fiction. In *Lord Jim* or *Victory*, for example, the Shakespearean allusions have a bearing on interpretation. Moreover, the notion of the 'dramatic' – and related concepts such as role-playing and pretence, portrayal and enactment, rehearsal and performance – is a recurrent feature of Conrad's novels and short stories. Similarly, although Shakespearean reference may be paramount, Conrad can be found alluding to specific forms and genre ranging from music hall, melodrama and opera through to shadow puppetry, *commedia dell'arte* and cinema. But the dramatic did not merely serve an allusive function: Conrad himself was a playwright.

I

There are three phases to Conrad's own attempts at playwriting. According to Zdzisław Najder, the adolescent Conrad wrote patriotic plays eulogizing

Polish nationalism, such as *The Eyes of King Jan Sobieski*.[2] The second phase did not come until the twentieth century with *One Day More* (an adaptation of his own short story 'To-morrow') staged in London in 1905 by the Stage Society and performed in translation in Paris in 1909. Conrad was encouraged to write the play by his friend and distinguished figure in the arts scene, Sidney Colvin, and Ford Madox Ford seemingly made some contribution to the script. The one-act play attracted some attention on the contemporary theatre scene, impressing theatre critics William Archer and Max Beerbohm, while George Bernard Shaw was, according to the author, 'extatic [*sic*] and enthusiastic' (*CL* 3:272). Undoubtedly, part of the reason for the enthusiastic reception from some quarters is that Conrad was seen as fulfilling the demand for an 'English Literary Theatre' which, from the late nineteenth century, had been seen as a Holy Grail to redeem the national dramatic scene, which, unlike the dramatic cultures in the rest of Europe, seemed to be in terminal decline. In the 1890s, the playwright Henry Arthur Jones lamented that English drama was in an antithetical condition, like a conjoined twin, with 'dramatic art … pinched and starving' and at the mercy of 'its fat, puffy, unwholesome, dropsical brother, popular amusement'.[3] In contrast, English prose was seen as being in excellent health, and hope was placed in the playwriting experiments of Henry James, J. M. Barrie, George Moore, Thomas Hardy and other novelists, even if the results were undeniably mixed. By the time of the Edwardian era – with notable playwrights such as George Bernard Shaw, Harley Granville Barker and John Hankin – the new theatre scene was nascent and adventurous, but attempts to coax respected 'men of letters' into writing for the theatre continued, not least as some still feared that English theatre was at risk of becoming moribund.

Conrad, for one, was less than sanguine about his own effort, and in the self-deprecating mood that characterizes his practical relationship with the stage he dismisses *One Day More*, recalling how the 'exceptionally intelligent audience stared it coldly off the boards' in what amounted to 'a fair and open execution' (*NLL*, 77). Although *One Day More* may be a modest work, it is not without interest. Aside from its status as an example of 'English Literary Theatre' as outlined above, the one-act form, popular in Continental Europe at the time, was comparatively neglected in Britain. With regard to the theme, especially the absurd Captain Hagberd, endlessly waiting for a 'to-morrow' that will never arrive, Conrad creates a work that is a precursor of Eugene O'Neill's *The Iceman Cometh* (1946) and the plays of Samuel Beckett.[4] In addition, *One Day More* is significant for placing Bessie Carvil centre-stage, thereby creating a particularly noteworthy female role in its Edwardian theatre context. Indeed, all of Conrad's plays are adaptations and, in a subtle reconfiguration of the original works of fiction, Conrad makes the women central, if not focal, characters.

The third and final phase of Conrad the playwright is the most impressive and extended: during the last few years of his life – mainly around the pivotal year of 1920 – Conrad became 'seriously interested in the theatre'.[5] He wrote stage adaptations of *The Secret Agent*, which enjoyed a West End production in 1922; 'Because of the Dollars' (as *Laughing Anne*, written for the London Grand Guignol but rejected and not produced in Conrad's lifetime); and played a key advisory role in Basil Macdonald Hastings' dramatization of *Victory*, which enjoyed a large-scale and successful run at the Globe in 1919, produced by, and starring, the actor-manager Marie Löhr.

Conrad even tried his hand at writing a screenplay with his agent, J. B. Pinker, adapting 'Gaspar Ruiz' into the un-produced film-script *Gaspar: The Strong Man*. Around the same time, in mid-1921, Conrad worked on his only published translation from Polish: an English rendering of Bruno Winawer's play *The Book of Job*.[6] In addition to these developed and completed works, Conrad can be found considering the possibility of other adaptations and collaborations. For example, acting as consultant on Hastings' *Victory* was a happy enough experience for him to propose that the two writers collaborate on a completely original play about a group of English people in Siena and a 'Faked old Master' painting (*CL* 6:135).

Theatre's potential as a creative medium for Conrad may be most developed in the three phases identified, but he also entertained the idea at other times, even if it seldom bore fruit. From the 1890s onwards, Conrad considered playwriting collaborations with Stephen Crane, the short-story writer Perceval Gibbon and Polish activist Józef H. Retinger. It is interesting to speculate why theatre became so important to Conrad around 1920, when he actively turned himself into a dramatist, screenwriter and theatrical translator. One reason is probably its potential financial reward – an argument Conrad had used some years before to justify the writing of *One Day More* (*CL* 3:117) – but it is also because the performing arts offered an irresistible 'escape from malaise and stagnation'.[7] The theatre, too, was more vibrant than it had been in the earlier days of Conrad's literary career, while cinema was burgeoning as an art form. The dramatic achievements of Shaw, John Galsworthy and others had prevailed, while theatrical censorship – denounced by Conrad in 'The Censor of Plays: An Appreciation' (*Daily Mail*, 12 October 1907) – had been forced to become more liberal in attitude, if not in legislation.

Ultimately, despite Conrad's investment of time and creative energy, the final dramatic phase went largely unrewarded. *Gaspar the Strong Man*, *Laughing Anne* and *The Book of Job* failed to secure productions. By contrast, the stage dramatization of *The Secret Agent* received a high-profile, if short, run at the Ambassadors Theatre in November 1922. Although some acquaintances of Conrad – including Hastings and Galsworthy – could be harsh in their condemnation of Conrad's theatrical *naïveté*, others were more supportive. Particularly noteworthy in this regard is Arnold Bennett, who believed that *The Secret Agent* as a play was 'the best I have seen for a very, very long time, and by a long way the best'.[8] As for its disappointing run, Bennett contended that the play was simply ahead of its time for a London theatre scene fed on 'dishonest pap'. For Bennett, the play's genuinely disturbing theme and treatment would have been welcomed and successful in the rest of Europe, but was doomed for tepid reception in Britain. To put it another way, although popular theatre audiences could have been forgiven for thinking that *The Secret Agent* was an example of the 'thriller' genre that had begun to take the West End stage by storm in the early 1920s, they were largely disappointed with the result: Conrad's play is a thriller of sorts, but not of the *Bulldog Drummond* variety.

All of Conrad's plays make more sense when viewed in a more global context. For instance, Galsworthy argued that the man without hands in *Laughing Anne* is an 'unbearable spectacle' which fatally flaws the play because 'Conrad probably never realised that … what you can write about freely cannot always be endured by the living eye'.[9] This argument becomes less convincing when one realizes that Conrad was writing a work specifically in the genre of Grand Guignol, the 'Theatre of Horror', an excessive form of theatre that deliberately explores the ostensibly unbearable and unendurable. Likewise, although it is true that the bleak themes of *The Secret Agent* may have shocked people when dramatized – including, astonishingly, Conrad himself – it is a play that would have been much more at home in the repertoire of German expressionist drama. This idea is further consolidated in the light of the technical challenges that Conrad posed in *Laughing Anne* and *The Secret Agent*. These were realized in the scenery of the latter production, of which one review stated rather conde-scendingly: 'some have called it "Expressionist"' (*Stage*, 9 November 1922).

Hastings' *Victory* is less 'difficult' than Conrad's self-written plays inas-much as the dramatization is predominantly a traditional stage melodrama with a happy ending, which resulted in the lambasting of Hastings by some theatre critics. What was not widely known at the time was that Conrad wholly encouraged Hastings' choice of dénouement claiming, with startling romanticism, that it was 'the end I have been dreaming of' (*CL* 5:655). Nevertheless, *Victory* remains the most successful theatrical dramatization of Conrad. This is explained, not least, by the fact that the original novel has enormous dramatic resonance. Conrad himself recognized that '*Victory* may make a libretto for a Puccini opera' (*CL* 5:452), and the novel was finally given an operatic adaptation with Richard Rodney Bennett's *Victory* (1970). The dramatic potential to the novel most obviously makes *Victory* seem as if it was 'aimed at Hollywood'.[10]

II

Cinema provides the real triumph of Conrad in adaptation. In 1919, coincidentally the same year as the stage *Victory*, there appeared the first of many cinematic adaptations of Conrad: *Victory*, directed by Maurice Tourneur. A major Hollywood release, it featured Lon Chaney as Ricardo, and can be seen as drawing on and consolidating paradigms of the genre of cinematic adventure melodrama that are never far away in subsequent screen adaptations of what remains the most frequently adapted Conrad novel. *Victory* enjoyed a proliferation of international adaptations in 1930–1, thanks to the productions made by Paramount in 'assembly line fashion'[11] in studios near Paris. As well as for the American film version, entitled *Dangerous Paradise* (William A. Wellman, 1930), the same set was used by a variety of production teams, resulting in near-simultaneous Polish, French, German and Swedish adaptations of *Victory*. A few years later, *Victory* returned to the screen (John Cromwell, 1940) starring the well-known actors Frederic March (Heyst) and Cedric Hardwicke (Mr Jones). *Victory* was subsequently adapted as an early example of live television drama – directed by Ernest Colling in 1945 – while another American television version was shown in 1960: 'the first television adaptation of Conrad to be made in colour'.[12]

As well as *Victory*, there has been a wide range of adaptations of other Conrad works, including, to particular acclaim, *Outcast of the Islands* (Carol Reed, 1952) and *Apocalypse Now* (Francis Ford Coppola, 1979), notwithstanding the irony that the latter fails to mention Conrad or 'Heart of Darkness', on which it is based, in the credits. *The Duellists* (1977), Ridley Scott's version of 'The Duel', has also been highly regarded. Although it remains the director's only overt Conrad adaptation, Scott sustained his Conrad interest, albeit tangentially, by naming the spaceship in *Alien* (1979) 'Nostromo'.

As well as the completed films, there are some notable unfulfilled cinematic Conrad projects. For example, David Lean died before he could make

Nostromo, and Harold Pinter's *Victory* screenplay has been published (2000) but never produced. When Orson Welles was headhunted by Hollywood after the Mercury Theatre's (in)famous radio adaptation of *War of the Worlds* in 1938, his first film proposal was *Heart of Darkness*. It was only because of irreconcilable budgetary problems that Welles was obliged to abandon the Conrad project and make *Citizen Kane* (1941) instead. Welles was a great fan of Conrad and always felt that the Conrad oeuvre had enormous potential for dramatization, stating of his *Heart of Darkness* project: 'My script was terribly loyal to Conrad. And I think that, the minute anybody does that, they're going to have a smash on their hands. Any of them. Think what *Lord Jim* could have been, if some attention had been paid to the original book.'[13]

Welles believed that all of Conrad's works provided templates for successful adaptation and his barbed comment about *Lord Jim* (directed by Richard Brooks, 1965) reveals what he regards as the peril of simplifying or tinkering with this most dramatic of novelists. Welles always regretted never filming *Heart of Darkness*, but he did succeed in making two radio versions of the novella. His radio adaptations – one for *Mercury Theatre on the Air* in November 1938 and the other for *This Is My Best* in March 1945 – are remarkable accomplishments and startlingly different in approach. For instance, although Welles plays Kurtz in both adaptations, in the *Mercury Theatre* dramatization he also plays an acquaintance of Marlow who recounts the tale (a strategy which successfully recreates the 'framing narrative' of the original novella), while, in the *This Is My Best* version, Welles plays Marlow himself.[14]

Radio dramatization has produced some of the most impressive versions of Conrad in any performance medium. The BBC's *Lord Jim* in February 1927 was the first radio adaptation of Conrad and, over the decades, British radio has continued to dramatize him with, to name but a few examples, Tim Crook's *Heart of Darkness* (Independent Radio, 1989), the four-part *Tales from the Islands* (BBC, 1997) and Zosia Wand's *The Inextinguishable Fire* (BBC, 2006), a biographical drama about Conrad's visit to Poland in 1914. In the United States, the pick of the radio adaptations include NBC's versions of *Lord Jim* (1948), *Heart of Darkness* (1949) and *Victory* (1950), while CBS chose to produce two less obvious adaptations as part of its 'Escape' series: 'Typhoon' (1947) and 'The Brute' (1948), the latter arguably improving one of Conrad's most maligned short stories.

To return to cinema, another film director drawn to Conrad was Alfred Hitchcock. The young Hitchcock was among the spectators at the stage production of Conrad's *The Secret Agent* in 1922 and, according to Daniel Spoto, it was Conrad's play (rather than the novel) which inspired him to adapt the novel as *Sabotage* in 1936.[15] It is also interesting to note that Hitchcock used one of the actors from *The Secret Agent* stage production when he cast Frank Vosper (Mr Vladimir in Conrad's play) as Ramon Levine in *The Man Who Knew Too Much* (1934). But aside from his one explicit adaptation of Conrad, there is also an argument that Hitchcock's tone, style and irony make him one of the most Conradian of film-makers. Another case in point is Werner Herzog who, although never producing a direct adaptation of Conrad, is frequently 'Conradesque'. *Aguirre, Wrath of God* (1972), the epic tale of a conquistador's disastrous journey up the Amazon, can be seen as a variation of 'Heart of Darkness'. Similarly, the jungle as location and metaphorical backdrop to the human condition gives a Conradian mood to Herzog's *Fitzcarraldo* (1982), the documentary *Julianes Sturz in den Dschungel* (2000) and the prisoner-of-war escape drama *Rescue Dawn* (2006).

Music, and in particular opera, was very close to Conrad's heart and can be seen to inform his work significantly. The composer John Powell approached Conrad in 1910 about adapting 'Heart of Darkness' into an opera, which seemed to cause offence, but a few years later Conrad suggested that Powell use the novella as material for a 'symphonic poem', an idea that inspired Powell's 1917 composition *Rhapsodie nègre*.[16] We have already mentioned Richard Rodney Bennett's 1970 opera of *Victory*, and other operatic adaptations of Conrad include John Joubert's *Under Western Eyes* (1969) and Romuald Twardowski's *Lord Jim* (1977), while Tadeusz Baird's *Jutro* (1966) brings the story of Conrad and adaptation full circle, being a musical drama based on 'To-morrow'.

As he adapted *The Secret Agent*, Conrad confessed: 'It is a terribly searching thing – I mean the stage. I will confess that I myself had no idea what the story under the writing was till I came to grips with it in this process of dramatisation' (*CL* 6:520). It is a remarkable admission, but reveals the power of both adaptation and intertextuality. Dramatization can play a major role in popularizing and even commercializing literary fiction but it can also be eviscerating and shocking in what it brings to the surface. As for intertextuality, Conrad provides a compelling demonstration of how a writer's stories and ideas can end up having lives of their own.

NOTES

1. Richard Curle, *The Last Twelve Years of Joseph Conrad* (London: Sampson Low, Marston, 1928), pp. 125–6.
2. Zdzisław Najder, *Joseph Conrad: A Life*, trans. Halina Carroll-Najder (Rochester, NY: Camden House, 2007), p. 33.

3. Henry Arthur Jones, *The Renascence of the English Drama* (1895; New York: Books for Libraries Press, 1971), p. 11.
4. See Richard J. Hand, *The Theatre of Joseph Conrad: Reconstructed Fictions* (London: Palgrave, 2005), pp. 37–40.
5. J. H. Stape, *The Several Lives of Joseph Conrad* (London: Heinemann, 2007), p. 236.
6. For a discussion of this, see Grazyna Branny, 'Bruno Winawer's *The Book of Job*: Conrad's Only Translation', *The Conradian*, 27.1 (2002), 1–23.
7. Frederick R. Karl, *Joseph Conrad: The Three Lives* (London: Faber and Faber, 1979), p. 838.
8. Arnold Bennett, *Letters of Arnold Bennett*. Vol. 1: *Letters to J. B. Pinker*, ed. J. Hepburn (Oxford: Oxford University Press, 1966), p. 317.
9. John Galsworthy, 'Introduction', in *Laughing Anne and One Day More* (London: J. Castle, 1924), p. vii.
10. Cedric Watts, *Writers and the Work: Joseph Conrad* (Plymouth: Northcote House, 1994), p. 40.
11. Gene M. Moore, ed., *Conrad on Film* (Cambridge: Cambridge University Press, 1997), p. 10.
12. Owen Knowles and Gene M. Moore, *Oxford Reader's Companion to Conrad* (Oxford: Oxford University Press, 2001), p. 437.
13. Orson Welles and Peter Bogdanovich, *This is Orson Welles*, ed. Jonathan Rosenbaum (London: Harper Collins, 1993), p. 32.
14. Richard J. Hand, 'Escape with Joseph Conrad! The Adaptation of Joseph Conrad's Fiction on American Old-Time Radio', *Conradiana*, 38.1 (2006), 17–58, pp. 20–1.
15. See Daniel Spoto, *The Dark Side of Genius: The Life of Alfred Hitchcock* (New York: Ballantine Books, 1983), pp. 68–9.
16. See Rolf Charlston, 'A Rhapsodic *Heart of Darkness*: John Powell's *Rhapsodie Nègre*', *The Conradian*, 26.2 (2001), 79–90.

CHAPTER 13

Translations

Mario Curreli

Conrad's experience of literature in translation began early. His father, Apollo Korzeniowski, translated works by Shakespeare, Dickens and Victor Hugo, and he himself read Polish and French translations avidly, recalling in *A Personal Record* 'how well Mrs. Nickleby could chatter disconnectedly in Polish and the sinister Ralph rage in that language' (71). Translations of Conrad's works began to appear during his lifetime, but his books were seldom translated shortly after their first English publication. His most widely translated works to date are *Lord Jim*, 'Heart of Darkness' and 'Typhoon', in a clear demonstration of the fact that nautical terminology posed an obstacle for translators, not for foreign readers.

The majority of translations are now available in over forty languages, mainly European, but including Hebrew, Icelandic and Yiddish. Oddly enough, given the locale of much of his fiction, there are virtually no Malay translations, with the exception of *Lord Jim*, published in Malayalam in 1983. A special case was the inclusion in 1920 in Harrap's Bilingual Series of seven different editions of 'The Idiots', with the English text and, on the page opposite, translations into French, Spanish, Italian, German, Russian, Danish or Dutch. In his introduction, the series' general editor, J. E. Mansion, noted that, having spent his early youth amid political unrest, Conrad's parents were 'the future writer's first examples of those tragic heroes, struggling gloomily yet bravely against Fate, which he was to adopt so often in later years', adding that in 'The Idiots' one can recognize the 'great breath of tragedy which inspired Æschylus and Sophocles, and which, until the advent of Mr Conrad, had remained foreign to western literature'.

Chronologically speaking, the first work to be translated was *Wyrzutek*, a poor and anonymous Polish version of *An Outcast of the Islands*, subsequently attributed to Maria Gąsiorowska. Serialized in the Warsaw weekly *Tygodnik Romansów i Powieści* from January to March 1897, this novel was 'miserably butchered in the attempt to domesticate it for its audience. The novel's Dutchmen were, oddly, turned into Germans; its nautical terms systematically cut; and its Malay words and phrases effaced'.[1]

From a cultural point of view, Conrad's international reputation began in France, rather than Poland, as French translations were instrumental in establishing his fame in non-English-speaking countries, both in Western and Eastern Europe, when English and its American variety had not yet reached their planetary hegemony.

WESTERN EUROPE

In 1894, while waiting for an answer from Fisher Unwin's readers, Conrad suggested to his distant Belgian relative, the writer Marguerite Poradowska, née Gachet, that they prepare a French version of *Almayer's Folly*, 'not as a translation but as a collaboration' (*CL* 1:165), for publication in the *Revue des Deux Mondes*. Nothing came of this. Instead, Poradowska produced a translation of 'An Outpost of Progress'. Long thought to be lost, this has been recently uncovered by Anne Arnold in a Parisian journal: 'Un Avant-poste de la civilisation', the first-known publication of Conrad's work in French translation, appeared in two issues, those of 22 and 29 January 1903, of *Les Nouvelles Illustrées*.[2]

Quite unhappy with his distant cousin's not too accurate version, Conrad authorized Henry-Durand Davray to translate 'Karain', published in 1906 by the *Mercure de France*. Conrad reduced Davray's manuscript by a third, saying the story was improved in this form.[3] In 1909, *The Nigger of the 'Narcissus'* was translated by Robert d'Humières for the *Mercure de France* editions. 'Typhoon', translated by the Belgian solicitor Joseph de Smet, appeared in *Le Progrès* in 1911, and *The Secret Agent*, translated by Davray, was issued in 1912 by the new publishing house just established in Paris by Gaston Gallimard. Many other early translations were promoted by Conrad's long-time admirer André Gide, who visited Capel House in 1911 and produced a new translation of 'Typhoon' for Hachette as *Le Typhon* (1918).

Gide supervised the translations of several other works for Gallimard, under the *La Nouvelle Revue Française* (*NRF*) imprint. Only ten volumes of the *Oeuvres complètes* were published between 1919 and 1938. *Almayer's Folly* was translated by Geneviève Seligmann-Lui, as *La folie-Almayer*, in 1919, and the following year both 'The Idiots', in Harrap's Bilingual Series, and *Under Western Eyes* – in a translation by Philippe Neel about which Conrad claimed 'Je suis très, très content' (*CL* 7:212) – appeared. He also judged 'magnifique' Neel's translation of *Lord Jim* (*CL* 7:550), while expressing alarm about it to another correspondent. *Within the Tides* was translated by G. Jean-Aubry (as *En marge des marées*, 1921), assisted by Conrad himself with the translation of the 'Author's Note' (*CL* 7:168–9). A musicologist who at first collaborated with Gide and later succeeded him as general editor of Gallimard's *Oeuvres complètes*, Jean-Aubry also commissioned the translation of the play version of *The Secret Agent*. He was soon one of Conrad's staunchest friends, completing a dozen translations altogether.

Conrad always showed a great interest in the progress of his French translators, whose work he liked 'to look over' before publication (*CL* 6:458). He provided translators with advice and constant encouragement, as long as they were Gide, Davray or Neel; with the latter he examined several options for the French title of *Victory* (*CL* 7:432–3); he made a few corrections to Jean-Aubry's French version of the preface to *The Arrow of Gold* and suggested changing the title from a tentative *La Flêche en Or* (*sic*; *CL* 7:197) to *La flèche d'or*. But, having in mind Poradowska's poor rendering of 'An Outpost of Progress', he had violent outbursts over female French translators of *The Arrow of Gold* and *Victory*, particularly when Gide told him that a woman, Madeleine Octavie Maus, was getting her hands on the former: 'Je vais protester de toutes mes forces' (*CL* 6:502), and again 'Une dame *c'est emparée* du livre' (*sic*, for *s'est emparée*; *CL* 6:515); 'I am afraid that I have quarrelled with Gide for good' (*CL* 6:517) – so much so that *The Arrow of Gold* was eventually translated by Jean-Aubry and published quite a few years after it had been reassigned to him by Gide.

These frequently reprinted early translations served French readers well into the 1980s, when Sylvère Monod provided them with his five Bibliothèque de la Pléiade volumes. In addition to coordinating the whole project, the General Editor himself introduced, annotated and provided chronologies or glossaries of nautical terms for each of these prestigious volumes (1982–92).

In Italy, even though Hilary Campioni's parallel text of 'The Idiots' – 'Gli idioti' – appeared in Harrap's Bilingual Series in 1920, Conrad's work went almost unnoticed during his lifetime; but from 1924 onwards a flood of new translations was produced, some of which, between the two world wars, were based on French versions. In April 1924 Henry Furst (1893–1967) praised *Lord Jim* as one of the finest creations of world literature. To demonstrate this, since no Italian translations were yet available, he translated the final episode of the novel and suggested that either *Lord Jim* or *Victory* should be translated into Italian. On 10 May 1924, Furst sent Conrad this article with a letter (now in the Berg Collection, *CL* 8:378) and, on 12 August 1924, he wrote an obituary in which he stated that

Conrad's greatest merit had been that of rescuing narrative art from deca-
dence and injecting new life into the sea-novel tradition. On 15 August 1924
Furst's translation of 'Youth' began to be serialized in the Roman journal *Lo
Spettatore Italiano*.

Lorenzo Gigli's translation of *Almayer's Folly* allowed the author to see
the first parts of *La casa sul fiume grande* serialized in the Turin weekly
Illustrazione del Popolo (July–December 1924). Shortly before he died,
Conrad received a letter (11 June 1924, Berg) from Giovanni Marcellini, a
translator from French and Spanish, who eventually translated 'The End of
the Tether', in 1928, followed in 1930 by 'The Inn of the Two Witches',
translated with the help of the Anglicist Salvatore Rosati.

The first book-form translation, *Cuore di tenebra* ('Heart of Darkness'),
was issued in December 1924 by Bottega di Poesia in Milan and, on
Christmas Day 1925, the Genoese daily *Il Lavoro* began serializing *Attesa*,
Santino Caramella's abridged translation of *Suspense*. Then, between 1925
and 1945, over fifty different translations appeared. The quality of these early
translations was generally poor; errors with unfamiliar nautical terms
abounded; omissions of single phrases and sentences were common and
whole paragraphs were censored: the Marxist photographer episode was
omitted from *Nostromo*, the (communist) term *compagno* ('comrade') was
either avoided or replaced by the (fascist) term *camerata*. Things were
even worse with *The Secret Agent*, in which there were not only omissions
but additions as well. In the first paragraph, 'nominally' was omitted and
Stevie was proleptically called *deficiente cognato* ('idiot brother-in-law'). In
Chapter 8 (here appearing as Chapter 4) readers were prematurely told that
Winnie was going to sew their home address on Stevie's overcoat, and,
moreover, to set events in a chronological order, the chapter sequence was
rearranged.

Censorship tolerated Conrad's sardonic denunciations of colonialism
since they were mostly concerned with images of what fascist propaganda
described as corrupt Judaic Masonic plutocratic democracies. The Tuscan
writer Emilio Cecchi (1884–1966) – who in 1919 had asked permission to
translate one of Conrad's stories (*CL* 6:400–1) – wrote perceptive criticism,
abstracted in the special 1924 issue of the *NRF* and re-used in 1956 as an
introduction to Giovanni Fletzer's translation of *Almayer's Folly*.[4]

The latter was the first tome of the 24-volume edition of the first
complete Italian collection of Conrad's works, published between 1949
and 1966 in Milan by Valentino Bompiani (1898–1992), under the general
editorship of the Tuscan critic and poet Piero Bigongiari (1914–97). Old,
un-revised translations were occasionally re-used and the editor's choice of

new translators did not always prove fortunate: many, although full of admiration for Conrad, were thoroughly imbued with French culture but had little or no experience of English colloquialisms and nautical technicalities.

The real strength and chief recommendation of the Mursia edition (1967–82) lies in the fact that a small number of professional translators were carefully supervised by Ugo Mursia (1916–82) himself in his three-fold capacity as translator, editor and publisher. Still the largest collection of Conrad works in any language, it includes *The Sisters*, the two *Congo Diary* notebooks, stage versions of *The Secret Agent*, *One Day More* and *Laughing Anne*, as well as the first-ever publication of the film-script *Gaspar: The Strong Man*.

The first stories to appear in Germany were 'Typhoon' and 'Amy Foster' (1908), followed by 'The Brute' (1912) and, during the next two years, *Under Western Eyes* and 'The Duel'. In 1926, Thomas Mann provided a foreword to Ernst W. Freissler's translation of *The Secret Agent*, praising the work's psychologically and morally profound narrative art while noting that Conrad's constant anti-Sarmatic satire was responsible for his limited reputation in Russia and Germany. The 22-volume Fischer Verlag edition was eventually completed in 1939. Only well after the Second World War was a new translation of the complete works undertaken, in the late 1950s by Suhrkamp – the first volume, *Tales of Hearsay*, appearing in 1961, the last in the 1980s.

Scandinavian readers would easily have had access either to the originals or to the Tauchnitz editions available in every European spa or railway-station kiosk. The first translation of Conrad to appear in book form in any language was *Tales of Unrest*, translated into Swedish by Karin Hirn in 1903, with a note by the translator's husband, Yrjö Hirn of Helsinki University.⁵ *Almayer's Folly* followed (1908), with *An Outcast of the Islands* and *The Secret Agent* in successive years, and other volumes appearing regularly, so that by mid-May 1920 Conrad was corresponding with Pinker about the price being charged for his volumes by the Stockholm publisher Albert Bonnier (*CL* 7:97).

Conrad's first collection to appear in Denmark, *Tales of Unrest*, was translated in 1904. *Almayer's Folly* followed in 1916, after which translations appeared regularly, with half of Conrad's oeuvre available in Danish translations by the time of his death.

EASTERN EUROPE

In Poland, the 'emigration of talents' controversy about the advantages derived from writing in languages other than one's own – raised in 1899 by Wincenty Lutosławski's interview with Conrad and fuelled by Eliza

Orzeskowa's inept nationalistic attack on the writer's choice of English as demonstrating a betrayal of his Polishness – may have contributed to the lack of interest in his work for a few years.[6] But *Lord Jim* appeared in Emilja Węsławska's translation in 1904, Maria Gąsiorowska translated *The Secret Agent* (in 1908), and other translations soon followed. In his introduction to an edition of six Conrad novels, published by the Warsaw firm Ignis (1923–6), the novelist Stefan Żeromski declared 'not a single fibre links Conrad's purely artistic achievement with Polish literature'.[7]

Among early Polish translators and reviewers one often finds the familiar names of writers Stefan Żeromski and Maria Dąbrowska, as well as those of Conrad's distant cousins Aniela (1881–1943) and Karola Zagórska (1885–1955), the sisters who, legally, held the Polish and Russian translation rights to his works (*CL* 7:358). When an almost complete 22-volume edition, *Pisma Zbiorowe Josepha Conrada*, was published between 1928 and 1939, 10 of its titles were translations by Aniela Zagórska, 'the best known translator of Conrad into Polish'.[8] In 1973, her old translation of *Lord Jim* was reissued in a printing of 50,000 copies.

Another 23-volume edition, published from 1956 to 1970, remained incomplete, Soviet influence predictably mandating that *The Secret Agent*, *Under Western Eyes*, *Notes on Life and Letters* and *Last Essays* be omitted. An almost complete 27-volume edition was published by PIW (the State Publishing Institute) in 1972–4 under Zdzisław Najder's editorship. In this edition, censorship forbade including some ideologically sensitive pieces; eventually, Najder collected these in a supplementary volume (1975).

Conrad's dislike of things Russian influenced his reception in that country and was responsible for the censorship both before and after the Bolshevik Revolution, with his 'decadent' work and his 'corrupt' ethical ideals serving only the world of wealthy capitalists and ship-owners whose primary object was the safety of cargo. Initially, interest was directed towards the short fiction: 'The Lagoon' and 'Karain' were translated in 1898, 'Youth' in 1901, and 'An Outpost of Progress' in 1902. But an instant Russian translation of *The Secret Agent* was published in 1908 in a small run of 1,500 copies. Between 1913 and 1925, 'Il Conde', 'An Anarchist', 'The Informer' and 'The Tale' appeared. The publication of Conrad's complete works in translation, launched in the year of the writer's death, was discontinued in 1926 after selling 70,000 copies. In 1959, a two-volume edition of selected works, excluding *Under Western Eyes*, was issued by the State Publishing House; in its introduction, N. Bannikov appreciated Conrad's criticism of white colonization, 'even though not everything he wrote is acceptable by us': it sold 225,000 copies.[9]

His first novel was translated into Ukrainian only as late as 1929, followed a year later by a translation of 'Typhoon'. In 1931, *The Shadow-Line* was translated into Slovene and into Serbo-Croatian, and translations of 'Youth' were published in Belgrade and Zagreb in 1948 and 1950, respectively.

In Prague, *Almayer's Folly* and *Under Western Eyes* appeared in 1919, followed in 1920 by 'The End of the Tether', and *Lord Jim* and *Nostromo* in the early 1930s. In Bulgaria, 'Youth' was translated in 1948. Hungarian translations of 'Youth', 'The Partner' and 'The Secret Sharer' were published in 1967. Translations into Dutch were few, most readers using either the originals or handy Tauchnitz copyright editions. After the 1920 Dutch translation of 'The Idiots' in Harrap's Bilingual Series, in July 1922 Conrad signed an agreement for Dutch translations of his work, 'the terms of which are distinctly good' (*CL* 7:490), but, apparently, nothing came of this.

Spanish translations of Conrad's works began appearing shortly after his death. *Almayer's Folly* and *Under Western Eyes* were published in 1925, followed across the decade by *Nostromo*, *Lord Jim*, *Tales of Unrest* and *Victory*, with a further nine volumes appearing by the mid-1930s. Many of these Spanish translations were subsequently reissued, some under slightly different titles, in Buenos Aires in the 1940s, with a translation of *Victory* also being reissued in Mexico City in 1941.

Lord Jim's translation into Portuguese in 1940 initiated other translations, beginning with *The Arrow of Gold* in 1941 and *Victory* in 1942. These Portuguese translations were either reissued or translated anew for the Brazilian market in the same decade.

ASIA

At the other end of the Mediterranean, Conrad was practically unknown in Turkey until translations of *Lord Jim* and *Nostromo* were published in Istanbul by the Ministry of Education as late as 1946. After a long hiatus, these were followed by *The Nigger of the 'Narcissus'* and *Victory* in 1982. New translations of *Nostromo* and *Lord Jim*, in 1985 and 1986, respectively, followed, and this resurgence of interest yielded Turkish translations of *Under Western Eyes*, also in 1986, and 'Heart of Darkness', in 1994. A complete translation into Turkish is under way in a series co-edited by Orhan Pamuk.

In Japan, as early as 1922, the English texts of 'Typhoon' and *The Nigger of the 'Narcissus'* were available in the Kenkyusha English Classics, introduced and profusely annotated in Japanese. Translations began with *Almayer's Folly* and *Chance* in 1926, after which they appeared at regular intervals, with a resurgence of interest in the mid-sixties, coinciding with Richard Brooks' film based on *Lord Jim*, starring Peter O'Toole. Fukizawa Tadashi's 1965 translation of the latter novel was closely followed by translations of *The Secret Agent* (1966), *Victory, Under Western Eyes, Nostromo* and another *Lord Jim* in 1967.

NOTES

1. J. H. Stape, *The Several Lives of Joseph Conrad* (London: Heinemann, 2007), p. 98. See also Marcin Piechota, 'The First Conrad Translation: *An Outcast of the Islands* in Polish', *The Conradian*, 30.1 (2005), 89–96.
2. Anne Arnold, 'Marguerite Poradowska as a Translator of Conrad', *The Conradian*, 33.1 (Spring 2008), 119–29.
3. Cited in Martin Ray, *Joseph Conrad: Memories and Impressions, An Annotated Bibliography* (Amsterdam and Atlanta, GA: Rodopi, 2007), p. 34.
4. See Mario Curreli, *Cecchi e Conrad: tre lettere inedite* (Viareggio: Pezzini, 1999).
5. Stephen Donovan, 'Conrad in Swedish', *The Conradian*, 31.2 (2006), 114–35, p. 120.
6. See Zdzisław Najder, *Conrad under Familial Eyes* (Milan: Mursia International, and Cambridge: Cambridge University Press, 1983), pp. 178–92.
7. Cited in Andrzej Busza, 'Conrad's Polish Literary Background and Some Illustrations of the Influence of Polish Literature on his Work', *Antemurale*, 10 (1966), 109–255, p. 203.
8. Zdzisław Najder, *Conrad's Polish Background* (London: Oxford University Press, 1964), p. 224.
9. Eugene Steele, 'Conrad in Russian (1912–1959)', *Conradiana*, 14.1 (1982), 57–62, p. 61; Ludmilla Voitkowska, 'Conrad in Russia: A Discipline in Absentia', *Conradiana*, 37.1–2 (2005), 147–64, p. 152.

1 Apollo Korzeniowski

2 Ewelina Korzeniowska

3 Joseph Conrad, 1863

4 Tadeusz Bobrowski

5 Joseph Conrad in Cracow, 1874

6 The *Duke of Sutherland*, Circular Quay, Sydney, 1871

7 The *Torrens* in the Southern Ocean, 1895

type wide / No title / No. 1

A tale of the Islands.

I.

When he stepped off the ~~straight and~~ narrow path of his peculiar honesty it was with the ~~inner~~ assertion of unflinching resolve to ~~fall~~ fall back again into the ~~safe~~ stride of virtue as soon as ~~his~~ little excursion into the wayside quagmires had produced the desired effect. It was going to be a short episode — a sentence in brackets — in the flowing tale of his life: ~~to be~~ done unwillingly yet neatly and to be soon forgotten. He imagined he could go on ~~after~~ ~~the~~ flowers in the small garden infront of his house.

He fancied that nothing would be changed; that he ~~would~~ ~~contempt~~ his pale yellow ~~wife~~ patronise his dark brother-in-law, who wore patent leather shoes on his little feet and was to humble ~~before~~ the white husband of the lucky sister.

Such were the delights of his life. ~~significance~~ of any ~~act of his could~~ ~~affect the~~ very nature of things, could ~~~~ dim the light of the sun

8 Manuscript leaf: An Outcast of the Islands

9 Jessie George

10 The Conrad
family, 1908

11 John Galsworthy

12 R. B. Cunninghame
Graham by Frederick
Hollyers (c. 1890)

13 Ford Madox Ford
by E. O. Hoppé, 1915

14 Edward Garnett by Lucia
Moholy, 1936

15 Joseph Conrad by De'Ath and Condon, *c.* 1913

Grasping
the true Ideal

"An ideal is often but a flaming vision of reality," writes Joseph Conrad in "Chance." Vision a pen that writes just when you want it to write, smoothly, easily, without pause, that suits your hand to a nicety, that never varies, a pen perfect in every respect—and you vision Reality. For your ideal of a pen is Waterman's Ideal—the pen with the International reputation.

Waterman's (Ideal) FountainPen

—used for the signing of most of the Peace Treaties of recent times.

16 Waterman pen advertisement

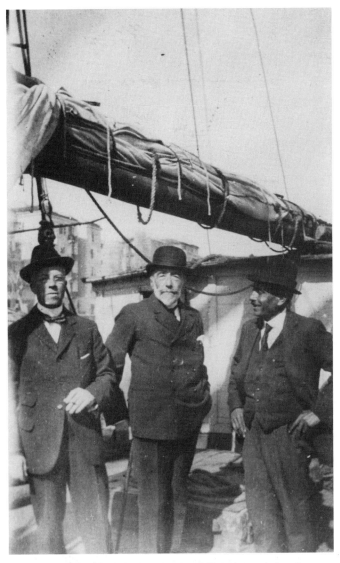

17 Conrad in Corsica with J. B. Pinker (left) and an unknown man,
February 1921

18 F. N. Doubleday

TIME

The Weekly News-Magazine

VOL. I, NO. 6   JOSEPH CONRAD
"Toward New Adventure"—See page 15   APRIL 7, 1923

19   *Time* magazine cover, 7 April 1923

20 Joseph Conrad arriving in New York, May 1923

PART III

Historical and Cultural Context

CHAPTER 14

Africa

Allan H. Simmons

In 1857, the year of Conrad's birth, Richard Burton and John Speke 'discovered' Lake Tanganyika, and the following year Speke 'found' Lake Victoria. Recalling his boyhood and education, in a late essay entitled 'Geography and Some Explorers', Conrad wrote: 'I stand here confessed as a contemporary of the Great Lakes' (*LE*, 14). Hitherto, the European powers had concerned themselves largely with the continent's margins – 'nibbling at the edges' (13), in Conrad's phrase – their interest crudely represented in names such as the Ivory Coast, the Gold Coast and the Slave Coast.

But European missionaries, including David Livingstone (1813–73), and explorers – like Mungo Park (1771–1806), James Bruce (1730–94), Burton (1821–90) and Speke (1827–64), all named in Conrad's essay – were steadily mapping the so-called 'Dark Continent'. In 1871, while searching for the Nile's source, Livingstone stumbled upon the Lualaba River; five years later, while attempting to cross Africa from east to west, Henry Morton Stanley showed this to be the River Congo's source. On this expedition he became the first European to sail down the Congo. It was while working as a journalist for the *New York Herald* in 1871 that Stanley found and resupplied Livingstone, providing the newspaper scoop and the legend: 'Dr Livingstone, I presume'. When Livingstone died two years later, his sun-dried body was brought back for burial in Westminster Abbey. But while such geographical exploration helped to fill in the map, the discovery of navigable rivers in the continent's interior meant that it was quickly overtaken by imperialist exploitation as European powers were attracted to its resources. If Livingstone's life provided one of the great adventure stories of Victorian times, popular interest in Africa was urged on by such fictions as H. Rider Haggard's *King Solomon's Mines* (1885), puffed by its publisher as 'the most amazing story ever written', and real-life imperial fantasies, such as the story of Cecil John Rhodes (1853–1902), who, sent to South Africa for his health, became a successful diamond prospector, forming the

De Beers Consolidated Mines Company, and used this fortune to pursue his imperial dream in southern Africa, looking northward beyond the Transvaal to Mashonaland and Matabeleland, which were eventually united to form Rhodesia.

Following the cessation of the Atlantic slave trade in the early nineteenth century, European interference was motivated by a new impulse: to save the Africans from themselves. Geographical exploration undertaken by such bodies as the Royal Geographical Society, the successor to the Association for Promoting the Discovery of the Interior Parts of Africa (founded in 1788), was complemented by religious zeal as missionary societies were launched in France, Portugal, Spain, Italy, Germany and the Scandinavian countries, as well as Britain. As the African adage has it, 'When the whites first came they had the Bible and we had the land; after a while, we found that things had changed: now they have the land and we have the Bible.' Facing British invasion, Ethiopian Emperor Theodore put it more starkly: 'I know their game. First, it's traders and missionaries. Then it's ambassadors. After that, they bring the guns. We shall do better to go straight to the guns.'[1]

The sheer speed with which Africa was appropriated by Europe in the last decades of the nineteenth century is astonishing. Where, by the mid-1870s – beyond coastal trading posts and a few strategically important colonies such as South Africa, which safeguarded Britain's access to the Indian Ocean and the lucrative spice trade – some 80 per cent of the continent remained under indigenous rule, by 1900 virtually the whole continent had been claimed by Britain, France, Germany, Portugal and Italy. Thus, for example, in just eighteen months, between 1883 and 1885, South West Africa, Togoland, the Cameroons and East Africa all came under German rule, their colonization characterized by Foreign Minister Bernard von Bülow, in 1897, as his country's right to 'a place in the sun'.

The partitioning of the world outside Europe and the United States into territories in the last quarter of the nineteenth century and the first quarter of the twentieth represented a new phase in empire-building, as colonialism based on military and economic might was translated into systematic imperialism, involving formal conquest, annexation and administration. In Africa, by 1914, only Ethiopia – which successfully resisted conquest by Italy – Liberia and a part of Morocco remained outside European control.[2]

A leader headed 'The Scramble for Africa', in *The Times* of 15 September 1884, begins:

Since Germany has joined in the game there promises to be something like a scramble among the three great European trading nations for the possession of at least the West Coast of Africa. It was recently stated in these columns that Africa's time had apparently come, that all the other continents had been virtually appropriated, and that the parcelling out of the heritage of Ham, which had been going on spasmodically for four centuries, would probably be completed in a few years.(8)

Although Conrad's maritime career (1874–93) took him to the edges of the continent – southern African ports like Cape Town and Port Elizabeth were regular stopping places (Conrad sojourned at the latter between December 1883 and February 1884), and the Suez Canal, that 'dismal but profitable ditch' produced when 'the French mind set the Egyptian muscle in motion' (*OI*, 12), through which he passed in 1889 – it was his brief experience in the Congo Free State in the employ of the Société Anonyme Belge pour le Commerce du Haut-Congo in 1890 on which he drew a decade later for his most famous work, 'Heart of Darkness' (1899). This experience, which he claimed never to have got over, opened his eyes to the reality of this 'scramble'.

On the Congo River, Conrad served in and briefly captained the steam-ship *Roi des Belges*, employment that provided the source for Marlow's journey in 'Heart of Darkness'. Scholarship has long established the degree to which the novella is haunted by its biographical origins and historical facts.[3] Part of the shock for the reader lies in discovering, for instance, that the characters Fresleven and Kurtz are partly based on actual people, while incidental details such as building the railway acquire added significance once we know that Roger Casement, whom Conrad first met at Matadi in June 1890, was himself working on the project.

African exploration and exploitation clearly fired Conrad's imagina-tion, yielding fictions that are shaped by and helped to shape their era's debates about colonialism. The short story 'An Outpost of Progress' (1897), described as 'the lightest part of the loot' he carried off from Central Africa (*TU*, vii), offers a scathing treatment of the atavistic notion whereby European contact with African culture leads to decay and death. Africa does not stand in isolation in Conrad's thought, but as part of his general attitude towards the imperialism in which, as a merchant seaman, he was involved and which he found repellent.

In the Congo Free State in 1890, his childhood boast to school friends – 'One day, putting my finger on a spot in the very middle of the then white heart of Africa, I declared that some day I would go there' (*LE*, 16) – had been realized, but at a price. Not only was the romance of exploration devalued – Stanley's 'rescue' of Livingstone, for instance, was in his view 'a prosaic newspaper "stunt"' – but the civilizing purpose behind European involvement in the Congo was seen as no more than a crude alibi for 'the vilest scramble for loot that ever disfigured the history of human conscience and geographical exploration' (*LE*, 17). The scramble for Africa would forever be associated with the figure of Belgium's King Leopold II, whose single colony at the heart of Africa provided extreme evidence of the atrocities and excesses perpetrated by European powers.

The reasons for the scramble at this particular moment were various: the desire for spoil; potential new markets; national pride; the belief, fuelled by a notion of racial superiority, that European civilization should be visited upon the Africans; an attempt to quash the Swahili and Arab slave trade now that Europe had abandoned the practice; and the evangelical revival in England, where pressure to abolish the slave trade led to Africa's becoming 'the focus for missionary zeal'.[4]

History abounds with such grim ironies. At the time of Conrad's sojourn, the Congo Free State, an area of approximately 1 million square miles (almost eighty times as large as Belgium) was administered not by the Belgian government but by Leopold II as his personal fiefdom. His interest in the Congo declared itself internationally in September 1876, when the king hosted the Geographical Conference of Brussels, where Europe recognized him as the leader of the crusade to civilize Africa by electing him president of the newly established International Africa Association. Ostensibly a crusade against the slave trade within the continent, Leopold emphasized the venture's nobility: 'to pierce the darkness which envelops whole populations, it is, I dare to say, a crusade worthy of this century of progress'. He expressed his real intentions in a letter to his London ambassador, Baron Solvyns, shortly afterwards: 'I do not want to miss a good chance of getting us a slice of this magnificent African cake.'[5] Nonetheless, Leopold's philanthropic pretence succeeded in hoodwinking the delegates: Viscount Ferdinand de Lesseps, who directed the Suez Canal's construction, called Leopold's plans 'the greatest humanitarian work of this time'.[6]

Acclaimed for his explorations in the Congo Basin, Stanley became Leopold's chief agent. The king commissioned him to create a chain of commercial and scientific stations across Central Africa, which were effectively armed garrisons of Empire. Stanley also launched steamer routes and made treaties with native chiefs. Mary Kingsley, another intrepid contemporary traveller in the Congo, claimed 'there is no other region in the world that can match West Africa for the steady kill, kill, kill that its malaria works on the white men who come under its influence',[7] and Conrad would attribute subsequent bouts of ill health to 'Reminders of Africa' (*CL* 1:123).

But quinine as much as the steamboat made possible wholesale invasion of the so-called 'White Man's Grave'. Rapacity was the watchword. In 1881, Leopold ordered: 'The treaties must be as brief as possible … and in a couple of articles must grant us everything'.[8]

Fifteen European powers were represented at the West Africa Conference of 1884–5 in Berlin to settle rival claims to Africa. Although not present himself, Leopold persuaded the European powers into accepting him as owner and ruler of the Congo, to preserve it as an international area of free trade rather than let it fall into the hands of one or other of the great powers. The Charter of the Congo Free State, subsequently endorsed by the Brussels Act of 1890, involved a trade-off among the imperial powers each driven by their own vested interests in West Africa. Wary of France's designs on British interests in the Lower Niger, for instance, Britain accepted Leopold as the price worth paying for German support in defending not only the Niger but also Egypt against French aspirations.

Welcoming delegates to the Berlin conference, 'Iron Chancellor' Bismarck piously restated Livingstone's lofty ideals, to introduce the '3 Cs' – commerce, Christianity and civilization – into Africa. But, as Pakenham wryly notes, from the African perspective, it was the unspoken fourth 'C' – conquest – that predominated in the scramble for Africa: 'the Maxim gun – not trade or the cross – became the symbol of the age in Africa'. British forces under Lord Kitchener killed 10,000 Sudanese in a single day at Omdurman in 1898. Comparable atrocities punctuate the colonial story throughout Africa. In 1904, in South West Africa, German General Lothar von Trotha, charged by Kaiser Wilhelm II with crushing a Herero revolt by 'fair means or foul', simply drove the whole tribe of 30,000 into the desert to die of drought and starvation.[9] Conrad's own 'Congo Diary', kept during his stay in Africa, records how cheaply native life was held: 'saw at a camp place the dead body of a Backongo. Shot? Horrid smell', and, the following day, 'Saw another dead body lying by the path in an attitude of meditative repose' (*LE*, 165). As Marlow says in 'Heart of Darkness', 'The conquest of the earth, which mostly means the taking it away from those who have a different complexion or slightly flatter noses than ourselves, is not a pretty thing when you look into it too much' (*Y*, 51).

Apart from the 'loot' he carried out of the Congo Free State, references to Africa generally in Conrad's work are incidental, such as the ordeal of the *Narcissus* off the notorious Cape of Storms. Instead, and fittingly, his was an imaginative encounter with the continent, met indirectly through the language and clichés of colonialism. In 'Heart of Darkness', Marlow is brutal about 'the great cause', perceiving in his aunt's designation of him as 'an exceptional and gifted creature … one of the Workers … Something like an emissary of light, something like a lower sort of apostle' an echo of the 'rot let loose in print and talk just about that time' (*Y*, 65, 59). Similarly, in 'An Outpost of Progress', whose very title is part alibi, part apologia, Carlier and Kayerts read in 'old copies of a home paper' of '"Our Colonial Expansion" in high flown language' that extols 'the rights and duties of civilization, of the sacredness of the civilizing work' (*TU*, 94). Typically, the Europeans whom Conrad brings to Africa are foolishly inspired by the propaganda they've ingested from their newspapers. This device allows him access to more representative imperialist fictions, which he then mocks by transposing them into incongruous settings.

Whether trade follows the flag or the other way round, imperialism and economics are intimately related. The scramble for Africa was driven by the continent's combination of resources and labour. Foodstuffs such as tea, sugar and cocoa supplied European grocers. Hobsbawm reminds us that West Africa was a source for the Quaker beverage and chocolate manufacturers.[10] But it was the wealth of minerals and raw materials, rather than Europe's sweet tooth, that generated imperial fervour. South Africa's gold and diamonds, and the copper belts of Northern Rhodesia (now Zambia) and the Congo (now DR Congo), proved irresistible. Filling in the blank spaces on the world map meant filling in the blank spaces on the map of world trade, and Leopold's interest in the Congo was primarily economic. While ivory provides the country's alluring source of wealth in Conrad's African fictions (where one is left to wonder at the absence of elephants), the real economic incentive for Leopold lay in the indigenous rainforests. At the dawn of the motor-car age, rubber trees yielded the new 'gold'. Replacing ivory as the chief source of loot, its extraction, in the equatorial jungles of both the Congo and the Amazon, involved the mass exploitation of indigenous people that in time drew international condemnation.

Leopold's ownership of the Congo Free State lasted from 1885 to 1907, when control of the country passed to the Belgian state. Although figures vary, it is estimated that, during this time, as many as 10 million natives may have lost their lives in Leopold's fiefdom. The accounts of observers, like Roger Casement and George Washington Williams, make grim reading in their detailing of widespread cruelty and abuse. Supported by photographs of mutilations, such reports attracted condemnation from, among others, Mark Twain.[11] To Conrad, 'the moral clock had been put back many hours' (*CL* 3:96). Despite a vigorous propaganda campaign, Leopold II was eventually brought to the bar of international justice for the atrocities committed in his name, his reign ended by the work of Casement and the Congo Reform

Association, founded by E. D. Morel, who, in a letter to Sir Arthur Conan Doyle, called 'Heart of Darkness' simply 'the most powerful thing ever written on the subject' (7 October 1909).

As Britain's interests in Egypt, invaded and occupied in 1882, and South Africa demonstrate, the nation's early involvement in Africa was motivated by the need to safeguard the route to India and the East Indies. But British sway in South Africa was complicated by the presence of the Boers, on whom a confederation was imposed by the Disraeli government in 1877. The country remained divided, composed of the British-controlled Cape Colony and Natal, and the Boer republics of Transvaal and Orange Free State, independent but under British suzerainty. What was expected to be a short war began in 1899 when High Commissioner Milner, having asserted British rights over the Boer republics, goaded them into attacking the Cape Colony. Unlike the usual colonial enemies, however, the Boers were well armed, with German weaponry. Despite suffering a series of defeats, the British succeeded in capturing the main Boer cities by 1900, but the Boers' resort to guerrilla tactics dragged the war out. The British response was to burn Boer farms, clear the veldt and herd Boer women and children into 'concentration camps'. The practice backfired when the high death toll in the camps led to public protests at home, ensuring that victory, when it came in 1902, was a pyrrhic one.

Conrad was exercised by the war, calling it the 'the Krüger–Chamberlain combination' (*CL* 2:302). His concerns voice a personal interest, as Ted (Edward) Sanderson, one of his first English friends and the dedicatee of *An Outcast of the Islands* (1896), was in uniform. Conrad's comments about the respective merits of British generals suggest a deeper fascination, too, and he correctly foresaw, in October 1899, that 'The victory – unless it is to be thrown away – shall have to be followed by ruthless repression. The situation will become repugnant to the nation. The *"reasonable English ideals"* (I am quoting Sir F Milner's words) are not attained in that way' (*CL* 2:211). And whilst Conrad laid the blame on 'the doings of German influence' (*CL* 2:230) – the Germans, established in South West Africa (Namibia), were already a power in the region – R. B. Cunninghame Graham, a lifelong friend of socialist commitment, saw the war as 'a fight between two burglars'.[12]

Conrad's experience of Africa in the late nineteenth century, though typical of many of the period, was transmuted into gold through his writing. Fiction, rather than sociology or history, these tales are none the less forever associated with the Scramble for Africa and helped to create the climate of opinion that would find its excesses intolerable.

NOTES

1. Cited in Basil Davidson, *The Story of Africa* (London: Mitchell Beazley, 1984), p. 167.
2. See Eric Hobsbawm, *The Age of Empire, 1875–1914* (London: Abacus, 1994), pp. 57–60.
3. See Norman Sherry, *Conrad's Western World* (London: Cambridge University Press, 1977).
4. Barbara Emerson, *Leopold II of the Belgians: King of Colonialism* (London: Weidenfeld & Nicolson, 1979), p. 72.
5. Thomas Pakenham, *The Scramble for Africa, 1876–1912* (London: Weidenfeld & Nicolson, 1991), pp. 21, 22.
6. Adam Hochschild, *King Leopold's Ghost* (New York: Houghton Mifflin, 1998), p. 46.
7. Mary Kingsley, *Travels in West Africa* (London: Macmillan, 1897), p. 681.
8. Hochschild, *King Leopold's Ghost*, pp. 71–2.
9. Pakenham, *The Scramble for Africa*, pp. xvii, 609.
10. Hobsbawm, *The Age of Empire*, p. 64.
11. According to Twain, 'Beside Leopold, Nero, Caligula, Attilo, Torquemada, Genghis Khan and such killers of men are mere amateurs' (in *New York World*, 3 December 1905).
12. Cedric Watts and Laurence Davies, *Cunninghame Grahame: A Critical Biography* (Cambridge: Cambridge University Press, 1979), p. 114.

CHAPTER 15

Anarchism

M. S. Newton

In January 1894, French authorities in Rouen mistook Conrad for an anarchist. The event occurred at a crucial moment: he was returning to his lodgings in London, where he would soon begin his literary career. In an atmosphere of tension and anxiety, following the throwing of a bomb in the Chamber of Deputies in Paris the previous month, official suspicion could have alighted anywhere. The misapprehension was swiftly resolved, but the fact remained: innocent, Conrad had none the less appeared guilty.

Only a month later, an anarchist outrage occurred at Greenwich Park, an event that forms the background to *The Secret Agent* (1907). Martial Bourdin, a young French anarchist working as a tailor in London, died in the Park when he stumbled and the bomb that he was carrying exploded prematurely. Various theories were offered to explain the incident: Bourdin was an *agent provocateur* or an idealist duped by one; he was on his way to France to aid anarchists there; he was testing a fuse; he had designs on the Royal Observatory. The solution to the problem remains out of reach; as Conrad says of Winnie Verloc's suicide in *The Secret Agent*, 'an impenetrable mystery' (*SA*, 307) is destined to hang forever over the event.

Although the link to the Greenwich Bombing of 1894 would have been apparent to many of the novel's first readers, Conrad was circumspect when discussing his sources and notoriously cagey when it came to the origins of his other anarchist fictions – the short stories 'An Informer' and 'An Anarchist', collected in *A Set of Six* (1908). For the 1920 edition of that collection, Conrad wrote a generally revealing account of the origins of the other tales, yet, when it came to these stories, he remarked:

Of 'The Informer' and 'The Anarchist' I will say next to nothing. The pedigree of these tales is hopelessly complicated and not worth disentangling at this distance of time. I found them and here they are. The discriminating reader will guess that I have found them within my mind; but how they or their elements came in there I have forgotten for the most part; and for the rest I really don't see why I should give myself away more than I have done already. (*SS*, ix–x)

Taking a different tack, the 'Author's Note' for *The Secret Agent* is at once tantalizingly open and guardedly obfuscatory. If, as a result, the context for these works is therefore somehow obscured, then that may be entirely apt: after all, anarchists were nothing if not secretive.

From the 1880s to the 1920s, Anarchism was a serious revolutionary political force. It had one essential tenet: all forms of law, authority and enforced social order are tyrannous. The interpretation of this core belief was immensely varied. Anarchism in Britain and elsewhere represented a spectrum of beliefs and practices ranging from anti-Parliamentarianism, through individualist Communism, to the outright celebration of crime. In 1894, shortly after the Greenwich Bombing, the London papers listed two varieties of anarchist: the violent type found in the Club Autonomie, and the philosophical kind in Grafton Hall.[1] This simplified the situation enormously. Anarchisms proliferated.

Among its diverse factions, activity was endless. Papers were printed; points of doctrine debated; conspiracies were planned; and revolutions foretold. Groups split and re-formed with bewildering irregularity. Immersing oneself in the history of the movement in the late 1880s and 1890s is to fall headlong into a flurry of bustle and what now seems largely purposeless industry. Although anarchists were everywhere in the popular British press – sinister, foreign and downright murderous – the reality was naturally different: a number of European refugees concentrated in the capital; a proportion of British workers and middle-class adherents to the labour movement in general in London and the provinces; a scattering of inveterate radicals; some freethinkers, some atheists, some revolutionaries.

Compared to the spectacular successes and acts of violence performed by anarchists in France, or Spain, or the United States, anarchist activity in Britain appears fragmented, docile and without significant influence, much as Conrad portrays it. The activists were outspoken but fundamentally timid. Anarchism in Britain was energetic, but, apart from the occasional intrusion into public awareness following an arrest for incitement to violence, for most people the movement remained largely shadowy and remote. Indeed, the fact that Anarchism seemed an affair of the shadows, a half-hidden manifestation of some imagined conspiratorial underground, accounted for much of its prestige and fascination. Conrad's anarchist fictions benefit from this mystique.

As is the case with Conrad himself, the British nature of Anarchism can only ever be part of the story. Far more important than the actions of British-based anarchists was the international basis of Anarchism, and alongside it the popular image of the nihilistic bomb-thrower, itself a widely dispersed cultural product, as vital in Chicago, Barcelona, Rio and Paris, as in London or Walsall. There was even anarchist activity in authoritarian Japan. The movement refused to recognize national boundaries. As the anarchist Farnara declared while on trial in London: "'For us there are no frontiers. The *bourgeois* are the same all the world over.'"[2] With its liberal asylum laws, London was a living symbol of Anarchism's internationalism, a meeting-point for activists and theorists from across the world, as reflected in *The Secret Agent*'s cosmopolitan cast of characters.

The period from 1880 to 1914 was one of bomb-throwing and assassination: it saw the murder of an Austrian empress, an Italian king, a French president, a Spanish prime minister and an American president, among many other public figures. Under the impact of these and other outrages, Anarchism began to be identified mainly with the practice and policy of 'propaganda by the deed'. Many, like William Morris, who were in part attracted to Anarchism's anti-authoritarian stance, were dismayed and alienated by the bomb outrages and assassinations of the 1890s. However, there were many ready to argue that violent acts (or other criminal deeds) worked better as critiques of Capitalism than the printed word or speeches. Such exploits embodied, more than words, the efficacy of action for its own sake. Yet the deeds themselves had to be enshrined, praised, condemned, examined within discourse – the press, the anarchists' own publications; the purity and impact of the deed depended on the mediation of print culture.

Indeed, the most likely way for Conrad to have formed an idea of Anarchism is through engagement with mainstream newspapers and magazines (rather than those radical journals parodied under the titles *The Gong* and *The Torch* at the start of *The Secret Agent*). The anarchist was, for instance, a stock figure in cartoons of the period. The nuances and genuine attractions of anarchist belief were a subject of interest for a coterie of radicals, intellectuals and activists. Most people relied instead upon such caricatures and upon the largely hostile reports of the mainstream press, the complex demonizations of popular fiction (the 'dynamite novel'), and the effects (reported and felt), spectacular and terrifying, of the many assassinations and bomb outrages that scarred these decades.

Yet, the 'media image' of the anarchist that Conrad would have encountered, and complexly re-invented, was a more nuanced one than a casual observer might at first assume. The anarchist terrorist was a figure poised between fear, derision and sympathy. The reporting of the Greenwich Bombing bears this out. The *Morning Leader* of 16 February 1894 begins harshly enough, praising the British policy of asylum for refugees and then asserting that an exception to this generous policy should be made for anarchists. It goes on to state that no matter what anyone felt about Bourdin, no one could pity him. Yet in the newspaper accounts, pity for the unfortunate Bourdin undoubtedly mingles with larger doses of disgust and contempt.[3] Moreover, anarchist statements were printed with regularity in the national press, such as 'An Anarchist's Apology for Outrage', which presents an interview with a French anarchist in the *St James' Gazette* of 16 April 1892. Similarly, Battolla's speech at the trial of the Walsall Anarchists, as reported in *The Times*, presented an image of the movement at variance with the popular mixture of comical ridicule and disdain. Battola affirmed: 'The Attorney-General did not know what anarchy meant; he said it was disorder. He himself asserted that it did not: it meant a state of society in which men lived together in harmony without laws.'[4] In this way even a hostile paper presented authentic anarchist views. For example, when David Nicoll was arrested for incitement to murder, the *Commonweal* article in which he declared that the anarchists in the Walsall trial had been entrapped by provocateurs was quoted in full by *The Times* and other newspapers. In the same trial, the press reported Nicoll's view that 'laws were made by force and must be destroyed by force. The law meant wrong and injustice.'

None the less, two dominant images that Conrad would have met with in press reports are those of anarchists as dangerous idealists, ready to murder in the cause of some obscure virtue, or more usually as madmen whose only intervention in the real world consisted of committing acts of terror and meaningless chaos. After all the complexity, this last is the dominant note of the mainstream press. For instance, we can trace again the reactions of the press to the bomb at Greenwich Park that, after all, killed only the man carrying the device. On the day after the explosion, the *Morning Leader* (16 February 1894) commented: 'Men like Ravachol, and Vaillant and Bourdin are the proclaimed enemies of society. They may be Frenchmen, Spaniards, Russians, or Englishmen, but, first and foremost, they are the foes of civilisation.' On the same day, the *Evening News* headed an article with the question 'Are Anarchists Lunatics?' The answer it helpfully supplies is: 'Yes'. Some years later, H. L. Adams wrote: 'One wonders how the blowing up of Greenwich Observatory would have helped their "cause". But as anarchism is undoubtedly a form of mental derangement, one must not look for reason on the part of those who espouse it.'[5] On 10 March 1894, *Tit-Bits* published a probably fictitious interview with an anarchist who declared his ultimate aim of killing as many people as possible, using what we would now call biological warfare:[6]

Have you ever reflected what splendid facilities are offered by modern science for carrying on a war to the death against society? To quote but one or two instances.

We could by pumping atmospheric air into the gas mains lay half of the principal thoroughfares in London in ruins. A few pounds' weight of corrosive sublimate thrown at night into any one of the reservoirs of the great water companies would carry sickness and death into thousands of homes. But even without resorting to comparatively costly methods such as these, there are plenty of simple means for taking a terrible revenge on any society which should dare to attack us. The commonest materials purchasable anywhere for a few pence will suffice.[7]

This clearly offers one of many similar precedents for The Professor's yearning for general extermination in *The Secret Agent*. Here is someone at war, not with laws and government, but with society as such. Anarchism and the practice of terrorism generally in the period began the erosion of the civilian/ soldier distinction that was to take devastating effect in the wars of the next century. For this very likely fictive anarchist, normality was the enemy.

Conrad certainly employs the popular view of Anarchism as a strange repudiation of social beliefs and shared practices. Both 'The Informer' and *The Secret Agent* touch on an image of Anarchism as utter nihilism, an example of incomprehensible Otherness. Often involved in Conrad's representation of the anarchist is the image of a comprehensive negation: the rejection of language, the abandonment of all social conventions. Anarchism allowed the writer to create an imagined space in which truth, beauty, honour, love, family, fidelity, loyalty, religion, meaning, and communication itself could all be denied. For anarchists envisaged in this way, social virtues were not inverted but genuinely annulled, and not so much refuted as erased. There could, then, be no rules for dealing with anarchists. As in *The Secret Agent*, in the face of such a foe, the police are essentially helpless or must, at the risk of repudiating civilized norms, resort to their enemies' methods.

In addition to newspaper reports and magazine editorials, Conrad had other, private, sources for his 'inside knowledge' of Anarchism. It is understood that the 'omniscient' friend who provided Conrad with the 'illuminating' details that inspired *The Secret Agent* was his fellow writer, Ford Madox Ford. Ford's actual knowledge of Anarchism may in fact have been rather limited.[8] Through Ford, however, Conrad very likely met Helen Rossetti, who, while a teenager and young woman in the early and mid-1890s, had been a prominent London anarchist. With her sister, Olivia, and her brother, Arthur, she had written and printed the revolutionary journal, the *Torch* (initially from a room in their parents' home in Primrose Hill). Helen Rossetti certainly was privy to a great deal of information regarding Anarchism, and particularly the story of Martial Bourdin and the Greenwich Bombing. Moreover, through his friendship with Edward Garnett, Conrad might also have picked up information regarding

British-based anarchists: Kropotkin, the leading anarchist theorist, was a
Garnett family friend, as had been the revolutionary Stepniak (although not
himself an anarchist). Moreover, Olive Garnett, Edward's sister, had also
met several of the actors involved in the real background to the Greenwich
Outrage. Conrad could also have learnt much about London Radicalism
from his socialist friend, Cunninghame Graham, an acquaintance of, and
correspondent with, Henry Benjamin Samuels (1860–1933), a London
anarchist once thought of as the 'original' for Verloc, the secret agent.[9]

Why Conrad turned to the subject of Anarchism in the period 1906–7
remains unclear. The heyday of anarchist atrocities was certainly the 1890s,
and the Greenwich affair, never highly important, may have seemed by 1907
somewhat remote. Bomb-throwing, revolutionary conspiracies and assassinations continued, of course, but the truly dangerous moment seemed to have
passed. It is a curious fact that both 'An Anarchist' and *The Secret Agent* take as
their subjects questions of guilt, innocence and responsibility. Although
convicted as such, the anarchist of the short story is not really an anarchist
at all, but is rather a marked man unjustly imprisoned in a penal colony. The
question of guilt pervades *The Secret Agent*, particularly in the figure of Stevie,
legally irresponsible through being not of sound mind, an innocent idealist,
and a persuaded terrorist ready to destroy. Blame for his death falls in different
ways on Mr Vladimir, who initiates the plot; on Yundt, who overexcites
Stevie; on The Professor, who provides the bomb; and on Verloc, who abuses
his brother-in-law's devotion. Similarly, Winnie justly murders Verloc,
although this act born of her 'freedom' puts her at the mercy both of an
unforgiving legal system and of the exploitative anarchist Ossipon. 'The
Informer' likewise offers at least two guilty parties – the police spy who betrays
the comrades he informs on, and the anarchists who entrap him (not to forget
the second 'informer' of the story, Mr X, the collector who tells the tale).

Of course, the complexity of Conrad's representation of anarchists does
not end here. Conrad's tales mirror the duality of the anarchists' representation in the papers and magazines (including *Blackwood's*). Taking on the
grotesque lineaments of their cartoon images, Conrad's anarchists are fairly
often shams (a word he used in a letter to R. B. Cunninghame Graham (*CL*
3:491)), as in *The Secret Agent*, or inauthentic middle-class poseurs, as in
'The Informer'. Yet the anarchists in the novel are both derided and
understood: even The Professor is granted the dignity of genuine extremism. The moral anarchists, Stevie and Winnie, may evoke the reader's
sympathy. In any case, the most radical voice in *The Secret Agent* is that of
Vladimir, who is not an anarchist at all but an autocratic diplomat at a
foreign embassy (presumably that of Tsarist Russia).

In several letters Conrad affirmed that it was not his intention to parody Anarchism in *The Secret Agent*, or to explore its philosophy. While finding its place within a complex cultural creation formed within the print-media, Conrad's representation of Anarchism goes beyond the instabilities of the popular image of the revolutionary. It represents a profound questioning of the basis of anarchist politics as such, in particular the foundation of such beliefs in the experience and philosophy of compassion. Moreover, it brings Anarchism back towards a searching critique of urban experience, trust, the provisional frame of the domestic and the dizzying abyss of 'freedom'. In his fictions of Anarchism, Conrad both draws upon the variety of images and representations available to him, in sources from the 'dynamite novel' to the editorials of *Blackwood's Magazine*, and presents from these materials his own version of the anarchist idealist or villain, refracted through a scornful and feeling irony. The energies present in the grotesques and victims of Conrad's anarchist fictions embody the forces present in the multifaceted images of Anarchism. More than any other fiction of the period, Conrad's *The Secret Agent* plunges into these ambiguities and makes of them an endlessly rewarding work of art.

NOTES

1. *Daily Graphic*, 17 February 1894, p. 3.
2. Hermia Oliver, *The International Anarchist Movement in Late Victorian London* (London: Croom Helm; New York: St Martins Press, 1983), p. 112.
3. For newspaper accounts of the bombing and its aftermath, see Mary Burgoyne, comp., 'Conrad among the Anarchists: Documents on Martial Bourdin and the Greenwich Bombing', in *The Secret Agent: Centennial Essays*, ed. Allan H. Simmons and J. H. Stape (Amsterdam: Rodopi, 2007), pp. 147–85.
4. *The Times*, 5 April 1892, pp. 8–9.
5. Hargrave Lee Adams, *C.I.D. Behind the Scenes at Scotland Yard* (London: Sampson Low, 1931), p. 166.
6. On the question of the article being a journalistic fraud, see the *Commonweal*, 31 March 1894.
7. *Tit-Bits*, 10 March 1894, p. 404.
8. See, for example, Michael Newton, 'Four Notes on *The Secret Agent*: Sir William Harcourt, Ford and Helen Rossetti, Bourdin's Relations, and a Warning Against Δ', in *The Secret Agent: Centennial Essays*, pp. 129–46.
9. See John Linklater, 'Anarchy in the UK: Who Inspired Conrad's *Secret Agent*?' in *Scottish Review of Books*, 12 August 2007, pp. 4–6. I am also indebted to Mark Samuels who passed on a copy of a letter addressed to H. B. Samuels, dated 9 July 1890, from Cunninghame Graham.

CHAPTER 16

Disease and medicine

Martin Bock

Disease and doctors were Conrad's lifelong companions. At an early age, he watched his parents die of tuberculosis and endured childhood ailments, which included serious fevers, headaches, gravel in the bladder, and nervous fits taken as symptoms of epilepsy.[1] And, when not ill, he was educated by men of medicine: Dr Izydor Kopernicki (1825–91), a medical anthropologist of some renown, and Adam Pulman (1846–?), a medical student in Cracow, who served as Conrad's tutor. Afterwards, life at sea brought its own perils. Jim's traumatic injury and hospitalization in *Lord Jim* draw on Conrad's own experience in 1887, when serving as first mate in the *Highland Forest*. Either before or after attaining his master mariner's certificate, he would have familiarized himself with standard handbooks on maritime medicine and had to call upon his medical knowledge when in command of the *Otago*'s ailing crew in 1888. His sea career was cut short by the illness contracted during his time in the Congo in 1890, when he suffered from dysentery and probably malaria, diseases that thereafter compromised his health. Several 'water cures' in Switzerland followed to ease his nervous symptoms, but neuralgic pains, touchy digestion, familial gout, rotten teeth and susceptibility to influenza and nervous breakdown troubled his adult life.

Conrad's life coincided roughly with what might be termed the first era of modern medicine, from the middle of the nineteenth century to the 1930s, by which time advances in therapeutic pharmacology and the study of antibiosis brought modern medicine to new levels of efficacy and optimism. In 1858 Rudolf Virchow founded modern cell science with his *Cellular-Pathologie*, which offered a new understanding of human tissue and disease: he discovered that cells are autonomous and beget other cells. Virchow's scientific theory and social ideology made him a vocal proponent of the miasmic theory of disease. This concept is prevalent in Conrad's Malay fiction. In *Almayer's Folly*, the narration foregrounds the tainted landscape: 'An acrid smell of damp earth and of decaying leaves ... The very air seemed dead in there – heavy and stagnating, poisoned with the corruption of countless ages' (*AF*, 167). Disease is endemic to locales where poisons inhere in the soil, water or air.

The other dominant contemporary model of disease transmission, germ theory,[2] emerged shortly after Conrad entered the British Merchant Marine, and evolved from the work of Pasteur, who studied what were called 'zymotic' diseases, thought to grow from microscopic seeds (like yeasts) and to ferment in the host organism. Pasteur's work led to his discovery of several strains of bacteria (1880) and the creation of vaccines for anthrax and rabies (1881–5).[3] But the mechanism for the transmission of bacterial disease was impressionistically understood until Robert Koch's work in the 1880s.[4] The main differences between germ theory and Virchow's miasmic theories were really the source of infection and the technology of transmission. Conrad's awareness of germ theory is evident in *The Nigger of the 'Narcissus'* (1897), which is set two years after Koch's discovery of the tubercle bacillus. The consumptive James Wait is depicted repeatedly coughing in the presence of the ship's crew and captain, the latter quarantining him, in keeping with then-standard medical practice.

No sooner is Wait aboard the *Narcissus* than he broadcasts his loud, ringing, metallic cough, explaining that he has a 'cold on [his] chest', to which a shipmate responds, '"should think 'twas something more"' (*NN*, 24). Neither 'consumption' (in its medical sense) nor 'tuberculosis' is ever mentioned by name, although the issue of Wait's illness is on the minds of the narrator and most other crew members, providing a spectrum of responses to illness and the fear of death. Wait, who suffers from the wasting disease, vacillates between denying his illness and using it as a means of avoiding work or garnering sympathy. As the crew variously respond with pity, the captain is impassive to the immediate danger of infection.

The awareness of epidemic disease only increased with a more precise knowledge about the transmission of diseases, which followed the ebb and flow of European interests and merchant ships around the world. But those same European interests recognized the need for preventing disease and, in 1876, inaugurated a series of International Congresses on Hygiene and Demography. In England, the Public Health Act of 1875 was instituted to give the government the power to regulate international travel with a Port Sanitary Authority. As a result, the role of the master mariner as medical doctor *pro tem* became an important aspect of merchant shipping. Indeed, the Merchant Shipping Act of 1867 outlines the responsibilities of ship-owners to provide a captain with a sanctioned medical guide and a 'scale of medicines' to care for the crew.[5] It is likely that Conrad had occasion to handle and use such a medical handbook. The *Singapore Free Press* noted on

2 March 1888 – when Conrad was commanding the ship – that 'The British bark *Otago*, bound from Bangkok to Sydney with a cargo of rice, put into port here last evening for medical advice as several of the crew are suffering from fever and the Captain wished to get a further supply of medicine.'[6]

Conrad betrays his apprehension about medical supplies as he prepares for his time in the Congo in 1890, writing to Karol Zagórski, 'If you knew all the bottles of medicine!', before citing the grim statistics of illness and emergency repatriation of the company employees home from Africa (*CL* 1:52). From Libreville, Gabon, Conrad wrote to Marguerite Poradowska on 10 June 1890 that he was 'awaiting the inevitable fever', which struck repeatedly in the ensuing months. By the end of September Conrad reports to Poradowska: 'I suffered from fever four times in two months, and then at the [Stanley] Falls … I suffered an attack of dysentery lasting five days. I feel somewhat weak physically and not a little demoralized … I shall be sent back to Europe by another attack of dysentery, unless it consigns me to the other world' (*CL* 1:62). We are offered a glimpse of Conrad's medical treatment of gunshot wounds and tropical fever, first-hand as it were, in his 'Congo Diary'.

Cut short by illness, Conrad's employment in the Congo Free State none the less left him with a lifelong susceptibility to the lingering effects of tropical fever and dysentery, complicated by the onset of neurasthenia and gout. Conrad's medical condition provides a pathology of the age, resonating with the *fin-de-siècle* quasi-medical theories of Max Nordau, whose alarmist *Degeneration* (1895) warned of various physiological and moral regressions in the modern, urban world, as well as a period of cultural and moral decline. But there were also significant advances in the study of tropical medicine. In the 1890s, parasitologists discovered that mosquitoes were transmitters of the parasites that cause yellow and malarial fevers. Such advances led to the founding of the London School of Hygiene and Tropical Medicine in 1899, and schools of tropical medicine in Liverpool and Edinburgh. Advances in parasitology and tropical medicine are registered in the composition history of *The Rescue*, begun in 1896 but only completed in 1919: the early chapters reveal little interest in insect life, but after the medical discovery that the *Anopheles* mosquito is the vector for malaria, and the tsetse fly the vector for sleeping sickness / Gambia fever, it is significant that the novel's characters, in later chapters, are plagued by clouds of insects and tropical fever.

Unsurprisingly, at the turn of the century medical scientists were busy reclassifying known diseases. Sir Thomas Clifford Allbutt, a self-described nosologist (or classifier of disease), was a leading figure in this enterprise. His magnum opus, *A System of Medicine by Many Authors* (1900–1), was praised as a comprehensive reclassification of known diseases and their treatments. Such advances spurred Conrad's hope for recovered health, prompting him to take several 'water cures' (in 1891, 1894, 1895 and 1907) at Champel-les-Bains, a Swiss hydropathic institute in Geneva's suburbs that focused on convalescence and the treatment of various nervous disorders, such as neurasthenia – weakening of the nervous system – neurasthenic dyspepsia, neuralgias and neuroses. There Conrad probably endured a wide range of baths and showers, both hot and cold, applied in gentle showers and quite vigorously – the 'active fire hose' in his own words (*CL* 1:212). In addition, he would have been treated with massage and possibly electro-therapy. He was comfortable with the atmosphere of Champel, as opposed to the large, more commercial Bavarian spas such as Carlsbad and Marienbad, which he had visited in 1883 with his uncle, Tadeusz Bobrowski. Conrad's last visit to Champel again restored his constitution but insufficiently to prevent his neurasthenic collapse in later years.

Human health in turn-of-the-century England was generally tenuous, as is documented in the poor health of working-class recruits during the Boer War.[7] The health of the Conrad family was no better. The Conrads' marriage began in 1896 with honeymoon bouts of fever and delirium, during which Conrad rambled in his native Polish. Since childhood, Conrad had grown accustomed to others attending to his illnesses, and this continued in his adult life, as Jessie often cared for him in a quasi-maternal way during his periods of illness with influenza, neuralgia, touchy digestion and gout. The introduction of children, Borys in 1898 and John in 1906, complicated this pattern: illnesses multiplied and Conrad found himself attending to the sick-needs of others when he needed time to write.[8] The early months of 1907, when the family was wintering in Montpellier, provide an extreme example: Borys, whom Conrad observed 'catches whatever's going' (*CL* 3:412), fell ill with infected adenoids, measles, bronchitis, and was finally tested for tuberculosis; then rheumatic fever and pleurisy set in, after which the infant John contracted whooping cough which he passed on to Borys. Between periods of writing, Conrad himself was ill with flu, suffered from bouts of gout, eczema and, not surprisingly, severe nervous strain. During this time he repeatedly refers to his family illnesses as a 'nightmare' (*CL* 3:402–47). The family travelled to Champel once the symptoms of contagious disease abated, and Borys' and Conrad's 'water cures' relieved their nervous disorders for the time being.

Jessie was an excellent care-giver but suffered from debilitating pain. In the autumn of 1904 while the Conrads were in London, Jessie fell and reinjured a knee hurt in a similar accident when she was seventeen. On

24 November, she was operated on by Bruce Clarke, a distinguished joint-surgeon, to repair displaced cartilage (*CL* 3:184). In the ensuing years, more than ten surgeries and worries about possible amputation are noted in Conrad's correspondence. Medical treatment later in life would lead to the Conrads' friendship with Sir Robert Jones, an eminent orthopaedic surgeon who operated repeatedly, in attempts to eliminate the infection that was causing Jessie's pain. Sir Robert became one of the three intimate friends to whom Conrad gave author's copies of his Collected Edition.

In 1910, Conrad experienced a 'complete nervous breakdown' (*CL* 4:321n1), the consequence of severe literary and personal difficulties. In deep financial debt to his friend and literary agent, J. B. Pinker (*CL* 4:298n5), Conrad was also making agonizingly slow progress on 'Razumov' (the working-title of *Under Western Eyes*), and due to ill health had delayed some instalments of his memoirs, which he was dictating for the *English Review*, a literary journal edited by his friend and collaborator Ford Madox Ford. In the autumn of 1909, he suspended work on his novel to write 'The Secret Sharer', a short story that reflects his mental agitation at the time, depicting a young captain on the brink of mental instability. In early January 1910, having completed 'Razumov', an argument with Pinker precipitated Conrad's complete collapse. Jessie Conrad recalls her husband gravely ill with gout and delirium in which he conversed in Polish with the characters he had just finished writing about.[9] Conrad remained in bed for some months, with only brief periods of work, and slowly regained his strength in the spring.

The First World War inaugurated a new set of medical problems and treatments. Most significantly, the style of modern warfare created a new kind of casualty: soldiers who showed the same symptoms as the typical neurasthenic and who, by early 1915, were pronounced 'shell-shocked'. In the twelve-month period ending on 30 April 1916, 1,300 officers and 10,000 soldiers of other ranks were being treated at special nerve hospitals in Britain, and, in the decade following the war, approximately 114,600 ex-servicemen applied for pensions for disorders related to shell-shock – what is now called Post-Traumatic Stress Disorder.[10] Borys Conrad was a victim of shell-shock and showed sighs of agoraphobia after serving in the war. He relates that, while hunting in open country, 'I was suddenly overcome by a sensation of exposure to great danger; I felt naked, defenceless and terrified, but eventually succeeded in pulling myself together sufficiently to stagger on to the boundary of the field … I have no idea how long I remained crouching there in a state of semi-consciousness.'[11]

Before the war's end, it was clear that some form of psychotherapy was needed to treat men affected by the shelling of trench warfare. Curiously, then, the war increased interest in Freudian theory, which had been embraced by few English psychologists in the first two decades of the twentieth century. Moreover, troop movements probably helped to spread the Spanish Influenza epidemic of 1918. On 18 December 1918, *The Times* reflected: 'It has been estimated that the war caused the death of 20,000,000 persons in 4½ years. In the same period, at its epidemic rate, [the flu] would have killed 108,000,000 … Never since the Black Death has such a plague swept over the face of the world.'[12] In fact, modern estimates suggest the influenza killed between 50 and 100 million people worldwide.[13] Conrad may have had a brush with this flu in June 1918 before it mutated into a more virulent and deadly strain of the pandemic (see *CL* 6:237–47).

Conrad's last years were characterized by personal and familial illness. He continued to suffer from periods of gout and depression. Borys Conrad showed renewed symptoms of neurasthenia (a tendency towards nervous breakdown), and Jessie Conrad's repeated operations on her knee ran up substantial medical bills. Hugh Walpole lamented that Conrad was 'preoccupied by money and gout', and Jacob Epstein, who made a bronze bust of the writer, noted in spring 1923 that his subject was 'crippled with rheumatism, crotchety, nervous, and ill'.[14] Battling emotional and physical illness, he became increasingly fatigued and felt his creative imagination fail. As John Stape observes, 'He was wearing out, as one severe attack of gout followed another. Drained of vitality, his face had taken on the leathery look of the heavy and inveterate smoker, the habit also slowly corroding his heart.'[15] In his final year, Conrad began to show symptoms of heart disease and, on 3 August 1924, died of a heart attack.

Conrad's attention to his physical and mental economy may, perhaps, seem the obsessions of a hypochondriac. Virtually every one of his volumes includes reference to illness and disease. Medical doctors are sometimes important characters, like Dr Monyham in *Nostromo*, or the Belgian doctor in 'Heart of Darkness' who asks Marlow, as he is presumably measuring his cranium, if there is a history of madness in his family. Craniology, phrenology and criminal anthropology were much in vogue at this time; and Conrad had received a request, from Tadeusz Bobrowski, to bring some human skulls back from Africa to give to his old anthropologist mentor, Dr Izydor Kopernicki. A country doctor narrates 'Amy Foster', a story some Conrad scholars suggest is an allegory for Conrad's sense of his exilic condition. In *The Nigger of the 'Narcissus'* and *The*

Shadow-Line, disease provides the *modus operandi* of plot; and many works
chart the physical or mental decline of a principal character. In the most
significant sense, disease functions as a central trope of Conrad's fiction: as
an index to moral being and a gauge of failure or success. Hence, to thrive
in the African wilderness and the corrupt colonialist enterprise, one must,
according to the Manager, have 'no entrails' (*Y*, 74) that are humanly
vulnerable; or to meet the onslaught of challenges and misfortunes that
command offers, one must have, like the young captain of *The Shadow-
Line*, invincible stamina and a charmed resistance to debility. Conrad's
intimate friend G. Jean-Aubry confirmed a dozen years after Conrad's
death that Conrad saw a direct link between one's moral being and
medical health. Jean-Aubry observed that since Conrad associated moral
problems with nervousness and attacks of gout, Conrad's 'most severe
[medical] crises always coincided with moral crises, which were therefore
nervous ones'.[16]

In her classic essay *Illness as Metaphor*, Susan Sontag offers a wide-ranging
exploration of the figurative valuation of illness in literature, making several
observations relevant to Conrad. She observes that 'fatal illness has always
been viewed as a test of moral character'.[17] Wait and Kurtz are characters
whose moral will is tested by their mortality. Analogously, Sontag argues
that 'Illnesses have always been used as metaphors to enliven charges that a
society was corrupt or unjust', and recognizes 'the analogy between disease
and civil disorder'.[18] The breakdown of order aboard the *Narcissus* and
ideological themes that are developed through Wait's decline are surely
reflected in his disease, and the anarchist Professor of *The Secret Agent* is last
seen disappearing into the urban landscape 'like a pest amid a crowd of men'
(*SA*, 231). Images of infection in Conrad's fiction and the work of his
contemporaries – one thinks of Wells' 'The Stolen Bacillus', or Kipling's
idea in 'The White Man's Burden' that colonists go 'to bid the sickness
cease' – reveal the *fin-de-siècle* preoccupation with disease and degeneration. But Conrad's interest in illness and disease is also intimately
associated with writing itself. If, as Sontag asserts, 'Disease is the will
speaking through the body, a language for dramatizing the mental: a form
of self expression',[19] then Conrad's curious comment does not seem
so strange: 'perhaps true literature (when you "get it") is something like
a disease which one feels in one's bones, sinews, and joints' (*CL* 2:368).
Conrad's gout often made the physical act of writing difficult; his mental
strain in the creative process is equally acute. For the modern writer, the
derangement and distemper of the body are an expression both of the self
and of being modern.

NOTES

1. Zdzisław Najder, *Joseph Conrad: A Life*, trans. Halina Carroll-Najder (Rochester, NY: Camden House, 2007), pp. 28–30.
2. For a full discussion of the competing ideas of miasmas and germ theory, see Laura Otis, *Membranes: Metaphors of Invasion in Nineteenth-Century Literature, Science, and Politics* (Baltimore: Johns Hopkins University Press, 1999), pp. 8–36.
3. Roy Porter, 'Medical Science', in *The Cambridge Illustrated History of Medicine*, ed. Roy Porter (Cambridge: Cambridge University Press, 1996), p. 184.
4. By isolating and culturing pure bacterial strains, Koch was able to demonstrate convincingly that the tubercle bacillus caused tuberculosis. The method of his proof consisted in satisfying what became known as Koch's postulates. Within twenty-odd years of his discovery of the tubercle bacillus (1882) and the cholera bacillus (1884), Koch and his followers were able to identify the bacterial pathogens of approximately twenty diseases.
5. Harry Leach, *The Ship Captain's Medical Guide*, 9th edn (London: Simpkin, Marshall, and Co., 1885), pp. v–vi.
6. Quoted in Najder, *A Life*, p. 124.
7. Boris Ford, *The Cambridge Guide to the Arts in Britain* (Cambridge: Cambridge University Press, 1989), vol. VIII, p. 14.
8. For a summary of the Conrad family health, see Owen Knowles and Gene M. Moore, *Oxford Reader's Companion to Conrad* (Oxford: Oxford University Press, 2000), pp. 149–51. David Miller discusses Conrad's sick-role and difficult adjustment to fatherhood in 'The Unenchanted Garden: Children, Childhood, and Conrad', *The Conradian* (Autumn 2006), 29–47, and John Stape, in *The Several Lives of Joseph Conrad* (London: William Heinemann, 2007), attends throughout to the Conrad family's illnesses and bedside manners.
9. See Jessie Conrad, *Joseph Conrad and His Circle* (London: Jarrolds, 1935), pp. 140–4.
10. See Anthony Babington, *Shell-Shock* (London: Leo Cooper, 1997), p. 80, and Elaine Showalter, *The Female Malady: Women, Madness, and English Culture, 1830–1980* (New York: Pantheon Books, 1985), p. 190.
11. Borys Conrad, *My Father: Joseph Conrad* (New York: Coward McCann, 1970), p. 155.
12. 'Influenza World Toll', *The Times*, 18 December 1918, p. 5.
13. John M. Barry, *The Great Influenza* (New York: Viking, 2004), p. 4.
14. Quoted in Najder, *A Life*, pp. 526, 568.
15. Stape, *Several Lives*, p. 199.
16. G. Jean-Aubry to Paul Wohlforth, 7 May 1936. Thanks are due to Owen Knowles for providing this information. Text TS Wellcome 8512/2; unpublished.
17. Susan Sontag, *Illness as Metaphor* (New York: Farrar, Straus, and Giroux, 1977), p. 41.
18. Sontag, *Illness as Metaphor*, pp. 72, 78.
19. Sontag, *Illness as Metaphor*, p. 44.

CHAPTER 17

Eastern Europe

Addison Bross

I

Writing in 1899 to a socialist friend who argued that peace could be achieved only by workers co-operating across national borders, Conrad confessed a deep-rooted aversion to 'international fraternity'. For him the 'national sentiment' must dominate all other political concepts, all collective aspirations. It must be carefully guarded against the erosive force of modernity (*CL* 2:158). In this remark Conrad bore witness to his roots in Eastern Europe and to a homeland erased from the map but persisting as an ideal and dream.

For most of his lifetime, four Empires in Eastern Europe had, with some success, stifled the national sentiments of several subjugated groups within their domains. Prussia (which by 1870 was leading its newly created German Empire), Russia, Austria and the Ottoman Empire held under restless subjection a number of diverse peoples, alien by culture and language to each other and to the Empire's ruling stock, peoples driven by nationalism to defy their overlords' secret police and armies, to scorn exile and death, indeed to challenge their oppressors' continued existence, ultimately to wring from them independence and to become autonomous. (The first three of these Empires, in fact, between 1772 and 1795 had thrice partitioned Poland's territories, each seizing various parts of the country's land until Poland ceased to exist.)

Combined with liberal demands for economic and political reform and cries for constitutions to limit monarchical prerogatives, the nationalist impulse would challenge the Empires in 1848, but only briefly. Despite the quick demise of the revolts of that year, nationalism, marked by a sense of violated ethnic identity and collective self-worth, would continue to rival the Empires' competition for territory and hegemony as a chief determinant of Europe's destiny. In 1914, a nationalist's act of assassination in Sarajevo would spark the conflagration that would obliterate three European

Empires and transform the fourth (Russia) into a nominally socialist state holding various peoples in subjection.

In dealing with Conrad the novelist, however, we must remember that cultural artefacts, as well as armed engagements and assassins, played a role in this era's nationalist movements. Poetry, drama, music, the visual arts and the writing of histories of subjugated peoples were crucial to keeping alive a fragile dream of independence.

Among the peoples of this region the Poles produced the most powerful writing for nurturing hope and arousing defiance, or simply for grasping cognitively the injustices history had committed against them – the loss of statehood and the defeat of three major insurrections (1794, 1830 and 1863). This was the emotionally intense literature of the Romantic insurrectionist tradition, which determined for many decades Poles' understanding of their situation and their role in history. It has been described as a literature that 'cursed God' and 'foamed with rebellion against reality'.[1] Not accidentally, the third of three Christian names given at birth to Józef Teodor Konrad Korzeniowski was taken from two fictional Konrads, who rebel against the reality forced upon Poland – central characters in two stirring narratives by the prophet-bard Adam Mickiewicz (1798–1855): *Konrad Wallenrod* (1828) and *Forefather's Eve, Part III* (1832).[2] Each of these figures, formerly oblivious to their nation's plight, undergoes a dramatic awakening, discovers his mission and pledges to relieve his people's suffering and free the homeland. The personal transformations in each work are full of passionate intensity.

Despite strict surveillance at the borders, most of these works – written in Paris or elsewhere in Western Europe and smuggled into the country, or simply memorized abroad – reached their audience. Amid these conditions, strikingly dissimilar from the contexts in which Western Europe's literatures have developed, Conrad in his early years found in the lyrical dramas of Mickiewicz, Julius Słowacki (1809–49) and Zygmunt Krasiński (1812–59) the potential that writing possesses for laying before a society a strong moral appeal, for protesting against unjust regimes and for offering an urgent, transformative interpretation of life. The moral intensity that marks Conrad's writings is, in part, his inheritance from the Romantic insurrectionist tradition.

II

In Conrad, nationalist sentiment was by no means a simple impulse. Underneath the apparently sincere avowal to his socialist friend mentioned above, his belief in the value of the national identity was undermined by doubt and wavering prompted by Poland's difficult history. Within the Romantic insurrectionist tradition, which defined this sentiment, lurked contradictions that would emerge dramatically as the century progressed. Furthermore, a rival conception of Polish patriotism, deriving from a movement called Positivism or 'organic work', would arise to challenge the Romantic insurrectionist version. The older tradition's embarrassing contradictions, along with its clash with the new one, never nullified Conrad's high estimation of nationalist feeling as a moral guide and mainstay. Nevertheless, they produced a painful dissonance, making 'Poland' a source of emotional disturbance and producing a mistrust of the dynamics of political phenomena generally that threads throughout his political fictions.

First, it should be noted that the Romantic tradition's influence on Conrad came to him in an extreme form through his father, Apollo Korzeniowski, a poet and nationalist agitator. Korzeniowski's conceptions were marked by dark melodrama, fierce condemnations of 'Muscovy' and unwavering idealizations of Poland. Melodramatic gloom pervades his poem on his son's christening, and black-and-white generalizations dominate his essay 'Poland and Muscovy' (1864),[3] written during exile in northern Russia under the sad knowledge that the January Rising, which Korzeniowski had supported, had become a bloody catastrophe. The Utopian dreams of Poles, he writes, necessarily fail amid the material world's inhospitable crassness, while in Muscovy, whose evil inhabitants are quite comfortable in this flawed realm, 'Poland's inspired fantasies have been reborn as rank, systematic lies.'[4]

Apart from its gloom and doctrinaire tone, the essay distorts the political and economic conditions on the eve of the Rising in Korzeniowski's home region of Ukraine (territory held by Poles from the sixteenth century but populated overwhelmingly by Ukrainian serfs serving Polish overlords). At issue is the likely disposition of landless Ukrainian serfs towards the planned revolt of their Polish masters, whose profits these peasants' unpaid labour provided under an agrarian system permitting land-ownership only to members of the *szlachta* (the numerous gentry class). Korzeniowski and his fellow insurrectionists knew they would need the peasants' help for a successful uprising, but – apparently forgetting that the peasants' economic interests and their natural class antagonism towards the *szlachta* would block any co-operation – they convinced themselves that such devoted self-sacrifice would be forthcoming, for 'the Polish spirit ... shines just as brightly whether under a [landowner's] velvet cape or a peasant's coat'.[5] Common among many insurrectionists was the myth of the peasant loyal to his lord, and Conrad, a half-century later, perpetuated it when he mistakenly claimed that 'all the Provinces' of pre-Partition Poland, including the overwhelmingly Ukrainian-populated eastern ones, took part in the insurrections 'with complete devotion' (*NLL*, 121).

One cannot be certain how Conrad responded to his father's morbid and mystical formulation of Polish patriotism or his distorted view of peasant–landowner relations. But given Conrad's characteristic scepticism, he must have experienced considerable dissonance between filial loyalty and his father's warped account of things. The intimate relation between father and son after Ewa Korzeniowska's death must have made the father's influence all the stronger, and, given this dissonance, intensified the son's later ambivalence towards that influence, towards the cause his father embraced and, perhaps, towards political questions generally.

Further to intensify the youthful Conrad's conflict, by the time of his departure from Cracow in 1874 a strong challenge to the Romantic tradition had appeared. In the aftermath of the failed January Rising, thinkers and activists – some known as Positivists, others as advocates of 'organic work' (*praca organiczna*), including in their number Conrad's maternal uncle, Tadeusz Bobrowski[6] – came to the fore, condemning the armed risings that had failed to win independence, exacted much in blood and property, obliterated the meagre autonomy enjoyed under Tsarist rule, and brought about a harsh programme of Russification. These anti-Romantics proposed Poland's redemption not by insurrection but by building up its feeble economy, improving its industry and education system, and fostering such socio-economic changes as the integration of the recently emancipated peasantry, freed by Alexander II in 1861.

In Conrad's story 'Prince Roman' (1911), this clash between Romantic and Positivist patriots is glossed over. The prototype of its main character, Prince Roman Sanguszko (1800–81), blended the two traditions. A hero of the November Rising, punished for his patriotism with forced labour in Russian mines, on his return from exile Sanguszko radically changed his understanding of the Polish cause, becoming a staunch advocate of 'organic work', an opponent of the January Uprising and a collaborator with the fiercely anti-insurrectionist Tadeusz Bobrowski in such strictly practical matters as estate-management and settling wills for various landowning families. In his memoirs, Bobrowski praises Sanguszko's untiring work to develop agriculture and industry in Ukraine – work pursued 'for the good of his society' – and applies to him the adjective most commonly applied to the Positivists: 'sober'.[7] In the story, however, Sanguszko's second, Positivist phase disappears: the Prince is simply an ageing patriot-martyr in the Romantic tradition, suffering from deafness (caused by his harsh life under deportation) and calmly tolerating the indifference of his daughter and son-in-law towards his Romantic insurrectionist past. The complex history of nineteenth-century Poland, physically present in the real-life Sanguszko, is replaced by Conrad with a simple Romantic story. By this truncation of the Prince's complexity, Apollo Korzeniowski's version of the national sentiment belatedly triumphed in his son's fiction.

In the rare instances where Poland appears in Conrad's writings, nationalist sentiment is highly honoured, even if only by overlooking its complexity, as in 'Prince Roman'. It is unquestionably valued in the pages of *A Personal Record* devoted to Conrad's early years, where, for instance, an uncle in one of Napoleon's Polish legions during the retreat from Moscow is admired for staving off hunger by eating dog – '*Pro patria!*' (35). In fiction that presents the tangled politics of other peoples, however, nationalist sentiment becomes realistically complex and morally ambiguous, even suspect. In *Nostromo*, it appears in such twisted forms as Decoud's highly unstable devotion to the national cause (adopted in part as a means of wooing Antonia Avellanos) and Charles Gould's destructive obsession with saving his country through alliances with 'material interests', represented by the naïve and arrogant Holroyd, the advocate of a coming American imperialism. The many questionable varieties of nationalist sentiment that pervade the novel are fittingly parodied by the senseless squawk of the Goulds' parrot: '*Viva Costaguana!*'

Despite the high value Conrad ascribed to national feeling in the letter cited above, his silent awareness of the conflicted politics of his captive homeland and the contradictions in the Romantic insurrectionist tradition made Poland an emotionally charged subject. According to Jessie Conrad, when asked by Polish friends in England about the possibility of his writing about Poland, 'Conrad seemed quite annoyed.'[8] When Aniela Zagórska read aloud to Conrad Słowacki's *Grób Agamemnona* (containing harsh complaints against the *szlachta* not unlike those levelled later, in Conrad's youth, by Positivists), his reaction surprised her: 'I looked up at Conrad and felt frightened. He sat immobile, looking angry and pained; suddenly he jumped to his feet and rushed out of the room, without saying a word or even looking at either my mother or myself, like a man deeply hurt.'[9]

Some of Conrad's comments on politics have the black-and-white, extremist quality of his father's expressions of disdain for Russia. Such strong emotion underlies Conrad's hasty attribution to all revolutionists of a carefree unscrupulousness: 'The revolutionary spirit ... frees one from all scruples as regards ideas. Its hard, absolute optimism is repulsive to my mind by the menace of fanaticism and intolerance it contains' (*PR*, xxi–xxii). He staunchly denied the revolutionary element at the centre of the Januarists' programme – their plan to win the peasants' support by granting them relief from serfdom, personal freedom and farmland. By this plan, the long-established restriction of land-ownership to the *szlachta* (the class structure on which Poland's economy and culture had long rested) would have been obliterated. Yet Conrad would have his readers believe that the Januarists did not intend 'the subversion of any social or political scheme of existence', nor did their plan for the 1863 armed insurrection involve more than 'moral resistance' (*PR*, ix–x).

A common type in Conrad's fiction is the private person caught up in political strife not by choice or from a wish to create a more just social order, but accidentally, often reluctantly and to no avail, or with unfortunate results. The most memorable characters of the political fictions have political activity violently thrust upon them. Charles Gould in *Nostromo* becomes politically involved (and obsessed) through his inherited managership of a silver mine, the working of which has been politicized by a series of sordid officials who exploit Costaguana for their own gain; the figure Nostromo does so by recruitment as a minor player in a grand political scheme undertaken by his superiors, in which he becomes corrupted morally; in *Under Western Eyes*, the chance appearance in his room of an acquaintance who has assassinated a Tsarist official leads ultimately to Razumov's recruitment, under pressure, as a police spy (that is, to self-betrayal); the unnamed mechanic in 'An Anarchist' becomes politicized by a moment of drunkenness when, egged on by men in a bar to shout anarchist slogans, he becomes finally the slave of an overseer on some remote grazing-lands of a meat-packing enterprise. In *The Secret Agent*, it is only by highly suspect motives – predominantly by selfish competition – that the more respectable characters take on the task of maintaining the social order. Inspector Heat, intent on building his career, strives to protect from suspicion the double-agent whom he in effect employs, upon whom he depends for his astounding and highly publicized discoveries of terrorist plots. As for the anarchists, they are so far from showing any grasp of radical collectivist thought or genuine commitment to changing society by violence or other methods that *The Secret Agent* cannot be said to explore the phenomenon of anarchism, or of any radical movement at all.

In most of Conrad's political fictions, the relieving foil to politics is family life and the women who sustain it amidst the cruel absurdities that crowd the public, political realm, and thus the motherly, nurturing qualities of Emilia Gould, Natalia Haldin and Winnie Verloc. These fictional women bring to mind the words in which Conrad recalled his own mother as one of the figures in his childhood, moving about the rooms in which his parents' clandestine committee held its meetings. She was:

a more familiar figure than the others, dressed in the black of the national mourning worn in defiance of ferocious police regulations. I have also preserved from that particular time the awe of her mysterious gravity which, indeed, was by no means smileless. For I remember her smiles, too. Perhaps for me she could always find a smile. (*PR*, xii)

Burdened as a youth with memories of an apparently endless struggle against an oppressor, waged by heroes caught in bitter internecine quarrels, Conrad has shown in an impressive series of narratives – as perhaps no other writer in English has done – the discouraging limitations of political involvement.

NOTES

1. Celina Wieniewska, ed., *Polish Writing Today* (Baltimore: Penguin, 1967), p. 16.
2. *Forefather's Eve* is available in English in *Polish Romantic Drama: Three Plays in English Translation*, ed. Harold B. Segel (Ithaca, NY: Cornell University Press, 1977); *Konrad Wallenrod*, in Irene Suboczewski, trans., *Konrad Wallenrod and Grażyna* (Lanham, MD: University Press of America, 1989).
3. Zdzisław Najder, ed., and Halina Carroll-Najder, trans., *Conrad under Familial Eyes* (Cambridge: Cambridge University Press, 1983), pp. 32–3, 75–88. Only a small part of 'Poland and Muscovy' is translated here.
4. 'Polska i Moskwa: Pamiętnik *** zaczęty 186 …', *Ojczyzna* (1864) 28, 1; 27, 2. Korzeniowski's essay 'Polska i Moskwa' was smuggled out of Chernikhov in Ukraine, his place of deportation, and published in this Polish émigré journal in Leipzig. To protect against Tsarist retaliation, it appeared anonymously, accompanied by a note stating that, although the author was deceased, his name was withheld to protect his family.
5. Najder, *Conrad under Familial Eyes*, p. 87.
6. Tadeusz Bobrowski, *Pamiętnik mojego życia* (Warsaw: Państwowy Instytut Wydawniczy, 1979), vol. II, p. 61.
7. Bobrowski, *Pamiętnik mojego życia*, pp. 387–8.
8. Jessie Conrad, *Joseph Conrad and His Circle* (London: Jarrolds, 1935), p. 49.
9. Najder, *Conrad under Familial Eyes*, p. 217.

CHAPTER 18

The Far East

J. H. Stape

Conrad first set foot in Asia on 14 March 1883, not at Bangkok, as planned, but at Muntok, Sumatra's principal western port, on Bangka Island. After numerous misadventures, his ship, the *Palestine*, had blown up and sunk when her cargo of coal caught fire. Arriving in small boats on the Sumatran coast, Conrad and his crewmates were then taken to Singapore by a British ship. An inquiry exonerated the ships' officers, and after a brief stay Conrad left the port, returning to Europe as a passenger. Recalled in 'Youth' (1898), these events are given a symbolic resonance altogether out of proportion with their sometimes banal reality. From another point of view, the story's emphasis on the East's glamour is consonant with the young seaman's expectations of his first encounter with it.

Conrad's own initial experience in the Far East set a pattern: his stays (always in ports and never far inland) were relatively brief, and he moved almost exclusively in shipping circles, having dealings mainly with fellow Europeans, particularly officialdom (harbour masters and consular officials). Although his fiction romanticizes the realities he encountered, it also demonstrates a surprisingly acute knowledge of a region with which he had only passing contact. To state the bald facts, he stopped at port towns on Sumatra, Java, Borneo and the Celebes, enjoyed longer stays in Singapore and Bangkok and, to broaden the Far East to include the Indian sub-continent, short ones in Madras, Calcutta and Bombay.[1] His highly nuanced appreciation of the region's life-ways was garnered during stops extending only from 1883 to 1888 when he left Singapore for the last time for Sydney. He knew nothing at all at first hand of China and Japan, although the Chinese figure in his fiction,[2] and his experience of India, which included a train journey from Madras to Bombay in 1884, provided little material for his writings.

'Conrad's Eastern World', as Norman Sherry notably characterized it, was composed of competing powers and conflicting commercial interests.[3] Large tracts of this world were under European control, with Britain, France, the

Netherlands, Portugal and Spain having a historical presence in the region. In some places, power effectively remained in local hands in arrangements that saw native states and colonial administration exist side-by-side.

Well-demarcated European maps represent what was at times, particularly in the hinterlands – as *Almayer's Folly* (1895) witnesses – only a nominal claim, fitfully maintained and more fiction than reality. For instance, the Dutch only effectively controlled Bali and the Celebes (now Sulawesi, Indonesia) early in the twentieth century, although they had gained a toehold in Java during the late fifteenth century and during the next two centuries established trading-posts throughout the Malay archipelago. In South-East Asia, only Siam (present-day Thailand) retained her independence; and on occasion this was a technicality, since the French, well entrenched in Indochina (present-day Laos, Cambodia and Viet Nam), exerted a strong influence on a state still undergoing consolidation and lacking a strong national identity, with the regions distant from Bangkok only gradually falling under central control. Nor was India, the jewel in the crown, wholly British: the Portuguese retained their foothold in Goa, gained in the early sixteenth century, and the French held on to Pondicherry, obtained in the seventeenth century. As Conrad's fiction testifies, the Arabs, who had come into South-East Asia during the thirteenth century and Islamized tracts of it, were still involved in the region's economy, as were (although their nations held no territory) Germans, Swiss and Danes, the latter an important presence in both the Royal Siamese Navy and the *gendarmerie*, just as the British dominated Siam's teak trade and were heavily involved in the mining of gems, with British ships overwhelmingly important in Siam's long-distance trade.

As a result of European economic interests in Asia, the rule of law, technology and scientific knowledge transfer, and the discoveries attendant upon the Industrial Revolution, had made their way unevenly across the region. In time, large, already-established entrepôts, such as Bangkok, adopted Western technologies, including electrification and the railway, while in the interior regions life was lived according to traditional patterns virtually unchanged for centuries, if not millennia. Batavia (later Djakarta and now Jakarta, Indonesia), a small backwater, grew under the Dutch, as did Singapore under British influence, with Sir Thomas Stamford Raffles (1781–1826) beginning the transformation of a Malay fishing village into an international trading-post that, by Conrad's time, had grown into one of the East's major colonial cities. 'The End of the Tether', a novella uneasily aware of 'changing times', describes this historical process and is aware of the boom-and-bust cycles characteristic of colonial economies where infrastructure and communication lines are installed in order to serve metropolitan needs.[4]

Along with these important economic developments, Conrad's fiction also testifies to vivid cultural contrasts, describing what at times was a violent, destabilizing contact for both parties: in *Almayer's Folly* (Chapter VI), Babalatchi, the one-eyed statesman of Sambir, in the Bornean jungle, plays a gramophone recording of an aria from Verdi's 1853 opera *Il trovatore*. Richly ironic, the scene plays up misunderstanding, cultural dominance and appropriation, and the clash of civilizations, all of which variously enter into, and underwrite, Conrad's fictions set in the Far East. The world he encountered was, moreover, one in transition, and, in some places, in dramatic upheaval. To recall Kipling's view of India's native states, with their transition to modernity only partly achieved: they touched 'the Railway and the Telegraph on the one side, and the days of Harun-al-Raschid on the other'.[5] In the Dutch East Indies, this was literally true, the first telegraph lines being laid between Batavia and Buitenzorg (present-day Bogor) in 1857 and the first railway begun on Java in 1873, while slavery, abolished by the Dutch administration in 1859, continued to flourish in the shade as local sultans continued to insist upon their time-honoured prerogatives.

The rule of law was, in any event, uneven, imposed more often than not for economic convenience rather than from noble motives, although the potency of the *mission civilisatrice*, despite efforts of revisionist historians, cannot wholly be discounted, as the early proselytizing by Roman Catholic missionaries in the region (highly successful in the case of the Philippines) amply witnesses. Piracy remained rife on the high seas as well as in riverine locations, and certain local rulers distant from the centres of power paid only lip-service to a central administration that made its presence felt occasionally. In *Almayer's Folly*, Conrad describes this state of affairs when the slaves are shunted off during a visit by Dutch officials, only to reappear again once they have departed.

The imposition of law from the outside not only met with varying success but also fomented nationalist aspirations. The Aceh War of 1873–80 in northern Sumatra, an anti-colonialist uprising against the Dutch, was of more recent memory in Conrad's time than the Indian Mutiny of 1857, and the clash between colonial powers and their subjects found several outlets as subject peoples became increasingly insistent on self-determination, also evidenced in the Philippine Revolution of 1896–8 against Spanish rule, which saw the first entry of the United States and its imperialist ambitions into the region. The Dutch novelist 'Multatuli' (pseudonym of Eduard

Douwes Dekker, 1820–87) exposed the inadequacy, corruption and brutality of administration in the Dutch East Indies in his novel *Max Havelaar*
(1860), making known to a complacent Netherlands the uglier side of her
imperialist adventure, a tack Conrad would follow in exposing Belgian
atrocities in King Leopold's Congo Free State in 'Heart of Darkness'.[6]

Conrad's fiction repeatedly demonstrates his fascination with Asia's
landscapes and cultures, a contemporary critic going so far as to acclaim
him 'the Kipling of the Malay Archipelago'.[7] His writing evidences a keen
awareness of the political arrangements he met with, of the deep cultural
complexities and extreme variety of peoples at differing stages of economic
and cultural development, and acute knowledge of both local and European
economic engagements. He also picked up a smattering of Malay, then the
lingua franca of regional shipping, learned in port as well as during his
service in the *Vidar*, in which he made four voyages out of Singapore in
1887–8 to various ports on the Celebes and Borneo, meeting the original for
his fictional Kaspar Almayer on the latter island: a Eurasian alienated from
his setting, engaged in local intrigues and adrift in several cultures.

Conrad's glancing encounters with several Asian peoples were in some
cases enriched by reading, as late-Victorian England, eager for travellers'
tales and fiction about then-exotic lands, saw a boom in scientific studies
as well as in popularizing accounts. Conrad went so far as to claim, for
instance, that his 'favourite bedside' book was *The Malay Archipelago,
The Land of the Orang-Utan and the Bird of Paradise: A Narrative of Travel
with Sketches of Man and Nature* (1869) by the naturalist Alfred Russel
Wallace (1823–1913),[8] a source that influences *Lord Jim* and *The Rescue*.
And he was keenly interested in the history of European imperialism
in the region (there were other imperialisms, empires of varying extent
having risen and fallen), particularly as exemplified by Sir James Brooke,
the first Rajah of Sarawak (1803–68). Brooke, who provides a part-model
for Lord Jim, dominated what in some views might be called the 'heroic'
phase of European imperialism in South-East Asia. As presented in
Wallace as well as in his own journals, Brooke's personality and exploits,
in addition to the world in which he operated, provided Conrad with
abundant raw material for *Lord Jim* as well as for his so-called 'Malay
trilogy', comprising *Almayer's Folly* (1895), *An Outcast of the Islands* (1896)
and *The Rescue* (1920).[9]

South-East Asia's variety of Islamic culture is variously reflected in
Conrad's fiction set in the Far East, which evidences background reading
in the Qur'an and *The Arabian Nights' Tales*, as well as in the work of
Sir Richard Burton (1821–90). He seems also to have picked up a casual

knowledge of the basic tenets of Buddhism (at least of its Theravada School, dominant in Siam) as well as of Chinese 'ancestry worship' and Malay animist belief, with a sharp appreciation of folkloric elements, local superstitions and taboos. There is, on the other hand, little acknowledgement in Conrad's fiction of Hindu mythology and culture, historically central to Siam, Cambodia and Java, and still a living presence on Bali.

Conrad inevitably presents the Asia he knew best both from his first-hand contact and from reading and thus focuses on what may broadly be called 'Malay culture', although the peoples, languages and cultural practices embraced by this term display enormous diversity, ranging geographically from the Straits Settlements (incorporated into present-day Malaysia and Singapore) under British administration, to parts of the Dutch East Indies – particularly the Javanese heartland, which Conrad encountered at Semarang – and to the Philippines. Aware of the racial variety and cultural confrontations in this vast area, Conrad's fiction depicts its Chinese, Arabs, Dyaks, Bugis, Javanese and Balinese, as well as Eurasians (Nina Almayer, or the Da Souzas in *An Outcast of the Islands*, for instance). Although the colonial administrator Hugh Clifford (1866–1941), who reviewed Conrad's early writings and whom Conrad himself reviewed, complained that Conrad 'didn't know anything about Malays', Clifford's own fiction set in the region suffers, by contrast, from too intimate a knowledge of its ways and often reads like undigested socio-anthropology.[10]

Conrad's sojourns in Australia and Mauritius brought him into contact with the Far East in diasporic forms, Australia already having well-established links to its geographic neighbours and an entrenched Chinese community whose origins lay in the gold rushes of the 1850s and 1860s, and Mauritius, formerly French, a large Indian community, established first as indentured labourers after Britain won control of the island in the wake of Napoleon's defeat. Thus, for instance, Conrad was in Port-Louis during the Hindu festival of light, Dewali, celebrated by the sizeable India population, and he recalls Sydney's Asian eating-houses in *The Mirror of the Sea* ('Sun-kum-on's was not bad' (122)), further evidence of large-scale Chinese economic migration across the region, which he had witnessed in Singapore and Bangkok. He specifically records it in the history of the coolie labourers of 'Typhoon' (1903), who, upon completing seven-year contracts in South-East Asia, are homeward bound with their earnings and, in dress and manner, appear wholly untouched by their expatriate experience.

Conrad's experience in Asia stands in vivid contrast to his later time in Africa. Asia's economic development was considerably more advanced, as was technology transfer and the introduction of modern science, and the experience of European rule was deeper and in some areas of long date. European territory and spheres of influence were relatively well marked out, although, as *Almayer's Folly* suggests, there were on-going local trade rivalries between the Dutch and the English, as there were between the French in Indochina and the English in Burma (annexed to India in 1886) over economic interests in Siam. 'Karain: A Memory' (1897) demonstrates an interest in internecine power struggles, and Conrad was no less cognizant of how individual Europeans could be complicit as suppliers of contraband arms. Captain Lingard in *The Rescue* is an example of the entrepreneurial adventurer operating on the margins of European administration, in effect engaging in private treaties with local rulers.

As he would later in the Congo Free State, Conrad witnessed the extension of communication lines as an integral factor of European economic expansion – 'The telegraph and railway follow the flag' might be an appropriate change rung on the time-honoured adage 'Trade follows the flag'. While Europe undoubtedly grew prosperous by dominating, or attempting to monopolize, trade throughout Asia, colonial administration inevitably imposed European languages on the region (at least in those territories held by the English and the French) as well as European norms: the Dutch suppressed head-hunting and ritual cannibalism in Borneo and the Celebes at the end of a gun-barrel in the late nineteenth century and the first decade of the twentieth, with James Brooke having earlier attempted, with only partial success, the suppression of endemic piracy and head-hunting in Sarawak.

Conrad's interest in imperialist history and the extension of colonial administration ran parallel with his curiosity about the history of European exploration and mapping of the Pacific region,[11] and his knowledge of the Dutch explorer Abel Tasman (1603–59) and Captain James Cook (1728–79) as is revealed in his 1924 essay 'Geography and Some Explorers' (*Last Essays*), which describes his childhood fascination with maps, exploration and explorers, at a time when the so-called 'dark places of the earth' were being annexed by Europe.

The Far East, as treated in Conrad's fiction, is partly confected of sympathetic imagination working in unison with memory and hearsay, and partly gleaned from what he characterized as 'dull wise books' (*CL* 2:130): works of history, travel accounts and scientific and anthropological studies. On whether these sources should serve as the basis for fiction, Conrad's contemporaries took opposite viewpoints, an English critic writing that 'There is certainly material for fiction in Borneo' and an American reviewer pontificating on the publication of *Almayer's Folly* that 'Borneo is a fine field for the study of monkeys, not men.'[12] At a time when international long-distance travel was limited mainly to emigration or was related to the business of Empire, Conrad's presentation of Asia, despite its inevitable 'Orientalism', served to make British readers aware of an area of the world in which their nation was importantly present, but about which they knew relatively little. Conrad's work significantly contributed to the discourse, then on-going, about Empire, and it documents in fiction, and thus with considerable nuance, the deeply human aspects of international trade relations and the cultural contact between Europe and South-East Asia towards the close of the nineteenth century.

NOTES

1. Conrad's biographers all deal with his time in the Far East in a general way. For a discussion of his contact with Siam, see Yasuko Shidara, 'Conrad and Bangkok', in *Journeys, Myths, and the Age of Travel*, ed. Karin Hansson (Karlskrona: University of Ronneby, 1998), pp. 76–96.
2. For a discussion, see Heliena Krenn, 'China and the Chinese in the Work of Joseph Conrad', *Conradiana*, 27 (1995), 83–96, and Agnes Yeow, 'Conrad and the Straits Chinese: The Politics of Chinese Enterprise and Identity in the Colonial State', *The Conradian*, 29.1 (2004), 84–98.
3. Norman Sherry, *Conrad's Eastern World* (Cambridge: Cambridge University Press, 1966).
4. See J. H. Stape in 'Conrad's Unreal City: Singapore in "The End of the Tether"', in *Conrad's Cities: Essays for Hans van Marle*, ed. Gene M. Moore (Amsterdam: Rodopi, 1992), pp. 85–96.
5. Rudyard Kipling, 'The Man who Would be King', in *The Phantom Rickshaw and Other Eerie Tales* (Allahabad: A. H. Wheeler & Co., 1888).
6. For a discussion, see Allan H. Simmons' essay on 'Africa' in the present volume.
7. Unsigned review of *Almayer's Folly, Spectator*, 19 October 1895, p. 530; rpt in *Conrad: The Critical Heritage*, ed. Norman Sherry (London: Routledge & Kegan Paul, 1973), p. 61.
8. Richard Curle, 'Joseph Conrad: Ten Years Later', *Virginia Quarterly Review*, 10 (1934), 431.
9. For a discussion of Conrad's borrowings from Wallace, see Amy Houston, 'Conrad and Alfred Russel Wallace', in *Conrad: Intertexts and Appropriations: Essays in Memory of Yves Hervouet*, ed. Gene M. Moore, Owen Knowles and J. H. Stape (Amsterdam: Rodopi, 1997), pp. 29–48.
10. 'Author's Note' (1919) to *A Personal Record*, p. iv. The most extended study of Clifford's work is Philip Holden's *Modern Subjects Colonial Texts: Hugh Clifford and the Discipline of English Literature in the Straits Settlements and Malaya, 1895–1907* (Greensboro, NC: ELT Press, 2000).

11. On this topic, see Robert G. Hampson: '"A Passion for Maps": Conrad, Africa, Australia, and South-East Asia', *The Conradian*, 28.1 (2003), 34–57.

12. Arthur Waugh, 'London Letter', *Critic*, 11 May 1895, p. 349, and unsigned review, *Nation*, 17 October 1895, p. 278; rpt in *Conrad: The Critical Heritage*, pp. 51, 60.

CHAPTER 19

Fin de siècle

Laurence Davies

Conrad began his literary career in the 1890s, a decade loud with talk of endings and beginnings, not so much a transitional period between 'Victorian' and 'Modern' as a liminal one with its own identity. Like Europe in the late eighteenth century, 'It was the best of times, it was the worst of times' and 'some of its noisiest authorities insisted on its being received, for good or evil, in the superlative degree of comparison only' (Dickens, *A Tale of Two Cities*, 1859). Although any era may feel unique to those experiencing it, the nineteenth was the first century to be comprehended as a cultural and historical whole.[1] Throughout Europe and the Americas, the sense of inhabiting a crucial period grew even stronger in its final decades, not least in Britain.[2] The Queen's Diamond Jubilee in 1897 elicited countless articles of the 'See how far we have come' variety, and as many triumphalist descriptions of the procession and service of thanksgiving, when 'The empire had come together to revere and bless the mother of the empire.'[3] It also occasioned Kipling's 'Recessional' with its warning against being 'drunk with sight of power' and its monitory refrain 'Lest we forget – lest we forget!' Scaling glory's heights could inspire a fear of falling.

In critical literature from the first half of the twentieth century, the term *fin de siècle* was associated with wilful decadence, melancholy, hedonism, dandyism, the religion of aestheticism, the aesthetics of religion and the doctrine of art for art's sake.[4] The emphases on art for art's sake, the pursuit of pleasure and the self as an artistic creation have now lessened, but the emphasis on decadence remains. We hear more about decadence in the eye of the indignant critic or observer, and less about its picturesque signifiers – less about absinthe, green carnations, patchouli, black masses celebrated on the bodies of naked virgins and fastidious prose, more about anxieties and the political and cultural movements that provoked them.

These anxieties stemmed from the conviction that society was under threat from enemies foreign and domestic, such as feminists, socialists, anarchists, freethinkers, rapacious capitalists, homosexuals, Little

Englanders and all those whom neurosis, shamelessness, selfishness, criminality, perversity, atavism, lassitude, avant-garde tendencies or in-breeding had made unfit to perpetuate the Anglo-Saxon race or beget a decent work of literature. Writing for *Blackwood's* four years before *Lord Jim*, the mountaineer Hugh Stutfield expressed the ideas of a strenuous man who took comfort in the survival of a

> large number of really cultivated people whose instincts are still sound and healthy, who disbelieve in 'moral autonomy', but cling to the old ideals of discipline and duty, of manliness and self-reliance in men, and womanliness in women; who sicken at Ibsenism and the problem play, at the putrid eroticism of a literature that is at once hysterical and foul.[5]

Other *Blackwood's* contributors such as G. W. Steevens, whose 'From the New Gibbon' appeared in the thousandth number along with the first instalment of 'The Heart of Darkness', deplored the debased popular press with its greedy owners and sensation-hungry readers. His imaginary future historian remarks that 'The student of the age will find melancholy evidence of degeneration in the printed records, and especially in the newspapers, of that time ... The empire, that magnificent fabric founded upon the generous impulse to conquer and to rule, was now formally regarded as a mere machine for the acquisition of pounds sterling.'[6] In other words, there was more than one narrative of degeneration. The term resonated among those gripped by Social Darwinism with its suggestion that evolutionary niches may be lost as well as won; those who feared that the Empire's fate would be that of previous Empires; those appalled by the doings of what the Marquess of Queensberry called 'somdomites' or the appearance of what Shaw gleefully called 'manly women and womanly men'; those who deplored the vulgarity or venality of contemporary life, whether from the point of view of the hearty out-of-doorsman, the seeker of spiritual truths or the confirmed aesthete – all those who felt they were living through a time of crisis.

The most notorious jeremiad of the period was Max Nordau's *Entartung* (1892–3; translated as *Degeneration* in 1895), whose first part is a fulmination in apocalyptic mode: 'Things as they are totter and plunge, and they are suffered to reel and fall, because man is weary, and there is no faith that is worth an effort to uphold them.'[7] For 500 pages, Nordau deplores the state of society and the arts, as exemplified by Ibsen, Tolstoy and the impressionists, following his initial bang with any number of whimpers. This hysteria did not go unchallenged: William James observed that 'If one were to apply Herr Nordau's method to the description of his own person, one could hardly help writing him down as a degenerate of the worst sort.'[8]

Two points stand out: while temptingly quotable, the silliest, most extravagant statements do not inevitably speak for a whole period; nevertheless, these statements tell us something about what people at a given moment chose not so much to believe as to quarrel over. Etymologically speaking, *decade* and *decadence* have distinct origins, but in the echo chamber of the 1890s, they resonated as if identical. A paradoxical result was that debates jumped confusingly among several time scales: an immediate one, featuring (to take 1895 as an example) such events as the trials of Oscar Wilde, the wrongful conviction of Dreyfus in France and the failure of Dr Jameson's attempted coup in the Transvaal, all of which had cultural as well as political reverberations; an imperial one, invoking centuries past and, whether promising fresh splendours or collapse, centuries still to come; a biological one, concerning the past and future of the human species; and one drawing upon the latest theories in physics and astronomy.

'*Fin de siècle*', Oscar Wilde's Lord Henry murmurs; '*Fin du globe*' replies his hostess, Lady Narborough.[9] Imagining a scale yet more cosmic than Nordau's, essayists and fiction writers such as Camille Flammarion, Anatole France and H. G. Wells contemplated the future of the universe, understood to be vastly larger and more ancient than believed a century or even fifty years before. Conrad was aware of such ideas and the pessimism they fostered. His long letter to R. B. Cunninghame Graham of 14–15 January 1898, with its doubts about reason, faith, language and the worth of human endeavour, anticipates twentieth-century patterns of thought while making a concise statement of *fin-de-siècle* cosmic bleakness: 'The mysteries of a universe made of drops of fire and clods of mud do not concern us in the least. The fate of a humanity condemned ultimately to perish from cold is not worth troubling about. If you take it to heart it becomes an unendurable tragedy' (*CL* 2:16–17). His immediate purpose would have been to challenge his friend Graham's devotion to Socialism (itself a sign of the times), but, in doing so, Conrad evokes the sombre background to his own stoical commitment to rendering 'the highest possible justice to the visible universe' (*NN*, 'Preface', xi). For all the scepticism and the pose of indifference, Conrad did trouble himself about the fate of the human beings visible to him and had his ways of taking them to heart.

Drawing upon such disparate earlier writers as Anatole France, Maupassant and Pater, the 'Preface' to *The Nigger of the 'Narcissus'* is a claim to literary independence. The novel was serialized in the *New Review* (August–December 1897), edited by W. E. Henley, a bluff man whose contempt for pain extended to his own considerable sufferings, an admirer of the force and determination that sifted 'the nations, / The slag from the metal, / The waste and the weak / From the fit and the strong' ('The Song of the Sword', 1890, dedicated to Kipling). He was, in other words, counter-decadence incarnate.[10] Disparaging references to 'pity' in the narrative suggest that Conrad concurred with Henley's agenda: 'Falsehood triumphed. It triumphed through doubt, through stupidity, through pity, through sentimentalism' (*NN*, 138).[11] Yet in the 'Preface' that accompanied the final instalment, Conrad diverged from Henley's line, distinguishing between sentimental pity and the pity owed to justice and compassion: although we are subject to the 'warlike conditions of our existence', 'part of our nature is … like the vulnerable body within a steel armour'. The artist 'speaks to our capacity for delight and wonder, to the sense of mystery surrounding our lives; to our sense of pity, and beauty, and pain' (*NN*, xii). Conrad distances himself from Henley without opting for any other allegiance: 'Realism, Romanticism, Naturalism, even the unofficial sentimentalism … all these gods must abandon' the writer; 'In that uneasy solitude the supreme cry of Art for Art itself, loses the exciting ring of its apparent immorality' (*NN*, xv). His solidarity with 'the disregarded multitude of the bewildered, the simple and the voiceless' (*NN*, xii) accords with neither the aesthetic position that only beautiful and witty people matter[12] nor the counter-decadent position that the race is always to the strong.

In the 1890s, Conrad's situation was paradoxical. He had lived more dangerously than most aesthetes, or, for that matter, most counter-decadents, and as a sailor had endured years of work demanding unlimited patience and the ability to keep one's head in the worst of circumstances, yet he had previously tried to kill himself, was prone to nervous illnesses, probably thought himself neurasthenic and perhaps feared insanity.[13] Although he played down the extent of his reading, his knowledge of French literature included the work of such decadent favourites as Gautier, Baudelaire and Barbey d'Aurevilly (*CL* 3:403, 224; 4:84, 78–9), and his admiration for Flaubert embraced *Salammbô*, a lush evocation of Carthaginian voluptuousness and cruelty, as well as *Madame Bovary*, with its relatively decorous Norman adulteries. He was also steeped in Polish Romantic literature, whose emphasis on suffering, courage and national vocation might have appealed to the counter-decadents, yet the Poles marshalled their virtues not in support of Empire but against it.

Conrad's work neither exemplifies the Nineties nor ignores its motifs and cultural obsessions. In *Almayer's Folly* (1895), Almayer, an object lesson in decay given to what Wilde calls 'the malady of reverie',[14] allows himself to slide into weakness, incompetence, drug addiction and self-pity, while the lovers, free of European restraints, play out their story against an exotic backdrop like that of orientalist opera. In *An Outcast of the Islands* (1896), Willems falls for Aïssa, whose hypnotic charms and willingness to kill seem to place her as that familiar menace in late-Victorian literature and painting, the *femme fatale*.[15] Yet such widely different critics as Ian Watt, Chris Bongie and Rebecca Stott have observed that the rich exoticism of these novels is purged by regular doses of irony.[16] The characters, moreover, fit no simple ideological grids: Almayer and Willems are not poets or dandies but shabby and ill-guided opportunists whose dreams are travesties, and Willems is hopelessly unsuited to playing the lover of a *femme fatale*; Mrs Almayer and Mrs Willems give the lie to the pathos of racial crossing, as dwelt upon by writers such as Pierre Loti;[17] the Arabs and Malays are colonizers, too; Babalatchi serenades his Muslim overlord with a miniature barrel organ playing an aria from Verdi's opera of Christian malfeasance *Il trovatore*; despite the narrator's allusions to Dain's 'savage nature' (*AF*, 69), he is more civilized than Almayer, and, although made in the heat of passion and disgust, Nina's decision to cleave to her Malay ancestry is, in the circumstances, sensible. Stott makes a revealing comparison with *Dracula*, a canonical representation of late-nineteenth-century fears: 'Unlike Stoker, whose vampire-hunters police the boundaries of binary oppositions between self and Other, male and female, good and evil, truth and falsity, health and sickness, Conrad writes of transgression, of the blurring of those boundaries and the dissolution of self.'[18]

When trying to place the stories of *Tales of Unrest* (1898), Conrad had his closest contacts with the 'decadent' magazines of the day. Writing to Edward Noble, another sailor with literary ambitions, in 1895, he described contributors to the *Yellow Book* as 'very aest[h]etic very advanced and think no end of themselves. They are certainly writers of talent' (*CL* 1:231). Two years later, Conrad thought of submitting 'The Return' there, but Edward Garnett, who knew the world of aesthetes and the wider market, apparently dissuaded him (*CL* 1:369, 386, 394), suggesting instead *Chapman's Magazine*, which specialized in stories about desperate marriages. Meanwhile, Conrad's first publication, 'The Idiots', had been taken by Arthur Symons, editor of the *Savoy*, a luxuriously produced magazine with art-work by Aubrey Beardsley, arguably more daring than the better-known *Yellow Book*. A list of favourite topics in the *Savoy* would include French and Celtic cultures, Roman Catholicism, peasant life, sexual revulsion and insanity. 'The Idiots' could not have found a more appropriate venue. Yet Conrad's treatment was not quite like anyone else's. He eschewed Yeats' reverence for peasant life and the detached, even clinical, coldness of the essays on rural psychopathology by Nordau's mentor, the criminologist Cesare Lombroso – one of which, 'A Mad Saint', had appeared there in April 1896, six months earlier than Conrad's story. Although Susan Bacadou kills her husband, she is neither specimen, nor demon, nor model of rustic nobility, but a desperate woman who has suffered terribly and defended herself against marital rape. Every one of the *Tales of Unrest* engages with the preoccupations of the Nineties: the exotic in 'Karain' and 'The Lagoon'; in 'The Return', the revolt of a wife who is not quite a New Woman, nor quite an Old one, and the revulsion of a husband who realizes, far too late, 'that morality is not a method of happiness' (*TU*, 183); the banality of bourgeois and petit-bourgeois culture in 'The Return' and 'An Outpost of Progress'; derangement in 'An Outpost of Progress' and 'The Idiots'; the power of involuntary memory in 'Karain'; also in 'Karain', identity as performance; and, to one extent or another, the unhomely and uncanny in them all, whether in the 'delightful world of crescents and squares' (*TU*, 134) or 'a little house, perched on high piles' by a 'stagnant lagoon' (*TU*, 189). Such topics were not unique to the Nineties, but, even if they had been, Conrad combined them in notably unusual ways.

The most remarkable case of Conrad's blending and transmuting *fin-de-siècle* elements into something that confronts but does not epitomize the cultural moment is 'The Heart of Darkness' (1899). Although the Congo Free State is unnamed, enough was known about its cruelties and philanthropic hypocrisies to identify the approximate location.[19] Yet Conrad's narrative is also measured by less immediate time scales: by the history of English trade and conquest, by the Roman Empire's fate, by the expanse of biological time, stretching back to 'the earliest beginnings of the world'. By these metrics, the 'little begrimed steam-boat' is 'like a sluggish beetle' (*Y*, 92, 95).

This conjunction of long-ago and present frames Kurtz, who, although of his time and place, belongs in a wider perspective. An *homme fatal*, he casts his spell upon the African woman and her kinsfolk, the Company hierarchy, the Harlequin, the Intended and, briefly, upon Marlow. An aesthete of all trades, symbolist painter, musician, journalist, procurer of ivory, master of arcane and sinister rituals, populist politician *manqué*, universal genius, he is the voice of what claims to be a 'new' imperialism, a member of the 'gang of virtue' which preaches Europe's superior virtues, an apostle of paternal benevolence and, eventually, genocide. More than any pathological show-piece from Lombroso, he behaves like an atavistic monster, literally crawling back to the jungle, fulfilling the worst nightmares of scientists such as Ray Lankester, who argued that 'the white races of Europe ... are as likely to degenerate as progress'.[20] And yet, in an orthodox sense, his may not even be a case of degeneration, for the wilderness has not so much brought him down as found him out. Has he ever been anything but a hollow man, like the more incompetent and thus less dangerous Kayerts and Carlier of 'An Outpost of Progress', the product of a hollow culture? Or the product of a dying one? The Company has sited its headquarters in a sepulchral city where weeds grow in the streets. Rather than Brussels, its actual locale, the city recalls Bruges, the scene of Georges Rodenbach's *Bruges-la-morte* (1892), one of the most influential of French 'decadent' novels.

In the period's popular African romances, such as H. Rider Haggard's *Allan Quatermain* (1887) or Willis Boyd Allen's *The Lion City of Africa* (1892), travellers to Africa find lost races or relics of former cultural glory; the alternative, as presented in sensational magazine entertainments by the likes of C. J. Cutcliffe-Hyne, is bloodthirsty fetishism. Conrad's novella offers neither: the unspeakable rites are presided over by an arch-European, and Marlow lacks the easy assurance that enables other fictional travellers to know the secrets of indigenous life.

Kurtz's fate is ironic, but he never seems capable of irony. Marlow does; his most telling comments about Kurtz come in the form of withering understatement, the product of savage indignation and restraint. For all its intensities, 'Heart of Darkness' is a chain of contradictions. Where the counter-decadents praised bluntness and self-confidence, and the aesthetes – Wilde especially – the art of beautiful lying, Marlow's portion of the narrative ends with a lie that might be taken as evasive, cowardly or kind, but, in any case, is shameful and inglorious. While many of his contemporaries claimed the sky was going to fall and others hailed a brilliant dawn, Conrad took the path of indirection and unknowing.

NOTES

1. Among periodicals, we find such names as *The Nineteenth Century* (London, founded 1877), *Il secolo XIX* (Genoa, 1886) and *El siglo diez y nueve* (Mexico City, 1841).
2. Stronger too in such dramatically changing polities as Meiji Japan and the Ottoman Empire, though without the calendar fetish.
3. G. W. Steevens, *Things Seen*, ed. G. S. Street (Edinburgh: Blackwood, 1900), p. 197, originally from an eyewitness account in the *Daily Mail*.
4. Such features were not unique to the Nineties. Influenced by Gautier, Baudelaire and Pater, the aesthetic movement in Britain emerged in the early Seventies, and by 1881 was familiar enough to be satirized in Gilbert and Sullivan's *Patience* and caricatured in *Punch*.
5. Hugh E. M. Stutfield, 'Tommyrotics', *Blackwood's Magazine*, 157 (1895), 845.
6. Quoted here from Steevens, *Things Seen*, p. 24; the unsigned original was in *Blackwood's Magazine*, 165 (1899), 241–9. Conrad told William Blackwood that 'Gibbon especially fetched me quite' (*CL* 2:162).

7. *Degeneration* (London: Heinemann, 1895), p. 13.

8. William James in *Psychological Review*, 2 (May 1895), 289–90.

9. Oscar Wilde, *The Picture of Dorian Gray* (1891; Oxford: World's Classics, 1998), p. 147.

10. Jerome Hamilton Buckley's *William Ernest Henley* (Princeton: Princeton University Press, 1945) remains a valuable source for the 'counter-decadence'.

11. Commonplace in Henley's circle, these ideas had multiple origins in Social Darwinism, Nietzsche's critique of slave morality and the literature of ancient Rome. Conrad's extant letters do not mention Nietzsche until 1899 (*CL* 2:188, 209, 218, 344).

12. Vivian, the protagonist of Wilde's 'The Decay of Lying: A Dialogue', asserts that 'We don't want to be harrowed and disgusted by the lower orders': *Nineteenth Century*, 25 (January–June 1889), 39.

13. See Martin Bock, *Joseph Conrad and Psychological Medicine* (Lubbock: Texas Tech University Press, 2002), pp. 21–60. Nordau approved of at least one Conrad novel, probably *The Nigger of the 'Narcissus'* (*CL* 2:121).

14. Wilde, *The Picture of Dorian Gray*, p. 107.

15. Bram Dijkstra's *Idols of Perversity* is a field-guide to this phenomenon.

16. Ian Watt, *Conrad in the Nineteenth Century* (Berkeley: University of California Press, 1979), pp. 41–55; Chris Bongie, *Exotic Memories: Literature, Colonialism and the Fin de Siècle* (Stanford: Stanford University Press, 1991), pp. 151–7; Rebecca Stott, *The Fabrication of the Late-Victorian Femme Fatale* (Basingstoke: Macmillan, 1992), pp. 126–62.

17. See his novels *Aziyadé* (1879) and *Madame Chrysanthème* (1887).

18. Stott, *The Fabrication of the Late-Victorian Femme Fatale*, p. 143.

19. Sir Charles Dilke denounced the behaviour of the Belgian Upper Congo Company in 'Civilisation in Africa', *Cosmopolis* (July 1896), 18–35; 'An Outpost of Progress' appeared in the same magazine a year later.

20. Lankester, *Degeneration: A Chapter in Darwin* (1880), cited in Sally Ledger and Roger Luckhurst, eds., *The Fin de Siècle: A Reader in Cultural History, c. 1880–1900* (Oxford: Oxford University Press, 2000), p. 4. Cedric Watts, in *Heart of Darkness: A Critical and Contextual Study* (Milan: Mursia, 1977), pp. 132–6, discusses Kurtz as an example of Nordau's 'highly gifted degenerate'.

CHAPTER 20

The First World War

Richard Niland

During the First World War, Conrad believed himself peripheral to a transitional historical moment, writing in November 1914: 'the thoughts of this war sit on one's chest like a nightmare. I am painfully aware of being crippled, of being idle, of being useless with a sort of absurd anxiety' (*CL* 5:427). In August 1915, he felt the 'world of 15 years ago is gone to pieces; what will come in its place God knows, but I imagine doesn't care' (*CL* 5:503). The political forces of nineteenth-century Europe that had fashioned Conrad's literature, notably imperialism and nationalism, were undermined and unleashed anew by the violence of the Great War and the uncertain legacy of the conflict. Conrad's close observation of Poland's fate throughout the war inspired 'A Note on the Polish Problem' (1916) and 'The Crime of Partition' (1919). While 1918 saw the political rebirth of Poland, antagonisms provoked by the redrawing of Europe's historical boundaries made Conrad uneasy. On Armistice Day, he wrote: 'The great sacrifice is consummated – and what will come of it to the nations of the earth the future will show. I can not confess to an easy mind. Great and very blind forces are set free catastrophically all over the world' (*CL* 6:302).

H. G. Wells observed in *Mr Britling Sees It Through* (1916) that 'the world-wide clash of British and German interests … had been facts in the consciousness of Englishmen for more than a quarter of a century. A whole generation had been born and brought up in the threat of this German war.'[1] From Erskine Childers' *The Riddle of the Sands* (1903) to William le Queux's *Invasion of 1910* (1906), the threat of Germany resonated throughout British society, and Michael Howard has written that, if the youth of the rival countries howled for war in 1914, 'it was because for a generation or more they had been taught to howl'.[2] Awareness of pervasive anti-German writing appears in *The Secret Agent* (1907), where Winnie Verloc describes how pamphlets of the Future of the Proletariat relate the story 'of a German soldier officer tearing half-off the ear of a recruit, and nothing was done to him for it. The brute! … The story was enough, too, to make one's blood boil. But what's the use of printing things like that? We aren't German slaves here, thank God' (*SA*, 60). *Victory* (1915), completed before the war, reveals Conrad's own engagement with anti-German sentiment prevalent in Britain. The 'Note to the First Edition' explained that animosity towards the Teutonic Schomberg was part of Conrad's Polish cultural inheritance: 'far from being the incarnation of recent animosities, he is the creature of my old, deep-seated and, as it were, impartial conviction' (*V*, viii). While antipathy to Germany had not prevented Conrad's sympathetic delineation of Stein in *Lord Jim*, it certainly informed 'Autocracy and War', which appeared in the *Fortnightly Review* in 1905. Conrad wanted the piece to be a 'sensation' (*CL* 3:272), and, while perceptively outlining recent trends in European history, he also orchestrated a crescendo of anti-Prussianism, concluding with 'a warning that, so far as a future of liberty, concord, and justice is concerned: *Le Prussianisme – voilà l'ennemi!*' (*NLL*, 114). In the *Review of Reviews* in July 1905, journalist W. T. Stead condemned Conrad, claiming he had the 'logic of the alarmist'.[3]

'Autocracy and War' positions Conrad as a representative of the Edwardian generation that engendered the language of rivalry before 1914. As Keith Carabine has noted, the 'ostensible stance of "Autocracy and War" is that of Joseph Conrad, the eminent English novelist, known to be of Polish origins, taking advantage of his unique position to warn his Edwardian public' of the threat posed by Germany.[4] Conrad prepared for hostilities at a time when journals 'exacerbated the existing tension' and only 'Germany had the capacity to upset the *status quo*; she alone, therefore, posed a threat to the peace of Europe'.[5] Conrad contributed in some degree to the discourse of antagonism in Europe, and he would later feel the accusation that such ideologies had encouraged war and sent youth off to fight and die.

Wyndham Lewis believed the 'curtain went down' on Conrad and Henry James in 1914.[6] Because he was in Poland between August and November 1914, Conrad was not summoned at the outbreak of the war by C. F. G. Masterman, head of the British War Propaganda Bureau, to a meeting of writers at Wellington House in London. Nevertheless, his wartime work responds to the consequences of this meeting. According to Samuel Hynes, Masterman, in recruiting ageing war propagandists such as Hardy, Kipling and Wells, initiated the concept of 'the Old Men, as the makers of the war and enemies of the young'.[7] This polarization of home front and battlefield saw Conrad accept the relative obsolescence of the writer during war: 'It seems almost criminal levity to talk at this time of books, stories, publication. This war attends my uneasy pillow like a nightmare. I feel oppressed even in my sleep and the moment of waking brings no relief' (*CL* 5:439). Conrad's fatigue was revealed when 'Poland Revisited', previously published in the *Daily News* and the *Boston Evening Transcript* in 1915, was offered to Edith Wharton for *The Book of the Homeless* (1916), a volume of propaganda whose proceeds aided Belgian refugees. 'Poland Revisited' recalled Conrad's 1914 journey to Poland in heightened Romantic language, featuring an elegiac, pastoral representation of pre-war Britain along with memories of Conrad's original arrival in a Dickensian London. Conrad recognized 'the futilities of an individual past', the traditional material for his fiction, noting instead the emergence of modern European history in 'the faint boom of the big guns at work on the coast of Flanders – shaping the future' (*NLL*, 173). 'Poland Revisited' captures Conrad's sense of history in flux: his journey to Poland revisiting and symbolically entombing the world of the nineteenth century.

Once he engaged with the conflict, when his son Borys enlisted in the Army Service Corps, Conrad proposed to write an 'early personal experience thing' (*CL* 5:441). This confirmed his position in 'Poland Revisited' that 'things acquire significance by the lapse of time' (*NLL*, 157). The renewed significance lay in Conrad's attempt to empathize with the experience of soldiers. Conrad insisted that there was 'no question here of any parallelism. That notion never entered my head. But there was a feeling of identity, though with an enormous difference of scale – as of one single drop measured against the bitter and stormy immensity of an ocean' (*SL*, vi–vii). Conrad's wartime fiction, *The Shadow-Line*, 'The Warrior's Soul' and 'The Tale', constitutes a dialogue with youth, one member of the older generation asking for understanding. Recalling the wartime composition of *The Arrow of Gold* (1919), Conrad wrote: 'If anything it is perhaps a little sympathy that the writer expects for his buried youth, as he lives it over again at the end of his insignificant course on this earth' (*AG*, 4–5). In this respect, the war influenced Conrad's posthumous reputation. In 1917, Conrad began producing Author's Notes, stressing 'the authenticity of the stories as based on his personal experiences and observations; this was later to become the dominant motif of his author's notes'.[8] Conrad alleviated his marginalization by portraying his own youthful initiation into experience.

The Shadow-Line had 'a sort of spiritual meaning' (*CL* 5:458). The story's dedication – 'To / Borys and all others / who like himself have crossed / in early youth the shadow-line / of their generation / With Love' – addresses the living and stands as a memorial to those already lost in the war. Conrad resurrected his characteristic literary voice, now endowed with a new

importance, as the remembered younger self articulated Conrad's identification with youth at the Front while the controlling narrative voice,
typically the ageing nostalgic, embodied Conrad's wartime position. *The
Shadow-Line* aligns the experience of the soldier with the experience of the
onlooker/artist. For the young captain facing the difficulties of his first
command, the sense of stasis before the storm at sea corresponded to the
anticipation of battle: 'In the tension of silence I was suffering from it
seemed to me that the first crash must turn me into dust. And thunder was,
most likely, what would happen next. Stiff all over and hardly breathing, I
waited with a horribly strained expectation. Nothing happened. It was
maddening' (*SL*, 113). *The Shadow-Line* saluted the youth of Europe
(Conrad's dedication, notably, is not partisan) going through the fire of
initiation to experience, while simultaneously portraying an ageing narrator
sidelined by history. In 'The Warrior's Soul', Conrad later wrote: 'And what
more desolate prospect for a man with such a soul than to be imprisoned on
the eve of war; to be cut off from his country in danger, from his family,
from his duty, from honour, and – well – from glory, too' (*TH*, 16). *The
Shadow-Line*, however, unites youth and age as Captain Giles collaborates
with the young captain, and the dénouement resolves the generational
discord that began the work.

As *The Shadow-Line* ran in the *English Review* and Conrad received
favourable reviews of *Victory* and *Within the Tides*, Siegfried Sassoon's
poetry was appearing in the *Cambridge Magazine*. Conrad was familiar
with Sassoon's anti-war stance. Anticipating a visit from him in 1918,
Conrad wrote: 'I know his verse only in extracts and I want to see it all
before I meet the man' (*CL* 6:310). Conrad's response to being on the
fringes of the war forms part of a wider trend in the psyche of Britain
between 1914 and 1918. In the *Tatler* in October 1916, Richard King wrote
that 'War – as we presently understand it – is the sacrifice of the young and
the innocent on the altar erected by the old and middle-aged.'[9] In April
1916, the *Cambridge Magazine* had published 'The Betrayal of the Young',
which acknowledged that 'between the old and the young there is to-day a
great gulf fixed'. A soldier noted that 'In the cavalry messes things are often
said which wouldn't please Lord Northcliffe and the old men who made the
war', while a private about to return to France vehemently announced the
soldier's alienation: 'You people at home are responsible for continuing this
slaughter. Secretly you know it. Individually you mostly acknowledge it.'[10]

'The Warrior's Soul', a tale of the Napoleonic Wars, appeared in *Land
and Water* in March 1917, registering Conrad's continued response to
generational conflict in English society. The story opened with a possible

address to soldiers, as the 'old officer with long white moustaches gave rein to his indignation', asking: 'Is it possible that you youngsters should have no more sense than that! Some of you had better wipe the milk off your upper lip before you start to pass judgement on the few poor stragglers of a generation which has done and suffered not a little in its time' (*TH*, 1). The veteran reminds the reader that 'we had our losses too' (*TH*, 5). 'The Warrior's Soul', however, accepts misgivings about the old guard: 'the innocent … found himself in distinguished company there, amongst men of considerable position. And you know what that means: thick waists, bald heads, teeth that are not – as some satirist puts it. Imagine amongst them a nice boy, fresh and simple, like an apple just off the tree' (*TH*, 9). Conrad echoes Sassoon's 'The Fathers', where old men sit at home in decaying complacency while the young soldier experiences battle. 'The Warrior's Soul' also treats perceived public enthusiasm for the war: 'People without compassion are the civilians, government officials, merchants and such like. As to the ferocious talk one hears from a lot of decent people in war time – well, the tongue is an unruly member at best, and when there is some excitement going there is no curbing its furious activity' (*TH*, 17). Most poignantly though, Conrad evoked a landscape disturbed by innumerable dead. In the 'general mourning I seemed to hear the sighs of mankind falling to die in the midst of a nature without life … a pathetic multitude of small dark mounds stretching away under the moonlight in a clear, still, and pitiless atmosphere – a sort of horrible peace' (*TH*, 20).

Conrad's peripheral experience of the war was increased by his paternal anxiety about his son's safety (Borys Conrad was shell-shocked but survived the war), the loss of soldier friends such as Edward Thomas, but also because of his reputation as a writer of adventurous stories and his knowledge that soldiers read his work. Writing to Conrad after a visit to the Front, press magnate Lord Northcliffe related: 'More than once have I found "Victory" being read by officers at the front. These men of action love your work.'[11] In February 1915, Jean Schlumberger, later co-founder of the *Nouvelle Revue Française*, serving in France, wrote to Conrad of his delight in coming across a copy of 'The Secret Sharer'. Conrad expressed satisfaction that his work resonated with the experience of the soldier: 'Proud that my little tale can be read amidst the din of war' (*CL* 5:443). Importantly, the outlets for Conrad's new fiction, the *English Review, Land and Water* and the *Strand*, were all to be found at the Front. Conrad was therefore conscious that he had a contemporary audience amongst soldiers, as the 'reviews, especially *Blackwood's*, the *English Review*, and the *Cornhill* were much appreciated' by the military.[12] In these periodicals, soldiers could estimate the indifference of the home front to the fate of the soldier. According to Paul Fussell, the 'standard officers' dugout required ... current copies of the *Bystander*, the *Tatler*, and *Punch*'.[13] In Theodore Wesley Koch's estimation, Conrad was popular in the trenches, and 'periodicals played a great part ... with the wounded soldier, *The Strand*, *The Windsor*, *The Red*, *Pearson's*, *The Wide World*, and *John Bull*'.[14] In 1917, Conrad maintained *The Shadow-Line* was written for soldiers, not the general market for fiction: 'I did not like the idea of it being associated with fiction in a vol of stories. And this is also the reason I've inscribed it to Borys – and the others' (*CL* 6:37). The 'Effect of the War on Literature', in the *Scotsman* on 15 May 1916, announced that 'Joseph Conrad had come into his own' in popularity since August 1914.[15]

'The Tale', characterized by 'infinite sadness', captures a society mourning soldiers from whom 'no answering murmur came' (*TH*, 59), and Conrad's work resonates with later interpretations of the war, articulated in the outpouring of war memoirs in the 1920s. Securities and realities from the pre-war world are redundant. In 'The Tale', the writer has become irrelevant, and the woman in the story delivers judgement on those who held authority before the war: 'You used to tell – your – your simple and – and professional – tales very well at one time ... You had a – a sort of art – in the days – the days before the war' (*TH*, 60). The war had altered artistic representation. Previously, stories such as Conrad's could be written, but the war had shifted aesthetic and ideological presuppositions. According to Walter Benjamin, 'men returned from the battlefield grown silent – not richer but poorer in communicable experience', and Fussell notes that 'the presumed inadequacy of language itself to convey the facts about trench warfare is one of the motifs of all those who wrote about the war'.[16] Language is scrutinized in 'The Tale' as an Officer and his acquaintance discuss the meaning of the word 'duty'. The officer claims the word 'contains infinities', but he is interrupted, his authority harshly undermined: 'What is this jargon?' (*TH*, 61).

Published in the *Strand Magazine* in October 1917, 'The Tale' resulted from Conrad's engagement in propaganda work and from his correspondence with Ford Madox Ford, stationed in France in 1916, about the difficulties of artistically representing the war. At the Admiralty's request, Conrad toured naval bases, went on a minesweeping expedition in the *Brigadier* in the North Sea, and tracked German submarines in the Q-ship *Ready* in autumn 1916. However, the importance of Conrad's propaganda activities should not be overstated. The short articles 'Flight' and 'The Unlighted Coast' 'contained no trace of propaganda and not even much optimism. This failure must have discouraged Conrad from further efforts, and, despite his own occasional mention of projects, he did not write any more articles about the war.'[17] One reason for this can be found in Conrad's scepticism about official doctrines of war aims. Despite his cordial relations with Lord Northcliffe, for whose *Daily Mail* Conrad wrote the article 'Tradition' in 1918, in a letter to John Quinn, Conrad expressed dissatisfaction with newspaper reporting of the war: 'A miserable affair no matter how much newspapers may try to write it up' (*CL* 5:446). Conrad remained sceptical during the Versailles Peace Conference, remarking that there 'is an awful sense of unreality in all this babble of League of Nations and Reconstruction … I ask myself who on earth is being deceived by all these ceremonies' (*CL* 6:349-51).

Ford Madox Ford described the Armistice as a 'crack across the table of history',[18] indicating the war had ruptured Europe's historical continuity. Despite his post-war observation of international politics, Conrad's Proustian engagement with memory meant the emerging legend of the *belle époque* held an easy fascination. While many post-war writers, such as Ford, Joseph Roth and Thomas Mann, returned to pre-war culture in their work, Conrad looked further back, returning to his youth in Marseilles in *The Arrow of Gold* (1919), concluding former artistic ideas in *The Rescue* (1920), and visiting the formative points of nineteenth-century history in *The Rover* (1923) and *Suspense* (1925). By placing himself in the nineteenth century and by employing conventional methods of representation, Conrad, with his health declining, experienced the solace of memory and historical escapism, but, with the ascendancy of high-modernist writers such as Joyce, Pound, Lewis and Eliot, and later Faulkner and Céline, perhaps saw his worst wartime fears of artistic marginalization ultimately realized.

NOTES

1. H. G. Wells, *Mr Britling Sees It Through* (London: Cassell, 1916), p. 123.
2. M. E. Howard, *Studies in War and Peace* (London: Temple Smith, 1970), p. 102.
3. W. T. Stead, '"Ghost, Ghoul, Djinn, Etc.": The Fantastic Rhetoric of Mr Conrad', *Review of Reviews*, 33.187 (July 1905), 51–2.
4. Keith Carabine, *The Life and the Art: A Study of Conrad's 'Under Western Eyes'* (Amsterdam: Rodopi, 1996), p. 84.
5. Keith Nelson and Zara S. Steiner, *Britain and the Origins of the First World War*, 2nd edn (Basingstoke: Macmillan, 2003), pp. 179, 189.
6. Wyndham Lewis, *Creatures of Habit and Creatures of Change: Essays on Art, Literature and Society 1914–1956*, ed. Paul Edwards (Santa Rosa, CA: Black Sparrow Press, 1989), p. 222.

7. Samuel Hynes, *A War Imagined: The First World War and English Culture* (London: Bodley Head, 1990), p. 26.

8. Zdzisław Najder, *Joseph Conrad: A Life* (Rochester, NY: Camden House, 2007), p. 495.

9. In Hynes, *A War Imagined*, p. 247.

10. *Cambridge Magazine*, 5.18 (1916), 407, 408.

11. J. H. Stape and Owen Knowles, eds., *A Portrait in Letters: Correspondence to and about Conrad* (Amsterdam: Rodopi, 1996), p. 108.

12. Theodore Wesley Koch, *Books in the War: The Romance of Library War Service* (Cambridge: The Riverside Press, 1919), pp. 182–3.

13. Paul Fussell, *The Great War and Modern Memory* (London: Oxford University Press, 1975), p. 67.

14. Koch, *Books in the War*, p. 258.

15. 'Effect of the War on Literature', *The Scotsman*, 15 May 1916, p. 7.

16. Walter Benjamin, *Illuminations*, ed. Hannah Arendt (London: Pimlico, 1999), p. 84; Fussell, *The Great War*, p. 170.

17. Najder, *A Life*, p. 490.

18. Ford Madox Ford, *A Man Could Stand Up* (London: Duckworth, 1926), p. 13.

CHAPTER 21

Intellectual movements

Richard Niland

In *The Historical Novel* (1937), Georg Lukács wrote that Walter Scott 'had no knowledge of Hegel's philosophy and had he come across it would probably not have understood a word'.[1] Conversely, Joseph Conrad's fiction incorporated a wealth of historical, philosophical and aesthetic ideas resulting from the writer's overt dialogue with nineteenth-century European thought. The philosophy of Rousseau, Herder, Hegel, the Polish Romantics and Positivists, Schopenhauer, Nietzsche and Bergson represents the intellectual backdrop to Conrad's explorations of individual and communal identity.

Conrad was born into a Polish culture dominated by nationalism and patriotism. The 'most powerful element' of Conrad's Polish inheritance 'was the work of the great Romantic poets, Adam Mickiewicz (1798–1855), Juliusz Słowacki (1809–49), and Zygmunt Krasiński (1812–59). Their Romanticism was of the continental kind, saturated with the spirit of communal and especially national responsibilities.'[2] Polish Romantic poetry formed part of the broader intellectual current of Polish Romantic historicism, the treatment of the philosophy of history by patriotic Polish writers, which flourished in the 1830s and 1840s. Essential to its development was its dialogue with the thought of G. W. F. Hegel, whose work gave philosophical validation to the power of the Prussian state. Hegel's philosophy posited that history is guided by a 'Geist', or 'Spirit', ensuring its logical progress towards freedom, which Hegel saw manifesting itself in the 'State'. Hegel's philosophy greatly informed contemporary historical debate. The 'controversy about Hegel was especially intense in partitioned Poland and [it] gave birth to a number of quite interesting philosophical systems'.[3] In 1838, August Cieszkowski published an important precursor of Marxist philosophy in *Prolegomena zur Historiosophie*, proclaiming that 'the totality of history must consist of the past and of the future, of the road already travelled as well as of the road yet to be travelled'.[4] Cieszkowski believed the philosophy of history must transcend Hegel's idealism, and 'the term "historiosophy" – which refers to the interpretation of time in a way that inscribes the past with meaning and offers predictions for the future – was of fundamental importance to Polish intellectuals in the 1830s and 1840s'.[5] Cieszkowski influenced Juliusz Słowacki, and in *Genesis from the Spirit* (1844) Słowacki endowed the past with significance only if it was historically constructive: 'But the teachings and experiences of the past ages were worthless if they did not give us the right directions for the future.'[6]

Conrad believed his exposure to the Polish Romantics and their concern with history gave his own writing its inimitability. In a letter to R. B. Cunninghame Graham, Conrad wrote: 'I look at the future from the depths of a very dark past, and I find I am allowed nothing but fidelity to an absolutely lost cause, to an idea without a future' (*CL* 2:161). In 'Heart of Darkness', Marlow affirms his historical inheritance: 'I don't think a single one of them [Africans] had any clear idea of time, as we at the end of countless ages have. They still belonged to the beginnings of time – had no inherited experience to teach them as it were' (*Y*, 103). For Marlow, history should be read in the Cieszkowskian tradition, inherited experience 'teaching' the way to the future. Marlow declares: 'The mind of man is capable of anything – because everything is in it, all the past as well as all the future' (*Y*, 96). *Nostromo* (1904), while also echoing the political thought of Edmund Burke, unveils Conrad's echoing of Polish Romantic philosophy. In her consideration of history, Mrs Gould asserts that 'for life to be large and full, it must contain the care of the past and of the future in every passing moment of the present. Our daily work must be done to the glory of the dead, and for the good of those who come after' (*N*, 520). The presence of the philosophy of Polish historicism in the poetry of Mickiewicz and Słowacki undoubtedly shaped Conrad's belief that fiction was a form of historiography, for 'a novelist is a historian, the preserver, the keeper, the expounder, of human experience' (*NLL*, 17).

After the failed 1863 Polish insurrection against Russian rule, Tadeusz Bobrowski and the Polish Positivists opposed the militant tradition, promoting a pragmatic approach to protecting Poland's national identity in which political independence would be forsaken in favour of strengthening the economic power and cultural bonds of the nation. The writings of prominent nineteenth-century British thinkers, such as Darwin, Spencer and Buckle, were fundamental to Polish Positivism. The novelist Bolesław Prus summed up the Positivist ethos when he wrote in the *Weekly Review* in 1887 that there were 'intermediate times between the idyll and the battle, when it is not possible to either live with a smile, or die with honour, only work, work, work'. The '"dream" became a common positivist trope, allowing them to contrast productive "work" with all sorts of lofty ambitions – most important those of the romantic nationalists'.[7] Conrad's *The Nigger of the 'Narcissus'* advocates the Positivist necessity of labour: 'No rest till the work is done. Work till you drop. That's what you're here for' (*NN*, 93). The crew 'boasted of our pluck, of our capacity for work, of our energy' (*NN*, 100). The emphasis on work also features in 'Youth': 'But they all worked. That crew of Liverpool hard cases had in them the right stuff' (*Y*, 25). This capacity for the task becomes a force in history, as it has 'a completeness in it, something solid like a principle, and masterful like an instinct – a disclosure of something secret – of that hidden something, that gift of good or evil that makes racial difference, that shapes the fate of nations' (*Y*, 28–9).

While critics cite the importance to Conrad of Thomas Carlyle's writings on the Victorian work ethic, the Polish Positivist approach to work, adapted from Hegel, along with Conrad's own formative experiences at sea, represents a significant context for Conrad's attitude to practical activity. In his lectures on aesthetics Hegel had earlier noted the contribution of work to individual identity: 'man is realised for himself by his *practical* activity … This purpose he achieves by the modification of external things upon which he impresses the seal of his inner being.'[8] In 'Heart of Darkness', Marlow advocates the position of work in the establishment of a stable concept of self: 'I don't like work – no man does – but I like what is in the work – the chance to find yourself. Your own reality – for yourself, not for others – what no man can ever know' (*Y*, 85). As Zdzisław Najder notes, Thomas Carlyle 'was not the father to but only a stepson of a certain political tradition, and therefore a comparison with him will drive us into a side-alley of the history of ideas'.[9]

Writing in 1924, Conrad insisted that 'the formative forces acting on me, at the most plastic and impressionable age, were purely Western: that is French and English' (*CL* 8:291). From his correspondence and the memoirs of his literary acquaintances, it is clear that Conrad, as R. B. Cunninghame Graham observed, had a mind 'steeped in the modern literature of Europe, especially in that of France' (*TH*, ix). In *A Personal Record*, Conrad recalled the work of Flaubert and Hugo, and Conrad's later admiration for the works of Balzac, Stendhal and Maupassant supports his recollection, late in life, that if his 'mind took a tinge from anything it was from French romanticism perhaps' (*CL* 7:616). However, Conrad's exposure to 'tones Hegelian, Nietzschean, war-like, pious, cynical, inspired' (*NLL*, 125) reveals that a broader German philosophical tradition featured significantly in the writer's work.

While Polish responses to Hegelian thought represented Conrad's introduction to German philosophy, Schopenhauer – the great opponent of Hegel – and Nietzsche became the subjects of Conrad's later investigations of German philosophy, with both thinkers excavating to different degrees the underlying condition of human nature in an advanced European civilization – and later in Conrad's case, at the outposts of European imperialism. Schopenhauer's philosophical scepticism in *The World as Will and Idea* (1818) is echoed ubiquitously in Conrad's early letters. In 1897, Conrad wrote to Cunninghame Graham: 'It is impossible to know anything tho' it is possible to believe a thing or two' (*CL* 1:370). *Victory* (1915) unveils a character deeply affected by the teachings of his father's Schopenhauerian (or, to some critics, Nietzschean) philosophy, with Axel Heyst battling, like Conrad, with his philosophical heritage. Schopenhauer, whose fame spread in Europe from the 1850s, identified the impossibility of satisfying the energy of the will as the root of human affliction, and Conrad's pessimism echoes a philosophy that sees life as an attempt at affirmation that simultaneously conceals, knowingly and often necessarily, a profound disappointment. Similarly, Nietzsche's prominence in nineteenth-century philosophical culture represents a major point of dialogue between Conrad and European intellectual thought. Conrad's scepticism about language and its ability to mask human impulses belongs to the cultural climate that engendered Nietzsche's studies of the etymology of ethics and morality in the Schopenhauer-influenced *The Birth of Tragedy* (1872) and *On the Genealogy of Morals* (1887). Conrad, however, in another example of his fascination with and resistance to German philosophy, while drawn artistically to the 'mad individualism of Niet[z]sche' (*CL* 2:188), refuses, owing to his own consistent concern with the position of the individual in larger communal groupings, to condone the popularly understood conclusions of Nietzsche's work. However, when Conrad pronounced 'what makes mankind tragic is not that they are the victims of nature, it is that they are conscious of it' (*CL* 2:30), it articulated his view of an unfeeling, awe-inspiring natural world opposing the struggles of mankind, thereby resonating with contemporary thought grappling with the death of God in a post-Nietzschean twilight.

When Conrad settled in England, late-Victorian Britain approached the new century with a discourse of evaluation on the experience of Empire and progress, embodied in the political sphere by the publication of J. A. Hobson's *Imperialism* in 1902, and in the arts by the translation of Max Nordau's polemical attack on burgeoning Modernism in *Degeneration* (1895). Following Darwin's seminal writings in the 1860s, Conrad's new setting was a society where 'it was not the physical but the biological sciences which had the deepest and the most pervasive effect upon the way man viewed his personal and historical destiny'.[10] In 1893, neo-Hegelian idealist David G. Ritchie published *Darwin and Hegel*, stating: 'Evolution is in every one's mouth now, and the writings of Mr. Spencer have done a great deal (along with the discoveries of Darwin) to make the conception familiar.'[11] Such discussions were also contemporary with resurgence in interest in the subjects of time and history in literature and philosophy. As one thinker noted in the journal *Mind* in 1898, 'it is clear that the idea of progress in its current acceptation is essentially knit up with time'.[12] While Conrad's representation of nature in *Almayer's Folly* and *An Outcast of the Islands* offers a Spencerian interpretation of Darwin's ideas, his engagement with time and memory in 'Karain', 'Youth', 'Heart of Darkness', *Lord Jim* and *The Secret Agent* can be read alongside contemporary British responses to Hegelian philosophy.

The pages of *Mind* in the late 1890s carried dialogue between prominent British neo-Hegelian idealists such as F. H. Bradley and Bernard Bosanquet over the inherent perplexities of time and history as subjects of philosophic study. The French philosopher Henri Bergson's *Matière et mémoire* (1896) had analysed how the human perception of time involved an amalgamation of both past and present states. Following Bergson, Bradley wrote in 1908 that 'no one can deny that in a sense we depend on past experience. For, apart from any other consideration, it is from past experience that in the main our minds are filled.'[13] Although Conrad was 'probably not directly exposed to the systematic theories of the neo-Hegelians, his explicit statements on politics and the dramatic structure of his novels both attest to the presence of his intellectual milieu'.[14] Conrad also interacted with English writing that echoed the Polish response to German Idealism. In the case of Carlyle, Conrad recognized a towering figure in English letters who, along with Coleridge, familiarized English literature with Goethe, Kant and Hegel. Carlyle represented a British tradition of historical philosophy, continued by F. H. Bradley, which questioned the respective values of a Romantic approach to history or a sceptical view of the past. The problems voiced in Carlyle's essay 'On History' (1830) and Bradley's later 'The Presuppositions of Critical History' (1874) reflected philosophical debate in Poland between the adherents of Romanticism and Positivism. In his final essay, 'Legends', left unfinished at his death in 1924, Conrad wrote that he still had 'nothing against a legend twining its tendrils fancifully about the facts of history' (*LE*, 44), articulating his career-long occupation with history and its representation.

The politics of nationalism in nineteenth-century European history represents a subject central to *Nostromo* (1904) and *Under Western Eyes* (1911), and embedded in these novels lies Conrad's response to Rousseau and Herder. Polish Romantics such as Mickiewicz and Cieszkowski drew from the philosophy of Rousseau and Herder, regarding national identity as an inherited spiritual bond founded on shared cultural traditions, historical memory and a stable political structure. Herder's position as the foremost exponent of cultural nationalism is important in Conrad's presentation of the nation, especially in the cultural diversity and plurality of Costaguana. While Conrad labelled Rousseau an 'artless moralist' in *A Personal Record* (95) for the unwieldy size of his *Confessions*, as Edward Said has pointed out, 'if Conrad's hatred of Rousseau was at all like his well-known hatred of Dostoevsky, it may have been that Conrad perceived in the loquacious Swiss a temperament uncomfortably similar to his own'.[15] The most problematic aspect of Rousseau's thought for Conrad was Rousseau's insistence on the subjection of the individual to the state, expressed in *The Social Contract* as follows: 'The better the constitution of a state is, the more do public affairs encroach on private in the minds of the citizens. Private affairs are even of much less importance, because the aggregate of the common happiness furnishes a greater proportion of that of each individual, so that there is less for him to seek in particular cares.'[16] Nevertheless, as in Conrad's writings on Poland, *The Social Contract* indicates a division of peoples into separate identity groups and analyses 'the rules of society best suited to nations', each of which Rousseau sees possessing its own unique 'character'.[17] In June 1907, Conrad wrote to John Galsworthy that a 'government – believe me – is either the expression of a people's character or an illustrated commentary on the same' (*CL* 3:454). In his understanding of Polish national identity, particularly in the face of Russian power, Conrad agreed with Rousseau that 'a patriotic community ... because of its strong traditional way of life, is able to withstand the shocks which bad political leaders and mediocre laws can give it. Such a community is, in a manner of speaking, protected by tradition against political extremism; it enjoys an internal non-political stability.'[18] As F. M. Barnard has stressed, while 'Herder and Rousseau saw the transition from national becoming to political becoming in divergent terms, there was full agreement between them that some matrix of national becoming must precede political becoming for the latter to be able to build upon the former'.[19] Conrad's language of nationality, particularly in *Nostromo*, featuring Giorgio Viola's overt references to Garibaldi and Cavour, and allusions to the political art of Goya, connects to a broad, populist tradition of nationalism in nineteenth-century Europe. Giuseppe Mazzini embraced Herder's philosophy with his 'Young Italy' movement of the 1840s, and Conrad's sympathetic depiction of Viola in *Nostromo* – Viola is 'the Idealist of the old, humanitarian revolutions'

(*N*, xix) and the inheritor of Mazzini's and Garibaldi's liberal nationalism – is consistent with his historical support for national independence movements, particularly those opposing the Empires that controlled Poland.

Under Western Eyes also subtly engages with a Western intellectual tradition represented by the polarization of Edmund Burke and Rousseau. Christopher GoGwilt notes that 'there is something historically important in the success with which [Conrad] makes Rousseau stand for a contestation of claims to inheritance of "the West"'.[20] It has been traditionally understood that 'Burke has a reverence for the past; Rousseau has a revolutionary's hatred of the present. Burke has a disposition to conserve; Rousseau, a rage to renovate or overturn. Burke's appeal is to experience; Rousseau's, to natural rights.'[21] In *Under Western Eyes*, Victor Haldin's radical philosophy can be aligned with this received view of Rousseau, while Razumov's beliefs can be located in the Burkean tradition of evolutionary political development. Razumov writes: 'History not Theory. / Patriotism not Internationalism. / Evolution not Revolution. / Direction not Destruction. / Unity not Disruption' (*UWE*, 66). The narrative's polarization of the Russian East of the story and the *Western Eye* of the narrator emphasizes that Conrad's scrutiny of the Russian nation occurs under the lens of Western intellectual tradition. Alfred Cobban has written that the 'modern Western European conception of the nation has largely been a product of the fusion' of the thought of Rousseau and Burke.[22] In *Under Western Eyes*, Conrad sought to portray a Russia lacking the foundation of any historical or cultural experience of nationhood according to the Western models of Rousseau and Burke. For Rousseau, 'Patriotism specifically, but more broadly the whole range of emotional commitments a citizen may feel for the state, will help to make the public self predominate and thus assist in creating the conditions necessary for a stable and legitimate political order.'[23] For Burke, 'Society is indeed a contract … a partnership not only between those who are living, but between those who are living, those who are dead, and those who are to be born'.[24] In Conrad's Russia, no legitimate political order exists or can be established, as Rousseau's patriotism and Burke's tradition have never emerged, thereby negating both Haldin's revolution and Razumov's political evolution.

NOTES

1. Georg Lukács, *The Historical Novel* (London: Merlin Press, 1962), p. 30.
2. Zdzisław Najder, 'Polish Inheritance', in Owen Knowles and Gene M. Moore, *Oxford Reader's Companion to Conrad* (Oxford: Oxford University Press, 2000), pp. 319–21, p. 320.

3. Andrzej Walicki, *Philosophy and Romantic Nationalism: The Case of Poland* (Oxford: Clarendon Press, 1982), p. 2.

4. August Cieszkowski, *Selected Writings of August Cieszkowski*, ed. and trans. André Liebach (Cambridge: Cambridge University Press, 1979), p. 51.

5. Brian Porter, *When Nationalism Began to Hate: Imagining Modern Politics in Nineteenth-Century Poland* (Oxford: Oxford University Press, 2000), p. 23.

6. Juliusz Słowacki, *Genesis from the Spirit*, trans. Col. K. Chodkiewicz, (1844; London: Col. K. Chodkiewicz, 1966), p. 26.

7. Porter, *When Nationalism Began to Hate*, pp. 50, 49.

8. G. W. F. Hegel, *On Art, Religion, and the History of Philosophy: Introductory Lectures* (Indianapolis: Hackett, 1997), p. 58.

9. Zdzisław Najder, 'Conrad and Rousseau: Concepts of Man and Society', in *Joseph Conrad: A Commemoration: Papers from the 1974 International Conference on Conrad*, ed. Norman Sherry (London: Macmillan, 1976), pp. 77–90, p. 78.

10. Ian Watt, 'Ideological Perspectives: Kurtz and the Fate of Victorian Progress', in *Joseph Conrad*, ed. Elaine Jordan, New Casebooks (Basingstoke: Macmillan, 1996), pp. 32–47, p. 32.

11. David G. Ritchie, *Darwin and Hegel* (London: Swan Sonnenschein, 1893), p. 42.

12. J. M. Baillie, 'Truth and History', *Mind*, 7 (1898), 506–22, p. 521.

13. F. H. Bradley, 'On Memory and Judgement', *Mind*, 17 (1908), 153–74, p. 156.

14. Avrom Fleishman, *Conrad's Politics: Community and Anarchy in the Fiction of Joseph Conrad* (Baltimore: Johns Hopkins University Press, 1967), p. 67.

15. Edward Said, *Joseph Conrad and the Fiction of Autobiography* (Cambridge, MA: Harvard University Press, 1966), p. 53.

16. Jean-Jacques Rousseau, *The Social Contract and Discourses*, ed. G. D. H. Cole (London: Dent, 1963), p. 78.

17. Rousseau, *The Social Contract*, p. 32.

18. David Cameron, *The Social Thought of Rousseau and Burke: A Comparative Study* (London: Weidenfeld & Nicholson, 1973), p. 124.

19. F. M. Barnard, *Herder on Nationality, Humanity, and History* (London: McGill-Queen's University Press, 2003), p. 40.

20. Christopher GoGwilt, *The Invention of the West: Joseph Conrad and the Double-Mapping of Europe and Empire* (Stanford, CA: Stanford University Press, 1995), p. 150.

21. Cameron, *Social Thought*, p. 5.

22. Alfred Cobban, *The Nation State and National Self-Determination* (London: Collins, 1969), p. 121.

23. Cameron, *Social Thought*, p. 124.

24. Edmund Burke, *Reflections on the French Revolution* (London: Dent, 1910), p. 93.

CHAPTER 22

Literary movements

Robert Hampson

Conrad is often thought of as a solitary writer. Adam Gillon's book, *The Eternal Solitary*, for example, begins by describing isolation as 'a dominant motif' in both Conrad's 'life and works'.[1] However, Conrad was involved with various literary movements during the course of his career. In fact, his involvement with these began even before his birth. The very name 'Conrad' is freighted with the political ideals of Polish Romanticism. As Zdzisław Najder notes, the name had been made popular in Poland through two works by Adam Mickiewicz: the narrative poem, *Konrad Wallenrod* (1827), and the poetic drama, *The Forefathers' Eve* (1832). The eponymous hero of *Konrad Wallenrod* is a young Lithuanian who becomes the Grand Master of the Knights of the Teutonic Order with the intention of destroying them from within. In *The Forefathers' Eve*, the young poet Gustav is reborn as Conrad, who becomes the leader and saviour of the nation in a movement from individualist isolation to collective national struggle. The significance for a young man born in partitioned Poland was unmistakable.

Under his father's tuition, Conrad was initiated into three cultures: Polish Romanticism, French fiction and English literature. During his exile in Chernikhov, Apollo Korzeniowski translated Victor Hugo's *Les Travailleurs de la mer*, Dickens's *Hard Times* and Shakespeare's *The Comedy of Errors*, and Conrad read all three translations. However, Polish Romanticism had the strongest immediate impact. In an interview in 1914, Conrad recalled his father reading to him Mickiewicz's *Pan Tadeusz*, *The Forefathers' Eve* and *Konrad Wallenrod*. As a schoolboy, he liked to recite poems, particularly those of Mickiewicz, although later he expressed a preference for Słowacki. According to Najder, the works of Mickiewicz, Słowacki and Krasiński 'formed the basic reading of every educated Pole', and Conrad's understanding of Poland and Polonism came from his reading of Mickiewicz and Słowacki. Their work was pervaded by ideas of 'moral and national responsibility' and the linkage of the two: 'the moral problems of an individual were posed in terms of the social results of his actions', and ethical principles were based on the idea that the individual is always a member of the group and 'responsible for its welfare'.[2]

Conrad moved to Marseilles in 1874. While ashore between voyages, he enjoyed the bohemian café culture of the port among an artistic set which included the poet Clovis Hugues, a protégé of Victor Hugo. At the same time, as Claudine Lesage suggests, Conrad could not have avoided contact with the Felibrige.[3] *Felibrisme*, the movement founded by the poet Mistral in 1854, was still active in the 1870s, and Gounod's opera, *Mireille*, based on a poem by Mistral, featured at the Opera in Marseilles in 1877.[4] *Felibrisme* represented a 'Provençal renaissance', 'restoring Provençal to its natural spelling' and celebrating the customs and culture of the region.[5] It took a language which had been reduced to the level of a *patois* and revived its status as a literary language. Alphonse Daudet, one of Conrad's youthful enthusiasms, was another native of Provence and a close friend of the Felibrists.[6] Conrad wrote an obituary essay on Daudet, and *Almayer's Folly* was criticized for being written too much in Daudet's style.[7] However, it was the works of Flaubert, Maupassant and Anatole France, in particular, that left their mark on his fiction. Jocelyn Baines noted that Conrad had 'served his apprenticeship' under Flaubert and Maupassant.[8] Conrad himself acknowledged that the 'spirit of Flaubert' hovered over the writing of *Almayer's Folly* (*PR*, 3) and feared the novel was 'too much under the influence of Maupassant' (*CL* 1:183). Ford, in *Thus to Revisit* (1921), observed that 'the literary influence of France is overwhelming over the style, the construction of the sentences, the cadence, the paragraph, or the building up of the effects'.[9] Yves Hervouet has demonstrated in detail Conrad's debts to French realist fiction, and the on-going engagement with it throughout his writing life.[10] His extensive familiarity with recent French fiction provided the basis for Conrad's literary friendship with Ford and James. Indeed, Conrad, James and Ford (along with James Joyce) can be seen as constituting a 'school of Flaubert' in English fiction.

In retrospect, Conrad's final voyage in the *Torrens* in 1893 might seem to have introduced him into English literary circles, since it was on this voyage that he began his lifelong friendship with John Galsworthy. However, Galsworthy, at this point, had not begun his literary career, and, although Conrad was friendly with both Galsworthy and (later on) Arnold Bennett, he was also critical of their over-attachment to the 'dogmas of realism' (*CL* 2:390). Instead, it was through T. Fisher Unwin's senior reader, Edward Garnett, and through the publication of his first novels that he actually became involved in English literary groups and movements. During 1896, he began a correspondence with H. G. Wells, who had written a positive review of *An Outcast of the Islands*, and he sent a copy of the novel to Henry James. During the same period, Garnett took pains to involve Conrad in the literary market-place through various business lunches with agents and publishers. Garnett also introduced him to Ford. When Conrad moved to the Pent in 1898, which he sublet from Ford, he had Wells and James as close neighbours. In 1899, Stephen Crane also moved into the area. For a decade, from 1898 to 1908, there was intense interaction between this group of writers.

Apart from the close social interactions of this group of 'writers in Romney Marsh', there were enough literary similarities for them to be seen as constituting a literary movement.[11] In the first place, Ford and James, like Conrad, were steeped in the French realist novel and were dedicated to 'the art of fiction'. Ford learned from James's 'scenic method' how to construct a narrative, while he later acknowledged that he had 'learned the greater part' of what he knew of 'the technical side of writing' from his collaboration with Conrad. In addition to whatever he learned specifically about the technicalities of novel writing, a concern for *le mot juste* and attention to cadences were two lessons Ford carried over into his poetry. In his interactions with Pound, from 1908 onwards, Ford was to pass on these Flaubertian lessons: they re-appear in the programme of Imagism and in what Pound called the 'prose tradition' in poetry.[12] Conrad, Crane and Ford were also grouped together by reviewers as 'impressionists' because of their placing of the individual consciousness at the centre of their work, and their attention to visual and aural phenomena. Conrad himself was privately critical of what he saw as the limitations of Crane's Impressionism.[13] Ford, on the other hand, in his 1914 essay 'On Impressionism', and in his memoir of Conrad (1924), later promoted the idea that he and Conrad, like Flaubert and Maupassant, had been writers of impressionist fiction.[14] Ford, at this point, was keen to promote 'Impressionism' in order to defend his own aesthetic position from that developed from it by *les jeunes* – Pound and his followers.

The *English Review* can be seen as the fruit of this movement. The first issue, December 1908, was put together at Conrad's home, Someries. Ford had founded the magazine with the intention of 'giving imaginative literature a chance in England'.[15] Max Saunders provides a useful gloss on this ambition: the importance of Flaubert for Ford was not just a matter of literary technique, it was also (as perhaps also for Conrad) about the attempt to write honestly about sexuality.[16] The *English Review* would inevitably reflect the concern of Conrad and Ford with literary quality, but it would also aim to advance 'the cause of civilisation' by treating its readers 'with the respectful consideration due to grown-up minds'.[17] Hence the inclusion in the first issue of a poem by Hardy that had been turned down by another editor as unsuitable for a magazine with young readers. This appeared alongside work by James, Conrad, Hudson and Wells. With the subsequent publication of work by Ezra Pound, D. H. Lawrence and Wyndham Lewis, the *Review* (under Ford's editorship) clearly signalled the beginnings of English Modernism.

While Conrad was involved with Ford and James and the art of fiction, he was also associated with another quite different group of writers. From early reviews of his fiction, he had been linked with writers of Empire such as Kipling, and his early Malay fiction, as well as his association with *Blackwood's Magazine*, served to confirm this image. His Malay novels had attracted the attention of Hugh Clifford, and from 1899 onwards he maintained a close friendship with Clifford. Through him he also met that other colonial-service writer of Malaysia, Frank Swettenham.[18] For Conrad, as Linda Dryden has shown, Clifford was always first and foremost a colonial administrator with hands-on experience of Malaysia, while Clifford had a more elevated conception of his own position as a novelist and approached Conrad as a fellow *Blackwood's* author. At the same time, Conrad also developed close relations with anti-imperialist writers such as Cunninghame Graham, who had first written to him (in 1897) in response to 'An Outpost of Progress'. It is indicative of his relative valuation of the two authors that, in his correspondence with Cunninghame Graham, Conrad engages more deeply with the technicalities of writing than he ever does in his correspondence with Clifford.

By the early years of the twentieth century, Conrad was an established author whose work appeared in a range of magazines. He had begun as a *Blackwood's* author, but, once he had taken on J. B. Pinker as his agent, he sought (and, indeed, was obliged to seek) publication with other magazines. But even before his involvement with Pinker, Conrad had not confined himself to *Blackwood's*. *The Nigger of the 'Narcissus'* was written for Henley's masculinist and imperialist literary journal, *New Review* (1897), while 'The Idiots' appeared in the diametrically opposed, aesthetic movement journal, the *Savoy* (1896). As this suggests, Conrad published with a wide range of literary magazines. He also published with a wide range of popular journals, from the high-circulation *Illustrated London News* to popular publications such as the *Strand* and *Pall Mall*, as well as more niche publications such as the shipping magazine *Blue Peter* or the *National Geographic*. His work was spread similarly widely in the United States, from popular magazines such as *Harper's* to the more eclectic *Ridgway's; a Militant Weekly for God and Country*. Once he ceased being a *Blackwood's* author, Conrad did not identify himself, through the placing of his work, with any particular literary movement. As he said, he was not a coterie writer. Apart from his brief period of involvement with the *English Review*, Conrad's publication in serial form was always a matter of taking advantage of the many publication options available, in both Britain and North America, as a result of the rapid growth in the market for short fiction in both countries in this period.

As part of his professional life as a writer, Conrad also attended Garnett's lunches at the Mont Blanc restaurant in Soho from 1905 onwards. Through these he met younger writers such as the journalist and travel-writer Richard Curle, who admired and promoted Conrad's work.[19] Conrad himself was also involved in the promotion of work by younger writers. He advised Norman Douglas, as he had Galsworthy earlier, and was instrumental in Douglas becoming assistant editor of the *English Review*, after it had passed out of Ford's hands. He subsequently introduced another aspiring novelist, Francis Warrington Dawson, to Douglas to try and promote his work. Stephen Reynolds had also served as assistant editor on the *English Review* and had a novel serialized in it. Conrad's correspondence testifies to the effort he put into advising and criticizing work by these writers. Hugh Walpole, a protégé of Henry James's, was another young writer who attached himself to Conrad. By contrast to the 'writers in Romney Marsh', this is a much less distinguished and coherent group. Galsworthy was a very successful novelist in the English social, moral realist tradition; Walpole also had considerable success during his lifetime; while Dawson was to found the Fresh Air Society, an anti-modernist movement that regarded contemporary culture as decadent, before withdrawing as an invalid to his apartment in Versailles.[20]

In 1914, Conrad revisited Poland for the first time in almost twenty-five years. He took advantage of the family's enforced stay in Zakopane to acquaint himself with recent Polish writing. The generation that had emerged in the 1890s, the literary movement 'Young Poland', had returned to Romantic revolt, the literary culture in which Conrad had his roots. This movement had reshaped this heritage through its interest in French Symbolism and other forms of neo-Romanticism, including the work of Hugo, Baudelaire and Mallarmé, and through the philosophical influences of Nietzsche and Schopenhauer. Conrad read works by the earlier, Positivist novelist Bolesław Prus, as well as the great 'Young Poland' poet and play-wright, Stanisław Wyspiański. In Zakopane, he met the romantic-realist novelist Stefan Żeromski, 'the conscience of Polish literature'. Perhaps through him, he also read the work of Wacław Sieroszewski who, like Żeromski, lived in Zakopane and had associations with the Polish Socialist Party. Żeromski, who was the most important Polish novelist of the time, subsequently wrote the preface for Aniela Zagórska's translation of *Almayer's Folly* and mediated between Conrad and a new Polish readership.

Similarly, when Conrad had met André Gide and Valery Larbaud in 1911, he made contact with a very specific section of the younger generation of French writers. Gide and Larbaud represent Conrad's recognition by the young writers associated with the *Nouvelle Revue Française*, a liberal journal, associated with the radical republican tradition. After the First World War, it became France's leading literary journal, publishing work by major modernist writers. Gide actively championed Conrad's work in France: he translated 'Typhoon' in 1917, and supervised the translation of Conrad into French. Also, as Russell West has shown, Gide's own writing clearly developed in dialogue with Conrad's.[21] When Conrad died, the *Nouvelle Revue Française* published a special memorial issue with essays by Conrad's friends Jean-Aubry, Curle, Galsworthy and Cunninghame Graham, as well as by a range of French writers including Gide, André Maurois and Paul Valéry.[22]

Conrad's association with literary movements also continued after his death. The most obvious of these posthumous literary involvements was with Modernism. Garnett, through his promotion of Conrad, Lawrence and others, was one of the midwives of Modernism. With the institutionalization of Modernism in the academy, 'Heart of Darkness' became a paradigmatic modernist text – with its unreliable narrator, its indeterminacies and its aura of suggestion. Conrad also had a paradoxical relationship with postcolonial writing. While many postcolonial critics, following Chinua Achebe's lead, would gladly have burned 'Heart of Darkness' for its alleged racism, many other postcolonial writers were empowered by Conrad. V. S. Naipaul's *Bend in the River*, for example, or David Dabydeen's *The Intended* clearly draw on 'Heart of Darkness'. As Jacqueline Bardolphe has shown, Ngugi Wa Thiong'o's *A Grain of Wheat* and *Petals of Blood* were modelled on *Under Western Eyes* and *Victory*, respectively. Ngugi relocates Conrad's treatment of guilt and betrayal from the Russian revolutionary movements to the anti-colonial struggle and rewrites Heyst's failed attempt at isolation as a study of a failed Messiah. In the same way, Conrad's fiction has also influenced the New Zealand novelist, Randolph Stow: *Visitants* is Stow's version of 'Heart of Darkness'. Its account of a young patrol officer 'going troppo' in the Trobriand Islands recalls Kurtz' degeneration in Africa. The narrative method of Stow's novel *Tourmaline* also recalls Marlow's narration in *Lord Jim*.

Conrad's engagement with the underside of political life in *The Secret Agent* and *Under Western Eyes* has similarly linked him with the development of the thriller and spy fiction – from John Buchan through Graham Greene to John le Carré. Perhaps more surprisingly, Conrad has also been linked with the development of science fiction. The 1890s was a boom period for British science fiction. *The Inheritors*, which picks up on Wells's interest in the 'fourth dimension' in *The Time Machine*, might even be seen as a pioneer of UK science fiction. As Leon Higdon noted, Michael Moorcock's *The Ice Schooner* (1969) was a rewrite of Conrad's *The Rescue*, while Kurtz re-appears in Brian Aldiss's *Starswarm* (1985). 'Heart of Darkness' is drawn on by Moorcock for his novel *The Land Leviathan*, which has a cameo appearance by Conrad himself as Captain Korzeniowski, master of the *Lola Montez*. The naming of the spaceships, the *Nostromo* and the *Sulacco*, in the *Alien* films similarly testifies to the retrospective association of Conrad with a literary genre, if not exactly a literary movement.

NOTES

1. Adam Gillon, *The Eternal Solitary: A Study of Joseph Conrad* (New York: Bookman Associates, 1960), p. 7.
2. Zdzisław Najder, *Conrad's Polish Background: Letters to and from Polish Friends*, trans. Halina Carroll (London: Oxford University Press, 1964), pp. 9, 10, 16, 15.
3. Claudine Lesage, *Joseph Conrad et le continent* (Paris: Michel Houdiard, 2003). The Felibrige was an association founded in the nineteenth century to maintain Provençal customs and language.
4. Lesage, *Joseph Conrad*, p. 57.
5. Frederic Mistral, *The Memoirs of Frederic Mistral* (Paris: Alyscamps Press, 1994), pp. 144, 81.
6. See Marie-Thérèse Jouveau, *Alphonse Daudet, Frederic Mistral: La Provence et le Felibrige* (Nimes: Imprimerie Bene, 1980), and Alphonse Daudet, 'The Poet Mistral', in Daudet, *Letters from My Windmill* (London: Penguin, 1978).
7. 'Alphonse Daudet', *Outlook*, 9 April 1898, collected in *Notes on Life and Letters*, pp. 25–31; Ford Madox Ford, *Joseph Conrad: A Personal Remembrance* (London: Duckworth, 1924), p. 16.
8. Jocelyn Baines, *Joseph Conrad: A Critical Biography* (1960; Harmondsworth: Pelican, 1971), p. 184.
9. Ford Madox Ford, *Thus To Revisit* (London: Chapman & Hall, 1921), p. 56.
10. Yves Hervouet, *The French Face of Joseph Conrad* (Cambridge: Cambridge University Press, 1990).
11. See Iain Finlayson, *Writers in Romney Marsh* (London: Severn House Publishers, 1986).
12. See Robert Hampson, '"Experiments in Modernity": Ford and Pound', in *Pound in Multiple Perspective*, ed. Andrew Gibson (London: Macmillan, 1993), pp. 93–125.
13. Ian Watt, *Conrad in the Nineteenth Century* (London: Chatto & Windus, 1980), p. 173.

14. See Ford, 'On Impressionism', *Poetry and Drama* 2 (June, December 1914), 167–75, 323–34; and *Joseph Conrad: A Personal Remembrance* (London: Duckworth, 1924).

15. Ford, *Thus to Revisit*, p. 58.

16. Max Saunders, *Ford Madox Ford: A Dual Life* (2 vols., Oxford: Oxford University Press, 1996), vol. 1, pp. 427–9.

17. Douglas Goldring, *South Lodge* (London: Constable, 1943), p. xviii; editorial for the first issue of the *English Review*.

18. See Robert Hampson, *Cross-Cultural Encounters in Conrad's Malay Fiction* (Basingstoke: Palgrave, 2000), for more on Conrad's literary relations with Clifford and Swettenham.

19. See Robert Hampson, 'Conrad, Curle and *The Blue Peter*', in *Modernist Writers and the Marketplace*, ed. Ian Willison, Warwick Gould and Warren Cherniak (Basingstoke: Macmillan, 1996), pp. 89–104.

20. See Dale Randall, *Joseph Conrad and Warrington Dawson: The Record of a Friendship* (Durham, NC: Duke University Press, 1968).

21. Russell West, *Conrad and Gide: Translation, Transference and Intertextuality* (Amsterdam: Rodopi, 1996).

22. 'Hommage à Joseph Conrad', *La Nouvelle Revue Française*, 1 December 1924.

CHAPTER 23

Modernism

Michael Levenson

The emergence of a self-conscious Modernism closely accompanied the early development of Conrad's career. In the last decades of the nineteenth century, and in many capitals, an adversary culture gained coherence and visibility; literary works broke with prevailing conventions; artists collaborated in new alliances; journals promulgated aggressive doctrines of artistic formation; and audiences, whether attentive or resistant, grew more absorbed by the spectacle. Conrad most often preserved a careful distance from the movements stirring round him. Still, his consciousness of a changing culture is unmistakable, and even as he worked to preserve his separateness, the modernist tumult affected both the course of his career and his own appraisal of its importance.

In a well-known letter to William Blackwood, Conrad defended the deliberate pace of his work, invoking the careers of Scott, Thackeray and George Eliot. 'But', he continues,

these are great names. I don't compare myself with them. I am *modern*, and I would rather recall Wagner the musician and Rodin the Sculptor who both had to starve a little in their day – and Whistler the painter who made Ruskin the critic foam at the mouth with scorn and indignation. They too have arrived. They had to suffer for being 'new'. (*CL* 2:418)

The use of the word 'modern' here, as well as 'new', is illuminating. At a moment of emergency, Conrad reaches for these descriptors, both because they offer the terms of his self-understanding and because, by invoking a lineage of the new (Wagner, Rodin, Whistler), he can parry the demands that he conform to the 'present public', which is incapable of 'fixing its attention for five consecutive minutes' (*CL* 2:418).

The recourse to such heroes of cultural modernity is significant. But so too is their status as strongly divergent individual artists, strong indeed in their difference from Conrad's own temperament. In the 'Preface' to *The Nigger of the 'Narcissus'* he famously repudiates what he calls 'the temporary

179

formulas' of the writer's vocation. Conceding that each suggests some portion of the truth, he still resists the call of orthodoxy: 'Realism, Romanticism, Naturalism, even the unofficial sentimentalism (which like the poor, is exceedingly difficult to get rid of,) all these gods must, after a short period of fellowship, abandon [the artist] – even on the very threshold of the temple – to the stammerings of his conscience and to the outspoken consciousness of the difficulties of his work'. The genuine artist is left in 'uneasy solitude' (*NN*, x–xi).

Here we come to a prominent feature of Modernism, as it assumed its shape in the last decades of the nineteenth century, namely, the division between grand individuals and collective movements. Conrad clearly located himself on the former side of this division. Like the three figures he names, but also like Flaubert, Turgenev and Maupassant, he saw himself as essentially a lone worker, whose achievement must reflect a solitary temperament. Yet for all his proud independence, he remained not only aware, but also often watchful, of the schools and theories, doctrines and dogmas that circulated rapidly in the *fin de siècle*.

The most conspicuous legacy of this emerging Modernism was for Conrad something broader than school or doctrine: it was the ideal of craft, a sense of the artistic vocation as self-generating and self-legitimated, as an independently justified human practice. Here Flaubert was the great epitome. His legendary pursuit of *le mot juste*, his dedication to the rhythm of sentences and the precise construction of narrative were consistently animating ideals for Conrad, who recalled the 'tempest of anger' that *Madame Bovary* had incited 'by the sheer sincerity of its method alone' (*CL* 2:445). The term 'method' remained a foundational one, frequently appearing in Conrad's attempts to explain his convictions. In the spring of 1902, he wrote that 'Out of the material of a boys' story I've made *Youth* by the force of the idea expressed in accordance with a strict conception of my method. And however unfavourably it may affect the business in hand I must confess that I shall not depart from my method' (*CL* 2:417). Maupassant, who himself learned so much from Flaubert, is the other presiding figure in this tenacious, but sometimes desperate, self-definition as a 'methodical' modernist. Conrad knew Maupassant's fiction well, so well that he worried that his influence ('thought, method, and all' (*CL* 1:185)) was too strong.[1]

The art of Flaubert and Maupassant neither pandered to the sensation-seeking public nor justified itself within the canons of religion or morality; this was a telling modernist recognition for Conrad. And yet, like his precursors, he believed that the labour of conscientious method could never be its own justification: it must point beyond itself to the world that it is uniquely suited to disclose. Art, as Conrad memorably put it in the 'Preface', 'may be defined as a single-minded attempt to render the highest kind of justice' to the world (*NN*, vii). This is, of course, a fundamentally realist aspiration, and much of the inspiration of his French predecessors came from the strenuousness of their representational labour. Literature would enact the severity of objectivity, uninterested in vaporous morality; the clarity of sentences and the precision of rhythm would mirror the structure of the external world.

To put it this way is to see how, for all his protestations, Conrad emerges from within a broadly realist aesthetic, although one that regards the represented world as only attainable through the refinements of literary craft. If he continually resisted the 'formulas' of Realism, that is partly because the Flaubertian legacy exalted the individual artist apart from any school. But it is also because of the particular turn in the realist tradition at the close of the nineteenth century. The prominence of the brothers Goncourt and especially of Émile Zola meant that Realism now assumed the more programmatic aspect of Naturalism. In *Le Roman expérimentale*, Zola held that a genuine modern literature would be as systematic as any science: the imaginative writer 'should operate on the characters, the passions, on the human and social data, in the same way that the chemist and the physicist operate on living beings. Determinism dominates everything.'[2] For Zola, moreover, a properly scientific fiction must excavate the sordid regions ignored by middle-class piety, the baser motives that are the real engines of social life: greed, power, desire, disgust. In the face of Zola's example, Conrad was outspoken: 'I wish to disclaim all allegiance to realism, to naturalism and – before all – all leaning towards the ugly' (*CL* 1:421).

But Conrad's place within the milieu of a modernizing Realism is more complex than this statement implies. 'Realism', after all, was not strictly an aesthetic category. It was equally a feature of the nineteenth-century philosophic and scientific context: the broad movement towards materialism and empiricism that contested religious and moral perspectives. Darwin's challenge to the Biblical narrative was inescapable, and Conrad came to maturity within the framework of a post-Darwinian universe. The 'Real' was no longer congruent with the theological, the metaphysical or the ethical; it resided in a play of causes and effects that now seemed only intelligible within a scientific rationalism. What Conrad most tellingly took from modern science – and in another aspect from the philosophy of Schopenhauer – was an impatience with a self-deceptive sentimentality, with a pious moralism and an unscrutinized faith ('masquerading philanthropy' (*CL* 1:294)). This is the 'realist' temper that, despite his protestations, links Conrad to Zola as well as to Maupassant. The long fall of Kurtz in 'Heart of Darkness' or the shattering of illusions in *Lord Jim* and *Nostromo* map an arc from idealist delusion to the sordid realist ground of 'desire, temptation, and surrender' (*Y*, 149), and if Conrad works to distinguish himself from Naturalism, that is partly because he knows how much he shares with a sceptical naturalist perspective on human motives.

The 1890s, and especially the middle and later years of the decade, saw a newly agitated scene within the transforming literary culture. Zola exerted one kind of pressure on young writers, but then he was hardly alone, and when Conrad met Stephen Crane in 1897, he recognized another current of experiment that suggested a turn in both the theory and practice of his fiction. The virtuosity of Crane's visual imagination in *The Red Badge of Courage* has persuasively been seen as an inspiration for *The Nigger of the 'Narcissus'*, as well as for its important 'Preface'. From Flaubert onward, the task of visual representation – of what is incontestably present to the artist's eye – had offered itself as a vocation in its own right. When Conrad speaks of his dedication to rendering the world 'in its forms, in its colours, in its lights, in its shadows' (*NN*, vii), he writes in solidarity with his early understanding of Crane.

There was also an early resistance, Conrad writing of Crane that 'He is *the only* impressionist and *only* an impressionist' (*CL* 1:416) – a judgement that he later softens but that reflects a productive tension in his own Modernism. The necessity of homage to the 'visible universe' gives clarity and definition to the modern artist; it avoids the loose indiscipline of popular writers, and it offers an antidote to sentimental opinion-making. But the visual surface alone cannot satisfy. It cannot provide the heft, weight and significance that Conrad asks from art. The double-sided modernist question pervading the formative phases of his career is how to overcome a poisonous and complacent idealism (in religion, in morality) with a rigorous craft that matched precise sentences to the real structure of the world, but also how to surpass the merely impressionist surface in pursuit of deeper, more probing reflections.

Here, the example of Henry James was indispensable. James too had recognized the towering precedent of Flaubert and shared an admiration, though more muted, for Maupassant. But he also offered distinct terms for the critique of both eminent predecessors. For James, as for Conrad, the heroic Flaubertian precision and the dignity of craft remained an emblem of Modernism. But James saw Flaubert's 'objective' method – the celebrated withdrawal of the artist and the artist's opinions from the fictive world – as containing a telling weakness, shown most clearly in *L'Éducation sentimentale*.

There, Flaubert had designed a complex historical canvas and had refined the precision of his style, but he had placed the burden of significance on a protagonist too weak to bear the weight. With no distinction of mind and no subtle responsiveness, Frédéric Moreau remained incapable of wresting meaning from complicated events. In closely similar terms, James regrets the lost opportunities in Maupassant – his fascination with the 'senses' at the expense of 'motives, reasons, relations, explanations'[3] – and a comparable loss in Zola, who ambitiously offers 'a picture of *numbers*, of classes, crowds, confusions, movements, industries' while the 'individual life is, if not wholly absent, reflected in coarse and common, in generalised terms'.[4]

James' contribution, decisive both to a wider Modernism and to Conrad, was to insist on the active mental reflection of characters within the fictional world. No more than Flaubert would the Jamesian novelist intrude into the work. But if the novelist must be silent, the novel must still find its way to self-consciousness. The guiding assumption was that human events are interesting only to the extent that individuals 'feel their respective situations' and create a 'fine intensification and wide enlargement' of meanings.[5] The resources of a character's consciousness, of a subtly responsive subjectivity, are what James missed in Flaubert, Maupassant and Zola; it is also what his fictional example confirmed in Conrad.

The invention of Marlow as a characterized narrator is Conrad's most salient contribution to the ambitious work of modernist subjectivity. Where James emphasized the rigours of interior life – the careful sifting of significance – Conrad, one might say, preferred the freer, more flexible play of a recollecting, narrating mind. Marlow not only ranges over meanings, but also ranges over space and time, and in following the associations of memory, rather than the chronology of event, he introduces a new form of temporality into modernist fiction. Marlovian time is ordered not by the logic of causal or calendrical sequence, but by the unpredictable movements of memory and the will to speech.

When Conrad met Ford Madox Ford (then still Ford Hueffer) at the end of the nineteenth century, he began a collaboration that would yield several jointly composed novels and – more immediately relevant – a joint and on-going reflection on the techniques of narrative. Ford shared many of Conrad's admirations, including that of James; and he too pondered the effects of a radically subject-centred narrative – later summarizing the effects of their 'Impressionist' experiments:

That we did succeed in finding *a* new form I think I may permit myself to claim, Conrad first evolving the convention of a Marlow who should narrate, in presentation, the whole story of a novel just as, without much sequence or pursued chronology, a story will come up into the mind of a narrator, and I eventually dispensing with a narrator but making the story come up in the mind of the unseen author with a similar want of chronological sequence.[6]

It should be clear here that the term 'Impressionism' endures a revealing shift of meaning in Conrad's career. At the end of the nineteenth century, it stood for the visual brilliance associated with James, Maupassant and Crane. But, even as Conrad and Ford elaborated their common practice, and under the pressure of Ford's theorizing, the term suggested the primacy, not of the visible world, but of the moving mind. As such, it participated in the excavations of consciousness central to the project of Modernism.

But a further aspect of Marlow deserves attention here. In Conrad, far more notably than in James or Ford, the turn to the responsive mind is an opening to effects that are as much symbolist as impressionist. The unnamed frame narrator of 'Heart of Darkness' describes how in Marlow's storytelling 'the meaning of an episode was not inside like a kernel but outside, enveloping the tale which brought it out only as a glow brings out a haze' (Y, 48). As Ian Watt has indicated, the image of an indeterminate outer meaning, shading off into impalpability, can be linked to the self-conscious and growing movement of Symbolism in the 1890s.[7] Its centre was Paris, and its leading figure the poet Stéphane Mallarmé, who called for a literature of evocation and suggestion, precisely in opposition to the realist/naturalist demand for clarity and intelligibility. 'To name an object', wrote Mallarmé, 'is to suppress three-quarters of the enjoyment of a poem'.[8] When E. M. Forster describes the 'central obscurity' of Conrad, whose 'secret casket … contains a vapour rather than a jewel',[9] he points to the broadly symbolist strain of the fiction, which avails itself of indeterminacy and inconclusiveness.

The Symbolism of the 1880s and 1890s, however, was most often the summoning of a metaphysical elsewhere, a conjuring of what Yeats described as 'something that moves beyond the senses'.[10] And while Conrad acknowledged the workings of inscrutable forces that exceed human understanding, his emphasis fell on complexities *within* rather than *without*, on the conundrum of the earth-bound psyche rather than unseen transcendent powers. In 'Heart of Darkness', Marlow remarks that the 'mind of man is capable of anything – because everything is in it, all the past as well as all the future' (Y, 96). Such a perception links Conrad to Freud, especially to the Freudian thought that no extremity is unknown to the psyche, that there can be no refuge in convention or normality – with 'a butcher round one corner, a policeman round another' (*Y*, 114) – and that the desires and temptations of others reside within each of us.

Indeed, this last thought sets the contours for Conrad's engagement with a modernist Primitivism, which, in his case, assumed its shape within the frame of this psychological perspective: the belief that nothing called 'primitive' is alien to any human mind. Like others of the period – Gauguin, Picasso and Lawrence amongst them – Conrad drew imaginative energy from an encounter with pre-industrial, pagan and non-European peoples. His treatment of them has come in for vehement critique, and there can be no doubt that Conrad, like so many European modernists, tended to select certain images from Africa and Oceania that were productive for aesthetic experiment but to set aside the wider contexts of a living culture. What makes Conrad's Primitivism demanding, however, is that, even as it represents the non-European population as 'Other', it also insists on continuity across geographies and generations, nations and ethnicities. Witnessing the Africans in their 'black and incomprehensible frenzy', Marlow remarks that 'what thrilled you was just the thought of their humanity – like yours' (*Y*, 139). The Africans are at once Other and the Same.

The insistence that the mind is 'capable of everything' is then both a socio-cultural and psychological provocation, and in both respects it is a challenge to the moral sense. No idealism or sentimentality, no dogma or convention, can stand as a bulwark against the press of desire and the fatality of weakness. Part of Conrad's exemplary modernity lay in his willingness to represent the human agon in its full post-religious, post-metaphysical, post-Darwinian bewilderment. But part, too, lay in the effort to sustain an ethics in the face of scepticism. He upheld certain root values – honour, fidelity, work – that seemed so fundamentally human that they might resist the corrosions of modern unbelief. More challengingly, he tried to articulate an ethics that could be generated from within subjectivity, consciousness turning back on itself in an act of primal restraint, as Kurtz' soul 'struggled blindly with itself'. Although Conrad dismissed the 'mad individualism' of Nietzsche (*CL* 2:188), this self-generated morality recalls Nietzsche's project of self-overcoming (where the self becomes 'the judge, the avenger, and the victim of its own law').[11]

During the late stages of Conrad's career, a younger generation of modernists pressed towards new limits of aesthetic extremity – in, for instance, the abstract painting of Kandinsky, the atonality of Schoenberg, the cult of technology among the futurists, the verbal experiments of Stramm and Apollinaire. From the standpoint of *les jeunes*, Conrad could appear as the bluff vestige of the previous era; his post-sceptical morality could seem like heavy nineteenth-century weather. In a revealing episode of the 1920s, T. S. Eliot attached an epigraph from 'Heart of Darkness' – Kurtz' testament of 'horror' – to his draft of *The Waste Land*, only to find Pound wondering whether Conrad was 'weighty enough to stand the citation'. Eliot replied that the quotation was 'much the most appropriate [he] could find' but yielded to Pound's doubts.[12] Then just a few years later he returned to 'Heart of Darkness' for the epigraph to 'The Hollow Men' ('Mistah Kurtz – he dead'). Eliot's poetic recognition here, alongside Ford's admiring volume *Joseph Conrad: A Personal Remembrance*, marks an acknowledgement that contended with the indifference (or even disdain) exemplified by Pound. It would be too strong to say that Conrad's standing in Modernism was ever in serious doubt, but right to hold that it had to await – and has always still to await – a fuller reckoning.

NOTES

1. For an extended discussion of the influence of French writing on Conrad, see Yves Hervouet's *The French Face of Joseph Conrad* (Cambridge: Cambridge University Press, 1990).
2. Émile Zola, *The Experimental Novel and Other Essays*, trans. B. M. Sherman (New York: Cassell, 1893), p. 18.
3. Henry James, 'Guy de Maupassant', in *The Art of Criticism*, ed. William Veeder and Susan Griffin (Chicago: University of Chicago Press, 1986), p. 205.
4. Henry James, 'Émile Zola', in *The Art of Criticism*, pp. 430–1.
5. Henry James, 'Preface', in *The Princess Casamassima* (New York: Charles Scribner's Sons, 1922), p. xii.
6. Ford Madox Ford, 'Techniques', in *Critical Writings of Ford Madox Ford*, ed. Frank MacShane (Lincoln: University of Nebraska Press, 1964), p. 68.
7. Ian Watt, *Conrad in the Nineteenth Century* (Berkeley: University of California Press, 1979), pp. 180–200.
8. Stéphane Mallarmé, *Oeuvres complètes* (Paris: Éditions de la Pléiade, 1961), p. 869.
9. E. M. Forster, 'Joseph Conrad: A Note', in *Abinger Harvest* (New York: Harcourt Brace and Company, 1936), p. 138.
10. W. B. Yeats, 'The Symbolism of Poetry', in *Ideas of Good and Evil* (London: A. H. Bullen, 1907), p. 255.
11. Friedrich Nietzsche, *Thus Spake Zarathustra*, trans. Walter Kaufmann (London: Penguin, 1978), p. 115.
12. T. S. Eliot, *'The Waste Land': A Facsimile and Transcript of the Original Drafts*, ed. Valerie Eliot (New York: Harcourt Brace Jovanovich, 1971), p. 125.

CHAPTER 24

Nationalism and Empire

Allan H. Simmons

Conrad's whole life was shaped by and responsive to nationalism and Empire. Born Józef Teodor Konrad Korzeniowski, to ardent Polish nationalists, he was, like them, a child of the Russian Empire. His early adult professional life was spent in the service of the British Empire as a sailor in the Merchant Service, during which time he became a naturalized British subject, on 19 August 1886 (although not officially released from the status of Russian subject until 2 July 1889). In the standard vision of nineteenth-century European history, the 'Age of Nationalism' precedes the 'Age of Empire', but 'History', as T. S. Eliot wrote, 'has many cunning passages, contrived corridors' ('Gerontion'), and Poland's futile attempts to re-emerge as a nation-state in successive revolts (1830, 1848 and 1863), together with Britain's imperial expansion in the last quarter of the century, meant that, for the self-styled Homo duplex Conrad, the personal experiences of nationalism and Empire were concurrent.

Conrad's conscious experience of nationalism came early and brutally. With Polish territory divided between Russia, Austria and Prussia since 1793, his was a homeland of the heart; before Conrad's fourth birthday, his father's clandestine anti-Russian activities led to arrest by the Russian authorities and imprisonment in the Warsaw Citadel, in whose courtyard, according to Conrad, 'characteristically for our nation – my childhood memories begin' (CL 1:358). A photograph of Conrad from this period bears the inscription 'To my dear Grandmama, who helped me to send pastries to my poor papa in prison'. It is signed 'Grandson, Pole-Catholic and *szlachcic* [gentleman], Konrad'.[1] The following year, the family was exiled to Vologda, 300 miles north-east of Moscow. Ewa Korzeniowska died in exile. Apollo Korzeniowski followed her within eighteen months of his release, leaving the eleven-year-old Conrad an orphan. His father's gravestone bears the inscription: 'victim of Muscovite tyranny'.

Poland's struggles for independence from Russia are consistent with the century's political impetus: the belief that inherited power could be toppled,

an impulse inherited from the French Revolution. Among Conrad's forebears, his maternal great-uncle Nicholas Bobrowski had served under
Napoleon against Poland's oppressor. As described in *A Personal Record*,
his dinner of Lithuanian dog during the catastrophic retreat from Moscow
in winter 1812 doubles as family inheritance and national parable.

The linkage of national identity and political power drove the nineteenth
century's revolutionary movements. In 1848, the year that saw the publication of Friedrich Engels and Karl Marx's *Communist Manifesto*, revolutions
shook Europe. Sparked by rebellions in Palermo and Paris, popular nationalist insurrection spread from Poland in the east to Ireland in the west.
Metternich, chancellor of the Austrian Empire, fell, as did the 'July monarchy' of France's Louis-Philippe. A map of the continent at mid-century
shows how the vast Russian and Austrian Empires had swallowed many
Eastern European 'nations', with Germany and Italy divided into numerous
petty states dominated by Austria. If the revolutionary movements of
1848 petered out, the *Risorgimento* for Italy's unification and the nationalist
movement in Germany would have far-reaching consequences.

Small wonder, then, that nationalism became such a potent force in the
century's revolutionary movements, leading to the emergence of a Europe
of nation-states. Poland's case was slightly different: historically subject to
foreign rule, hers was a struggle to re-emerge as a state. Yet this historic
nation failed to win autonomy or independence, despite being a persistent
thorn in the Russian Empire's side. In the light of Conrad's espousal of
British nationality in his adult life, it is intriguing to find that the English
Chartist poet, Ernest Jones, in his 'March of Freedom' (1848), not only
likens the Whig prime minister, Lord John Russell, to Tsar Nicholas, but
also describes Ireland as 'The Poland of the West'.[2]

Professionally, Conrad's two careers wedded him to the life of his
adopted nation, then in her imperialist heyday. A sailor in the British
Merchant Service, he served in the workhorse of Empire. As he began to
make his name in English letters, a national backlash was perhaps inevitable. It took the form of a debate in the Polish weekly *Kraj* – ironically,
once edited by Conrad's father. Responding to an article entitled 'The
Emigration of Talent', the novelist and feminist Eliza Orzeszkowa accused
Conrad of deserting his homeland, neglecting his patriotic duties and
besmirching his famous name while writing 'popular and very lucrative
novels in English'.[3]

That this charge was made in 1899, when Conrad was still scraping a
living by his writing, is by the bye. The attack stung, as it was intended to.
Conrad returns to the theme a dozen years later in *A Personal Record*: 'The

part of the inexplicable should be allowed for in appraising the conduct of men in a world where no explanation is final. No charge of faithlessness ought to be lightly uttered' (*PR*, 35). In ways that neither he nor Orzeszkowa could have predicted, his words would reach Poland in another hour of darkness. Recalling his experiences in the Polish Resistance during the Second World War, Jan Józef Szczepański records: 'The situation created the moral climate of a Conrad novel. For us Conrad was more topical than ever before. His books became a collection of practical recipes for men fighting lonely battles in the dark that was dense enough to hide personal defeats and therefore represented an additional challenge.'[4]

Conrad's Polishness would again be a matter of public debate in 1907 when reviewers began referring to him as a 'Slav'. In the light of the Russian Empire's grand nationalist concept of 'Pan-Slavism' in the nineteenth century, this must have seemed a lazy and insensitive attribution, as his reaction demonstrates: 'You remember always that I am a Slav (it's your *idée fixe*) but you seem to forget that I am a Pole. You forget that we have been used to go to battle without illusions' (to Edward Garnett, *CL* 3:492). Written in 1918, 'The Crime of Partition' expresses Conrad's concern about Poland's fate in post-war Europe, particularly because of the invitation to Russia to attend the Versailles Peace Conference. He fulminated to Richard Curle: 'The mangy Russian dog having gone mad is now being invited to sit at the Conference table, on British initiative!' (*CL* 6:350).

Writing to a fellow Pole in 1899, Conrad spoke of the liberty 'which can only be found under an English flag' (*CL* 2:230). He adopted British nationality in an age that paraded its nationalism in patriotic celebration expressed as imperial pageant. Colonial premiers and troops paraded in Queen Victoria's Diamond Jubilee celebrations of 1897, and Edward Elgar marked the year with his *Imperial March*. If Kipling was the poet of Empire, Elgar provided its soundtrack. 'Land of Hope and Glory', written by A. C. Benson to a tune by Elgar, was incorporated into the 'Coronation Ode' for Edward VII in 1902 and all but replaced 'God Save the Queen' as the national anthem. Coupled with the international focus of his writing, the fact that Conrad does not respond to such events as Victoria's Jubilee or death in his letters suggests that he looked beyond nationalism – and something of his thoughts of Empire, too, can be gleaned from 'Karain, A Memory' (1897) where Queen Victoria's cameo appearance is as an image on a Jubilee sixpence. Conrad has a reputation as a 'man's writer'; his novels describe the male-centred worlds of seafaring or colonial adventure. Ironically, while Victoria lent her name to the age, Britain's contact with Empire involved women only peripherally. In Conrad's fiction, women

such as Edith Travers or Emilia Gould are presented as victims of (male)
imperial ambitions. Neither does he deal with officialdom. Rather, his concern is with the human types Empire threw up: in 'An Outpost of Progress',
Kayerts and Carlier, the bureaucrat and the soldier, are emblematic comic
figures and colonial archetypes.

Empire was *the* fact of British life in the late nineteenth century. ('Empire
Day' was established in 1902.) It was during this period that Britain
increased its territory by some 4 million square miles. Conrad's personal
experiences inevitably involved him in mixed national sentiments. Having
left a colonized Poland, the Boer War, for instance, meant that he had 'by
his own choice … become a citizen of a country engaged in a war aimed
primarily at enlarging the empire'.[5] His antipathy to the war is well known.
He viewed it as 'a struggle against the doings of German influence' and a
distraction from the real threat posed by German and Russian expansionism
in the Far East, writing to Ted Sanderson: 'the danger to the Empire is
elsewhere' (*CL* 2:230, 211).

In Eric Hobsbawm's designation, the years from 1875 to 1914 constitute
the 'Age of Empire'. Conrad spent the first half of this period furthering the
cause of Empire, and the second half writing about it. From his vantage on
the deck of a merchant ship, Conrad's view of the world was necessarily
coloured by what Hobsbawm calls 'the major fact about the nineteenth
century': 'the creation of a single global economy, progressively reaching
into the most remote corners of the world'.[6] Conrad's fictions of Empire
demonstrate that the partitioning of the world by a handful of European
states had economic and cultural dimensions never achieved on such a scale
in history.

When Conrad turned professional author with the publication of
Almayer's Folly in 1895, his first-hand experiences of Empire provided a
rich creative source. So much so that, leaving aside his collaborations with
Ford, not until *The Secret Agent* was published in 1907 did Conrad's novels
look beyond the colonial world for their setting – and even here, at the heart
of London, that 'monstrous town … cruel devourer of the world's light'
(*SA*, xii), the Assistant Commissioner yearns for a return to his days as a
police official in the colonial service.

With *Almayer's Folly* and, a year later, *An Outcast of the Islands*, critics
decided that Conrad had 'annexed' the island of Borneo.[7] Beginning his
second novel, Conrad himself exclaimed to Marguerite Poradowska: 'You
see how Malays cling to me! I am devoted to Borneo' (*CL* 1:171). *Almayer's
Folly* initiated a trilogy-in-reverse, the final part of which, *The Rescue*, was
begun in 1896 but abandoned and only completed in 1919, and published

the following year. Chronologically, these novels recount stages in the story of Captain Tom Lingard. Nicknamed the 'Rajah Laut' or 'King of the Seas', the English independent adventurer-trader in the archipelago is drawn from stories about William Lingard and his nephew, Jim, seamen-traders in the area at the time of Conrad's visits. There are also recognizable echoes of Sir James Brooke (1803–68), the first Rajah of Sarawak, in the characterization. But while Conrad praised 'the greatness of [Brooke's] character and the unstained rectitude of his purpose' (*CL* 7:137), the Lingard trilogy traces a career of waning influence, beginning in *The Rescue* with his tragic failure to honour his word and restore Prince Hassim to power in Wajo in the Celebes (now Sulawesi) by overthrowing its Dutch-supported rulers.

In this manner the trilogy provides a tale of disillusionment, poignantly contrasting European colonial history with a vibrant world of local nationalism. In competition for the lucrative spice trade, Dutch and British rivalry in the East Indies extended back at least as far as the early seventeenth century, by which time each country had established its own East India Company. Glimpses of the popular forces at work within a world of competing Dutch and British imperialism which they mirror and parody are often discernible only in the texts' margins, as it were, leading to what Cedric Watts has defined as 'covert plots', available to the careful reader but evading such self-absorbed characters as Almayer.[8]

Conrad repeatedly portrayed the Malay archipelago as a conflicted trading sphere, in which local traders are more than a match for the interloping 'specimens of the superior race' (*OI*, 63) and where economics provides the basis for aspirations and alliances, political and personal, and conveys the larger forces of history and nationalism. For instance, in *Almayer's Folly*, Dain Maroola arrives in Sambir against a backdrop of colonial conflict, hoping to enlist Almayer's assistance in a plot to obtain gunpowder for his father, the Rajah of Bali, 'at the time when the hostilities between Dutch and Malays threatened to spread from Sumatra over the whole archipelago' (*AF*, 81). Here, as elsewhere, commerce is a function of imperialism as the unevenness of the conflict makes the illegal trade in gunpowder, quite literally, a matter of national survival. Conrad's colonial fiction charts different stages in the process of European expansion from colonialism to imperialism, from isolated trading outposts at the edges of Empire to formal conquest, annexation and administration. Set in the world of Greater Britain, Conrad's fictions have casts that are, typically, multinational. In *Lord Jim*, Europe is represented by characters from England, Scotland, Germany, France, Scandinavia, Italy, Switzerland, Denmark and Portugal in a Far East of Chinese, Javanese, Arabs, Malays and Bugis. The novel's international scope is everywhere – often present in the hybrid form of the half-caste, such as the brigantine captain – resulting in complex cultural configurations: Gentleman Brown's Solomon Islander has deserted from an American ship; Brown's French schooner is captured by a Spanish patrol cutter and taken into a Philippine bay; Stein & Co. trade in Patusan thanks to a permit from the Dutch authorities; the *Patna*, Chinese-owned, Arab-chartered, skippered by a German, plies her trade between Singapore and Jeddah, and, after her collision, is rescued by a French gunboat and towed to the British port of Aden. Although unmentioned by name, scenes also occur in India and Penang. In this way *Lord Jim* transcends the specific context of Eurocentric values during the Age of Empire to engage with the wider cultural dialogues from which they emerged. In Patusan, Jim acts out a colonial fantasy, wielding authority and meting out justice to the native inhabitants while pursuing his private dream of honour.

'Heart of Darkness' is indebted to Conrad's presence in the Congo Free State in 1890, in the employ of the Société Anonyme Belge pour le Commerce du Haut-Congo. He claimed never to have recovered from his six-month experience of the 'Scramble for Africa', when systematic European imperialism led to the continent's rapacious division – 'this magnificent African cake' as Leopold II called it – between a handful of powers in a feeding frenzy. Marlow, seeing the map of Africa in the Company's offices, recognizes the partitioning as a reflection of Europe's own partition into cultural and national stereotypes: 'There was a vast amount of red – good to see at any time, because one knows that some real work is done in there, a deuce of a lot of blue, a little green, smears of orange, and, on the East Coast, a purple patch, to show where the jolly pioneers of progress drink the jolly lager-beer' (*Y*, 55).

While the novella largely eschews geographical precision in the interests of universality and allusion, history and biography identify the exploited territory as the Congo, the personal property of Belgium's King Leopold II. Yet, it is in 'Heart of Darkness' that Conrad voices his most scathing reaction to British imperialism. All the more potent for being smuggled in under the guise of the frame narrator's hymn to Empire, the references to Britain's maritime glory are double-edged. Those to Drake and Franklin certainly evoke exploration and courage, but subtly anticipate looting and probable cannibalism. The rhetorical apostrophe to the Thames that follows concludes with a paragraph-break – 'The dreams of men, the seed of commonwealths, the germs of empires. | The sun set' (*Y*, 47) – that bathetically undermines the Victorian truism about the sun's never setting on the British Empire. This is reinforced when Marlow takes up the narration, drawing an analogy between the late-nineteenth-century empires of the

European powers and the Roman Empire. The reminder of the transience of Empire is arguably Conrad's most prescient, and certainly his most damning, comment upon the British Empire.

Kipling's catchphrase of 1899, 'Take up the White Man's burden', was an injunction not to Britain but to the United States, which, recovered from the Civil War at mid-century, had expressed its longing for a new and larger role on the world stage by taking over the Philippines. Conrad addressed American imperialism and, with it, the face of Empire changing into global Capitalism, in *Nostromo* (1904). Lured by the wealth of the San Tomé silver-mine, the American financier Holroyd underwrites restoring the derelict mine inherited by Charles Gould, a young Englishman whose family history in Costaguana, a country on the Pacific coast of South America, is bound up with the history of the mine. One vision of national expansion in the late nineteenth century depicts the British as 'reluctant imperialists'.[9] Following in his forebears' footsteps, Charles Gould appears to typify this. But if a sense of injustice initially spurs him to take up the responsibilities of the family concern, once backed by the American dollar, this interest develops into a ruthless obsession, and he is ultimately prepared to destroy the mine by dynamite, 'to send half of Sulaco into the air' (*N*, 204), rather than surrender his claim.

Demonstrating the inexorable power of foreign financial investment, Holroyd's boast that he is 'running a man' extends to running a country. What strikes the contemporary reader is the prescience of *Nostromo*, as Holroyd's claim about American expansion continues to reverberate:

We shall be giving the word for everything: industry, trade, law, journalism, art, politics, and religion, from Cape Horn clear over to Smith's Sound, and beyond, too, if anything worth taking hold of turns up at the North Pole. And then we shall have the leisure to take in hand the outlying islands and continents of the earth. We shall run the world's business whether the world likes it or not. The world can't help it – and neither can we, I guess. (*N*, 77)

In the final phase of his writing career, Conrad turned to the Napoleonic Empire for inspiration. Both his last completed novel, *The Rover* (1923), and *Suspense* (1925), left unfinished on his death, are set during the period. In turning to Napoleon Bonaparte, who redrew the map of Europe a century previously, Conrad engaged once again with the dynamics of national and imperial belonging. Such constant recourse to the manner in which Empires rise, fall and are reconfigured is unsurprising. Conrad's was a life caught in the contradictions and vicissitudes of nationalism and Empire: born in a Poland that had no territorial existence but whose national identity survived the loss of its political institutions, he would become a subject of Queen Victoria when the British Empire was at its height. Despite this, Empire provided a conflicted space. Where Kipling asked 'what can they know of England who only England know?', G. K. Chesterton responded with a question of his own: 'What can they know of England who know only the world?'[10] No sooner had Conrad settled into life as a professional writer than the Conservative government's Aliens Act of 1905 restricted immigration into Britain for the first time. Constantly beset by laws of inclusion and exclusion, Conrad reflected these pressures in his writing. After all, in his essay 'Henry James: An Appreciation' (1905), he wrote: 'Fiction is history, human history, or it is nothing' (*NLL*, 17).

NOTES

1. John Stape, *The Several Lives of Joseph Conrad* (London: Heinemann, 2007), p. 14.
2. In A. N. Wilson, *The Victorians* (London: Hutchinson, 2002), p. 116.
3. In Zdzisław Najder, ed., *Conrad Under Familial Eyes*, trans. Halina Carroll-Najder (Cambridge: Cambridge University Press, 1983), p. 187.
4. In Najder, ed., *Conrad Under Familial Eyes*, p. 279.
5. Zdzisław Najder, *Joseph Conrad: A Life*, trans. Halina Carroll-Najder (Rochester, NY: Camden House, 2007), p. 300.
6. Eric Hobsbawm, *The Age of Empire: 1875–1914* (London: Abacus, 2002), p. 62.
7. See reviews of *Almayer's Folly* in *Daily News*, 25 April 1895, p. 6, and *Critic*, 11 May 1895, p. 349; reprinted in Norman Sherry, ed., *Conrad: The Critical Heritage* (London: Routledge & Kegan Paul, 1973), pp. 47, 50.
8. Cedric Watts, *The Deceptive Text: An Introduction to Covert Plots* (Brighton, Sussex: Harvester Press, 1984).
9. H. C. G. Matthew and Kenneth O. Morgan, *The Oxford History of Britain: The Modern Age* (Oxford: Oxford University Press, 1992), pp. 42–8.
10. Rudyard Kipling, 'The English Flag' (1890); G. K. Chesterton, *Heretics* (London: John Lane, 1905), p. 42.

CHAPTER 25

Politics

Allan H. Simmons

The period of Conrad's life corresponds with momentous political upheavals on several continents: the Boer War, the struggle for Irish Home Rule, the Spanish–American War, the First World War, the Bolshevik Revolution and the emergence of Capitalism and *Weltpolitik*. Domestically, the clamour for workers' rights that led to the foundation of the Labour Party at the turn of the century, the rise of the women's movement and the waning faith in the idea of Empire had their impact upon national identity and definition. Internationally, Conrad's was an age of revolution that saw the birth of the nation-state.

Conrad is generally considered a political conservative. But this definition is nuanced, as shown, for instance, by his public hostility to censorship of drama or, in 1910, by his adding his name to a petition to Prime Minister Asquith in favour of a bill extending suffrage to women. While it is usual to think of Conrad as not interested in small-'p' politics, his letters reveal an awareness of their broader social expression. For instance, those written from his last berth, the *Adowa* in Rouen harbour, testify to the outbreak of anarchist activity in France and England in the 1890s that included Auguste Vaillant's attack on the Chamber of Deputies. Similarly, holidaying in Montpellier in 1906, the Conrads arrived to discover 'the whole town an amazing mixture of carnival and political riots' (*CL* 3:316), the latter occasioned by a bill to separate the French state from the Roman Catholic Church.

The circumstances of his birth and upbringing in what he called 'The Country of Remembrances' (*CL* 1:359) ensured that Conrad's was a politicized life from its outset. When, shortly before his seventeenth birthday, he journeyed to Marseilles to take up a sea career, he had left behind him a Poland that was only notional, still absorbed into the Russian, Prussian and Austro-Hungarian Empires that, because of his father's unwavering and idealistic commitment to the cause of Polish independence, had claimed the lives of both of his parents. Indeed, one interpretation of his upbringing must be that his father, Apollo Korzeniowski, sacrificed himself and his family to political issues. Conrad's early political sense, an inheritance of patriotism and nationalism, left him with a lifelong suspicion of Russia, expressed in *The Secret Agent* (1907), *Under Western Eyes* (1911) and his political essay 'Autocracy and War' (1905).

Conrad's decision to jump ship, as it were, from the French to the British Merchant Service may also have been politically motivated: as a subject of the Tsar, he was liable for service in the Russian army. Almost a decade later, on 19 August 1886, Conrad became a naturalized British subject, whose sworn allegiance was to Queen Victoria rather than Tsar Alexander III (although he was only formally released from his status as a Russian subject in 1889). Enlisting in the British Merchant Service meant that Conrad, who would describe himself as 'a Polish nobleman, cased in British tar' (*CL* 1:52), engaged with the day-to-day practicalities of Empire – but this world of Greater Britain was itself an expression of political forces in Westminster as Empire dominated British foreign politics in the second half of the nineteenth century. For instance, it was in 1886, too, that William Gladstone's decision to espouse Home Rule for Ireland split the Liberal Party, bringing an end to decades of alternating Liberal and Conservative governments and ushering in twenty years of virtually uninterrupted Conservative rule sustained by an anti-Gladstone, anti-Home-Rule alliance. The popular perception was that the Liberals could not be trusted with the Empire.

By contrast, the Conservatives were seen as the party of Empire. Benjamin Disraeli enhanced this view through, among other things, the purchase of shares in the Suez Canal, gaining a controlling interest for Britain in 1875, and proclaiming Victoria 'Empress of India' the following year. In a speech at the Crystal Palace in late June 1872 Disraeli referred to England as 'a great country – an Imperial country – a country where your sons, when they rise, will rise to paramount positions, and obtain not merely the respect of their countrymen, but command the respect of the world'.[1]

Thus, the Britain of Conrad's choice was aggressively imperial, and Empire, the great fact of British life, provided him with a living and a sense of communal recognition and belonging. A sailor in the British Merchant Service engaged in the practical realities of Empire, he was part of the great web of communication that assimilated remote areas of the world into the British economy. While Conrad's family history may complicate his political allegiance to an Empire composed of territories whose boundaries took no account of tribal origins, it would none the less be surprising if his political allegiances were not Conservative. Conrad reveals these allegiances in his letters to Kliszczewski of 13 October and 19 December 1885.[2] In the first he admits to reading the (Conservative) *Daily Telegraph* sent to him in Singapore by Spiridion 'expecting great things' in the wake of the Liberal government's defeat by a Conservative budget-amendment in June 1885; while the second contains his comments on the election in November that year: 'I and the rest of the "right thinking" have been grievously disappointed by the result of the General Election' (*CL* 1:12, 15–16). The elections yielded a Conservative victory, but with a minority government.

Conrad's political sentiments formulate a sense of his Polish diasporic history: ethnically he was Polish; politically he could not be, as Poles were without a parliamentary voice. Having pinned his hopes on the Conservatives to form an anti-Russian alliance with Germany, his despondence about Britain's limited influence on Continental affairs shows: following the election, he lamented, 'Joy reigns in St. Petersburg, no doubt, and profound disgust in Berlin' (*CL* 1:16). In time Conrad would come to warn that German expansionism could lead to a divided Europe – but, by then, German imperialism had already declared its hand, not least in Kaiser Wilhelm's congratulatory telegram sent to President Kruger on 3 January 1896 on his successfully repulsing Jameson's invasion of the Transvaal. (Kipling later called the Jameson Raid 'the first battle in the war of 14–18 – a little before its time but necessary to clear the ground'.)[3] In fairness, Conrad's volte-face reflects the general ambivalence of British attitudes towards Germany. The Kaiser's Germany was also the Germany of Goethe, admired for its culture. In *Lord Jim*, Stein, who quotes both Shakespeare and Goethe, provides a notable counterpoint to the boorish German skipper of the *Patna* with his Bismarckian '"blood and iron" air' (14).

While Empire dominated Britain's foreign policy during the late nineteenth and early twentieth centuries, the major shaping force upon her domestic policy was Democracy. In fact, as has been argued, foreign and domestic politics were in opposition: 'Empire preserved overseas something of the aristocratic paternalism that was withering in the face of economic liberalism at home.'[4] Forces for social and political change were widespread. At home, the plight of the urban worker was publicized in studies such as *London Labour and the London Poor* (1861–2), by Henry Mayhew, and *In Darkest England* (1890), by William Booth, founder of the Salvation Army – and the political landscape of Britain would be further transformed by the First World War, as the demobilized Army, now with voting rights, returned to the job-market. The landed and salaried might have resented gains made by organized labour, and feared the Labour Party, but the 1918

Representation of the People Act, which was also the beginning of female suffrage in Great Britain, almost trebled the size of the electorate, to 21 million, roughly half of the population.[5] According to the economist J. A. Hobson, the war 'had advanced state socialism by half a century'.[6]

Social unease and change characterized the period as the market-place echoed to the clamour for workers' rights. For example, the increasingly virulent campaign against unemployment in the mid-1880s led to the clash between protestors and the Metropolitan Police in Trafalgar Square on 'Bloody Sunday' in November 1887. The Great London Dock Strike of 1899 occurred two years after the publication of *The Nigger of the 'Narcissus'*, in which the seditious Donkin announces to the fo'c'sle: 'I stood up for my rights like a good 'un. I am an Englishman, I am' (*NN*, 11–12). Although unmentioned in Conrad's correspondence, another dock strike, that of 1890, may well have contributed towards his seeking employment abroad, in Belgium. Conrad's attitudes can only be guessed, but he had encountered labour problems in Australia two years before, when, under his captaincy, the *Otago*, bound for Mauritius, had narrowly made it out of Sydney harbour during a shipping crisis, with a general strike threatened.

Grass-roots politics, including educational reform, Poor Law reform, women's suffrage and industrial relations defined the era's political agenda. The extension of the franchise across the nineteenth century led not only to revised political issues but also to the commonplace that Britain was a democracy, even while all women and a third of adult men were still excluded from the parliamentary vote. Added to this, the great social movement of the century, the migration of workers from countryside to towns and cities, acutely focused social problems. By 1901, 80 per cent of the population was urbanized,[7] and if, as the social historian Eric Hobsbawm points out, the word 'imperialism' first became part of the political and journalistic vocabulary at this point 'in the course of arguments about colonial conquest', it is also the case that the word 'unemployment' entered the language soon afterwards.[8]

Conrad described 'The Return', one of his earliest short stories, as depicting 'the gospel of the beastly bourgeois' (*CL* 1:393). Although he would later claim 'Class for me is by definition a hateful thing' (*CL* 7:595), his early disdain towards 'social-democratic ideals' is palpable in references to the 'infernal doctrines born in continental back-slums' (*CL* 1:16). He had, after all, signed off from two English ships with the aristocratic particle 'de Korzeniowski'. None the less, his circle of English friends quickly included such anti-establishment figures as Edward and Constance Garnett and Robert Bontine Cunninghame Graham, pioneer socialist and Scottish nationalist, imprisoned for his part in the Bloody Sunday protest. The colourful 'Don

Roberto' Graham became a lifelong friend, and their correspondence contains some of Conrad's most revealing political sentiments.[9] For example, he supported Graham's opposition to the Spanish–American War of 1898 while describing it as 'a miserable affair whichever way you look at it' (*CL* 2:60). Seeing Graham's 'ideals of sincerity, courage and truth' as 'strangely out of place in this epoch of material preoccupation', Conrad chided: 'What you want to reform are not institutions – it is human nature' (*CL* 2:25). Two decades later, Conrad would define the difference between himself and H. G. Wells, socialist turned utopian, as 'fundamental': 'You don't care for humanity but think they are to be improved. I love humanity but know they are not!'[10]

Typically, political circumstances in Conrad's writing highlight the plight of the individual alienated from, yet trapped within, broad national and historical forces. Initiating the Malay fiction, *Almayer's Folly* (1895) is set in a remote trading-post in the Dutch East Indies where rival British claims in the region, registered through reference to the British Borneo Company and the Union Jack that flies over the compound of Lingard and Co., cast the present-tense action into political relief. In the resulting palimpsest, European politics are overlaid on local politics in a way that confirms the richness of the latter while threatening the former's claims to superiority. The politics of imperialism are reduced as the Dutch flag becomes, quite literally, a flag of convenience, hastily run up as the Dutch soldiers approach. Similarly, the machinations of Babalatchi, the ironically named statesman of Sambir, render him indistinguishable from his frock-coated nineteenth-century European counterparts: cynical, untrustworthy and self-seeking – Talleyrand in a sarong, as it were – he becomes emblematic of politicians in general. Equivalences between these cultural groupings – if only because all of them confirm Conrad's scepticism about human motivation – ensure that *Almayer's Folly* transcends the imperial prejudices of its age. Conrad's fictions repeatedly emphasize egoism rather than altruism as the basis for individual action. Writ large on the canvas of colonial politics, it is this attitude that ultimately renders the *mission civilisatrice* ineffectual, whether represented by the economic adventurer Captain Lingard or the altruistic Jim.

Drawn largely from his first-hand experiences as a seaman, Conrad's fictional world is international. While this chimed with the popular appeal of exotic fiction, whose fascination had already been proved by colonial administrators turned writers such as H. Rider Haggard, its consequence is that surprisingly little of Conrad's fiction is set in Britain. Critically overlooked now, *The Inheritors* (1901), Conrad's first collaboration with Ford Madox Ford, mingles science fiction with a political *roman à clef* whose portraits include those of Conservative leader and future prime minister, Arthur Balfour, and Leopold II of Belgium. *Chance* (1914), which brought the financial success that had eluded Conrad for nearly twenty years, caught the popular mood of the country by addressing the 'Woman Question'.

Despite his early experiences, it was only in 1905, with 'Autocracy and War', that Conrad turned his attention to Russian politics, having been enmeshed in British politics to this point. But, even as he does so, it is not Russia itself that engages him. Instead, England's involvement in an anti-German alliance with Russia spurs him to write the essay. It was in 1905, too – and six years after his assurances to Aniela Zagórska, on Christmas Day 1899, that liberty 'can only be found under the English flag all over the world' (*CL* 1:229) – that the Conservative government restricted immigration into Britain for the first time. One opponent of the Aliens Act was Winston Churchill, then a young Liberal, who, in a letter to *The Times*, defended 'the old tolerant and generous practice of free entry and asylum to which the country has so long adhered and from which it has so often greatly gained' (31 May 1904, p. 10).

Perhaps unsurprisingly in light of his personal experiences, Conrad's attitude towards politics was sceptical. He famously praised Anatole France for recognizing that 'political institutions, whether contrived by the wisdom of the few or the ignorance of the many, are incapable of securing the happiness of mankind' (*NLL*, 38). At the heart of his fictional oeuvre is the political trilogy – composed of *Nostromo* (1904), *The Secret Agent* (1907) and *Under Western Eyes* (1911) – that, most critics agree, constitutes his crowning achievement as a novelist and which expresses scepticism of governance, suggesting that it is a necessary evil, always corruptible and tending towards despotism of some kind. Despite the central novel in this sequence being set in London – it is Conrad's great metropolitan novel – the trilogy mainly demonstrates his fascination with *Weltpolitik* rather than national politics and, with this, the development of a prophetic vision, whether of the global economic role of the United States of America, in *Nostromo*, or of the tensions of the Cold War, in *Under Western Eyes*.

Nor do alternatives to political tyranny escape censure, whether Giorgio Viola's Republicanism in *Nostromo* or democracy – described by Natalia Haldin as the West's 'bargain with fate' in *Under Western Eyes*. For example, one of Garibaldi's 'immortal thousand in the conquest of Sicily' (*N*, 20), Giorgio Viola accompanied his leader to South America forty years before the opening of the novel's action to fight 'for the cause of freedom' (30) in Uruguay. Yet, for all his 'austere contempt for all personal advantage', and belief that 'Too many kings and emperors flourished yet in the world which

God had meant for the people' (31), the old Garibaldino is a puppet of political forces that feed off his sentimental idealism: by the conclusion, and symbolically detached from the continent he has served, Viola unwittingly guards Nostromo's silver hoard on the Great Isabel, his very isolation proclaiming the link between political commitment and solipsism.

The First World War distracted Conrad's attention from the writing-desk and towards the world of politics. An ill-timed holiday to Austrian Poland in July 1914 afforded him an eye-witness view of mobilization and necessitated an anxious return to England. His elder son's enlistment in September 1915 gave the conflict a personal dimension, as did the Admiralty's invitation to inspect naval bases in 1916, to which Conrad responded enthusiastically. Coincident with the war was the Irish uprising of Easter 1916, towards which Conrad was antipathetic, claiming that, had it succeeded, 'The Island Republic (if that is what they wanted) would have become merely a strongly held German outpost – a despised stepping stone towards the final aim of the Welt-Politik' (*CL* 5:596).

The war revived Conrad's interest in Polish affairs. 'A Note on the Polish Problem', a memorandum to the Foreign Office, was drafted in June 1916 at the instigation of his friend, Józef H. Retinger, and depicts Poland as an 'advanced outpost of Western civilisation' and Polonism as forever separate from either Germanism or Slavonism. Characteristically clear-eyed, Conrad's opinion on the ceasefire, expressed on 11 November 1918, was that 'Great and very blind forces are set free catastrophically all over the world' (*CL* 6:302). Anticipating that the United States' intervention in the war 'has got to be paid for' by the Western powers, and anxious over Poland's fate at the peace negotiations – 'Poland will have to pay the price of some pretty ugly compromises … The mangy Russian dog having gone mad is now being invited to sit at the Conference table, on British initiative!' – he accepted that 'The old order had got to die' (*CL* 6:349–50).

As one possible expression of these newly released 'Great and very blind forces', Conrad's enduring interest in Napoleon Bonaparte, already dramatized in 'The Duel' (1908) and 'The Warrior's Soul' (1917), provides the historical backdrop for his late novels *The Rover* (1923) and the unfinished *Suspense*, published posthumously in 1925. Like many Poles, Conrad's forebears had fought in Napoleon's armies as wild geese against Russia. *A Personal Record* details how his maternal great-uncle, Nicholas Bobrowski, survived the disastrous retreat from Moscow in the winter of 1812 and was never disillusioned about Napoleon's cynical use of the Poles as cannon fodder in advancing his own political aims, while holding out a vague promise of restoring the Polish nation-state. Napoleon, who rose to fame by taming the forces unleashed by the French Revolution, and whose subsequent career is described in the opening of 'The Duel' as having 'the quality of a duel against the whole of Europe' (*SS*, 165), offers a fitting example of Conrad's political anxieties and hopes in the wake of the First World War.

In his fiction, Conrad emerges as a special kind of political novelist – one who is so fine *because* of (and not in spite of) his intensely sceptical attitude to the modern political spectacle. To George Orwell, Conrad possessed 'a sort of grown-upness and political understanding which would have been almost impossible to a native English writer at the time'.[11] One can see what he means: by virtue of his European scope and his sophisticated interest in the impersonal machinery of autocracy, Capitalism, Globalism and other political '-isms', Conrad's vision is simply of a different order from that of his contemporaries Wells, Forster, Lawrence and Galsworthy. If he does not believe in political solutions to societal issues, he certainly shows why we all writhe in absolute misery at the decisions made by others 'in our name' and at the impersonal forces unleashed by the world's Holroyds. In Conrad's 'big' novels, the machinery of state or *Weltpolitik* is invariably a given, and the questions he raises always seem to follow on that fact. What attitude to take to these forces? How do we live with them? Is it possible to sustain a purely moral vision of any kind? Does individual action count for anything? In sum, enmeshed within the machinery of state, we are all confronted with Mikulin's question to Razumov: '"Where to?"' (*UWE*, 99). Conrad's sophistication as a political novelist is such that, in order to describe his habitual human territory, we need epithets (however clumsy) of a hyphenated kind: 'psycho-political', 'politico-moral' and 'socio-political'.

NOTES

1. 'Mr. Disraeli at Sydenham', *The Times*, 25 June 1872, p. 7.
2. Kliszczewski is listed as Josef Spiridion in the 1881 Census and he did business under this name for a couple of decades, suggesting that, like Conrad, his assimilation into the English context included changing his name. In a letter to Charles Chassé of 31 January 1924, Conrad refers to having 'preserved the secret of my origins under the neutral pseudonym of "Joseph Conrad"' (*CL* 8:290).
3. Letter to Herbert Baker, 12 January 1934, quoted in Andrew Lycett, *Rudyard Kipling* (London: Weidenfeld & Nicolson, 1999), pp. 296–7.
4. John Davis, *A History of Britain, 1885–1939* (New York: St Martin's Press, 1999), p. 12.
5. Of these 21 million voters, 8.5 million were women. See A. J. P. Taylor, *English History 1914–1945* (Oxford: Oxford University Press, 1990), pp. 115–16.

6. In Kenneth O. Morgan, *Consensus and Disunity* (Oxford: Oxford University Press, 1979), p. 21.

7. H. G. C. Matthew and Kenneth O. Morgan, *The Oxford History of Britain: The Modern Age* (Oxford: Oxford University Press, 1992), p. 12.

8. Eric Hobsbawm, *The Age of Empire* (London: Abacus, 2002), p. 60. According to Hobsbawm, 'Emperors and empires were old, but imperialism was quite new. The word (which does not occur in the writings of Karl Marx, who died in 1883) first entered politics in Britain in the 1870s, and was still regarded as a neologism at the end of that decade. It exploded into general use in the 1890s' (*ibid.*, p. 60). The *Oxford English Dictionary* gives 1888 as the date of first usage of the word 'unemployment'.

9. See Cedric Watts, ed., *Joseph Conrad's Letters to R. B. Cunninghame Graham* (Cambridge: Cambridge University Press, 1969).

10. Cited in Owen Knowles and Gene M. Moore, *Oxford Reader's Companion to Conrad* (Oxford: Oxford University Press, 2000), p. 400.

11. George Orwell, *The Collected Essays, Journalism and Letters of George Orwell*. Vol. IV: *In Front of Your Nose 1945–1950* (Harmondsworth: Penguin, 1970), p. 550.

CHAPTER 26

Popular culture

Stephen Donovan

Cosmopolitan origins, extensive travel and long residence near London gave Conrad an unusually varied experience of what is now called 'popular culture'. As a boy, he read Jules Verne and thrilled to lurid accounts of savages and sea monsters in the Cracow magazine *Wędrowiec*. At sea, he came to know the shanties, jigs and yarns of traditional sailing life as well as the shore-based pleasures of marionettes, carnivals, shadow theatres and magic shows. As a professional writer, he saw Charlie Chaplin features, educational films and magic shows, read the *Daily Mail* and the humorous magazines *La Vie Parisienne* and *Punch*, and took holidays in the Mediterranean resorts of Capri and Corsica, as well as in the Belgian seaside town of Knocke-sur-Mer.

Numerous passing references in Conrad's writing – billiards in *An Outcast of the Islands* (1896), pigeon-fancying in 'Heart of Darkness' (1902), boxing in 'Typhoon' (1903) and stage illusions in *Chance* (1914) – illustrate how popular culture had become the 'material unconscious' of literary production by the turn of the century.[1] But there existed as yet no collective name for this sprawling and fast-evolving range of activities. In English, the term 'culture' had long been synonymous with the arts and tastes of the genteel classes, with 'folk culture' only gaining currency late in the nineteenth century as a designation for traditions now under siege by the 'popular' forces unleashed by modernization. With the gradual erosion of high culture's dominance and the spread of new leisure activities, the word 'popular' began to acquire a secondary and less pejorative meaning: not merely as vulgar or working-class, but as appealing simply to the majority.

In Britain, this cultural shift had its origins in a cluster of economic, demographic and technological developments during the second half of the nineteenth century: the maturing of an industrial capitalist economy; rapid population growth, especially in the cities; and major advances in transport and communication. Rising wages coupled with a fall in basic living costs increased the disposable income of most citizens, particularly the middle classes, stimulating demand for new commodities, among them patent foods and colonial imports such as the meat extract Bovril which Conrad satirizes in 'An Anarchist' (1906). While consumption patterns continued to function as powerful markers of class, a measure of social convergence was discernible in the domestic sphere with its rituals of Sunday dinner, family excursions and Christmas festivities.

Most striking, however, was the expansion of leisure. Albeit unevenly and with notable exceptions, the working week was standardized and shortened, thanks in part to the rise of an organized labour movement, and by the 1900s most middle-class and some working-class Britons could look forward to a week's unpaid annual holiday. Package tours and hotels enabled them to visit seaside resorts and other popular destinations which offered a host of diversions as well as souvenir photographs, picture postcards and tourist kitsch. At home, the public's recreational needs were increasingly well served by municipal parks, museums, galleries and libraries. Traditional pastimes, which had often been characterized by gambling and rowdiness, gave way to more organized and respectable commercial entertainments. Participation in new pastimes such as golf and hiking grew apace, and sports became mass spectator events organized into national leagues. The Olympic Games, revived in the preceding decade, came to London in 1908, and football, now firmly established as the national game, was described by one commentator as exciting 'more emotion than art, politics and the drama, and [awakening] local patriotism to the highest pitch'.[2] Popular interest in Britain and its Empire, meanwhile, was reflected in the crowds which flocked to exhibitions, parades and military shows, and the phenomenal success of the Scouting Movement made its founder, Robert Baden-Powell, according to one biographer, 'after Shakespeare, the most widely read British writer of all time'.[3]

The popularity of cycling well illustrates the reciprocal influence of popular culture and social change at this time. Convenient and affordable, the bicycle was both harbinger and symbol of several kinds of mobility. When press magnate George Newnes held a competition in *Tit-Bits* in 1884, the first prize of an editing job on the famous miscellany was won by a teenager named Arthur Pearson who had cycled sixty miles to his nearest library every Sunday for three months. Pearson went on to found a stable of journals – among them *Pearson's Weekly* (1890), *Pearson's Magazine* (1896), *Mainly About People* (1897), *Royal Magazine* (1898) and *Novel Magazine* (1905) – which promoted, among other things, modern diversions such as cycling to a readership comprised substantially of women. And it was the popularity of a female cycling correspondent which alerted Alfred Harmsworth, while editor of Coventry's *Cycling News*, to the historic opportunity presented by the new enthusiasms of female and younger readers. The phenomenon was registered by Conrad and Ford Madox Ford in their science-fiction romance, *The Inheritors* (1901), a satire on the manipulation of public opinion by journalists, in which the sinister agent of a conspiracy to destroy 'a whole fabric, a whole plane of society' (*I*, 208) is a bicycle-riding woman.

Conrad, who had submitted his first attempt at fiction to another *Tit-Bits* competition in 1886, followed these developments with concern, calling social progress and radical reform 'milestones on the road to ruin' (*CL* 1:17) and portraying the labour agitator Donkin, in *The Nigger of the 'Narcissus'* (1897), as someone who 'never did a decent day's work in his life ... discoursing with filthy eloquence upon the right of labour to live' (*NN*, 172). His lack of enthusiasm for leisure time, echoed in Marlow's grouchy aside that it 'must be got through somehow' (*C*, 135), was reinforced by a low opinion of how his contemporaries chose to spend it. From the pornography sold in Verloc's shop in *The Secret Agent* (1907) to Massy's addiction to the lottery in 'The End of the Tether' (1902), popular leisure activities in Conrad's fiction are almost always associated with spiritual or aesthetic loss. He was sceptical of new reproduction technologies, particular when it concerned high cultural forms closer to his heart: the music box in *Almayer's Folly* (1895) with which Babalatchi unsteadily cranks an aria from Verdi's *Il Trovatore* (1853) in a 'mournful round of tearful and endless iteration' (*AF*, 89); the mechanical piano in *The Secret Agent* whose 'aggressive' rendering of the traditional folk song 'Blue Bells of Scotland' fills a seedy Soho restaurant with 'painfully detached notes' (*SA*, 61, 79); and the oleograph, an inexpensive technique for simulating oil painting, condemned in *Under Western Eyes* (1911) as 'oppressively odious – in its unsuggestive finish: the very perfection of mediocrity' (*UWE*, 203). The aim of the 'artistic' photographer, Conrad declared satirically, is 'to obliterate every trace of individuality in his subject' (*CL* 2:105).

One of the fastest-growing entertainments was music hall, which by the turn of the century had emerged as a respectable venue for nationally famous performers. The narrator of Conrad's semi-autobiographical 'Youth' recalls travelling from Falmouth to London to catch a variety show, and a pen-and-ink sketch which Conrad drew in 1896 attests to his own enjoyment of chorus-line dancing. Although an observer in 1912 could remark that middle-class men and women 'go as readily to the first and second "houses" of the variety theatre as to the "legitimate" theatre',[4] residual doubts about the status of music hall most likely prompted Conrad's show of reluctance to attend a comic revue at London's Alhambra Theatre in 1914. In turn, musical and variety shows appear in unflattering light in his fiction. In 'The Informer', an anarchist cell operating under the cover of a 'shabby Variety Artists' Agency' for 'performers in inferior music-halls' includes a 'long-faced' fellow who sings 'comic songs for the entertainment of a joyless proletariat' (*SS*, 91). And in *Victory* (1915), Axel Heyst rescues Lena from an all-female touring orchestra which provides erotic diversion for the patrons of sleazy hotels.

The variety and scale of visual entertainment grew rapidly during these years, bringing music hall stars, waxwork exhibitions, *tableaux vivants*, magic lantern shows, pyrotechnic displays and theatrical performances to those living outside major cities. In 1899, London's Earl's Court staged a full-scale re-enactment of the repulse of Ndebele warriors by members of the British South Africa Company Police, a spectacle mediated to an even larger audience by the new cinematograph. Well before Conrad wrote a screenplay of 'Gaspar Ruiz' for Lasky-Famous Players, film had shaken off its original identity as a music hall or fairground diversion and established itself as a major narrative art form with permanent exhibition venues. By the time he saw an adaptation of *Victory* at a cinema in Canterbury in 1919, the overwhelming majority of films screened in Britain were being made in Hollywood.

For authors, the most important developments were taking place in publishing. With the demise of the expensive three-decker novel format in 1895, and an exponential increase in publishers' advertising budgets, book sales rose dramatically, making the fortunes not only of writers such as Grant Allen, Marie Corelli and Hall Caine, whom Conrad dismissed as 'popular because they express the common thought' (*CL* 2:137–8), but also of H. G. Wells, whose work he held in high regard, and W. W. Jacobs, whose humorous maritime tales he read aloud to his children. This was the heyday of the cheap reprint series: Henry Morley's Universal Library (1886); W. T. Stead's Books for the Bairns (1895) and Masterpiece Library (1895); Thomas Nelson and Sons' New Century Library (1900) and Sixpenny Classics (1900); Grant Richards' World's Classics (1901); and the Temple Shakespeare (1894) and Everyman's Library (1906) of J. M. Dent, who became Conrad's own publisher. The approving portrait in *The Nigger of the 'Narcissus'* of the tattooed sailor, Singleton, reading Edward Bulwer Lytton's popular classic *Pelham* (1828) in what is presumably a cheap reprint, contrasts sharply with Conrad's scepticism towards the flood of new titles, 'common books of commerce … hired books published by ordinary publishers' (*NLL*, 66).

The periodical press, meanwhile, was transformed by a massive influx of capital investment, advances in printing technology and, above all, a revolution in advertising methods. A new breed of professional journalist, its ranks now swelled by war reporters, special correspondents, interviewers, photo-journalists and undercover investigators, catered to the interests of a mass readership of national newspapers whose appetite for sensation prompted one of Fleet Street's elder statesmen to lament: 'Never till now has there been such an inpour of startling reports, unexpected developments, surprising portents, keys to the situation, revelations of the most authorised description.'[5] Conrad was equally pessimistic, calling journalism 'the most demoralizing form of human activity, made up of catch phrases of mere daily opportunities, of shifting feelings' (*CL* 6:56). Nevertheless, his compositional method relied heavily upon extensive reading of newspapers, and journalists and journalism figure prominently in *The Inheritors*, *Nostromo* (1904), *The Secret Agent*, *Under Western Eyes* and 'The Planter of Malata' (1914). In 'Heart of Darkness', Kurtz' murky past includes 'writing for the papers' (*Y*, 68).

After the boom of the 1890s, the industry entered a phase of consolidation as the media groups of Newnes, Pearson and Harmsworth fought to dominate market sectors with competing journals whose audiences numbered in the hundreds of thousands. These included penny and halfpenny daily newspapers (*Westminster Gazette* (1893), *Daily Express* (1900), *Daily Mail* (1896)), weekly women's magazines (*Woman's Life* (1895), *Home Notes* (1894), *Home Chat* (1895)) and sixpenny monthly fiction magazines (*Strand* (1891), *Pearson's*, *Harmsworth* (1898)). By 1910, the fifty titles controlled by Harmsworth's Amalgamated Press were selling more than 8 million copies every week, and a decade later the *Daily Mail*'s circulation topped 1,350,000, making it the largest daily paper in the world.

In addition to writing reviews and features for several Amalgamated Press titles, Conrad allowed his work to appear in over fifty other newspapers, including the *Dallas Morning News*, the *Daily Chronicle*, the *New York Herald*, the *Los Angeles Times* and the *Star* of London. But it was as a contributor to popular magazines – the *Illustrated London News*, *Pall Mall*, *Harper's*, *McClure's*, *Hampton's*, *Munsey's*, the *Strand*, *Romance*, *Lloyd's*, *Pictorial Review* and many others – that he benefited most directly from the boom in periodical publishing. Packed with fiction, feature articles, illustrations, self-help advice, competitions, sporting news and celebrity gossip, mass-circulation magazines at the turn of the twentieth century had become what Richard Ohmann, writing of the American context, has called the nation's 'major form of repeated cultural experience'.[6] Aggressive and ingenious self-promoters, they brought Conrad's name and writings into the mainstream of a mass culture which they themselves had helped create. 'An ultra-popular magazine', the *New York Times* noted dryly in May 1912, 'has made a new short story of [Conrad's] the basis of advertising in the subway'. Thanks to its large advertising section, an 'ultra-popular' magazine like *Metropolitan*, which was serializing Conrad's 'Freya of the Seven Isles' in April 1912, could slash its cover price to below the cost of production, thereby effectively selling the attention of its million-strong, mostly female readership to manufacturers like Chiclets and Nabisco that were desperate to reach their target demographic. Writers with mass appeal profited handsomely from this new arrangement. Lucrative rates of reimbursement and a steady demand for fiction, particularly short stories, enabled many novelists to depend financially upon magazine serialization. Conrad was more fortunate than most in having a ready fund of material on subjects popular with magazine readers – maritime adventure ('Typhoon', 'The Partner', 'The Secret Sharer') and exotic colonial tales ('The Lagoon', 'Because of the Dollars', 'The Planter of Malata') – and he willingly tried his hand at other popular themes: Anarchism ('The Informer', 'An Anarchist'); aristocratic drama ('Il Conde', 'The Duel', 'Prince Roman'); the supernatural ('The Black Mate', *The Shadow-Line*); the macabre ('The Inn of the Two Witches', 'The Tale'); and, rather less successfully, domestic melodrama ('The Return').

As mass-circulation periodicals drew almost every aspect of contemporary life into their ambit, the public's fascination with national celebrities extended beyond actors, politicians and socialites to include literary professionals. 'Between 1880 and the First World War', writes John Gross, 'there must have been proportionately more popular interest in authors and the world of authors than at any time before or since'.[7] Not only Conrad's literary activities but also his opinions, health, holidays and wartime escape from Vienna were widely covered on both sides of the Atlantic. Literary pages and interviews with writers were staple features of periodicals across the board, and serial fiction was promoted using an array of marketing gimmicks: Edgar Wallace offered large cash prizes for correctly guessing the solution to his thriller-mystery *The Four Just Men* (1904); a serial story by Arthur Morrison in *Tit-Bits* gave clues to the location of buried gold sovereigns; and readers of Newnes' penny weekly, the *Million*, advanced the serialization of an interactive 'Novel Novel' by submitting their own chapters. In 1909, the *Daily Mail* provoked Conrad to fury by inviting him to review books found in the possession of the fugitive murderer, Dr Crippen; and after his death, the *Saturday Review of Literature* serialized *Suspense* in tandem with a prize contest for the best outline of how the unfinished novel should end.

The new relationship between author and popular audience created by advertising had other profound consequences for the composition and reception of literary works. On the production side, Conrad's fraught correspondence records commercial and ideological pressures which magazines exerted on both his writing and his interactions with agents, editors and publishers. On the consumption side, the context in which Conrad's works first appeared was qualitatively different from, and considerably more complex than, the ordered calm of the book. Organized into instalments, formatted with double columns and inter-titles, and supplemented by illustrations and plot summaries, they formed part of a reading experience that promoted more than just chewing-gum and biscuits: a historically new world-view predicated upon social consensus and consumption. Above all, such magazines made 'culture', a concept encompassing familiarity with the work of prestigious authors like Conrad, into the mainstay of a larger project to reshape class society.

Conrad's fictional portrayal of popular culture as corrupting and debasing bears comparison with numerous works of this period: George Gissing's *New Grub Street* (1891), Henry James' 'The Papers' (1903), H. G. Wells' *Tono-Bungay* (1909) and Rose Macaulay's *Potterism* (1920). His references to 'the newly enfranchised idiots' (*CL* 1:16) and his descriptions in *The Arrow of Gold* (1919) of the 'Carnivalesque lunacy' (*AG*, 273) echo, too, contemporary denunciations of the riotous celebrations of the relief of Mafeking on 18 May 1900, a 'democratic saturnalia' that, according to economist J. A. Hobson, had broken down 'the most sacred distinction of classes' and laid bare the 'mob-mind' of music hall, 'the most powerful instrument of such musical and literary culture as the people are open to receive'.[8] And Conrad's antipathy was undoubtedly genuine. Mocking the 'inherent horrors' of the ABC tea-room chain (*LE*, 104), and the 'state of near lunacy' induced by cricket,[9] he penned fictional satires on the credulity of spiritualists, the philistinism of tourists, the cynicism of advertisers and the faddishness of walking enthusiasts. Yet close scrutiny of his writing shows popular culture as a more significant influence than he cared to admit – indeed, one that perhaps mirrored his own substantial presence in the media of his day. 'Out of the material of a boys' story I've made *Youth*' (*CL* 2:417), he confided to the publisher William Blackwood, and to his friend Richard Curle he confessed to having been compelled to write *Under Western Eyes*, a densely personal novel whose writing cost him more than any other, 'by the rubbishy character of stories about Russian revolutionists published in magazines'.[10]

NOTES

1. Bill Brown, *The Material Unconscious: American Amusement, Stephen Crane, and the Economies of Play* (Cambridge, MA: Harvard University Press, 1996), p. 4.

2. Pamela Horn, *Pleasures and Pastimes in Victorian Britain* (Stroud: Sutton Publishing, 1999), p. 154.

3. Michael Rosenthal, *The Character Factory: Baden-Powell and the Origins of the Boy Scout Movement* (London: Collins, 1986), p. 13.

4. Simon Gunn, *The Public Culture of the Victorian Middle Class: Ritual and Authority and the English Industrial City, 1840–1914* (Manchester: Manchester University Press, 2000), p. 90.

5. Frederick Greenwood, 'The Newspaper Press: Half a Century's Survey', *Blackwood's Edinburgh Magazine*, 161 (May 1897), 711.

6. Richard Ohmann, *Selling Culture: Magazines, Markets, and Class at the Turn of the Century* (London: Verso, 1998), p. 29.

7. John Gross, *The Rise and Fall of the Man of Letters: English Literary Life Since 1800* (London: Weidenfeld and Nicolson, 1969), p. 200.

8. J. A. Hobson, *The Psychology of Jingoism* (London: Grant Richards, 1901), pp. 3, 31, 32, 40.

9. John Conrad, *Joseph Conrad: Times Remembered* (Cambridge: Cambridge University Press, 1981), p. 164.

10. Jocelyn Baines, *Joseph Conrad: A Critical Biography* (London: Pelican, 1986), pp. 444–5.

CHAPTER 27

Publishing

Aaron Zacks

When Joseph Conrad deemed *Almayer's Folly* fit for publication in 1894, rather than submit his manuscript officially to a publishing house, he sent it to Edmund Gosse, later Librarian at the House of Lords but then a reader reviewing manuscripts for William Heinemann. Directly soliciting a publisher's reader was unconventional, if not unprofessional, especially for an unknown writer. In Conrad's first publishing act, we observe him attempting to circumvent the conventions of the market-place by appealing to Gosse on a personal level. One of the most distinguished 'men of letters' of the Victorian era, a prolific intellectual who published scholarship, fiction and poetry and editions of other poets' work, Gosse was one of 'the *right people*' whose attention Conrad sought and whose company he hoped one day to share (*CL* 1:405). In approaching Gosse, Conrad was announcing, with naïve impudence, his intention to enter the Victorian literary tradition – one, in fact, eroding rapidly.

The era in which Conrad entered Britain's literary market-place saw prominent authors dramatizing the palpable threat to the traditions of Victorian authorship and publishing. In 1891, George Gissing published *New Grub Street*, a novel satirizing the degradation of Victorian literary culture through the industrialization of the market-place. Another of Conrad's literary models, Henry James, published a series of fables in the 1890s about authors struggling against market-place forces.[1] One of these stories, 'The Middle Years', first published in *Scribner's Magazine* in May 1893, portrays the gradual demise of Dencombe, a semi-autobiographical 'fingerer of style' who has fled the deleterious bustle of the London market-place for the recuperative air of a seaside resort.[2] The 'death' of the Victorian literary sensibility was a ramification of the widespread democratic reforms that revolutionized British culture in the nineteenth century. The expansion of the electorate, through the Reform Acts of 1832, 1867 and 1884, in conjunction with the gradual establishment of compulsory schooling by the Education Acts of 1870 and 1880, endowed new sectors of the population with the agency to attain knowledge. Contemporaneous technological advances, such as the transition from steam, gas and water power to electricity and the perfection of the rotary press, enabled the widespread distribution of literature of all kinds, particularly in periodical form.

The periodical market grew exponentially during the nineteenth century. The 1890s saw the proliferation of a new kind of monthly miscellany, represented by Newnes' *Strand* and *Pearson's Magazine*, each of which had circulations of a quarter-million by 1900. By diverging from the Victorian tradition of serializing novels over multiple issues, these and other popular magazines Conrad despised did much to nurture the short story in Britain. The growth of the periodicals threatened the book publishing magnates – Constable, Macmillan, Blackwood's and Smith, Elder.

From the 1810s until the century's final decade, these houses resisted democratizing trends by their commitment to the three-decker novel. At a time when an average labourer made approximately 24 pence (2 shillings) per week, the three-decker sold at an astronomical 10 shillings and sixpence per volume. Keeping new fiction out of the reach of the growing middle class insulated the Victorian literati from the perceived threat of mass culture. The three-decker flourished only because of the publishers' arrangement with the circulating libraries, which charged an annual 1s subscription fee. But towards the end of the century, a new generation of publishers recognized the economic advantage in bypassing the intermediary libraries and appealing directly to the reader with new, affordable literature. The most successful of these were Conrad's first publisher, T. Fisher Unwin (est. 1883), John Lane of the Bodley Head (est. 1889), Algernon Methuen (est. 1889), William Heinemann (est. 1890) and Grant Richards (est. 1897). Growth led to consolidation and, generally speaking, a more equitable market-place. Walter Besant founded the Society of Authors in 1883; the Associated Booksellers was established in 1895; and the Publisher's Association followed the very next year. The reign of the three-decker came to an end in 1894, when the circulating libraries refused to comply with the publishers' demands regarding price and republication rights.[3] Conrad's first publication the following year thus situates him firmly in the era of modern book publishing.

Gosse and Heinemann rejected *Almayer's Folly*, but Unwin, on the advice of his readers W. H. Chesson and Edward Garnett, accepted the manuscript. This was an unusual beginning to a writing career. Fiction writers of the late-Victorian period typically entered the profession through periodicals, many supplementing their income by contributing to what Conrad referred to as the 'degradation of daily journalism' (*CL* 2:34). Arnold Bennett published journalism and criticism in newspapers and magazines – *Fortnightly Review*, *Pall Mall Gazette* and *Saturday Review* – for several years before he took 'up fiction for a livelihood' in 1898.[4] H. G. Wells published a series of quasi-scientific essays about time travel in W. E. Henley's *National Observer* while he was publishing fictional renderings of his concepts in a wide range of periodicals, including the *Graphic, Illustrated London News* and *Strand*. Heinemann published the book version of *The Time Machine* in 1895.

At the beginning of his second career, Conrad was seemingly averse to the idea of magazine publication and sold the book rights to his first two novels – six years of work – to Unwin for the combined sum of £70.[5] Unwin was certainly taking a risk by publishing an unknown author, but Conrad's payments were absurdly low considering that at mid-century an author could expect between £50 and £200 for the rights to a new novel.[6] In 1897, the Conrads rented a farmhouse outside Stanford-le-Hope for £28 per year.[7] To make a proper living, Garnett convinced Conrad that he had to write short stories. Although Edward Garnett was just beginning his career when he met Conrad, he had industry connections through his father, Richard, Keeper of Printed Books at the British Museum. Over the course of his career, Garnett would serve as a reader with Heinemann, Duckworth, Grant Richards, John Lane and Jonathan Cape, but he was much more than a publisher's reader. Garnett used his intermediary position in the publishing process to discover and nurture the talents of Conrad, D. H. Lawrence and Henry Green, among others. Personally and professionally, Conrad's friend did much to nurture the development of literary Modernism in Britain.[8]

Conrad began to write short stories in 1896, and he and Garnett set out to place them before 'the *right people*' (*CL* 1:405). The results were varied. Conrad's first appearance was an awkward one. He had written 'The Idiots' in the naturalist style, hoping it would appeal to an avant-garde magazine such as *Cosmopolis* or *Cornhill*. When these publications rejected the story, Conrad took Garnett's advice and submitted it to *Savoy*, a decadent periodical edited by Arthur Symons intended to rival the *Yellow Book*. The story appeared in October 1896, out of place alongside Aubrey Beardsley's illustrations. 'The Lagoon' appeared in *Cornhill* (January 1897), a competitor with *Macmillan's* in the genre of high-priced glossy monthlies. Established in 1860, the *Cornhill* had been 'the premier literary magazine of the High Victorian period', reaching a circulation of 110,000.[9] The bitterly ironic 'An Outpost of Progress' could not have been more out of place in *Cosmopolis* (June–July 1897); its first instalment abutted an article called 'The Reign of Queen Victoria' by Sir Richard Temple

extolling 'the expansion of the Empire, its material development, its progress in all matters'.[10] However compromised Conrad might have felt his
literary ideals to be, he could not deny the necessity of periodical publication:
'An Outpost of Progress' alone earned £45, more than the much longer
Almayer's Folly.

These early magazine publications were important for Conrad moneta-
rily, but it was the serialization of *The Nigger of the 'Narcissus'* in W(illiam)
E(rnest) Henley's *New Review* (August–December 1897) that Conrad
would later describe as 'the first event in my writing life which really
counted' (*CL* 3:115).[11] Also editor of the *Scots Observer* (later *National
Observer*), Henley was an esteemed poet, man of letters, good friend of
Kipling's and an outspoken advocate of imperialism. The *New Review*
published many authors Conrad admired, including Wells, James, George
Moore, R. B. Cunninghame Graham and Stephen Crane, and Conrad felt
his appearance there put him before 'the *right people*'. Heinemann, 'a
pioneering new firm' that published Crane and Wells, as well as *New
Review*, bought the book rights to *The Nigger of the 'Narcissus'*.[12] The story
was also a success financially, earning Conrad £100 combined from serial
and book rights, in addition to royalties (15 per cent on the first 2,000 and
20 per cent thereafter).

After this success, Garnett suggested Conrad send a story to *Blackwood's
Magazine*, founded in 1817, shortly after the innovation of the high-priced
three-decker novel. *Maga*, as it was fondly referred to, had a long tradition
of serializing fiction. It was a tradition in which Conrad was eager to be
included, even though he disparaged his submission, 'Karain: A Memory',
as 'magazine'ish' (*CL* 2:57). *Blackwood's*, represented by David S. Meldrum,
bought 'Karain' for £40 and requested first refusal of any future stories by
Conrad. It was the kind of patronage the fledgeling author had desperately
been seeking, and he clung to it for the next four years.

During Conrad's 'Blackwood period', *Maga* serialized 'Karain', ' Youth'
(September 1898), 'The Heart of Darkness' (February–April 1899), *Lord
Jim* (October 1899 – November 1900) and 'The End of the Tether' (July–
December 1902). And the firm published *Lord Jim* (1900) and *Youth:
A Narrative and Two Other Stories* (1902) in volume form. In addition to
the steady income, Blackwood's patronage provided Conrad with liberties
of style and timetable that other publishers most likely would not have
granted. *Lord Jim* is the most significant example. Conrad began the novel
as a story to fill two instalments of *Maga*, but the story grew, and, under the
advice of Meldrum, Blackwood permitted Conrad to run with it. *Lord Jim*
wound up spanning fourteen instalments. Conrad earned £500 for *Lord*

Jim: £300 for serial rights and a £200 advance on royalties of approximately 17 per cent.[13] Given the combination of financial security and artistic freedom that Conrad received from Blackwood's, it is not unreasonable to credit Meldrum and Blackwood with enabling Conrad to develop the style of his major period.

Conrad would later reflect to his agent J(ames) B(rand) Pinker that *Blackwood's Magazine* presented him before 'a good sort of public. There isn't a single club and messroom and man-of-war in the British Seas and Dominions which hasn't its copy of Maga' (*CL* 4:506). But, as early as January 1901, Conrad had desired 'to reach another public than Maga's' (*CL* 2:321). Conrad first dealt with Pinker in 1900 over *The Inheritors* (1901), the *roman à clef* Conrad co-authored with Ford Madox Ford (then Hueffer). Conrad engaged Pinker as his personal literary agent later that year, although he waited until 1903 to announce this to the loyal Blackwood, at which time their friendship and business relationships became hopelessly severed.

The figure of the literary agent arose in the 1880s in response to the growing complexity of the literary market-place. The growth of the newspaper and magazine markets, as well as the development of the syndicates, and the extension of American copyright to British writers provided by the 1891 Chace Act (US Congress), made the literary market-place an increasingly unwelcoming and disorienting place for the author to conduct his business. For 10 per cent commission, an agent would solicit publishers and arrange advantageous contracts, enabling the writers to exploit the publishing opportunities in what was 'a golden age for the working writer'.[14] With the help of a tactful agent, a fiction writer could earn upwards of six or more payments for a single piece of work, including payments for British and American serial rights, book and reprint rights, imperial rights, translation rights and rights for foreign publication in English.[15]

Pinker worked for the *Levant Herald*, acted as a publisher's reader and edited *Pearson's Magazine* before setting up his agency in 1896. He represented, among many others, Bennett, Crane and Wells, and, after convincing him to turn his back on Heinemann in 1898, Henry James. Pinker placed 'Typhoon' in *Pall Mall* (est. 1893), a large-circulation monthly comparable to the *Strand*, the first of its kind in which Conrad appeared.[16] Although the £100 Conrad received for 'Typhoon' was beggarly in comparison to the £1,500 *Pall Mall* paid for Rider Haggard's *Joan Haste* in 1894,[17] this publication represents 'a threshold moment' in Conrad's 'accommodation to the sensibilities of a popular magazine audience'.[18] During his 'Blackwood period', Conrad had worked almost in a vacuum, writing for one specific magazine without the pressures of firm deadlines. Pinker, 'the ever-alert transatlantic commuter and maker of deals', brought Conrad '"upon the market"' while at the same time insulating him from the business side of publishing (*CL* 2:xxiii, 425). Late in life, Conrad would state, somewhat hyperbolically, that his literary achievements owed 'their existence to Mr Pinker as much as to me' (*CL* 5:619); indeed, Pinker's influence on Conrad's literary output is inestimable.

In addition to managing Conrad's finances, essentially acting as a bank to the prodigal writer, Pinker attuned Conrad to the rhythms of modern literary production by supplying him with writing assignments for periodicals, both fiction and non-fiction, while he toiled at his novels. Although Conrad always had difficulty meeting deadlines, Pinker forced Conrad to prioritize his tasks and goaded him into becoming more efficient. Conrad once bragged to Wells that he was composing *Nostromo* during the day and dictating occasional essays (collected in *The Mirror of the Sea*) 'without effort at the rate of 3000 words in four hours' at night (*CL* 3:112). Pinker was especially important in developing Conrad's reputation in America. *Harper's Monthly Magazine*, 'the most widely respected magazine of its kind in America at the time', published several stories of Conrad's middle period, but the serialization of *Chance* in the Sunday supplement of the *New York Herald* in 1912 vaulted Conrad to the ranks of celebrity and made him rich.[19] In 1918, a single essay fetched Conrad £250 from the *Daily Mail*.

But the appearance of 'Typhoon' in the populist *Pall Mall* did not mean Conrad had given up his hostility towards serials – he had merely decided to ignore them. Pinker placed *Nostromo* (Harper/Harper, 1904) in *T. P.'s Weekly* (January–October 1904), a slightly more literary version of *Tit-Bits* or *Pearson's*. Conrad called it 'T P's horror' and, upon the editor's request for abridgement, wrote to Pinker, 'I have no objection to the compression of the story for the purpose of serial pub^{on} ... as long as I am not called upon to do the compressing myself ... I would stipulate also that no proofs should be sent to me' (*CL* 3:91–2). This detachment carried over to the serialization of *The Secret Agent* (Methuen/Harper, 1907) in *Ridgway's Magazine: A Militant Weekly for God and Country* (October–December 1906), 'a down-market magazine' primarily dealing in genre fiction.[20] Conrad wrote to Pinker, 'Ridgway's are sending me their rag. It's awful – and it don't matter in the least. I see they are "editing" the stuff pretty severely' (*CL* 3:369). Conrad added about 26,000 words to *The Secret Agent* for book publication. Contrast Conrad's attitude towards periodical publication with a letter he wrote to Pinker regarding Harper's American book publication of *Nostromo*: 'Whatever happens I must have proofs of the book … I can't let a book of mine go into the world without a careful personal revision' (*CL* 3:92). Publication context remained important for Conrad through-out his career, and in 1914 he begged the literary collector John Quinn not to read *Victory* in *Munsey's Magazine*, writing, 'I don't want you to see it in double columns and crowded type … A book is written for the eye' (*CL* 5:403).

Early in his career, Conrad may have suffered from 'his peregrinations among publishers' (largely the result of a search for the most favourable terms), but over the course of his career Conrad did not spread his books among publishers as liberally as some of his more popular contemporaries.[21] In his middle and late career, Conrad published with Harper's, Methuen and Dent. In America, Conrad published almost exclusively with Harper's between *Nostromo* (1904) and *Chance* (1913) but then became a major Doubleday author. By contrast, the popular novelist Eden Phillpotts, on the other hand, published titles with Osgood, McIlvaine, Bliss, Sands & Foster, French, Methuen, Simpkin, Harper, Newnes, Chapman & Hall, John Lane, John Murray, Cassell, Macmillan, Duckworth, Heinemann, Hutchinson and Smith, Elder – all during Conrad's career. Wells, a more literary writer than Phillpotts, also appeared under more imprints than Conrad.

In his 1905 appreciation of Henry James, Conrad reflected that the lack of a collected edition of James' work signified his modernity, his refusal to put 'forth a hasty claim to completeness' in the fashion of Dickens, Thackeray and Hardy.[22] As Conrad was writing, though, James and Pinker were in negotiations with Scribner's for the New York Edition. Conrad actively participated in the production of the first collected editions of his work published by Heinemann in Britain and Doubleday in America (both 1920–1). These de luxe, limited editions, which were supplemented by Dent's more modestly priced, popular edition (1923–8), helped secure Conrad's canonical status, particularly in America, and earned him £5,500.[23]

NOTES

1. These fables of authorship include 'The Lesson of the Master' (*Universal Review*, 16 July and 15 August 1888), 'The Real Thing' (*Black and White*, 16 April 1892), 'The Middle Years' (*Scribner's Magazine*, May 1893), 'The Death of the Lion' (*Yellow Book*, April 1894), 'The Coxon Fund' (*Yellow Book*, July 1894), 'The Next Time' (*Yellow Book*, July 1895) and 'The Figure in the Carpet' (*Cosmopolis*, January and February 1896).

2. Henry James, 'The Middle Years', in *The Complete Tales of Henry James*, Vol. IX: *1892–1898*, ed. Leon Edel (London: Rupert Hart-Davis, 1964), pp. 53–76, 63.
3. In *A History of British Publishing* (London: Croom Helm, 1988), p. 55, John Feather reports that the number of three-deckers published dropped from 183 in 1894, to 52 in 1895 and to a mere 4 in 1897. Detailed accounts of the three-decker's decline can be found in Margaret D. Stetz, 'Publishing Industries and Practices', in *The Cambridge Companion to the Fin de Siècle*, ed. Gail Marshall (Cambridge: Cambridge University Press, 2007), pp. 113–30, and John Sutherland, *Victorian Novelists and Publishers* (Chicago: University of Chicago Press, 1976).
4. Arnold Bennett, *The Journals of Arnold Bennett, 1896–1910*, ed. Newman Flower (London: Cassell, 1932), pp. 79–80.
5. Conrad received £20 for *Almayer's Folly* and £50 for *An Outcast*, with 10 per cent royalty, rising to 12.5 per cent after the first 2,000 copies and to 15 per cent after 4,000 copies.
6. Richard D. Altick, *English Common Reader: A Social History of the Mass Reading Public, 1800–1900* (Chicago: University of Chicago Press, 1957).
7. Jeffrey Meyers, *Joseph Conrad: A Biography* (London: Murray, 1991), p. 155.
8. Garnett's impact on Conrad's creative process has been examined by Cedric Watts in 'Edward Garnett's Influence on Conrad', *The Conradian*, 21 (Spring 1996), 79–92. See also George Jefferson, *Edward Garnett: A Life in Literature* (London: Jonathan Cape, 1982).
9. Michael Ashley, *The Age of the Storytellers: British Popular Fiction Magazines, 1880–1950* (London: The British Library, 2006), pp. 250–2.
10. Richard Temple, 'The Reign of Queen Victoria', *Cosmopolis*, 6 (June 1897), 621–36.
11. This comment must be taken with a grain of salt, as Conrad made it in memoriam to Henley, who died in 1903.
12. Peter McDonald, *British Literary Culture and Publishing Practice, 1880–1914* (Cambridge: Cambridge University Press, 1997), p. 15.
13. Cedric Watts, *Joseph Conrad: A Literary Life* (Basingstoke: Macmillan, 1989), p. 76.
14. Introduction to Joseph Conrad's *Notes on Life and Letters*, ed. J. H. Stape (Cambridge: Cambridge University Press, 2004), p. xxvii.
15. In Germany, Tauchnitz published translated editions of many of the most accomplished British writers, including several Conrad titles.
16. Ashley, *The Age of the Storytellers*, p. 149, contends that the *Pall Mall*'s one-shilling price lent it a more 'elitist feel' than such sixpenny monthlies as the *Strand*. *Pall Mall* would subsequently publish four more of Conrad's stories as well as a few of the essays collected in *The Mirror of the Sea*.
17. Ashley, *The Age of the Storytellers*, p. 149.
18. Stephen Donovan, *Joseph Conrad and Popular Culture* (Basingstoke: Palgrave, 2005), p. 180.

19. S. W. Reid, 'American Markets, Serials, and Conrad's Career', *The Conradian*, 28.1 (2003), 57–100, p. 66.
20. Watts, *A Literary Life*, p. 103.
21. Frederick R. Karl, *Joseph Conrad: The Three Lives – A Biography* (London: Faber & Faber, 1979), p. 381.
22. Conrad, 'Henry James: An Appreciation', in *Notes on Life and Letters*, ed. Stape, p. 15.
23. Watts, *A Literary Life*, p. 128.

CHAPTER 28

Reading

Linda Dryden

In 1913, Conrad wrote to Alfred A. Knopf, then a clerk at Doubleday: 'When it comes to popularity I stand much nearer the public mind than Stevenson who was superliterary, a conscious virtuoso of style; whereas the average mind does not care much for virtuosity' (*CL* 9:257). Conrad was conscious of Stevenson's reputation for popular literature and of his wide readership, a fact he envied because it brought popularity and much-needed cash. Conrad was persuading Knopf to advocate *Chance* to Doubleday, and his fortunes were about to change. *Chance* marked a breakthrough for Conrad whose subject matter had previously attracted a largely male readership – specifically his work for *Blackwood's Magazine* – and who had been chided by no less than H. G. Wells for not making 'the slightest concessions to the reading young woman who makes or mars the fortunes of authors'.[1] In the event, *Chance* sold 10,000 copies in America alone during its first week of publication.

Writing in 1918 to Doubleday, by then his main American publisher,[2] Conrad claims inclusivity rather than exclusivity for his work: 'I want to be read by many eyes and all kinds of them, at that. I pride myself that there is no sentence of my writing, either thought or image, that is not accessible' (*CL* 6:333). He is speaking of *The Arrow of Gold*, which had just begun serialization in *Lloyd's Magazine* and was to be published in America by Doubleday. Despite Conrad's aspirations to appeal to a wide audience, Stephen Donovan speaks of his 'unconcealed contempt' for his fellow citizens 'whom he variously labelled "the herd of idiotic humanity" (*CL* 1:17), "a great multitude whose voice is a shout" (*CL* 3:13), "the great Public (which has the sails of windmills for brains)" (*CL* 5:165) and "the Democracy of the book-stalls" (*CL* 5:173)'. As Donovan says, 'Conrad protested on many occasions (albeit rarely to his agent or publishers) that he had no desire to be popular', while complaining of not earning enough from his fiction.[3]

Yet, in his early writing career, Conrad found it hard to escape the shadow of others' successes: Rudyard Kipling had captured the public imagination with *The Jungle Book* (1894), Stevenson was immensely popular, and Rider Haggard had created a buoyant market for imperial fantasies. The public taste for this imperial and adventure fiction was exploited by Conrad in early novels like *Almayer's Folly, An Outcast of the Islands* and *Lord Jim.* With tales set in the exotic East, Conrad thus found himself compared with others who were writing about the Empire: a reviewer of Conrad's first novel suggested that 'he might become the Kipling of the Malay Archipelago', while his second was declared to be 'like one of Mr Stevenson's … grown miraculously long and miraculously tedious'.[4] Conrad's awareness of the saleability of such fiction is evident in his collaboration with Ford Madox Ford on *Romance* (1903), where they consciously aimed to write an adventure novel to 'tap the audience for Stevenson, Anthony Hope, and Rider Haggard'.[5] Despite Conrad's disparaging comments about Stevenson, an unsigned review of *Typhoon* (1903) in the *Speaker* hails him as a successor to the Scotsman: 'There are times in reading his work when we think that Stevenson with new experiences has taken up his work when it broke off in his noble fragment *Weir of Hermiston*.'[6] Stevenson was still very much in the public mind, and this comparison must have stung Conrad, who regarded himself as 'modern' and Stevenson as belonging to an earlier age.

Edward Garnett recalls that in their second meeting in 1894 he had tried to persuade Conrad to ignore public opinion and 'follow his own path'. Conrad's response was 'emphatic': "But I *won't* live in an attic!" he retorted. "I'm past that, you understand? I *won't* live in an attic!"[7] David Meldrum confided to William Blackwood in 1900: 'I wish I could believe that he would ever be "popular" in the popular sense, but he is too good for that.'[8] To Donovan, Meldrum's remark 'highlights the slipperiness of the term "popular" for literary producers of Conrad's generation'.[9] Nevertheless, popularity was necessary to stave off poverty, eventually leading to Conrad's accepting the promotion of his work through advertising, despite earlier contempt for the practice.[10] By 1901 he was actively urging his agent, J. B. Pinker, to encourage publishers to make a 'fuss' over 'Typhoon': "'Mr. J Conrad's new tale Typhoon begins in … etc etc." That kind of thing. The public's so used to the guidance of Advertis[e] ment! Why! even I myself feel the spell of such emphasis' (*CL* 2:319). In the early twentieth century, commercialization was becoming essential to gaining a readership, even for authors of Conrad's integrity, as his enthusiasm here testifies.

This example of how Conrad had to accept the power of advertising highlights the fact that his career as a writer spans a period of some thirty years, from the publication of *Almayer's Folly* in 1895 to his death in 1924. This period of huge social, political and cultural change had an enormous impact on the literary market-place and the tastes of the reading public. Conrad began writing as the three-decker novel became obsolete, the high Victorian realist novel was on the wane, and Naturalism was about to flourish briefly. As a consequence, Conrad's writing, with its experimental form and technique, occupies a liminal position between two centuries – as Frederic Jameson says, 'floating uncertainly somewhere in between Proust and Robert Louis Stevenson'.[11]

The Victorian age in Britain had ushered in a new reading public: books and fiction were not new but 'what was new was the emergence of new fictions, new types of books and a new reading public'.[12] The 1871 Education Act had produced a new class of readers whose literary tastes required these new genres, and whose thirst for literature resulted in a fiction publishing boom. Peter Keating comments that, by the *fin de siècle*, a vast amount of fiction was being published in various forms, citing Walter Besant's lament in 1895 that the opening chapters of eight new novels would appear in one new publication alone.[13] Over a decade earlier, Bernard Shaw had complained of failing to find a publisher for his first novel, *Immaturity* (1879), because of the public desire for a new type of literature. As John Carey notes: 'Publishers were finding that people wanted not George Eliot nor the "excessively literary" Bernard Shaw, but adventure stories like Stevenson's *Treasure Island* and *Dr Jekyll and Mr Hyde*.'[14] Keating feels that it is understandable that 'writers like Conrad, James and Gissing who could rely on only a handful of people to read their novels should have taken a jaundiced view of all of this activity' in the world of fiction publications. Libraries afforded cheap and easy access for working-class readers: 'given the choice, most readers, regardless of class, would prefer Ouida to George Eliot, Mrs Henry Wood to Thackeray'.[15] In such a crowded market-place, it is inevitable that Conrad felt the need to embrace the hitherto disdained practice of advertising.

Conrad was in competition for an audience with a host of popular writers who were responsible for the emergence of new genres of fiction, like the detective novel (Conan Doyle), cowboy fiction (Bret Harte) or science fiction (H. G. Wells).[16] In an attempt to capitalize on the public taste for fantasy fiction, Conrad collaborated again with Ford on an unsuccessful scientific romance, *The Inheritors* (1901), a tale of dimensional travel. It was Wells, however, who had captured the public imagination with *The Time Machine* (1895), a novel to which *The Inheritors* is indebted. Wells was a best-selling author of scientific romances (as science fiction was then called) well into the twentieth century. W. H. Hudson was also writing fantastical fiction, notably *Green Mansions* (1904), a fantasy set in Venezuela, and the futuristic novel *A Crystal Age* (1887). Even Henry James tried his hand at the weird and fantastic in *The Turn of the Screw* (1898). Despite his lack of success with the genre, Conrad's attempt with *The Inheritors* signals his sensitivity to the literary market-place.

H. Rider Haggard's popular, fantastical, imperial romances were familiar to many of Conrad's early readers, who often expected something similar from Conrad's pen, leading some to misinterpret Conrad's intent: the *Manchester Guardian*'s anonymous review of 'Heart of Darkness' on 10 December 1902 asserts that Conrad is not attacking 'colonisation, expansion, even Imperialism' because in 'no one is the essence of the adventurous spirit more instinctive'.[17] Reflecting the public appetite for romance and adventure, Haggard's first novel and a major bestseller, *King Solomon's Mines* (1885), was a response to his brother's challenge to write something as successful as *Treasure Island*. Conrad's tales of human fallibility set against exotic landscapes could not match the saleability of such blockbusters, yet he had read Haggard: Garnett recalls that in that conversation in 1894 Conrad had 'stigmatised' Haggard as '"too horrible for words"', adding that he 'objected specifically to the figure of Captain Goode, as well he might!'[18] Rather than emulate fiction like Haggard's, Conrad was writing anti-romance that leaned towards Modernism, thus alienating those readers hungry for traditional imperial adventure stories.

There was also an established readership for sensation fiction: Marie Corelli's *The Sorrows of Satan* appeared in the same year as *Almayer's Folly*. Even Arnold Bennett could boast to his friend George Sturt: 'I believe I could fart sensation fiction now.'[19] Conrad could appeal to this audience by implying the supernatural in such tales as *The Nigger of the 'Narcissus'*, 'The Secret Sharer' and 'The Inn of the Two Witches'; but he was more concerned with form and artistic intent. However, as Mary Hammond argues, like other literary genres, Modernism 'had very ill-defined and permeable boundaries', and 'the art/market opposition was less a divide than a negotiating table'. In such a competitive market-place, modernists like Conrad, Joyce and Woolf were obliged, in each case unsuccessfully, to attempt to publish in the mass-circulation publication *Tit-Bits*, where writers like Haggard found favour, and which launched Bennett's career.[20]

Before trying to break into this more commercial market, Conrad had depended on the conservative *Maga*, as *Blackwood's Magazine* was affectionately known, where he found a guaranteed audience of men at home and in the colonies for his tales of Empire. By 1901, however, he realized that he needed to widen his readership, declaring to Pinker that there were several reasons why he wished to leave *Maga*, 'one of them being that I wish to reach another public than *Maga's*' (*CL* 2:321). He found a more domestic audience for the serialization of 'Typhoon' (1902) with *Pall Mall*, which published writers as diverse as Bram Stoker and Thomas Hardy. In the early years of the twentieth century he went on to publish in a variety of magazines aimed at a broad readership, among them *McClure's*, *Outlook*, *Metropolitan*, *English Review*, *Munsey's*, *Harper's* and *T. P.'s Weekly*, and found success in America with *Chance* and the *New York Herald*. As with *Pall Mall*, Conrad sought publication in magazines whose readership was diverse, and whose contributions ranged from the popular romance to the amateur lady poet and essayist, to the experimental and modernist. As the twentieth century progressed, it was clear that Conrad could no longer rely on the exclusive readership of a magazine like *Blackwood's*: financial security demanded that he publish alongside forays into literature by genteel ladies and retired generals, and best-selling writers like Haggard.

The term 'best-seller' was first coined in the 1890s and included novels like Anthony Hope's *The Prisoner of Zenda* (1894), Mary Cholmondley's *Red Pottage* (1899) and Horace de Vere Stackpole's *The Blue Lagoon* (1908). One the most prolific of the early twentieth-century best-selling authors was E. Phillips Oppenheim, who began his writing career in 1887 with *Expiation* and ended it, over 100 novels later, with *The Last Train Out* in 1940. So successful was his formula of suspenseful, melodramatic thrillers and romances that Oppenheim's *The Great Impersonation* sold over a million copies in 1920: Conrad must have been envious, even though, as the grand old man of English letters, he had by that time become a household name and a commercially successful author. Conrad rarely wrote potboilers: his tales were of human, moral and political dilemmas, like *The Secret Agent*, and rapidly produced 'page-turners' like Oppenheim's were formidable competition.

Despite appearing on the eve of the First World War, when the public may not have actively sought stories of romance, Conrad had finally tapped the commercial market he had both mocked and yearned for when he published *Chance*. The Edwardian era still embraced tales by Kipling, Haggard, and John Buchan's *Prester John* (1910), which celebrated the Empire. It also witnessed the emergence of influential new authors like G. K. Chesterton, Compton Mackenzie, E. M. Forster, Galsworthy, Saki, Walpole, and the beginnings of the careers of some of the giants of Modernism like Joyce and Woolf. Tastes were again changing, and it is an irony that, as the twentieth century emerged into full view, Conrad's best work was arguably behind him, yet the success for which he had so long striven came with novels commonly regarded as not belonging to his 'major phase'.[21] As Keating notes, the rise of the best-seller would have been proof for writers like Conrad of 'Britain's cultural decadence', evidence that the future could be guaranteed only by the 'sensitive' few. Reviewing *A Portrait of the Artist as a Young Man* in 1917, Ezra Pound

noted sarcastically that Joyce could not expect 'members of the "Fly-Fishers" and "Royal Automobile" clubs, and of the "Isthmian"' to read his book, but that no longer mattered, as a new kind of reader was coming into being: 'The last few years have seen the gradual shaping of a party of intelligence, a party not bound by any central doctrine or theory.'[22]

For the modernists, including Conrad, patience was all: these new 'intelligent' readers were a discerning minority. The modernists certainly had a readership, but nothing to compare with the sales of a Galsworthy, a Wells or a Bennett. While reserving her gratitude for Conrad, Hardy and Hudson, Virginia Woolf famously denounced Wells, Bennett and Galsworthy who, she felt, 'excited so many hopes and disappointed them so persistently'. Conrad's readership was diverse, but, as Woolf explains, he was also rather exclusive: 'Schoolboys of fourteen, driving their way through Marryat, Scott, Henty, and Dickens, swallowed him down with the rest; while the seasoned and the fastidious, who in process of time have eaten their way to the heart of literature and there turn over and over a few precious crumbs, set Conrad scrupulously upon their banqueting table.'[23] Writing in the mid-1920s, Woolf was responding to very different social and cultural conditions from those that prevailed when Conrad began his writing career. Universal literacy was no longer a distant dream, and escapism through literature was available to a wide audience. Clive Bloom notes how in the 1920s 'writers like Ethel M. Dell catered for "women with tiring and monotonous jobs; housekeepers, governesses, lady companions, maids [and] nurses"'.[24] *Chance* may well have attracted such an audience too. Certainly, from its publication in 1913 to his death in 1924, Conrad earned a comfortable living from his writing and a considerable reputation amongst the intelligentsia of the day. However, it is not for this commer-cially successful novel that Conrad's reputation endures: he may have sought popularity for financial gain, and perhaps as proof of his artistic appeal, but it is in the power and integrity of a literature that conveys the truths of solidarity with, and fidelity to, humankind that Conrad's legacy really lies.

NOTES

1. In J. H. Stape and Owen Knowles, eds., *A Portrait in Letters: Correspondence to and about Conrad* (Amsterdam and Atlanta, GA: Rodopi, 1996), p. 21.
2. See Owen Knowles and Gene M. Moore, *Oxford Reader's Companion to Conrad* (Oxford: Oxford University Press, 2000), pp. 110–11.
3. Stephen Donovan, *Joseph Conrad and Popular Culture* (Basingstoke: Palgrave, 2005), pp. 10, 9.
4. In Norman Sherry, ed., *Conrad: The Critical Heritage* (London: Routledge & Kegan Paul, 1973), pp. 61, 70.
5. Frederick R. Karl, *Joseph Conrad: The Three Lives – A Biography* (London: Faber & Faber, 1979), p. 438.
6. In Sherry, ed., *Conrad: The Critical Heritage*, p. 158.
7. Edward Garnett, ed., *Letters from Conrad: 1895 to 1924* (Bloomsbury: Nonesuch Press, 1928), p. xiii.
8. William Blackburn, ed., *Joseph Conrad: Letters to William Blackwood and David S. Meldrum* (Durham, NC: Duke University Press, 1958), p. 122.
9. Donovan, *Joseph Conrad and Popular Culture*, p. 7.
10. Donovan cites Conrad's protest to Unwin 'against the abominable advertisement being put opposite [his] dedication' in *An Outcast of the Islands*, and various other objections to the practice, as evidence that in his early career Conrad was concerned about 'a medium whose power over literary production could no longer be ignored or denied' (Donovan, *Joseph Conrad and Popular Culture*, p. 117).
11. Frederic Jameson, *The Political Unconscious: Narrative as Socially Symbolic Act* (London: Methuen, 1981), p. 206.
12. Clive Bloom, *Cult Fiction: Popular Reading and Pulp Theory* (Basingstoke: Macmillan, 1996), p. 49.
13. Peter Keating, *The Haunted Study: A Social History of the English Novel 1875–1914* (London: Fontana Press, 1991), pp. 46–7.
14. John Carey, *The Intellectuals and the Masses: Pride and Prejudice among the Literary Intelligentsia, 1880–1939* (London: Faber & Faber, 1992), p. 6.
15. Keating, *The Haunted Study*, pp. 401, 437.
16. Though, of course, neither Wells nor his readers would have recognized the term 'science fiction', only coined in the 1920s.
17. In Sherry, ed., *Conrad: The Critical Heritage*, p. 135.
18. Garnett, ed., *Letters from Conrad*, pp. xiii–xiv.
19. In Keating, *The Haunted Study*, p. 84.
20. Mary Hammond, *Reading, Publishing and the Formation of Literary Taste in England, 1880–1914* (Aldershot: Ashgate, 2006), p. 6.

21. The term refers to Jacques Berthoud's important work, *Joseph Conrad: The Major Phase* (Cambridge: Cambridge University Press, 1978).
22. Keating, *The Haunted Study*, p. 445.
23. Virginia Woolf, *The Common Reader*, First Series (London: The Hogarth Press, 1968), pp. 185, 282–3.
24. Clive Bloom, *Bestsellers: Popular Fiction Since 1900* (Basingstoke: Palgrave Macmillan, 2002), p. 69.

CHAPTER 29

Religion

John Lester

The messianic expectancy that pervaded the first half of the nineteenth century assumed a national character in Poland. In works by Adam Mickiewicz (1798–1855), Juliusz Słowacki (1809–49) and, most explicitly, in *Dawn* (1843) by Zygmunt Krasiński (1812–59), Poland itself was likened to Christ: crucified for the sins of the world, the nation would, on its own Third Day, rise again as the herald of God's Kingdom on Earth. As Conrad confirmed in a letter to Marguerite Poradowska, his Franco-Belgian relation by marriage, 'Don't forget that with us religion and patriotism go hand in hand' (*CL* 1:174). This kind of passionate religious nationalism led to the deaths of both of Conrad's parents and, in adulthood, Conrad claimed that 'from the age of fourteen' he had always 'disliked the Christian religion' (*CL* 2:468–9). Nevertheless, his works show a detailed knowledge of the King James version of the Bible, which, whether for religious or literary reasons, he could only have read as an adult.[1]

In Poland, fervent Catholicism was integral to nationalistic identity. Shortly after Conrad's birth, a group of priests calling themselves the 'Catholic Clergy of the Kingdom of Poland' proclaimed Catholicism as the country's national religion.[2] Indeed Conrad's first sense of identity, written with the aid of a guiding hand on the back of a photograph sent to his grandmother, was that of 'Pole, Catholic, nobleman'.[3] Although, in time, each of these markers would fade, he retained some sense of Catholic identity to the end of his life, once declining to join a London club on the grounds that 'one of the conditions of membership is to be a Protestant' (*CL* 8:190). 'I was born a R[oman] C[atholic]', he reminds his correspondent, 'and though dogma sits lightly on me I have never renounced that form of Christian religion'.

Despite the bold claims of its clergy, however, the Poland of Conrad's childhood was as oppressed in religion as in other matters, with an Orthodox Russian at the head of the Church, restrictions placed on the content of sermons and direct contact with the Vatican forbidden. Indeed, the Polish clergy received no encouragement from Rome, which, as the 1847–63 Concordat between the Pope and the Tsar revealed, remained an ally of autocracy, unlikely to support a revolt against established authority.

In Russia herself, the Orthodox Church was firmly linked to government, and Conrad reflects this in *Under Western Eyes*, where the old priest reveals to Natalia Haldin and her mother that he has been ordered to spy on them and dare not disobey: 'He did not wish to spend the evening of his days with a shaven head in the penitent's cell of some monastery – "and subjected to all the severities of ecclesiastical discipline; for they would show no mercy to an old man", he groaned' (*UWE*, 139). Elsewhere Conrad revealed that:

the parish priests of the Greek Church … tried to soothe the passions of the excited peasantry and opposed rapine and violence whenever they could, with all their might. And this conduct they pursued against the express wishes of the authorities. Later on some of them were made to suffer for their disobedience by being removed abruptly to the far north or sent away to Siberian parishes. (*PR*, 61)

The Catholic Church under Pius IX soon faced a crisis at its very heart. The dogma of papal infallibility was proclaimed in 1870, but, soon after, Victor Emmanuel II absorbed the Papal States (including, crucially, Rome) into the Kingdom of Italy. The resulting impasse between Church and state existed throughout Conrad's adulthood. During his time in Marseilles he was aware of the Church's support for the Carlists, whose unrealistic attempt to restore the monarchy in Spain provides the backdrop to *The Arrow of Gold*. Years later, he spoke scathingly of a Catholic Association whose members 'engaged themselves with all their might and power to work for the restoration of the temporal power of the Pope. Conceive you that imbecility!' (*CL* 8:191).

If the Roman Catholic Church provided no bulwark against Poland's political enemies, neither did it appear to offer Apollo Korzeniowski the succour he needed on his wife Ewa's death. Conrad described his father's 'strong religious feeling degenerating after the loss of his wife into mysticism and despair' (*CL* 2:247). In light of such an inheritance, it is unsurprising that Conrad's attitudes towards Christianity are at best ambivalent. His letters are often dismissive, referring to its beginnings as an 'absurd oriental fable' (*CL* 5:358), and claiming that the 'business in the stable isn't convincing' (*CL* 2:469). Elsewhere, he speaks of the 'idiotic mystery of Heaven' (*CL* 1:268). He married in a civil ceremony, and he refused to allow his son John to learn any religion until he was six years old – whereupon he was amused by his son's description of the crucifixion as 'disgusting'.[4] But John Conrad also records his father saying: 'Don't assume that because I do not go to church that I do not believe, I do; all true seamen do in their hearts.'[5] In this, Conrad appears to be sharing the outlook of Giorgio Viola in *Nostromo* who, 'Though he disliked priests, and would not put his foot inside a church for anything, he believed in God' (*N*, 29).

Whatever Church they belong to, the priests and acolytes of Christianity fare badly in Conrad's fiction. Most obviously, there are religious fanatics, like the self-righteous Podmore, in *The Nigger of the 'Narcissus'*, or the hypocritical Thérèse, in *The Arrow of Gold*. More sympathetically, Captain Whalley's faith, in 'The End of the Tether', that God will keep him healthy for his daughter's sake is proved unfounded. In 'Heart of Darkness', the evangelizing mission becomes an excuse for the rape of Africa. Marlow's aunt sees him as a colonial 'emissary of light' and part of the grand design that involves 'weaning the ignorant millions from their horrid ways' (*Y*, 59). This gives an added ironic edge to the repeated description of the colonists as 'pilgrims'.

The Protestant clergy often seem naïve and out of touch with reality. In *Lord Jim*, Marlow pictures Jim's father, safe in the parsonage of a cosy English village, dwelling 'in the inviolable shelter of his book-lined, faded and comfortable study, where for forty years he had conscientiously gone over and over again the round of his little thoughts about faith and virtue, about the conduct of life and the only proper manner of dying' (*LJ*, 341). Yet Jim remains sure that he 'wouldn't understand' the predicament of his son (*LJ*, 79). The same book contains a missionary who believes he is converting Gentleman Brown, whilst Brown is actually planning to seduce the missionary's wife (*LJ*, 384).

The failings of Catholic clergy are most evident in *Nostromo*. The sadistic Father Beron willingly serves the ruthless dictator Guzman Bento by extorting confessions by torture, thus perverting the confessional (*N*, 373), whilst, at Bento's behest, 'a solemn Mass of thanksgiving … sung in great pomp in the cathedral of Sta. Marta' is celebrated by a 'trembling' and 'subservient' archbishop (*N*, 139). Nostromo's comment that no 'fat padre' would have come out to the dying Teresa except 'perhaps' under his protection (*N*, 268) reveals most clergy in Costaguana as self-seeking and cowardly. Father Corbelan is fearless but his main objective seems to be 'the restitution of confiscated Church property' in the country (*N*, 188–9), an insistence that continues to the end of the book and which seems to be approved of in Rome (*N*, 478). This echoes the situation in Poland where Church lands were also confiscated. The ignorance and superstition of many Polish priests and their flocks are echoed by the priests in *Nostromo* informing a credulous 'barefoot multitude' that Bento's body has been taken away by the devil (*N*, 47). Even the likeable Father Roman, by claiming that Europe is 'a country of saints and miracles' (*N*, 103), is perpetuating ignorance and superstition among the Indians and may be revealing his own. His perplexity that Mrs Gould seems 'angelic' despite being 'evidently a heretic' (*N*, 399) illustrates the Catholic/Protestant divide in the book, which becomes competitive at the end when Father Corbelan's 'elevation to the purple' (appointment as cardinal) is believed to be 'a counter-move to the Protestant invasion of Sulaco organized by the Holroyd Missionary Fund' (*N*, 509). Protestantism, therefore, is seen as no improvement. Little wonder that Giorgio Viola has no belief 'in saints, or in prayers, or in what he called "priest's religion"' (*N*, 16).

Unsurprisingly, the priest in *The Rover* has royalist sympathies (*Ro*, 152) and can only prescribe repentance and a convent for the anxious Arlette, which, according to Peyrol, 'only shows what an ass the curé is' (*Ro*, 230). Arlette instead prays for and achieves a life-fulfilling relationship with Lieutenant Réal, in contrast to the life-denying advice of the abbé. Her aunt, Catherine, is a victim of the doctrine of celibacy, when she falls in love with a priest (*Ro*, 89) and feels 'cast out from the grace of God' (*Ro*, 232). In her case, too, religion has been antithetical to human love. That such priestly doctrines may be unthinking is suspected by Rita in *The Arrow of Gold*, when she considers that the cry of her uncle, a gaunt Basque priest – '"The road to Heaven is repentance"' – may reflect 'a mere unmeaning superstition, a mechanical thing' (*AG*, 116).

Conrad's voyages to the Far East gave him a wider experience of other belief systems. His visits to Bangkok brought him into contact with Theravada Buddhism, then beginning, in a less specific form, to attract the West's interest, for instance through Sir Edwin Arnold's *The Light of Asia* (1879), with the first British Buddhist Society established in 1906.[6] In 'Heart of Darkness', Marlow's pose is that of 'a meditating Buddha' (*Y*, 162), but in 'Falk' the narrator refers negatively to 'the distant temple of Buddha, like a lonely hillock on the plain, where shaven priests cherish the thoughts of that Annihilation which is the worthy reward of us all' (*T*, 210). Religion in its Eastern garb also pervaded the philosophy of Schopenhauer, who, considering life to be phenomenal, had recourse to Hindu scriptures to describe how the goddess Maya veils its reality, leaving us only representations and illusions.[7] Conrad himself comments that 'all are within the same eternal smile of the inscrutable Maya' (*CL* 1:421), and describes the 'aim of creation' as being 'purely spectacular' (*PR*, 92–3).[8] However, as his Malay fiction demonstrates, it was his introduction to Islam during his voyages in the Malay archipelago that made the most lasting impression upon Conrad.

Here too Victorian England was taking an interest: by 1880 there were three English translations of the Qur'an (first translated into Polish in 1858). Conrad had read Sir Richard Burton's *Personal Narrative of a Pilgrimage to El-Medinah and Meccah* (1855–6), drawing on it for much of his Malay fiction,[9] and he mentions Burton when commenting on *Mogreb-El-Acksa: A Journey in Morocco* (1898), written by his friend R. B. Cunninghame Graham (*CL* 2:125). Conrad's familiarity with Alfred Russel Wallace's *The Malay Archipelago* (1869) provided him with a textual source for Islamic customs that he may casually have observed, such as the Muslim burial procedures described in *The Rescue*.

Islam does not appear in 'Heart of Darkness' – nor, indeed, do any missionaries – but Conrad makes a veiled reference to Christian/Islamic rivalry in Africa when referring to 'the yet unbroken power of the Congo Arabs' in 'Geography and Some Explorers' (*LE*, 17). He would certainly have been aware of the activities in the Sudan of the Mahdists, who, in 1885, conquered Khartoum and killed General Gordon – an event much publicized by the British press. In 1889, there were rumours (unfounded) that this violent messianic movement, whose leader called for a *jihād* against infidels, would strike south, to Stanley Falls, 1,000 miles away from Khartoum. Conrad was at Stanley Falls just a year later.

References to Islam appear most frequently in his Malay fiction and often serve to highlight the shortcomings of Europeans. Babalatchi's comment that white men 'worship many gods' and are marked for destruction by any woman's hand (*OI*, 60), is borne out by Willems' sexual obsession for Aïssa, which leads to disaster. Almayer, in his equally obsessive attitude towards his daughter, Nina, is likened to 'a devout and mystic worshipper, adoring, transported and mute; burning incense before a shrine, a diaphanous shrine of a child-idol with closed eyes; before a pure and vaporous shrine of a small god' (*OI*, 320). In *Lord Jim*, the comfortable rural Christianity of Jim's youth fails to sustain him on the *Patna*, where the Arab's 'prayer of travellers by sea' beseeching 'blessings … on the secret purposes of their hearts' (*LJ*, 15) would have been fulfilled had he stayed on the vessel.

Muslims are also used to reflect European failings. In *The Rescue*, for example, Belarab's comment that 'It would be even in a manner a sin to begin a strife in a community of True Believers' (*Re*, 435) echoes that of Lingard's Christian mate, Shaw, whose 'grandfather was a preacher' and who thinks that war is 'Sinful … Unless with Chinamen, or niggers, or such people as must be kept in order and won't listen to reason' (*Re*, 22). Despite these key roles, however, Conrad's Muslims are frequently cut-throats like Babalatchi and Lakamba or hypocrites like Abdulla, who ponders: 'Where was the use to wonder at the decrees of Fate, especially if they were propitious to the True Believers' (*AF*, 109).

Victorian England saw many new Christian movements come into existence, either in the wake of 1844 (a year of messianic expectation, literally interpreted by Seventh Day Adventists and others) or with special concerns such as Christian Science, with its emphasis on natural and spiritual healing,[10] and the Salvation Army (both formally established in 1878). Already, though, all Christian Churches were under threat. Darwin's *The Origin of Species* (1859) and the theory of evolution that this developed challenged a literal interpretation of the Bible, particularly the creation stories of Genesis. The move from 'In the beginning was the Word' to 'In the beginning was the Bang' 100 years later was under way. Instead of developing new spiritual insights to meet this challenge, many of the Churches fell back on dogmatic and increasingly unsustainable assertions that had remained unchanged since the fourth century. This was especially apparent in the public debate between Bishop Wilberforce and T. H. Huxley, where the clergyman showed himself to be an unrealistic fundamentalist, and his desire to know through which parent Huxley derived his descent from monkeys simply demeaned his position in any impartial eyes.

Scepticism about religion was reflected in the philosophies of the day, most notably those of Schopenhauer and Nietzsche, both of whom find echoes in Conrad's work. Indeed, Nietzsche claimed, assertively: 'God is dead' (Introduction to *Thus Spake Zarathustra* (1883–5)). Often, the predicament of the Conradian character seems to reflect the uncertainties of humanity in a new faithless age. In *Almayer's Folly*, Taminah the Siamese slave girl 'knew of no heaven to send her prayer to' (*AF*, 118–19); in 'The Idiots', the Bacadou children provide 'a reproach to empty heaven' (*TU*, 58); whilst Heyst, in *Victory*, 'regretted that he had no Heaven to which he could recommend' Lena (*V*, 354).

In the wake of Darwin, as science filled the vacuum created by religious doubt, the philosophies of Schopenhauer, Nietzsche and Bergson (among others) challenged inherited beliefs in rational awareness, emphasizing instead the force of human instinct. As Natural Selection gained increasing acceptance, human existence was also viewed in terms of science and mechanization, famously voiced by Conrad when he compares society to a 'knitting machine' that has 'made itself without thought, without conscience, without foresight, without eyes, without heart' (*CL* 1:425). It also meant that fanaticism could be transferred virulently from religion into science. This can be seen in *The Secret Agent*, where The Professor's father is referred to as 'an itinerant and rousing preacher of some obscure but rigid Christian sect' (*SA*, 80), for the 'puritanism' of the son is directed towards bomb-making and destruction.

Conrad's early life in some ways exemplifies the philosopher Kierkegaard's concerns that religious institutions were stifling spirituality, causing spiritual outlets to be sought disastrously elsewhere. His fiction shows numerous examples of this as religious terms become attached to individual obsessions (such as Almayer's for his daughter) or collective ones, such as the attitudes towards Russia and revolution manifested in *Under Western Eyes*.

Thus, both the shortcomings of orthodox religion and the crises it faced, that seemed destined to undermine it, find echoes in Conrad's work. In some ways he was his own philosopher, adapting and refuting the insights of others according to his own observations and experience. Into his vocation he poured the devotion appropriate to a religion and spoke, indeed, of approaching his task 'in a spirit of piety' (*CL* 4:113). This made his art all-important and, indeed, his criticisms of Christianity all came when some aspect of the religion threatened to impinge on his latest creation (such as sales of the *Youth* volume being affected by the advent of Christmas). During his early days at The Pent, he writes: 'We live like a family of anchorites. From time to time a pious pilgrim … comes to pay a visit to the celebrated Joseph Conrad – and to obtain his blessing' (*CL* 2:132). However mocking the tone, there is the suggestion here that a successful writer becomes a kind of literary holy man. When he describes M. George's obsession with Rita de Lastaola as 'the state like that of some strange wild faiths that get hold of mankind with the cruel mystic grip of unattainable perfection, robbing them of both liberty and felicity on earth' (*AG*, 140), he could equally well be writing of his own state as an author, for the agonies of composition torment his correspondence. The intense devotion Apollo had given to Poland, Conrad gave to literature, but the wild faith of the son proved more productive than that of the father.

NOTES

1. See Dwight H. Purdy, *Joseph Conrad's Bible* (Norman: University of Oklahoma Press, 1984).
2. R. F. Leslie, *Reform and Insurrection in Russian Poland 1856–65* (London: Athlone Press, 1963), p. 107.
3. Zdzisław Najder, ed., *Conrad's Polish Background: Letters to and from Polish Friends* (London: Oxford University Press, 1964), p. 8.
4. Jessie Conrad, *Joseph Conrad and His Circle* (London: Jarrolds, 1935), p. 151.

5. John Conrad, *Joseph Conrad: Times Remembered* (Cambridge: Cambridge University Press, 1981), p. 152.

6. Christmas Humphreys, *Buddhism* (Harmondsworth: Pelican, 1951), p. 224.

7. Arthur Schopenhauer, *The World as Will and Representation*, trans. E. F. J. Payne (2 vols., India Hills, CO: Falcon's Way Press, 1958), vol. 1, p. 8.

8. It has indeed been suggested that Schopenhauer may have been a source for Conrad's knowledge of Buddhism. See, for instance, William W. Bonney, 'Eastern Logic Under My Western Eyes: Conrad, Schopenhauer and the Orient', *Conradiana*, 10 (1978), 225–52, and Bruce Johnson, '"Heart of Darkness" and the Problem of Emptiness', *Studies in Short Fiction*, 9 (1972), 387–400.

9. Detailed comparisons are given in John Lester, 'Conrad and Islam', *Conradiana*, 13 (1981), 166–8.

10. Christian Science was founded in the United States by Mary Baker Eddy (1821–1910), whom Conrad mentions ironically and bathetically when noting that an undiscriminating public has, among other things, 'swallowed Christianity, Buddhism, Mahomedanism and the Gospel of Mrs Eddy' (*CL* 4:387).

CHAPTER 30

Science and technology

Matthew Rubery

'The sacrosanct fetish of to-day is science' (*SA*, 31), declares the foreign diplomat Mr Vladimir in Conrad's *The Secret Agent* (1907). No institution embodied this authority more visibly during Conrad's lifetime than the Royal Observatory at Greenwich, whose prominent position overlooking the Thames established the building as a monument to Britain's maritime power. Greenwich Mean Time had become internationally accepted as the basis of the world's time zones in 1884, less for its geographical location than for its conventional use: nearly half the world's shipping sailed under the Red Ensign. Hence the assignment given to *agent provocateur* Mr Verloc to blow up the Observatory is a symbolic attack on the great regulator of the nation's time, and, by extension, its transport, trade and industry across the world. Few targets could have been more appropriate for an anarchist agenda intent on undermining the nation's centralized political authority. Based upon the Greenwich Outrage of 1894, this attack against one of Britain's premier scientific institutions expresses how central, if controversial, this field of knowledge had become to everyday life by the end of the nineteenth century. The prestige accrued by science and technology made them indisputable sources of economic, industrial and military strength. The retelling of this anarchist plot in *The Secret Agent* is one indication of Conrad's refusal to accept without misgivings the triumphalist version of scientific progress. Instead, the novel captures both the era's optimism and its scepticism towards the increasingly prominent role played by science and technology in people's lives.

Conrad's was an era of rapid technological change, referred to in retrospect as the 'Second Industrial Revolution'.[1] Numerous technologies having a profound impact on everyday life were introduced in the decades preceding the First World War: wireless telegraphy, electric light bulbs, synthetic aspirin, heroin, typewriters, vacuum cleaners, air conditioning, domestic refrigerators and the machine gun, to name but a few. Simple innovations such as gas lighting had dramatically influenced the quality of life at this

237

time, and progress was relentless: fifty 'electric illuminants' were introduced into Stanford-le-Hope in 1898, after the Conrads had left. Many of these inventions transformed the way people apprehended the world around them, in terms of sound (telephone, gramophone, radio); vision (telescope, photography, film); and transport (motor-car, bus, aeroplane). According to a historian of the era, 'Western industrial technology has transformed the world more than any leader, religion, revolution, or war.'[2]

Technological innovations in sound and vision directly influenced Conrad's conception of the arts. His documented opinions regarding photography and, towards the end of his life, cinema were almost uniformly hostile, even if this did not stop him from earning money for film rights or adapting the story 'Gaspar Ruiz' for silent cinema in 1920. The basis of modern photography had been developed earlier in the century by William Henry Fox Talbot, whose photographic process improved on earlier versions such as the 'calotype' and 'daguerreotype' through the reproduction of multiple copies from a single negative. In 1888, George Eastman distributed the first portable Kodak camera under the slogan: 'You press the button – we do the rest.' Simple, inexpensive designs were beginning to make technology available to amateurs everywhere. While references to the Kodak appear in such novels as *The Inheritors* (1901, co-written with Ford Madox Ford), Conrad often defined his own literary method against the visual transparency of the photograph. He deemed artistic perception superior to the indiscriminate mechanical reproduction of the camera when it came to capturing the interior world hidden beneath sensory experience. Indeed, the credulousness of audiences is called into question by Conrad's 'The Black Mate' (1908) through its satiric interest in such dubious media as spirit photography, which used the sleight-of-hand technique of double exposure to capture the appearance of ghostly figures in the portrait's background. Despite Conrad's distaste, publishers nevertheless relied on photographs in the process of 'selling' him to the public: he had become inescapably part of the technological advances of his time.

The modern age of telecommunications began in 1837 with patents for the first telegraph equipment by Samuel Morse in America and Charles Wheatstone in England. Reuters was the first news agency to use overland telegraph and undersea cable facilities to provide newspapers with reports from around the world. The telegraph dramatically altered the ability to communicate with distant regions, even if Conrad's Lord Jim is still able to remain incognito in the remote Malayan settlement of Patusan 'three hundred miles beyond the end of telegraph cables' (*LJ*, 282). The transmission of voice likewise became a technological reality with the patenting of the telephone by Alexander Graham Bell in 1876. The following year Thomas Alva Edison introduced a device for recording sound called the phonograph, which could play music from indentations on a tinfoil sheet wrapped around a grooved cylinder. The playing of a Verdi opera on a primitive chief's hand-organ in the Bornean jungle presents an incongruous mingling of Eastern and Western cultures in *Almayer's Folly* (1895). During a visit to Glasgow in September 1898, Conrad listened to Polish pianist Ignacy Jan Paderewski on one of the first commercially manufactured phonographs. This same visit gave him the chance to make an X-ray – referred to by the press as the 'New Photography' – of his hand, using the equipment of radiologist Dr John McIntyre. A letter describes the sequence of events that evening: 'dinner, phonograph, X rays, talk about *the* secret of the universe and the non-existence of, so called, matter. The secret of the universe is in the existence of horizontal waves whose varied vibrations are at the bottom of all states of consciousness' (*CL* 1:94–5). As the erudite dinner conversation suggests, Conrad was unusually informed about scientific issues for a man of letters. A similarly scientific vocabulary of sound vibrations and electric waves informs the description of Kurtz's voice as a 'current', 'flow' and 'stream of light' in 'Heart of Darkness' (*Y*, 118, 114).

As with many modern novelists, Conrad's impressionistic narrative method has been compared with scientific attempts to record how human beings apprehend objects of consciousness. The 'Author's Note' to the 1920 edition of *The Secret Agent* compares the writer's mental labours to the chemical process in which a tiny drop precipitates the process of crystallization in a test tube. Scientific advances in astronomy, chemistry and physics in particular offered little consolation to the author by undermining the traditional world-view in which humankind held a privileged position in a divinely ordered universe.

Many of the scientific ideas put forward at this time directly challenged Victorian faith in progress. Conrad's pessimistic conception of the cosmos arose partly from Lord Kelvin's second law of thermodynamics, or law of energy dissipation, which predicted a gradual loss of heat in the universe, leading to such outcomes as the extinction of the sun – known as 'heat death'. This gave rise to Conrad's vision of the planet's eventual demise in 'cold, darkness and silence' (*CL* 2:17). Such pessimism underlies Conrad's description of the character Singleton in *The Nigger of the 'Narcissus'* (1897) under the sway of 'the eternal decree that will extinguish the sun, the stars one by one, and in another instant shall spread a frozen darkness over the whole universe' (*CL* 1:423). In Conrad's eyes, humans suffered less from their subjection to the inexorable laws of nature than from a melancholy awareness of their plight, setting them apart from other species.

His world-view might be characterized as Darwinian in its perspective on life characterized by struggle, chance and absurdity. The publication of Darwin's *The Origin of Species* (1859) and *The Descent of Man* (1871) introduced the idea of natural selection, a process by which favourable characteristics best suited to an environment are reproduced in successive generations. This theory of evolution offered a bleak portrait of life as a struggle with no ultimate goal. It was difficult for post-Darwinian novelists like Conrad to maintain a conception of life as other than a random field of conflict ungoverned by a presiding deity. Instead of occupying a central position within a universe designed by a higher power, humans were now thought to reside within a hostile environment indifferent to their survival. In a letter to R. B. Cunninghame Graham of 1897, Conrad compared the universe to a blind instrument dictating men's lives:

There is a – let us say – a machine. It evolved itself (I am severely scientific) out of a chaos of scraps of iron and behold! – it knits. I am horrified at the horrible work and stand appalled. I feel it ought to embroider – but it goes on knitting ... And the most withering thought is that the infamous thing has made itself; made itself without thought, without conscience, without foresight, without eyes, without heart. It is a tragic accident – and it has happened. You can't interfere with it. (*CL* 1:425)

This vision, of a universe governed by the impersonal laws of physics, leaves little room for human intervention of any meaningful kind. Over the next several decades, Einstein's special theory of relativity (1905) and general theory of relativity (1915) would further challenge the prevailing view among scientists of a rational Newtonian universe.

Pseudo-scientific theories involving eugenics, phrenology and criminology are an equally important context for understanding Conrad's fiction. One has only to recall Marlow's cranium being measured by a company doctor before departing for Africa. The absurdity of taking such measurements to understand a patient's psychology gestures towards Conrad's recognition of the limitations of scientific methodology when applied to human problems. As Conrad would later complain, 'There are times when the tyranny of science and the cant of science are alarming' (*NLL*, 74). It was such questionable pseudo-scientific method that brought Darwin's ideas into the service of racial supremacists. Appalling, no doubt, to the modern reader, it is important to remember how seriously these ideas were taken by many in Conrad's lifetime. To take one example, Darwin's cousin Francis

Galton drew upon evolutionary thought to justify the management of human reproduction through selective breeding. Galton, who coined the term 'eugenics' in 1883, sought to apply to humans the kinds of artificial selection practised by pigeon fanciers. Intervention by such measures as the state regulation of marriages through eugenic health certificates would supposedly speed up the progress of evolution by ensuring the selective reproduction of more intelligent and healthier individuals. Belief in the importance of managing the racial qualities of future generations was accompanied by fears that the racial qualities of the present generation were deteriorating. In *The Secret Agent*, the specious theories of Cesare Lombroso and Max Nordau lie behind Comrade Ossipon's suspicion of Winnie Verloc as a degenerate type identifiable through her physiognomy. Ossipon's so-called 'scientific' inspection of her cheeks, nose, eyes, ears and teeth goes little way towards understanding Winnie's actual psychological state before her suicide (*SA*, 297).

Anxieties about cultural decline extended beyond London to Britain's relationship with the rest of the world. Many of Conrad's fictions set outside Europe, from Malaya to the fictitious South American republic of Costaguana, draw upon anthropological debates about culture. As a Polish émigré able to speak several languages fluently, he was sensitive to the difficulties of understanding another culture. Unease over potential dangers arising from cross-cultural contact between 'civilized' and 'primitive' societies is a key theme in his colonial fiction, where European figures such as Kurtz in 'Heart of Darkness' and Willems in *An Outcast of the Islands* (1896) negotiate whether it is possible to maintain a distinct cultural identity or whether instead to succumb to the temptation of 'going native' when immersed in foreign environments. These ideas were given further currency by Sigmund Freud's model of the human psyche torn between civilized conscious thought and unconscious primitive urges linking us to our bestial forebears. More projection than reality though these atavistic fears may have been, they nonetheless presented a disturbing and contradictory portrait to a confident British imperialism marching across the globe.

Technological improvements in transportation placed Conrad among the first generation to travel by steamer, automobile and aeroplane. Britain's merchant marine had developed into one of the largest fleets in the world when Conrad enlisted as an apprentice seaman in 1878. Sails gave way to steam power during Conrad's lifetime, as the maritime world of his own fiction reflects in the elegiac transition from the clipper *Narcissus* to the steamer *Nan-Shan*. Advances in hydrodynamics, steam propulsion and ship design made this transition inevitable. Prior to electricity and the internal combustion engine, steam was the dominant source of power driving land and sea transport during an era dubbed 'the age of steam'. Charles Parsons' invention of the steam turbine in 1884 for the generation of electricity marked a departure in steam technology, which remained the primary source of energy up to the First World War. Conrad referred to his as an 'age of mechanical propulsion, of generated power' (NLL, 245). Ships became faster, safer and more reliable. The replacement of wooden hulls by steel, paddle wheels by screw propulsion and reciprocating engines by more powerful steam turbines was a death knell to the picturesque sailing ships like the *Torrens* in which Conrad had served. In his eyes, the transition entailed more than a loss of romance: 'The sailing ship made men', he complained; 'Sailors today are little more than factory hands.'[3] Territorial expansion was now more affordable than at any previous point in history. In 1869, the completion of the Suez Canal – 'a dismal but profitable ditch', in Conrad's words (OI, 12) – had a dramatic effect on world trade by allowing the globe to be circled in record time, thereby increasing European penetration of Africa.

The extent to which technology shaped the world in which Conrad lived is vividly illustrated by the sinking of the *Titanic*, then the largest transatlantic passenger steamship in the world. Conrad irreverently referred to this marvel of naval engineering as 'a 45,000 ton hotel' (NLL, 218). On the night of 14 April 1912, this reputedly 'unsinkable' vessel collided with an iceberg in the North Atlantic on her maiden voyage. With a loss of over 1,500 lives, it was one of the worst maritime disasters in history. Conrad described the incident as a warning to 'blind trust in material and appliances' in place of more circumspect attitudes towards the potential risks entailed by technology (NLL, 218).

His sea-career over, Conrad became an enthusiast of the automobile. Horse-drawn vehicles had been the main source of private transportation prior to the car. The bicycle in many senses paved the way for the automobile during the 1880s by motivating road improvements and, more importantly, increased demand for long-distance travel apart from the railways. Gottlieb Daimler, William Maybach and Carl Benz made automotive travel possible by designing the gasoline engine, which surpassed the steam engine and electric motor in terms of speed, power and weight. In 1908, the Ford Motor Company introduced the first affordable mass-market car when it brought out the famous Model 'T', a basic 20-horsepower machine. Prior to acquiring one of these models, Conrad purchased his first car, a second-hand Cadillac affectionately christened 'the puffer' by the family, on 13 August 1912. A letter from Henry James the following year described this vehicle as 'the most dazzling element for me in the whole of your rosy legend'.[4] This was the first in a series of increasingly expensive cars owned by the Conrads, including a Ford, Daimler, Humber, Studebaker and Panhard. He even became a member of the Royal Automobile Club in Pall Mall, whose sole criterion for membership was car ownership. John Conrad humorously describes his father treating the first car like a horse-drawn carriage, though he later notes his father's delight in reaching speeds of 60 miles per hour in a friend's Rover Tourer.

The aeroplane was not far behind. Orville and Wilbur Wright made the first official flight in history on 17 December 1903 at Kitty Hawk, North Carolina, aboard their 'flyer', a tailless biplane powered by a 12-horsepower petrol engine of their own manufacture. This landmark flight of 12 seconds marked a turning-point in air transport, which for the previous century had been restricted to balloon travel. The essay 'Flight' (1917) recounts Conrad's own 80-minute flight aboard a Short biplane from the Royal Naval Air Station at Yarmouth on 18 September 1916, during wartime.

Nowhere is the link between imperialism and technology more evident than in the lopsided conflicts between Europeans and Africans after 1870. The superior firepower among industrial nations had far-reaching political consequences. The frontal assaults favoured by soldiers from the Sudan to South Africa were courageous but futile against rifles such as the Martini-Henry or Winchester used against the natives in 'Heart of Darkness'. In 1884, Hiram Maxim developed the first truly automatic machine gun. Unlike Richard Gatling's earlier hand-cranked model, Maxim's weapon was almost as easy to use as the Kodak camera – a soldier had only to hold down the trigger. The advantage on the battlefield was overwhelming. Kitchener's use of Maxim machine guns alongside other weaponry at the Battle of Omdurman in 1898 resulted in the disproportionate body count of 11,000 Sudanese in comparison with just 48 British casualties.[5] African natives could hardly be blamed for being unable to tell whether an explorer or an enemy stood before them in the figure of Henry Morton Stanley, who armed himself with a Maxim gun for his last major journey, the Emin Pasha Relief Expedition of 1886–8. As one historian observed, 'Soon the Maxim gun – not trade or the cross – became the symbol of the age in Africa.'[6] The very technological superiority in terms of weaponry and transport that enabled European colonization in the first place only increased demand for resources such as the rubber extracted by force from the Congo.

Untempered optimism in technological progress was difficult for anyone to maintain after the experience of the First World War, during which the deadly apparatuses of gas, artillery, tanks, Zeppelins and bombers accounted for unprecedented slaughter on the battlefields of Europe. The Great War's remorseless 'logic of technology, science and planning' accounted for atrocities on a scale never before experienced.[7] The psychiatric illness described as 'shell-shock' was one result of exposing soldiers to these new forms of mechanized warfare. (Conrad's own son, Borys, in the Mechanical Transportation division of the Army, narrowly escaped death and was gassed and shell-shocked.) The brutality inflicted upon the enemy by new technologies witnessed on the battlefield must have seemed almost inconceivable to soldiers born in the previous century: 'A generation that had gone to school on a horse-drawn streetcar now stood under the open sky in a countryside in which nothing remained unchanged but the clouds, and beneath these clouds, in a field of force of destructive torrents and explosions, was the tiny, fragile human body.'[8] Conrad's fiction was among the first to recognize the decisive role science and technology would play in human affairs beneath the unchanged clouds. As one of his prescient fictional characters recognized at the turn of the century, 'Science reigns already. It reigns in the shade maybe – but it reigns' (*SA*, 305).

NOTES

1. Robert Bud, Simon Niziol, Timothy Boon and Andrew Nahum, *Inventing the Modern World: Technology since 1750* (London: Dorling Kindersley, 2000), p. 98.
2. Daniel R. Headrick, *The Tools of Empire: Technology and European Imperialism in the Nineteenth Century* (New York: Oxford University Press, 1981), p. 4.
3. James Walter Smith, 'Joseph Conrad – Master Mariner and Novelist', in *Joseph Conrad: Interviews and Recollections*, ed. Martin Ray (Basingstoke: Macmillan Press, 1990), p. 185.
4. Quoted in J. H. Stape and Owen Knowles, eds., *A Portrait in Letters: Correspondence to and about Conrad* (Amsterdam: Rodopi, 1996), p. 90.
5. Thomas Kingston Derry and Trevor I. Williams, *A Short History of Technology from the Earliest Times to A.D. 1900* (Oxford: Clarendon Press, 1960), p. 305.
6. Thomas Pakenham, *The Scramble for Africa, 1876–1912* (London: Weidenfeld & Nicolson, 1991), p. xvii.
7. Daniel Pick, *War Machine: The Rationalisation of Slaughter in the Modern Age* (New Haven: Yale University Press, 1993), p. 165.
8. Walter Benjamin, *Illuminations*, ed. Hannah Arendt, trans. Harry Zohn (New York: Schocken Books, 1968), p. 84.

CHAPTER 31

Sea

Robert Foulke

I

In the title *The Mirror of the Sea* (1906) Conrad found the perfect image for his complex attitudes towards the oceans he sailed on and wrote about. In the volume's Preface (1919), he confessed his passion for the sea, 'defying the disenchantment that lurks in every day of a strenuous life'. He claims the ocean 'has ever been a friend to the enterprising nations of the earth', yet also contends 'the sea has never been friendly to man' (*MS*, viii, 101, 135). Such contradictions seem illogical and confusing until we realize that they represent different moods and subtle shifts of perspective, not fixed dogma. The fact that Conrad composed all but two of the volume's essays at different times for serials accounts for their distinctive attitudes and tones. As his rhetoric builds in 'Initiation', leading to the story of a chance encounter with a sinking brig, the sea becomes an 'accomplice of human restlessness' and 'dangerous abettor of world-wide ambitions' (*MS*, 135). It cannot be understood in human terms: 'the ocean has no compassion, no faith, no law, no memory' (*MS*, 135). Of course, Conrad was writing before nautical archaeologists began to recover fragments of the past from sunken ships, but his essential vision of the ocean's ever-volatile surface holds.

Created by human ingenuity and manned by those whose skill is essential to keep them afloat, sailing ships, in particular, are seen as key players in a human drama and he consistently personifies them. At the end of a long voyage, the ship seems conscious of closure, 'with a slight deep shudder of all her frame. By so much is she nearer to her appointed death' (*MS*, 22). In Conrad's day, ships had figureheads that represented their names, often allegorical images, and were only tangentially connected to land. And ships developed reputations, for speed and sea kindliness or for 'wicked' behaviour, as he reveals in 'The Brute'. Even ships with good characters had idiosyncrasies, but only rarely do steamships receive the same sympathetic treatment: in the *Nan-Shan* in 'Typhoon', the chief engineer skilfully cuts back the throttle to keep the propeller from spinning wildly as each enormous wave lifts the stern out of the water.

Conrad's treatment of the men sailing in them is much more complex. The officers and seamen in both sailing ships and steamships run the gamut from the highly skilled to the incompetent, from those faithful to their calling to others who bring shore concerns on board and disrupt their ships' working. Among them are malingerers and steadfast hands; the officers range from unimaginative time-servers to accomplished seamen and leaders. Conrad recognizes both ends of this human scale and gradations in between, including good men who harbour a potentially fatal flaw, like Lord Jim.

Elements of an implicit creed of the sea become themes for elaboration and variation in *The Mirror of the Sea* and the essays, and they inform the high rhetoric of authorial judgements and narrators' interpretation in the voyage tales. In a letter near the beginning of his writing career, Conrad 'rejects all formulas dogmas and principles of other people's making' and insists that 'Everyone must walk in the light of his own heart's gospel' (*CL* 1:253). Yet looking backward in the 'Familiar Preface' to *A Personal Record* (1912), he explicitly states a creed: 'Those who read me know my conviction that the world, the temporal world, rests on a few very simple ideas … It rests notably, among others, on the idea of Fidelity' (*PR*, xxi). That idea, or more frequently its violation, becomes the centrepiece of moral drama in his voyage fiction.

It works through a kind of reduction. Although the sea is never friendly, an unstable and unpredictable element, it affords a simpler environment, 'untroubled by the sound of the world's mechanical contrivances and the noise of its endless controversies' (*LE*, 28). For those who have spent time at sea within the circle of the horizon, especially in a sailing ship, the clutter of shore life and its conflicting obligations disappear. There is nothing beyond the contained society of the ship and no chance to escape a voyage's central purpose: to arrive at one's destination intact, to explore a part of the ocean world, to win a race, to set a record. The link between the sea and the complexity of human motive and behaviour is the ship, which Conrad unrestrainedly personalizes. And she becomes both the source and scene of moral drama as officers and men either devote themselves entirely to serving her needs or fail to do so through varieties of egoism – fear of death, desire for fame, false pride, jealousy, laziness, greed, submission to illusions. In Conrad's terms, fidelity to duty, usually associated with the solidarity of the crew, is the key to the ship's survival and the moral core of the men who sail in her.

Its mode of expression is not words but acts, and seamanship is not as simple as those unfamiliar with it might think, especially on board the large square-riggers of Conrad's day. Seamanship is based upon the science of moving efficiently through two fluids, the art of handling complicated ships skilfully, and accumulated ocean experience through millennia of seafaring. It requires extensive knowledge, technical precision, constant attention to detail, understanding of a given ship's peculiarities, anticipation of changes in wind and sea conditions, 'a just appreciation of means and ends', and sometimes in difficult situations 'fierceness of conception' combined with 'certitude of execution' (*MS*, 33). Above all, it demands, in Conrad's view, sincerity rather than 'self-seeking', a sense of vocation that raises it to art: 'To forget one's self, to surrender all personal feeling in the service of that fine art, is the only way for a seaman to the faithful discharge of his trust' (*MS*, 34, 30). And for the reader of Conrad's voyage tales some knowledge of the seamanship involved is essential for understanding crucial points of the action – the risk Captain Allistoun takes in not cutting away the upper masts of the *Narcissus*, the problematic tack at the end of 'The Secret Sharer', Captain MacWhirr's scorn for 'storm strategy' in 'Typhoon'.

The creed implicit in the traditions of the British Merchant Service becomes explicit in *The Mirror of the Sea* and parts of *A Personal Record*, and dominant in the late essays. In the fiction, it appears in fragments. It is easy to assume that fidelity and solidarity were inherent in the Service itself and that Conrad merely transferred these from his experience to his fiction, that he got his ethic as well as his material from sea-life. When he realizes his artistic goal of snatching 'from the remorseless rush of time, a passing phase of life' (*NN*, x), such commentaries serve as sign-posts for readers unfamiliar with the conditions of seafaring. They point the way to partial interpretation of events at sea and the motives of characters, but fail to provide the surrounding context. To learn what has been changed and what is missing one requires a sense of the state of the British Merchant Service in Conrad's era.[1]

II

In 1874, at the age of sixteen, Conrad began his seafaring on French ships out of Marseilles to the West Indies, but from 1878 to 1894 he served in ships of the British Merchant Service, formally established by the Merchant Shipping Act of 1854. There was precedent for it in the Maritime Service of the Honourable East India Company, which maintained naval discipline until its monopoly expired (1833), yet when the British Merchant Service replaced the old traditions with laws, ship-owners complained that 'the confidence between the sailor, his officers, his captain, and his owner' had been destroyed.[2] That process, begun in 1840, continued apace until the end of Conrad's sea career, with Parliament passing eighty-one acts dealing with merchant shipping.[3]

This growing legalism responded to more radical changes in the economics of shipping that started just before mid-century, when much faster American ships began capturing segments of world trade. Longer and leaner than Britain's Blackwall frigates, the so-called 'clippers' carried a huge press of sail. Like their American predecessors, British clippers were also doomed to obsolescence by the opening of the Suez Canal in 1869. The 'big ditch' did not immediately usurp their dominance of routes to the Far East because steamships required a geographical spread of coaling-stations, and for a number of years they could not go faster than sailing ships.

The saga of the British clippers in Conrad's essays and fiction obscures the story of the decline of sailing ships during his service. Among the factors accounting for this was the abandonment of the traditional form of ship-ownership divided into sixty-four shares, some often taken by captains, and others controlled by major investors interested in a line's reputation. As new forms of corporate ownership offered limited liability and attracted a wider set of small investors, it was easier for speculators to gain control for their own profit, leading to abuses.[4] Unlike the clippers, most ships during Conrad's era were consigned to the less lucrative trades, carrying bulk cargoes like coal or nitrates that required no speed. As a result, sailing ships became larger, clumsier and more difficult to handle, rising in average tonnage from 1,500 tons in 1870 to 1,800 in 1880 and 2,000 in 1890; by the end of the decade, during the first phase of Conrad's writing life, some had grown to more than 3,000 tons – an almost unmanageable size – to compete with tramp steamers.[5] The largest Conrad sailed in was the *Tilkhurst* (1,527 tons), and his favourite, the *Torrens*, was only 1,276 tons; he defined an ideal size for a square-rigger as 1,400 tons and considered anything over 2,000 as 'overgrown', 'dangerous' and 'rather helpless' if seriously damaged (*LE*, 67–8).

With reduced rates for cargoes in the slow trades, financially pinched ship-owners cut corners, sending ships out overloaded and with smaller crews. Unseaworthy relics like Conrad's *Palestine* put to sea for long voyages with dangerous cargoes: among coal-laden ships sailing from British ports, twenty-three were lost to spontaneous combustion in 1873 and fifty in 1874.[6] Just as Conrad was beginning his connection with the British Merchant Service, Samuel Plimsoll (1824–98) introduced, and Parliament passed, a flurry of legislation to stop ship-owners' abuses, especially overloading – which reduced freeboard (distance between deck and sea level) and made decks dangerously awash in heavy weather – and under-manning, which cut the crew's effectiveness as they wrestled with sails aloft. Although statistics fluctuated, they remained appalling during the height of Conrad's sea career: during 1883–4, 121 ships were lost at sea, including his *Palestine*, and 2,245 men perished.[7]

Under these conditions, Conrad's guardian Tadeusz Bobrowski was not off the mark in chiding his nephew for risking his life on such a vessel. As early as 1876, two years after Conrad reached England, ship-owners at a mass protest meeting blamed such losses on 'the decrease in the number and deterioration in the quality of British seamen'.[8] Altogether, two decades of rapid change in the conditions of seafaring under sail (remote, sometimes uncaring, ownership; increasing regulations; loss of lucrative cargoes; more dangerous ships; and the coming dominance of steamers) were unlikely to attract the young. Some, like Conrad, were attracted by the 'romance' of sailing ships and had practical reasons for escaping land. Some followed in their sea-going fathers' footsteps, while many in coastal areas saw going to sea as a way of avoiding the drudgery of apprenticeships. Yet others came out of the Industrial School Ships (for paupers, waifs, truants, unruly apprentices or potential delinquents), independent ships (for the homeless and destitute) and reformatory ships (for convicted delinquents). One MP complained that there were no opportunities for 'the children of respectable and honest parents' and that the school ships recruited from 'the dregs of society'.[9] Crews, often multi-national, were clearly a mixed lot. Incompetence, dereliction of duty and unbridled violence were not rare, and the men, in many cases petty criminals and drifters from the slums, were not the sort who customarily responded to ideals such as 'fidelity' and 'loyalty'. As espoused by Conrad, that creed exaggerates the force of sea tradition.

Discipline was more regulated and less harsh than on the notorious Yankee 'hell ships', but living conditions in stuffy forecastles or deckhouses awash with boarding seas in heavy weather were primitive, usually without heat or light. Isolated in crowded conditions for months, sometimes with contaminated food and water, men were vulnerable to disease, even scurvy. On deck, they were exposed to tropical heat and arctic cold in the Southern Ocean's endless gales, and furling or reefing sails while balanced on foot-ropes below wildly swaying yards always carried the threat of a fall to death. Some long-voyage seamen in sail, like Singleton in *The Nigger of the 'Narcissus'*, survived many voyages, but most were worn out at an early age.

Life ashore was chaotic. Beyond the desire for a fling, seamen were trapped by several features of the merchant shipping system. Sailing ships in this era of competition with steamships often waited long for cargoes. As a result, ship-owners discharged all but a skeleton crew upon reaching port and paid them off three to five days later. That pay was not much, averaging 60–75 shillings per month; much of it had already disappeared in an advance-note. Crimps, usually boarding-house owners, plied incoming crews, liquor in hand, luring the men to their establishments. During the gap between discharge and pay, men lived on credit and sometimes racked up bills larger than their pay. To settle those, crimps took their discharge certificates to captains looking for crew and sold the men to the ship for a two- to three-month advance. Because the advance was not valid until the ship had been at sea ten days, crimps made sure the men joined the ship, often by getting them drunk or drugging them. Ship-owners and captains tolerated this system because they filled crews, but the men lost out and could only break out of the trap with help from their families or other shore connections.[10] Sailors' Homes and charitable organizations for seamen rose to combat conditions that were often appalling.[11]

Men not wholly dependent upon their scanty wages never fell into this vicious cycle and moved rather quickly from forecastle to afterguard, using their sea time to qualify for Board of Trade examinations. (They could sit for these at an early age, especially if they went to sea as boys: seventeen for second mate, nineteen for first mate, and twenty-one for master.) In some ways, reaching command 'through the hawse hole' was faster than coming from the more prestigious 'gentleman's ships', the *Worcester* and *Conway*. That route, however, involved time as apprentices, and, whatever their path, young mates frequently worked alongside foremast hands, and increasingly so as crews became smaller and ships larger. They had better, although compact, living quarters and more varied food, yet their pay was still parsimonious, averaging £6 a month for mates in good sailing ships. In 1884, Conrad earned £5 a month as the *Narcissus*'s second mate; the able seamen in his charge got £3, the chief mate £8.[12]

Judging the quality of the officers and masters is risky, but many complaints were made during the last three decades of the nineteenth century. In 1872, scattered reports from British consuls accused masters of drunkenness, ignorance, recklessness and dishonesty.[13] In 1887, the Report of the Royal Commission on the Saving of Life at Sea blamed increased collisions and strandings on the masters' or officers' neglect of 'the *most ordinary rules and precautions of seamanship*'.[14] As sailing-ship trade declined, so did career opportunities – poor pay, gaps in employment and fewer chances of promotion or command offered an unpromising future. Many officers decided to 'give up the sea and go into steam'.

In this context, what are we to make of Conrad's words on 'the last days of sailing ships': 'the pathos of that era lies in the fact that when the sailing ships and the art of sailing them reached their perfection, they were already doomed. It was a swift doom, but it is consoling to know that there was no decadence' (*LE*, 46)? That is a fair summary of the years when clipper ships flourished, but not of what followed as the transition to steam proceeded. Conrad berates Basil Lubbock, a maritime historian whom he respects, for repeating a detail that is not credible about the feats of one of the first American clippers. This respects both 'the celebration of the era of fair ships sailed with consummate seamanship' and insists that facts 'must be in a sort of fundamental accord with the nature of the life they record' (*LE*, 47, 46). That is the double vision embedded in Conrad's voyage fictions, creating their integrity and enabling the persistent ironies between what is seen and what is said. Conrad renders the details of his sea world with impeccable accuracy and projects a whole range of attitudes towards it, including a highly idealized version of British Merchant Service traditions.

NOTES

1. For a more detailed treatment, see Robert Foulke, 'Life in the Dying World of Sail, 1870–1910', in *Literature and Lore of the Sea*, ed. Patricia Ann Carlson (Amsterdam: Rodopi, 1986), pp. 72–115.
2. Thomas Brassey, *British Seamen: As Described in Recent Parliamentary and Official Documents* (London: Longmans, Green and Company, 1877), p. 30.
3. Edward Blackmore, *The British Mercantile Marine: A Short Historical Review* (London: Griffin, 1897), p. 127.
4. For more detail on the effects of changing ship-ownership, see Blackmore, *The British Mercantile Marine*, pp. 141–5.
5. R. J. Cornewall-Jones, *The British Merchant Service: Being a History of the British Mercantile Marine from the Earliest Times to the Present Day* (London, 1898), pp. 252–3.
6. Robert White Stevens, *On the Stowage of Ships and Their Cargoes*, 7th edn (Plymouth and London: Longmans, Green, Reader, & Dyer, 1878), pp. 125–6.
7. Blackmore, *The British Mercantile Marine*, p. 119.
8. Blackmore, *The British Mercantile Marine*, p. 148.
9. Brassey, *British Seamen*, pp. 52–9, 67.
10. For further discussion of crimping and advance-notes, see Brassey, *British Seamen*, pp. 24, 152–9, 178–200.

11. Brassey, *British Seamen*, pp. 293–6.

12. Brassey, *British Seamen*, p. 358, and 'Agreement and Account of the Crew of the *Narcissus*' reproduced in Jocelyn Baines, *Joseph Conrad: A Critical Biography* (London: Weidenfeld & Nicolson, 1960), between pp. 292 and 293.

13. On this topic generally and on Conrad's experience, see Alston Kennerley, 'Joseph Conrad at the London Sailors' Home', *The Conradian*, 33.1 (2008), 69–102.

14. Brassey, *British Seamen*, p. 124.

CHAPTER 32

Society

Amar Acheraïou

Conrad is a figure of transition, straddling the Victorian and Edwardian periods. The decades preceding his arrival in England in 1878 saw industrial and agrarian revolutions, urbanization, economic prosperity, social and cultural transformations, class and gender struggles and colonial expansionism. The technologies of steam and the telegraph made communications faster and more efficient. The railway made travel quicker, improved the postal service and facilitated the circulation of news. Improvements were also perceptible in education and literacy. Owing to developments in the publishing sector, alongside a growth of the cheap fiction market from the 1830s on, more people from the lower rungs of society began to have access to books and newspapers. Colleges for Victorian women were founded from the 1870s on, paving the way for their social and economic emancipation.

Economically, the mid-Victorian period was one of growth and prosperity, as signalled by the 1851 Great Exhibition, which attracted over 6 million visitors and marked the beginning of mass consumer culture that was to characterize British society in the late nineteenth and twentieth centuries. The variety of domestic and international products on display and the remarkable amount of print devoted to the event were 'the first outburst of the phantasmagoria of commodity culture'.[1] In the late-Victorian era, mass entertainment was reflected in the British enthusiasm for football and cricket, music halls and, from 1895 onwards, cinema. Like his contemporaries Conrad indulged in the leisure generated by the new media,[2] yet his taste was elitist, leaning towards high rather than popular culture: opera appealed more to him than did the working-class music hall.

Victorian Britain was undoubtedly a leading economic power, but not a fair distributor of wealth. Instead of reaping the reward of industrialization, the majority of the country workers lured into cities were ensnared in ruthless capitalist exploitation and paucity. In 1849, for instance, 14,000 Londoners died of cholera. In 1866, typhus caused 5,000 deaths and typhoid claimed hundreds of lives.[3] Charles Dickens' novels and Henry Mayhew's study, *London Labour and the London Poor* (1861),[4] for example, offer telling pictures of the destitution of the London slums' working population. The workers' exploitation and distress, persisting throughout the Victorian era, often led to strikes and marches in London and other industrial cities. How much of this social context is registered in Conrad's works? How did Conrad relate to the Victorian values and key issues of his time? And, above all, how did he fit into the British society?

Conrad's integration into British society is evidenced by his natural-ization in 1886; marriage to an English woman, Jessie George, a decade later; desire to become an English gentleman; and choice of English as his medium of writing. It is also suggested by the many British friends of standing with whom he socialized and collaborated, and from whom he received literary and financial support.[5] Despite his integration, Conrad was seen by several contemporary critics and writers as a 'bloody foreigner', to evoke his own words. His friend Arnold Bennett, who encouraged him in his career, described his manners as 'Oriental', an attribute that marked Conrad as a racial other. The epithet was repeated by his friends Ford Madox Ford, Richard Curle, Henry Newbolt and by Jessie Conrad, too, who referred to her husband as an 'almost Oriental aristocrat'.[6] H. G. Wells stressed Conrad's 'ineradicable' foreignness. Rudyard Kipling likewise insisted on Conrad's un-Englishness, observing: 'When I am reading him … I always have the impression that I am reading an excellent trans-lation of a foreign author'.[7] Similarly, in her obituary of Conrad in the *Times Literary Supplement*, Virginia Woolf spoke of him as 'our guest', consigning him to a state of perpetual exile.

This exclusionary rhetoric is perhaps best understood in the light of the Victorian notions of Englishness, culture and race that informed Conrad's contemporaries. Douglas Lormier remarks that the British grew more racist during the 1850s and 1860s.[8] This racism, filtering through the works of authors like William Makepeace Thackeray and Thomas Carlyle, increased steadily with British imperial expansionism. The issue of racism is prominent in *Almayer's Folly*, *An Outcast of the Islands*, 'An Outpost of Progress' and 'Heart of Darkness', and has generated much criticism and controversy.[9] Within Conrad's fiction, however, 'Amy Forster' is the work that exposes most forcefully the Victorian cultural and ethnic exclusiveness. The Kentish villagers' rejection of the shipwrecked Polish protagonist, Yanko Gooral, reflects their adherence to a strict sense of Englishness. Metaphorically, Yanko's exclusion symbolizes Conrad's own alienation, or, more precisely, his adopted countrymen's reluctance to accept him com-pletely as 'one of us'.

The Britain of the 1880s and 1890s in which Conrad settled continued to thrive, although its economic supremacy began to be seriously challenged by its rivals: France, Germany and the United States. Affluence and deprivation went hand in hand during this period. Parallel to manifest national prosperity, working-class indigence was rampant, as shown by Charles and William Booth's social diagnosis.[10] The depression of the 1880s, for instance, caused a steady increase in unemployment, which led to marches and social unrest. In the year of Queen Victoria's Golden Jubilee (1887), in particular, which Conrad evokes in 'Karain: A Memory', several unemployment demonstrations were organized in London in the weeks preceding the celebrations. The 'Bloody Sunday' march degenerated into a violent confrontation with the police, causing the death of three and injuring hundreds of others.[11]

The Jubilee reinstated the Queen as 'mother of the nation' after years of disfavour caused by her withdrawal from public life following Prince Albert's death in 1861. Conrad conveys the popular enthusiasm occasioned by the event, but makes no mention of the strikes. As a subject of the Queen, Conrad might have thought it more appropriate to join in the celebratory mood than dwell on social discontent. However, the Victorian social and class conflicts absent from 'Karain' surface in 'The Return', *The Nigger of the 'Narcissus'* and *Nostromo*. In 'The Return' Conrad claims to represent 'the gospel of the beastly bourgeois' (*CL* 1:393). The attribute 'beastly' associated with the word 'bourgeois' sounds like Conrad's critique of the Victorian ideology of *laissez-faire*, while the term 'gospel' reflects the Victorian devotion to money and 'material interests' that Conrad, following George Eliot in *Silas Marner* (1861), condemned in his fiction, essays and letters. In *The Nigger of the 'Narcissus'*, it is the rowdy Donkin who brings class warfare to the fore. His discourse 'upon the right of labour to live' (172) sounds like Conrad's advocacy of a fairer labour system. In Donkin's comments, work amounts to a means of survival, but the idea of work in this novel, and in Conrad's fiction generally, goes beyond Donkin's philosophy of survival. It has a transcendental dimension, as in 'Heart of Darkness' where Marlow talks of work in terms of self-discovery and self-accomplishment. This conception is in tune with the Victorian work ethic as formulated by Samuel Smiles, who saw work as a means of character-building and self-improvement.[12]

The work ethic is also a central issue in *Nostromo*. As Conrad shows its erosion by imperial greed and abuse, he finely depicts the social and political state of Costaguana, with a focus on political violence and class conflicts. Both the Monterists and Ribierists are dismissed as greedy and brutal groups for which the working classes are mere tools to serve their political ends. Likewise, Gould's silver-mine represents a source of unscrupulous gain based on ruthless exploitation of the indigenous workers. Significantly, Conrad's denunciation of material interests and the workers' objectification stems more from his sympathy for human suffering than from adherence to the socialist doctrine, which he criticizes through his ironic portrayal of the man of the people, Nostromo. Concomitantly, his distance from Socialism may read as a rejection of the Labour Movement's Radicalism, which revived after the 1880s depression.

Nostromo's discussion of labour politics offers hints about the late-Victorian class tensions, yet the topic of imperialism renders best the spirit of the age. This novel registers Britain's move from nation-state colonialism to monopolistic financial imperialism in the late 1880s and 1890s. The growth of monopoly, symbolized by Gould's silver-mine, seriously challenged *laissez-faire* economics. With the transition to financial imperialism, entrepreneurs such as Gould and his American ally Holroyd shunned ideologies that did not serve their interests. This transformation is implied in Gould's deviation from the ideals of progress and justice that the mine initially stood for. Conrad's critique of monopolistic imperialism is reminiscent of Kipling's views in 'The Peace of Dives' where he strongly denounces the financiers. Further, in 'The Islanders', Kipling attacks the late-Victorian culture of luxury and mass entertainment, targeting equally 'the flannelled fools at the wicket or the muddied oafs at the goal'.

Kipling's exhortation to shift attention from games and mass entertainment to military discipline expresses the British anxiety about Empire, a theme explored in 'Heart of Darkness'. It also gives the measure of the cultural, social and technological transformations occurring at the turn of the century. The year 1895 forms the ideological matrix of the late-Victorian period. This date is important on many counts. For instance, it is the year of the discovery of X-rays by Wilhem Konrad Röntgen and of the invention of the cinematograph by the Lumière brothers. It also saw the publication of Conrad's first novel, *Almayer's Folly*, Thomas Hardy's last and most controversial novel, *Jude the Obscure*, and Oscar Wilde's highly publicized trial and imprisonment. Wilde's challenge to the late-Victorian morality crystallizes the spirit of contest that imbued the era about to be born – a period of tremendous change that some scholars associated with a 'revolution'.[13]

The Edwardian era (1901–14) was no doubt a time of transformation, but is more fittingly defined in terms of continuity and rupture, its break from the Victorian spirit being incomplete. The earlier social and political struggles did not fade; they merely took a more assertive and combative turn. Another feature of the age is the emergence of new aesthetic and philosophical preoccupations, resulting from the influence of artistic movements from the Continent, notably France and Russia. Like A. C. Swinburne, George Moore, Arthur Symons and Oscar Wilde, who familiarized English writers and the public with the French literary movements, Conrad was receptive to the innovations brought about by these trends. He pursued his aesthetic explorations, giving British literature an unprecedented Continental dimension. Conrad virtually welded the British and French literary scenes, grafting, as it were, onto the inherited Victorian literary traditions the new ideas and techniques gleaned from Continental literary movements: French Realism, represented by Conrad's literary models, Flaubert and Maupassant; Decadence; aestheticism; Naturalism; and Impressionism. Together with influencing Conrad's aesthetic and epistemological outlook, these movements impacted upon Edwardian culture. The 'social criticism' alongside the aesthetic innovations inspired by the Continental artists contributed to the Edwardian spirit of change and contest. This boisterous climate, seeping through Conrad's writing, was dominated by a set of issues, most of which were a Victorian legacy. Among these are: women's suffrage,[14] the tension between city and country, industrial unrest and class conflict, urban poverty and crime, scientific progress and fear of degeneracy, excessive concern with health and hygiene, censorship and religion. Conrad addressed most of these issues in his letters, essays and fiction. The 'Women Question', for instance, at the heart of political and literary debates during the Edwardian era, is central to *Chance* (1913).

Conrad was, of course, no feminist activist,[15] nor is *Chance* a feminist novel in the sense that Emma Frances Brooke's *The Story of a Modern Woman* (1894) or Mona Caird's *Gallia* (1895) are. However, its focus on a female character, Flora de Barral, and on the topical issues of marriage and women's independence reflects the impact of women's struggles on Conrad. This influence is justified given that Conrad worked on this novel when the militancy of the suffragette movement was at its height. Interestingly, Conrad's treatment of Flora draws attention to the overlapping of the Victorian and Edwardian gender politics. In Marlow's description, Flora becomes a spatio-temporal hiatus, combining qualities from both periods. She is at once 'too simple to understand my intention' (*C*, 236) and an 'intelligent girl' (*C*, 238). The first statement considers Flora a Victorian female prototype, cast in a state of infantilism and ignorance; whilst the second portrays her as a modern independent-minded woman, gifted with intelligence and, implicitly, with a potential for an autonomous existence. This rhetorical twist suggests the emergence of Flora, by extrapolation the

Edwardian woman, as a rational subject, a representation which contrasts with the Victorian conception of women as repositories of emotion and cosy domesticity. The narrative implies none the less that the women's transition from Victorian infantilism to Edwardian maturity is not radical. The fact that Flora is 'metaphorically imprisoned'[16] on board the ship by Anthony indicates the persistence of the Victorian patriarchal order.

While Edwardian gender politics resonates in *Chance*, *Victory* gives vent to the period's epistemological anxieties, embodied in the detached, lonely protagonist, Axel Heyst. The age's disquiet is even more cogently spelled out in the 'Author's Note' to *An Outcast of the Islands*: 'The discovery of new values in life is a very chaotic experience; there is a tremendous amount of jostling and confusion and momentary feeling of darkness' (*OI*, vii). In 'Falk', the Edwardians' excessive concern with health and hygiene, implied by 'Hermann's notions of hygienic clothing' (*T*, 167), is subtly derided. *The Secret Agent* registers instead the period's preoccupation with scientific progress, the relation between heredity and crime enacted through Lombroso's theories, and racial degeneracy embodied by Stevie and Winnie. Through the central theme of terrorism and anarchy, on the other hand, Conrad relates the British fear of Republicanism, born in the early 1870s when numerous republican clubs were established in Britain.[17] That the novel's anarchism is instigated by Russian agents gives the attack on the Royal Observatory at Greenwich a particular significance, for at the turn of the century Russia was seen as a serious threat. Along with enacting the fear of Republicanism, Conrad voices his own concern with the dangers of technology when it falls into the hands of dogmatic social reformers. As he implicitly argues for an ethical orientation that would humanize 'progress', Conrad initiates in *The Secret Agent* a new aesthetics that gives domestic issues and settings primacy over global preoccupations and the remote, exotic lands where his earlier novels were located.

The Edwardian quest for an alternative ethics and aesthetics, implied in Conrad's works and explicitly articulated in G. E. Moore's *Principia ethica* (1903), is underpinned by an 'epistemological crisis'[18] caused in large part by the erosion of Christianity, whose dismantling began in the years following the publication of Darwin's *The Origins of Species* (1859) and intensified during the Edwardian period. Religion obviously receded as a structuring social and moral agency, but it became a privileged field of experimentation for the period's writers. On rejecting Christian dogmas, authors such as Wilde, Conrad and E. M. Forster 'felt free to use it, for while they did not need religion they did need religious metaphors'.[19] Conrad uses abundantly religious metaphors, and these images often dramatize the Christian doctrinaires' hypocrisy and thirst for power. Catholicism in *Nostromo* is reduced to a vehicle of superstition and political oppression; so, too, is the Orthodox Church in *Under Western Eyes*, as suggested by Mrs Haldin: 'With us in Russia the church is so identified with oppression, that it seems almost necessary when one wishes to be free in this life, to give up hoping for a future existence' (*UWE*, 103).

Conrad's work operates as a resonance chamber, registering the key issues of late-Victorian and Edwardian societies. He depicted these contexts not from the perspective of a political activist or social reformer, but from the standpoint of a sharp, scrupulous artist who had a keen eye for detail and a sense of completeness. Conrad was a unique portraitist of his age, at once sufficiently involved in his society to see into its depths and detached enough soberly to record its transformations. The portrait he offers of his time is compelling, but as a Continental by training and origin, Conrad cannot be strictly fitted into a literary tradition or period. A transnational subject that defies monolithic narratives of the self and nation, Conrad may be more appropriately defined as a trans-epochal writer whose writings transcend the confines of the times that shaped them.

NOTES

1. Thomas Richards, *The Commodity Culture of Victorian England: Advertising and Spectacle* (London: Verso, 1990), p. 18.
2. See Stephen Donovan, *Joseph Conrad and Popular Culture* (Basingstoke: Palgrave, 2005).
3. Granville Hicks, *Figures of Transition: A Study of British Literature at the End of the Nineteenth Century* (New York: Macmillan, 1939).
4. Henry Mayhew, *London Labour and the London Poor* (London: Griffin, 1861).
5. See J. H. Stape, *The Several Lives of Joseph Conrad* (London: Heinemann, 2007).
6. Jeffrey Meyers, *Joseph Conrad: A Biography* (London: Murray, 1991), p. 136.
7. Meyers, *Joseph Conrad*, p. 209.
8. Douglas A. Lormier, *Colour, Class and the Victorians* (Leicester: Leicester University Press, 1978).
9. See Peter Firchow, *Envisioning Africa: Racism and Imperialism in 'Heart of Darkness'* (Lexington: University Press of Kentucky, 1999).
10. Charles Booth, ed., *Life and Labour of the London People* (London: Macmillan, 1892–7); William Booth, *In Darkest England and the Way Out* (Chicago: Laird and Lee, 1890).
11. Hicks, *Figures of Transition*, p. 42.
12. Samuel Smiles, *Self-Help* (Boston: Tinker and Fields, 1842).
13. Roy Hattersley, *The Edwardians* (New York: St Martin's Press, 2004), p. 1.

14. In 1887, Lydia Becker and Millicent Fawcett founded the National Union of Women's Suffrage societies.

15. Conrad, however, endorsed the women's struggle for political rights, as suggested by his signing the Writer's Memorial Petition that was sent to Asquith in May 1910 in support of a women's suffrage bill.

16. Susan Jones, *Conrad and Women* (Oxford: Oxford University Press, 1999), p. 113.

17. See John Lucas, ed., *Literature and Politics in the Nineteenth Century* (London: Methuen, 1971).

18. Ian Watt, 'Impressionism and Symbolism in "Heart of Darkness"', in Norman Sherry, ed., *Joseph Conrad: A Commemoration: Papers from the 1974 International Conference on Conrad* (London: Macmillan, 1976), p. 40.

19. Richard Ellmann, ed., *Edwardians and Late Victorians* (New York: Columbia University Press, 1960), p. 116.

Further reading

CHRONOLOGY OF COMPOSITION AND PUBLICATION

Hand, Richard J. *The Theatre of Joseph Conrad: Reconstructed Fictions*. London: Palgrave, 2005.

Jefferson, George. *Edward Garnett: A Life in Literature*. London: Jonathan Cape, 1982.

Knowles, Owen, and Gene M. Moore. *Oxford Reader's Companion to Conrad*. Oxford: Oxford University Press, 2000.

Law, Graham. *Serializing Fiction in the Victorian Press*. Basingstoke: Palgrave, 2000.

Moore, Gene M., Allan H. Simmons and J. H. Stape, eds. *Conrad between the Lines: Documents in a Life*. Amsterdam: Rodopi, 2000.

Najder, Zdzisław. *Joseph Conrad: A Life*. Trans. Halina Carroll-Najder. Rochester, NY: Camden House, 2007.

Saunders, Max. *Ford Madox Ford: A Dual Life*. 2 vols. Oxford: Oxford University Press, 1996.

Stape, J. H. *The Several Lives of Joseph Conrad*. London: Heinemann, 2007.

Stape, J. H., and Owen Knowles. '"In-between man": Conrad – Galsworthy – Pinker', *The Conradian* 31.2 (2006), 48–61.

eds. *A Portrait in Letters: Correspondence to and about Conrad*. Amsterdam and Atlanta, GA: Rodopi, 1996.

LANGUAGE

Coleman, A. P. 'Polonisms in Conrad's *Chance*', *Modern Language Notes* (November 1931), 463–8.

Hervouet, Yves. 'Joseph Conrad and the French Language', *Conradiana* 11.3 (1979), 229–51.

Knowles, Owen, and Gene M. Moore. *Oxford Reader's Companion to Conrad*. Oxford: Oxford University Press, 2000.

Monod, Sylvère. 'On Translating Conrad into French', *The Conradian* 9 (1984), 69–80.

Moutet, Muriel. 'Les Voix étrangères dans *Lord Jim* – l'exemple du lieutenant français', in Josiane Paccaud Huguet, ed. *Joseph Conrad – l'écrivain et l'étrangeté de la langue*. Caen: Lettres Modernes, Éditions Minard, 2006.

Niedzielski, H. 'Polish and English Pseudo-reflexives', *Papers and Studies in Contrastive Linguistics* 4 (1976), 167–98.

Pulc, I. M. 'The Imprint of Polish on Conrad's Prose', in W. T. Zyla and W. M. Aycock, eds. *Joseph Conrad: Theory and World Fiction*. Lubbock: Texas Tech University Press, 1974.

Putnam, Walter. 'Conrad under French Eyes', *Conradiana* 21.3 (1989), 173–83.

Ray, M. S. 'The Gift of Tongues: The Languages of Joseph Conrad', *Conradiana* 15.2 (1983), 83–109.

Smith, C. S. *The Parameter of Aspect*. Dordrecht: Kluwer, 1991.

Sullivan, W. J. 'Active and Passive Sentences in English and Polish', *Papers and Studies in Contrastive Linguistics* 5 (1976), 117–52.

Swan, O. 'Toward a Contrastive Analysis of Tense and Aspect in Polish and English', *Papers and Studies in Contrastive Linguistics* 13 (1981), 127–31.

West, Russell. *Conrad and Gide: Translation, Transference and Intertextuality*. Amsterdam: Rodopi, 1996.

BIOGRAPHIES AND MEMOIRS

Baines, Jocelyn. *Joseph Conrad: A Critical Biography*. London: Weidenfeld & Nicolson, 1960.

Batchelor, John. *Joseph Conrad: A Critical Biography*. Oxford: Blackwell, 1994.

Conrad, Jessie. *Joseph Conrad and his Circle*. London: Jarrolds, 1935.

Ford, Ford Madox. *Joseph Conrad: A Personal Remembrance*. London: Duckworth, 1924.

Jean-Aubry, G., ed. *Joseph Conrad: Life and Letters*. 2 vols. London: Heinemann, 1927.

Karl, Frederick R. *Joseph Conrad: The Three Lives – A Biography*. London: Faber & Faber, 1979.

Meyer, Bernard C. *Joseph Conrad: A Psychoanalytic Biography*. Princeton: Princeton University Press, 1967.

Meyers, Jeffrey. *Joseph Conrad: A Biography*. London: Murray, 1991.

Najder, Zdzisław. *Joseph Conrad: A Life*. Trans. Halina Carroll-Najder. Rochester, NY: Camden House, 2007.

Stape, J. H. *The Several Lives of Joseph Conrad*. London: Heinemann, 2007.

Watts, Cedric. *Joseph Conrad: A Literary Life*. Basingstoke: Macmillan, 1989.

CRITICAL RESPONSES

Berman, Jeffrey. *Joseph Conrad: Writing as Rescue*. New York: Astra Books, 1977.

Bloom, Harold, ed. *Joseph Conrad: Modern Critical Views*. Modern Critical Interpretations. New York: Chelsea House, 1986.

Carabine, Keith, ed. *Joseph Conrad: Critical Assessments*. 4 vols. Robertsbridge: Helm, 1992.

Erdinast-Vulcan, Daphna. *The Strange Short Fiction of Joseph Conrad*. Oxford: Oxford University Press, 1999.

Jordan, Elaine, ed. *Joseph Conrad.* New Casebooks. Basingstoke: Macmillan, 1996.
Karl, Frederick R., ed. *Joseph Conrad: A Collection of Criticism.* Contemporary Studies in Literature Series. New York: McGraw-Hill, 1975.
Knowles, Owen. *An Annotated Critical Bibliography of Joseph Conrad.* London: Harvester Wheatsheaf, 1992.
Knowles, Owen, and Gene M. Moore. *Oxford Reader's Companion to Conrad.* Oxford: Oxford University Press, 2000.
Moore, Gene M., ed. *Conrad on Film.* Cambridge: Cambridge University Press, 1997.
  Conrad's Cities: Essays for Hans Van Marle. Amsterdam: Rodopi, 1992.
Murfin, Ross C., ed. *Joseph Conrad: 'Heart of Darkness': A Case Study in Contemporary Criticism.* New York: St Martin's Press, 1989.
Sherry, Norman, ed. *Conrad: The Critical Heritage.* London: Routledge & Kegan Paul, 1973.
  Joseph Conrad: A Commemoration: Papers from the 1974 International Conference on Conrad. London: Macmillan, 1976.
Simmons, Allan H., and J. H. Stape, eds. *Conrad: The Contemporary Reviews.* 2 vols. Cambridge: Cambridge University Press, forthcoming.
Stallman, R. W., ed. *The Art of Joseph Conrad: A Critical Symposium.* East Lansing: Michigan State University Press, 1960.
Stape, J. H., ed. *The Cambridge Companion to Joseph Conrad.* Cambridge: Cambridge University Press, 1996.
Wollaeger, Mark A. *Joseph Conrad and the Fictions of Scepticism.* Stanford, CA: Stanford University Press, 1990.

DRAMATIC AND OTHER ADAPTATIONS

Baxter, Katherine, and Richard J. Hand, eds. *Joseph Conrad and the Performing Arts.* London: Ashgate, 2008.
Galsworthy, John. 'Introduction', in *Laughing Anne and One Day More.* London: J. Castle, 1924.
Hand, Richard J. 'Conrad and the Reviewers: *The Secret Agent* on Stage', *The Conradian* 26.2 (2001), 1–67.
  'Escape with Joseph Conrad! The Adaptation of Joseph Conrad's Fiction on American Old Time Radio', *Conradiana* 38.1 (2006), 17–58.
  'Producing *Laughing Anne*', *Conradiana* 34.1–2 (2002), 43–62.
  The Theatre of Joseph Conrad: Reconstructed Fictions. London: Palgrave, 2005.
Joy, Neill R. 'The Conrad–Hastings Correspondence and the Staging of *Victory*', *Conradiana* 35.3 (2003), 184–225.
Moore, Gene M., ed. *Conrad on Film.* Cambridge: Cambridge University Press, 1997.
Wheatley, Alison E. 'Conrad's *One Day More*: Challenging Social and Dramatic Convention', *The Conradian* 24.1 (1999), 1–17.
  '*Laughing Anne*: An Almost Unbearable Spectacle', *Conradiana* 34.1-2 (2002), 63–76.

TRANSLATIONS

Conrad, Joseph. *Oeuvres*, ed. Sylvère Monod. 5 vols. Paris: Gallimard, 1982–7.
Opere, ed. Mario Curreli. 2 vols. Milan: Bompiani, 1990–5.
Opere, ed. Ugo Mursia. 5 vols. Milan: Mursia, 1967–82.
Curreli, Mario. 'Cecchi critico Conradiano, con nuovi documenti inediti', *Italianistica* 28.2 (1999), 251–64.
Ehrsam, Theodore George. *A Bibliography of Joseph Conrad*. Metuchen, NJ: Scarecrow Press, 1969.
Knowles, Owen, and Gene Moore. *Oxford Reader's Companion to Conrad*. Oxford: Oxford University Press, 2000.
Lothe, Jakob. *Conrad in Scandinavia*. Lublin: Maria Curie-Skłodowska University; Boulder: Social Science Monographs, 1995.
Monod, Sylvère. 'Editing Conrad … for Whom?' in M. Curreli, ed. *The Ugo Mursia Memorial Lectures*. Milan: Mursia, 1988.
'The French Conrad', *Con-texts* 2–3 (1999), 6–17.
'On Translating Conrad into French', *The Conradian* 9 (1984), 69–80.
Mursia, Ugo. *Scritti Conradiani*, ed. Mario Curreli. Milan: Mursia, 1983.
Stape, J. H., and Owen Knowles, eds. *A Portrait in Letters: Correspondence to and about Conrad*. Amsterdam: Rodopi, 1996.

AFRICA

Achebe, Chinua. 'An Image of Africa: Racism in Conrad's "Heart of Darkness"', *Massachusetts Review* 18.4 (1977), 782–94. Rpt in *Hopes and Impediments: Selected Essays*. London: Heinemann, 1988.
Brantlinger, Patrick. *Rule of Darkness: British Literature and Imperialism, 1830–1914*. Ithaca, NY: Cornell University Press, 1988.
Fincham, Gail, and Myrtle Hooper, eds. *Under Postcolonial Eyes: Joseph Conrad after Empire*. Rondebosch: University of Cape Town Press, 1996.
Firchow, Peter Edgerly. *Envisioning Africa: Racism and Imperialism in Conrad's Heart of Darkness*. Lexington: University of Kentucky, 2000.
Hampson, Robert. '"Heart of Darkness" and "The Speech that Cannot be Silenced"', *English* 39.163 (1990), 15–32.
Lange, Attie de, and Gail Fincham, eds. *Conrad in Africa: New Essays on 'Heart of Darkness'*. New York: Columbia University Press, 2002.
Moore, Gene M. *Joseph Conrad's Heart of Darkness: A Casebook*. Oxford: Oxford University Press, 2004.
Zins, Henryk. *Joseph Conrad and Africa*. Nairobi: Kenya Literature Bureau, 1982.

ANARCHISM

Cahm, Caroline. *Kropotkin and the Rise of Revolutionary Anarchism, 1872–1886*. Cambridge: Cambridge University Press, 1989.

Garnett, Olive. *Tea and Anarchy! The Bloomsbury Diary of Olive Garnett, 1890–1893,* ed. Barry C. Johnson. London: Bartletts Press, 1989.

Goldman, Emma. *Living My Life.* 2 vols. New York: Knopf, 1931.

Hamilton, Carol Vanderveer. 'Revolution from Within: Conrad's Natural Anarchists', *The Conradian* 18.2 (1994), 31–48.

Howe, Irving. *Politics and the Novel.* New York: Horizon Press, 1957.

Joll, James. *The Anarchists.* London: Eyre & Spottiswoode, 1964.

Marsh, Margaret. *Anarchist Women, 1870–1920.* Philadelphia: Temple University Press, 1981.

Marshall, Peter. *Demanding the Impossible: A History of Anarchism.* 1992; London: Fontana Press, 1993.

Nataf, André. *La Vie quotidienne des anarchistes en France, 1880–1910.* Paris: Hachette, 1986.

Rossetti, Olivia, and Helen Rossetti [under the pseudonym, Isabel Meredith]. *A Girl among the Anarchists.* London: Duckworth, 1903.

Sherry, Norman. *Conrad's Western World.* Cambridge: Cambridge University Press, 1971.

Swingewood, Alan. *The Novel and Revolution.* London: Macmillan, 1975.

Woodcock, George. *Anarchism: A History of Libertarian Ideas and Movements.* New York: World Publishing, 1962.

DISEASE AND MEDICINE

Beard, George M. *A Practical Treatise on Nervous Exhaustion (Neurasthenia): Its Symptoms, Nature, Sequences, Treatments.* New York: E. B. Treat, 1905.

Bock, Martin. 'Joseph Conrad and Germ Theory: Why Captain Allistoun Smiles Thoughtfully', *The Conradian* 31 (2006), 1–14.

Joseph Conrad and Psychological Medicine. Lubbock: Texas Tech University Press, 2002.

Creighton, Charles. *A History of Epidemics in Britain.* Vol. II. London: Frank Cass, 1965.

De Kruif, Paul. *Microbe Hunters.* New York: Harcourt Brace, 1926.

Jacobs, Robert G. 'Comrade Ossipon's Favorite Saint: Lombroso and Conrad', *Nineteenth Century Fiction* 23 (1968), 74–84.

Lombroso, Cesare. *Criminal Man.* New York: G. P. Putnam's Sons, 1911.

McLendon, M. J. 'Conrad and Calomel: An Explanation of Conrad's Mercurial Nature'. *Conradiana* 23 (1991), 151–6.

Micale, Michael. *Approaching Hysteria: Disease and Its Interpretations.* Princeton: Princeton University Press, 1995.

Nordau, Max. *Degeneration.* London: Heinemann, 1895.

Osler, Sir William. *The Principles and Practice of Medicine.* 4th edn. New York: Appleton, 1902.

Savage, Sir George. *Insanity and Allied Neuroses: A Practical and Clinical Manual.* New York: Funk & Wagnalls, 1910.

Smith, W. Johnson. *A Medical and Surgical Help for Shipmasters and Officers in the Merchant Navy Including First Aid to the Injured.* London: Charles Friffin, 1895.

EASTERN EUROPE

Branny, Grażyna. 'Conrad in Kraków', in Andrzej Ciuk and Marcin Piechota, eds. *Conrad's Europe: Conference Proceedings.* Opole, Poland: Opole University Publishing House, 2005.
Bross, Addison. 'Conrad's "Skepticism" and the Internecine Struggles among Polish Patriots, 1860–1874', in Lalitha Ramamurthi and C. T. Indra, eds. *Joseph Conrad: An Anthology of Recent Criticism.* New Delhi: Pencraft International, 1998.
'The January Rising and Its Aftermath: The Missing Theme in Conrad's Political Consciousness', in Alex S. Kurczaba, ed. *Conrad and Poland.* Boulder: East European Monographs; New York: Columbia University Press; Lublin, Poland: Maria Curie-Skłodowska University, 1996.
Busza, Andrzej. 'Conrad's Rhetoric and Ideology in *Under Western Eyes*', in Norman Sherry, ed. *Joseph Conrad: A Commemoration.* London: Macmillan, 1976.
Crankshaw, Edward. 'Conrad and Russia', in Norman Sherry, ed. *Joseph Conrad: A Commemoration.* London: Macmillan, 1976.
Davies, Norman. *God's Playground: A History of Poland.* Vol. II: *1795 to the Present.* New York: Columbia University Press, 2005.
Lewitter, L. R. 'Conrad, Dostoyevsky, and the Russo-Polish Antagonism', *Modern Language Review* 79.3 (July 1984), 653–63.
Mikoś, Michael J. *Polish Romantic Literature: An Anthology.* Bloomington, IN: Slavica, 2002.
Miłosz, Czesław. 'Apollo N. Korzeniowski: Joseph Conrad's Father', *Mosaic* 6.4 (1973), 121–40.
The History of Polish Literature. 2nd edn. Berkeley: University of California Press, 1969.
Segel, Harold B. *The Columbia Guide to the Literatures of Eastern Europe since 1945.* New York: Columbia University Press, 2003.
Wandycz, Piotr Stefan. *The Lands of Partitioned Poland, 1795–1918.* Seattle: University of Washington Press, 1974.
Weeks, Theodore R. 'Defining Us and Them: Poles and Russians in the "Western Provinces", 1863–1914', *Slavic Review* 53.1 (1994), 26–40.
Nation and State in Late Imperial Russia: Nationalism and Russification on the Western Frontier, 1863–1914. De Kalb: Northern Illinois University Press, 1996.
Wheeler, Marcus. 'Russia and Russians in the Works of Conrad', *Conradiana* 10.1 (1980), 23–36.

FAR EAST

Clemens, Florence. 'Conrad's Malaysia', *College English* 2.4 (1940–1), 338–46.
Dryden, Linda. *Joseph Conrad and the Imperial Romance.* Basingstoke: Macmillan, 2000.

Fernando, Lloyd. *Cultures in Conflict: Essays on Literature and the English Language in South East Asia.* Singapore: Graham Brash, 1986.

GoGwilt, Christopher. *The Invention of the West: Joseph Conrad and the Double-Mapping of Europe and Empire.* Stanford, CA: Stanford University Press, 1995.

Hampson, Robert. *Cross-Cultural Encounters in Joseph Conrad's Malay Fiction.* London: Palgrave, 2000.

Stein, William Bysshe. 'Conrad's East: Time, History, Action, and *Maya*', *Texas Studies in Literature and Language* 7.3 (1965), 265–83.

White, Andrea. *Joseph Conrad and the Adventure Tradition: Constructing and Deconstructing the Imperial Subject.* Cambridge: Cambridge University Press, 1993.

FIN DE SIÈCLE

Arata, Stephen. *Fictions of Loss in the Victorian Fin de Siècle.* Cambridge: Cambridge University Press, 1996.

Brantlinger, Patrick. *Rule of Darkness: British Literature and Imperialism, 1830–1914.* Ithaca, NY: Cornell University Press, 1988.

Daly, Nicholas. *Modernism, Romance, and the Fin de Siècle.* Cambridge: Cambridge University Press, 1999.

Dijkstra, Bram. *Idols of Perversity: Fantasies of Feminine Evil in Fin-de-siècle Culture.* New York: Oxford University Press, 1986.

Dowling, Linda. *Language and Decadence in the Victorian Fin de Siècle.* Princeton: Princeton University Press, 1986.

Gilman, Sander L. *Degeneration: The Dark Side of Progress.* New York: Columbia University Press, 1985.

Kermode, Frank. *The Sense of an Ending.* New edn. Oxford: Oxford University Press, 2000.

Ledger, Sally, and Roger Luckhurst, eds. *The Fin de Siècle: A Reader in Cultural History, c. 1880–1900.* Oxford: Oxford University Press, 2000.

MacLeod, Kirsten. *Fictions of British Decadence: High Art, Popular Writing, and the Fin de Siècle.* Basingstoke: Palgrave Macmillan, 2006.

Marshall, Gail, ed. *The Cambridge Companion to the Fin de Siècle.* Cambridge: Cambridge University Press, 2007.

Pykett, Lynn, ed. *Reading Fin de Siècle Fictions.* London: Longman, 1996.

FIRST WORLD WAR

Berthoud, Jacques, ed. 'Introduction: Autobiography and War', in *The Shadow-Line.* London: Penguin, 1986.

Buitenhuis, Peter. *The Great War of Words: Literature as Propaganda, 1914–18 and After.* London: Batsford, 1989.

Cecil, Hugh, and Peter H. Liddle, eds. *Facing Armageddon: The First World War Experienced.* London: Leo Cooper, 1996.

Eksteins, Modris. *Rites of Spring: The Great War and the Birth of the Modern Age.* London: Papermac, 2000.

Kingsbury, Celia M. "'Infinities of Absolution'": Reason, Rumor, and Duty in Joseph Conrad's "The Tale'", *Modern Fiction Studies* 44 (1998), 715–29.

Messinger, Gary S. *British Propaganda and the State in the First World War.* Manchester: Manchester University Press, 1992.

Orel, Harold. *Popular Fiction in England, 1914–1918.* Lexington: University Press of Kentucky, 1992.

Schwarz, Daniel R. *Conrad: The Later Fiction.* London: Macmillan, 1982.

Steiner, Zara. *The Lights that Failed: European International History, 1919–1933.* Oxford: Oxford University Press, 2005.

Tuchman, Barbara W. *The Proud Tower: A Portrait of the World before the War, 1890–1914.* New York: Ballantine, 1996.

Winter, J. M. 'Britain's "Lost Generation" of the First World War', *Population Studies* 31 (1977), 449–66.

INTELLECTUAL MOVEMENTS

Brodsky, Stephen G. W. 'Conrad's Two Polish Pasts: A History of Thirty Years of Critical Misrule', in Alex S. Kurczaba, ed. *Conrad and Poland.* Conrad: Eastern and Western Perspectives 5. Lublin: Maria Curie-Skłodowska University; Boulder, CO: East European Monographs, 1996.

Bross, Addison. '*Almayer's Folly* and the Polish Debate about Materialism', in Laura L. Davis, ed. *Conrad's Century: The Past and Future Splendour.* Conrad: Eastern and Western Perspectives 7. Lublin: Maria Curie-Skłodowska University; Boulder, CO: East European Monographs, 1998.

'The January Rising and Its Aftermath: The Missing Theme in Conrad's Political Consciousness', in Alex S. Kurczaba, ed. *Conrad and Poland.* Conrad: Eastern and Western Perspectives 5. Lublin: Maria Curie-Skłodowska University; Boulder, CO: East European Monographs, 1996.

Busza, Andrzej. 'Conrad's Polish Literary Background and Some Illustrations of the Influence of Polish Literature on his Work', *Antemurale* 10 (1966), 109–255.

Eile, Stanisław. *Literature and Nationalism in Partitioned Poland, 1795–1918.* Basingstoke: Macmillan, 2000.

Kaplan, Carola M. 'Conrad's Narrative Occupation of/by Russia in *Under Western Eyes*', *Conradiana* 27.2 (1995), 97–114.

Knowles, Owen. "'Who's Afraid of Arthur Schopenhaeur?'": A New Context for "Heart of Darkness'", *Nineteenth-Century Literature* 49 (1994), 75–106.

Mallios, Peter. 'Undiscovering the Country: Conrad, Fitzgerald, and Meta-National Form', *Modern Fiction Studies* 47.2 (2001), 356–90.

Najder, Zdzisław, ed. *Conrad's Polish Background: Letters to and from Polish Friends.* Trans. Halina Carroll. London: Oxford University Press, 1964.

Niland, Richard. 'Conrad's Language of Retrospection: Youth, Poland, and the Philosophy of History', *The Polish Review* 50.2 (2005), 155–86.

Watt, Ian. *Conrad in the Nineteenth Century.* London: Chatto & Windus, 1980.
Wollaeger, M. *Joseph Conrad and the Fictions of Skepticism.* Stanford, CA: Stanford University Press, 1990.

LITERARY MOVEMENTS

Bardulphe, Jacqueline, 'Ngugi Wa Thiong'o's *A Grain of Wheat* and *Petals of Blood* as Readings of Conrad's *Under Western Eyes* and *Victory*', *The Conradian* 12.1 (1987), 32–49.
Donovan, Stephen, Linda Dryden and Robert Hampson, eds. *Conradiana* 40.1–2 (2008). Special Double Issue: 'Conrad and Serialization'.
Eile, Stanisław. *Literature and Nationalism in Partitioned Poland, 1795–1918.* Basingstoke: Macmillan, 2000.
Gillon, Adam, and Ludwik Krzysanowski, eds. *An Introduction to Modern Polish Literature.* London: Rapp & Whiting, 1968.
Higdon, David Leon. 'Conrad in Outer Space', *The Conradian* 12.1 (1987), 74–7.
Krzyżanowski, Julian. *A History of Polish Literature.* Warsaw: Polish Scientific Publications, 1976.
Miłosz, Czesław. *The History of Polish Literature.* Berkeley: University of California Press, 1983.
Saunders, Max. *Ford Madox Ford: A Dual Life.* 2 vols. Oxford: Oxford University Press, 1996.
Senn, Werner. 'The Conradian Intertext in the Fiction of Randolph Stow: *Tourmaline* and *Lord Jim*', *The Conradian* 15.1 (1990), 12–29.

MODERNISM

Armstrong, Paul B. *The Challenge of Bewilderment: Understanding and Representation in James, Conrad, and Ford.* Ithaca, NY: Cornell University Press, 1987.
Berthoud, Jacques. *Joseph Conrad: The Major Phase.* Cambridge: Cambridge University Press, 1978.
Coroneos, Con. *Space, Conrad, and Modernity.* Oxford: Oxford University Press, 2002.
Erdinast-Vulcan, Daphna. *Joseph Conrad and the Modern Temper.* Oxford: Oxford University Press, 1990.
Levenson, Michael. *A Genealogy of Modernism.* Cambridge: Cambridge University Press, 1984.
Parry, Benita. *Conrad and Imperialism: Ideological Boundaries and Visionary Frontiers.* London: Macmillan, 1983.
Peters, John G. *Conrad and Impressionism.* Cambridge: Cambridge University Press, 2001.
Watt, Ian P. *Conrad in the Nineteenth Century.* Berkeley: University of California Press, 1979.
Winner, Anthony. *Culture and Irony: Studies in Joseph Conrad's Major Novels.* Charlottesville: University Press of Virginia, 1988.

NATIONALISM AND EMPIRE

Brantlinger, Patrick. *Rule of Darkness: British Literature and Imperialism, 1830–1914*. Ithaca, NY: Cornell University Press, 1988.

Clifford, James. 'On Ethnographic Self-Fashioning: Conrad and Malinowski', in Thomas C. Heller, Morton Sosna and David E. Wellbery, eds. *Reconstructing Individualism: Autonomy, Individuality, and the Self in Western Thought*. Stanford, CA: Stanford University Press, 1986.

Crankshaw, Edward. 'Conrad and Russia', in Norman Sherry, ed. *Joseph Conrad: A Commemoration*. London: Macmillan, 1976.

Hampson, Robert. 'Conrad and the Idea of Empire', *L'Époque Conradienne* (1989), 9–22.

Kurczaba, Alex S., ed. *Conrad and Poland*. Conrad: Eastern and Western Perspectives 5. Lublin: Maria Curie-Skłodowska University; Boulder, CO: East European Monographs, 1996.

Morf, Gustav. *The Polish Heritage of Joseph Conrad*. London: Sampson Low, Marston, 1930.

Najder, Zdzisław. 'Introduction' to Najder, *Conrad's Polish Background: Letters to and from Polish Friends*. Trans. Halina Carroll. London: Oxford University Press, 1964.

POLITICS

Bantock, G. H. 'Conrad and Politics', *English Literary History* 25.2 (1958), 122–36.

Fleishman, Avrom. *Conrad's Politics: Community and Anarchy in the Fiction of Joseph Conrad*. Baltimore: Johns Hopkins University Press, 1967.

Hay, Eloise Knapp. *The Political Novels of Joseph Conrad: A Critical Study*. Chicago: University of Chicago Press, 1963.

Hewitt, Douglas. 'Joseph Conrad and the Politics of Power', in Hewitt, *English Fiction of the Early Modernist Period*. London: Longman, 1988.

Howe, Irving. *Politics and the Novel*. New York: Horizon Press, 1957.

Jameson, Fredric. *The Political Unconscious: Narrative as Socially Symbolic Act*. London: Methuen, 1981.

Searle, G. R. *A New England?: Peace and War, 1886–1918*. Oxford: Oxford University Press, 2005.

Watts, Cedric. *A Preface to Conrad*. 2nd edn. London: Longman, 1993.

POPULAR CULTURE

Carey, John. *The Intellectuals and the Masses: Pride and Prejudice among the Literary Intelligentsia, 1880–1939*. London: Faber & Faber, 1992.

Charney, Leo, and Vanessa R. Schwartz, eds. *Cinema and the Invention of Modern Life*. Berkeley: University of California Press, 1995.

Daley, Nicholas. *Modernism, Romance, and the Fin de Siècle: Popular Fiction and British Culture, 1880–1914*. Cambridge: Cambridge University Press, 1999.

Donovan, Stephen. *Joseph Conrad and Popular Culture*. Basingstoke: Palgrave, 2005.

Flanders, Judith. *Consuming Passions: Leisure and Pleasure in Victorian Britain*. London: HarperCollins, 2006.

Fraser, W. Hamish. *The Coming of the Mass Market, 1850–1914*. London: Macmillan, 1981.

Garvey, Ellen Gruber. *The Adman in the Parlour: Magazines and the Gendering of Consumer Culture, 1880s–1910s*. New York: Oxford University Press, 1996.

Jackson, Kate. *George Newnes and the New Journalism in Britain, 1880–1910: Culture and Profit*. Aldershot: Ashgate, 2001.

Reed, David. *The Popular Magazine in Britain and the United States*. London: British Library, 1998.

Storey, John. *Inventing Popular Culture: From Folklore to Globalization*. Oxford: Blackwell, 2003.

PUBLISHING

Anesko, Michael. *'Friction with the Market': Henry James and the Profession of Authorship*. New York: Oxford University Press, 1986.

Bloom, Clive, ed. *Literature and Culture in Modern Britain*. Vol. 1: *1900–1929*. London: Longman, 1993.

Brake, Laurel. *Print in Transition, 1850–1910: Studies in Media and Book History*. London: Palgrave, 2001.

Donovan, Stephen, ed. *Conrad First*. www.conradfirst.net.

Eliot, Simon. '"From Few and Expensive to Many and Cheap": The British Book Market, 1800–1890', in Simon Eliot and Jonathan Rose, eds. *A Companion to the History of the Book*. Malden, MA: Blackwell, 2007.

Gillies, Mary Ann. *The Professional Literary Agent in Britain, 1880–1920*. Studies in Book and Print Culture. Toronto: University of Toronto Press, 2007.

Gross, John J. *The Rise and Fall of the Man of Letters: A Study of the Idiosyncratic and the Humane in Modern Literature*. New York: Collier, 1970.

McAleer, Joseph. *Popular Reading and Publishing in Britain: 1914–1950*. Oxford: Clarendon, 1992.

Sullivan, Alvin. *British Literary Magazines: The Victorian and Edwardian Age, 1837–1913*. Westport, CT: Greenwood Press, 1984.

Vidan, Ivo. 'Conrad in His Blackwood's Context: An Essay in Applied Reception Theory', in Mario Curreli, ed. *The Ugo Mursia Memorial Lectures*. Milan: Mursia, 1988.

Weedon, Alexis. *Victorian Publishing: The Economics of Book Production for a Mass Market, 1836–1916*. Burlington, VT: Ashgate, 2003.

READING

Conrad, Joseph. *Heart of Darkness*, ed. Paul Armstrong. Norton Critical Edition. 4th edn. London: W. W. Norton, 2006.

Cox, Michael, ed. *The Concise Chronology of English Literature*. Oxford: Oxford University Press, 2004.

Dryden, Linda. *Joseph Conrad and the Imperial Romance*. Basingstoke: Macmillan, 1999.

Finkelstein, David. *The House of Blackwood: Author–Publisher Relations in the Victorian Era*. University Park: Penn State University Press, 2002.

Jackson, Holbrook. *The Eighteen Nineties: A Review of Art and Ideas at the Close of the Nineteenth Century*. New York: Capricorn Books, 1966.

Ledger, Sally, and Roger Luckhurst, eds. *The Fin de Siècle: A Reader in Cultural History, c. 1880–1900*. Oxford: Oxford University Press, 2000.

McDonald, Peter D. *British Literary Culture and Publishing Practice, 1880–1914*. Cambridge: Cambridge University Press, 2002.

Said, Edward. *Culture and Imperialism*. London: Chatto & Windus, 1993.

Simmons, Allan H. *Joseph Conrad*. London: Palgrave, 2006.

White, Andrea. *Joseph Conrad and the Adventure Tradition*. Cambridge: Cambridge University Press, 1993.

RELIGION

Burgess, C. F. 'Conrad's Catholicism', *Conradiana* 15 (1983), 111–26.

Ducharme, Robert. 'The Power of Culture in *Lord Jim*', *Conradiana* 22.1 (1990), 3–24.

Heyer, Friedrich. *The Catholic Church from 1648 to 1870*. London: A. & C. Black, 1969.

Hunter, Allan. *Joseph Conrad and the Ethics of Darwinism: The Challenges of Science*. London: CroomHelm, 1983.

Lester, John. *Conrad and Religion*. London: Macmillan, 1988.

O'Hanlon, Redmond. *Joseph Conrad and Charles Darwin: The Influence of Scientific Thought on Conrad's Fiction*. Edinburgh: Salamander Press; Atlantic Highlands, NJ: Humanities Press, 1984.

Purdy, Dwight H. 'The Manuscript of *Victory* and the Problem of Conrad's Intentions', *Journal of Modern Literature* 10.1 (1983), 91–108.

Steiner, Joan E. 'Modern Pharisees and False Apostles: Ironic New Testament Parallels in Conrad's "Heart of Darkness"', *Nineteenth Century Fiction* 37.1 (1982), 75–96.

Watts, Cedric. *A Preface to Conrad*. 2nd edn. London: Longman, 1993.

SCIENCE AND TECHNOLOGY

Greenslade, William P. *Degeneration, Culture and the Novel, 1880–1940*. Cambridge: Cambridge University Press, 1994.

Headrick, Daniel R. *The Tools of Empire: Technology and European Imperialism in the Nineteenth Century*. New York: Oxford University Press, 1981.

Hobsbawm, Eric. *The Age of Empire, 1875–1914*. New York: Vintage Books, 1989.

Kern, Stephen. *The Culture of Time and Space, 1880–1918*. Cambridge, MA: Harvard University Press, 1983.
Luckhurst, Roger, and Josephine McDonagh, eds. *Transactions and Encounters: Science and Culture in the Nineteenth Century*. Manchester: Manchester University Press, 2002.
Marsden, Ben, and Crosbie Smith. *Engineering Empires: A Cultural History of Technology in Nineteenth-Century Britain*. Basingstoke: Palgrave Macmillan, 2005.
Otis, Laura, ed. *Literature and Science in the Nineteenth Century: An Anthology*. Oxford: Oxford University Press, 2002.

SEA

Auden, W. H. *The Enchafèd Flood, or The Romantic Iconography of the Sea*. New York: Random House, 1950.
Carlson, Patricia Ann, ed. *Literature and Lore of the Sea*. Amsterdam: Rodopi, 1986.
Domville-Fife, Charles W., ed. *Square Rigger Day; Autobiographies of Sail*. Barnsley: Seaforth Publishing, 2007.
Foulke, Robert D. 'Life in the Dying World of Sail, 1870–1910', *Journal of British Studies* 3.1 (1963), 105–36. Rpt in *Literature and Lore of the Sea*, ed. Patricia Ann Carlson. Amsterdam: Rodopi, 1986.
  The Sea Voyage Narrative. New York: Twayne Publishers, 1997.
Guerard, Albert J. *Conrad the Novelist*. Cambridge, MA: Harvard University Press, 1958.
Hattendorf, John B., ed. *The Oxford Encyclopaedia of Maritime History*. 4 vols. New York: Oxford University Press, 2007.
Philbrick, Thomas. *James Fenimore Cooper and the Development of American Sea Fiction*. Cambridge, MA: Harvard University Press, 1961.
Villiers, Peter. *Joseph Conrad; Master Mariner*. Rendlesham, Suffolk: Seafarer Books, 2006.
Watt, Ian. *Conrad in the Nineteenth Century*. London: Chatto & Windus, 1980.

SOCIETY

Achebe, Chinua. '"An image of Africa": Racism in Conrad's "Heart of Darkness"', in *Hopes and Impediments: Selected Essays, 1965–67*. Oxford: Heinemann, 1988.
Acheraïou, Amar. *Rethinking Postcolonialism: Colonialist Discourse in Modern Literatures and the Legacy of Classical Writers*. London: Palgrave Macmillan, 2008.
Batchelor, John. *The Edwardian Novelists*. New York: St Martin's Press, 1982.
Brooks, David. *The Age of Upheaval: Edwardian Politics, 1899–1914*. Manchester: Manchester University Press, 1995.
John, Juliet, and Alice Jenkins, eds. *Rethinking Victorian Culture*. London: Palgrave Macmillan, 2000.

Lester, John. *Conrad and Religion*. New York: St Martin's Press, 1988.
Miller, Jane Eldridge. *Rebel Women: Feminism, Modernism and the Edwardian Novel*. London: Virago Press, 1994.
Simmons, Allan H. *Joseph Conrad*. London: Palgrave, 2006.
Wilson, A. N. *The Victorians*. London: Hutchinson, 2002.

Index